CliffsNotes®
TExES™ PPR EC-12 (160)

CliffsNotes®
TExES™ PPR EC-12 (160)

by
Sandra Luna McCune, Ph.D., and Vi Cain Alexander, Ph.D.

Houghton Mifflin Harcourt
Boston • New York

About the Authors

Sandra Luna McCune, Ph.D., is a former Regents professor in the Department of Elementary Education at Stephen F. Austin State University, where she received the Distinguished Professor Award. She now is a full-time author and consultant.

Vi Cain Alexander, Ph.D., is a former professor and Reading Education Coordinator in the Department of Elementary Education at Stephen F. Austin State University, where she received the Teaching Excellence Award. Presently, she provides consultation services.

Acknowledgments

The authors thank our family members and dear friends for their constant love and support. We extend our gratitude to Greg Tubach and our agent Grace Freedson for making this opportunity possible. Thanks to the editorial staff, especially to Christina Stambaugh for her invaluable guidance during the writing of this book, to Lynn Northrup for her keen insights, and to Carolyn Stufft for her brilliant technical editing contributions.

Editorial

Executive Editor: Greg Tubach

Senior Editor: Christina Stambaugh

Production Editor: Jennifer Freilach

Technical Editor: Carolyn J. Stufft, Ed.D.

Copy Editor: Lynn Northrup

Proofreader: Susan Moritz

CliffsNotes® TExES™ PPR EC-12 (160)

Copyright © 2020 by Houghton Mifflin Harcourt Publishing Company

All rights reserved.

Library of Congress Control Number: 2019950859
ISBN: 978-0-358-07386-4 (pbk)

Printed in the United States of America
DOO 10 9 8 7 6 5 4 3 2 1

For information about permission to reproduce selections from this book, write to trade.permissions@hmhco.com or to Permissions, Houghton Mifflin Harcourt Publishing Company, 3 Park Avenue, 19th Floor, New York, New York 10016.

www.hmhbooks.com

Note: If you purchased this book without a cover, you should be aware that this book is stolen property. It was reported as "unsold and destroyed" to the publisher, and neither the author nor the publisher has received any payment for this "stripped book."

THE PUBLISHER AND THE AUTHOR MAKE NO REPRESENTATIONS OR WARRANTIES WITH RESPECT TO THE ACCURACY OR COMPLETENESS OF THE CONTENTS OF THIS WORK AND SPECIFICALLY DISCLAIM ALL WARRANTIES, INCLUDING WITHOUT LIMITATION WARRANTIES OF FITNESS FOR A PARTICULAR PURPOSE. NO WARRANTY MAY BE CREATED OR EXTENDED BY SALES OR PROMOTIONAL MATERIALS. THE ADVICE AND STRATEGIES CONTAINED HEREIN MAY NOT BE SUITABLE FOR EVERY SITUATION. THIS WORK IS SOLD WITH THE UNDERSTANDING THAT THE PUBLISHER IS NOT ENGAGED IN RENDERING LEGAL, ACCOUNTING, OR OTHER PROFESSIONAL SERVICES. IF PROFESSIONAL ASSISTANCE IS REQUIRED, THE SERVICES OF A COMPETENT PROFESSIONAL PERSON SHOULD BE SOUGHT. NEITHER THE PUBLISHER NOR THE AUTHOR SHALL BE LIABLE FOR DAMAGES ARISING HEREFROM. THE FACT THAT AN ORGANIZATION OR WEBSITE IS REFERRED TO IN THIS WORK AS A CITATION AND/OR A POTENTIAL SOURCE OF FURTHER INFORMATION DOES NOT MEAN THAT THE AUTHOR OR THE PUBLISHER ENDORSES THE INFORMATION THE ORGANIZATION OR WEBSITE MAY PROVIDE OR RECOMMENDATIONS IT MAY MAKE. FURTHER, READERS SHOULD BE AWARE THAT INTERNET WEBSITES LISTED IN THIS WORK MAY HAVE CHANGED OR DISAPPEARED BETWEEN WHEN THIS WORK WAS WRITTEN AND WHEN IT IS READ.

Trademarks: CliffsNotes, the CliffsNotes logo, Cliffs, CliffsAP, CliffsComplete, CliffsQuickReview, CliffsStudySolver, CliffsTestPrep, CliffsNote-a-Day, cliffsnotes.com, and all related trademarks, logos, and trade dress are trademarks or registered trademarks of Houghton Mifflin Harcourt and/or its affiliates. TExES is a trademark of the Texas Education Agency, which does not endorse this product. All other trademarks are the property of their respective owners. Houghton Mifflin Harcourt is not associated with any product or vendor mentioned in this book.

Table of Contents

Introduction 1
   General Description 1
   Question Formats. 1
      Single Question Format. 1
      Clustered Questions Format 1
   The TExES PPR EC-12 Test Domains and Competencies 2
      Domain I: Designing Instruction and Assessment to Promote Student Learning. 2
      Domain II: Creating a Positive, Productive Classroom Environment 2
      Domain III: Implementing Effective, Responsive Instruction and Assessment 3
      Domain IV: Fulfilling Professional Roles and Responsibilities 3
   The Role of the TExES PPR EC-12 Test in Teacher Certification. 3
   Registration and Policies for the TExES PPR EC-12 Test. 3
   Passing Score for the TExES PPR EC-12 Test 3
   How to Use This CliffsNotes Book 4
   How to Prepare for the Day of the Test. 5
   What to Do During the Test 5

PART 1 - DOMAIN I: DESIGNING INSTRUCTION AND ASSESSMENT TO PROMOTE STUDENT LEARNING 7

Chapter 1: Developmentally Appropriate Practice 9
   Competency Descriptive Statements 9
   Development and Learning 10
   Types of Play 11
   Piaget 12
   Physical Developmental Characteristics of Children. 14
   Psychosocial Developmental Characteristics of Children 16
   Kohlberg 17
   Erikson 18
   Summary. 20

Chapter 2: Diversity. 21
   Competency Descriptive Statements 21
   Learning Styles 21
   Modality Preferences 23
   Field Independence/Field Dependence 25
   Gregorc's Mind Styles. 26
   Multiple Intelligences 26
   High-Ability Learners 27
   Struggling Learners 29
   Gender Patterns. 30
   Response to Intervention (RtI). 31
   Accommodations for Eligible Students with Disabilities 32
   English Language Proficiency Levels 35
   Embracing Diversity 43
   Summary. 45

Chapter 3: Instructional Design and Planning 47
   Competency Descriptive Statements 47
   Effective Planning. 47
   TEKS 49
   Instructional Objectives 50

Table of Contents

    Levels of Content Complexity 52
    Lesson Cycle Model 53
    5E Model. 54
    Interdisciplinary Units 55
    Selecting Technology 56
    Summary. 57

Chapter 4: Learning Principles 59
    Competency Descriptive Statements 59
    Motivational Strategies. 60
    Teacher Expectations 62
    Attributions and Locus of Control. 64
    Mindset. 64
    Bruner. 65
    Vygotsky 66
    Behaviorism and Constructivism 67
    Summary. 69
    Domain I Sample Questions and Answer Explanations 70
        Sample Questions 70
        Answer Explanations. 71

PART 2 - DOMAIN II: CREATING A POSITIVE, PRODUCTIVE CLASSROOM ENVIRONMENT 73

Chapter 5: Classroom Climate 75
    Competency Descriptive Statements 75
    Creating Supportive Classroom Climates 75
    Physical Layout 77
    Maslow's Hierarchy of Needs. 78
    Praise 78
        Effective Praise 79
        Ineffective Praise 79
    Learning Environment Accommodations for Learners with Special Educational Needs 80
    Summary. 81

Chapter 6: Classroom Management 83
    Competency Descriptive Statements 83
    Effective Classroom Management 83
    Kounin. 87
    Procedures and Rules. 88
    Discipline Management 89
    Conflict Resolution Strategies 90
    Positive Behavioral Interventions and Supports (PBIS). 91
    Summary. 92
    Domain II Sample Questions and Answer Explanations 93
        Sample Questions 93
        Answer Explanations. 94

PART 3 - DOMAIN III: IMPLEMENTING EFFECTIVE, RESPONSIVE INSTRUCTION AND ASSESSMENT 95

Chapter 7: Communication 97
    Competency Descriptive Statements 97
    Verbal and Written Communication 97
    Nonverbal Communication 98

Facilitating Class Discussions 100
    Before Discussions 101
    During Discussions 101
    After Discussions 102
Skillful Questioning 103
Brainstorming 105
Critical and Creative Thinking 106
    Critical Thinking 106
    Creative Thinking 107
Logical Reasoning 109
Graphic Organizers 110
Summary 112

Chapter 8: Instructional Delivery 113
Competency Descriptive Statements 113
Instructional Methods 113
    Direct Instruction 114
    Lecture Method 114
    Constructivist Instruction 115
        Discovery Learning 115
        Inquiry-Based Learning 115
        Project-Based Learning and Problem-Based Learning 115
    Reciprocal Teaching 116
    Simulations, Role Playing, and Games 116
    Differentiated Instruction 116
    Individualized Instruction 116
    Independent Student Centers 117
    Peer Tutoring and Cross-Age Tutoring 117
    Thematic Learning 117
    Interdisciplinary Instruction 117
Cooperative Learning 119
Marzano's High Yield Instructional Strategies 121
Modeling 124
Problem Solving 124
Scientific Inquiry 125
Second Language Acquisition Instruction in Texas 126
    English Language Proficiency Standards (ELPS) 127
    Proficiency Level Descriptors (PLDs) 130
    Texas English Language Proficiency Assessment System (TELPAS) 130
Second Language Development 131
Krashen's Theory of Second Language Acquisition 135
Marzano's Six-Step Process for Academic Vocabulary Development 136
Basic Interpersonal Communication Skills (BICS) and Cognitive Academic
   Language Proficiency (CALP) 137
Useful Second Language Acquisition Terms to Know 138
Summary 139

Chapter 9: Technology 141
Competency Descriptive Statements 141
Digital Literacy 141
Benefits of Using Technology in the Classroom 143
Technology Terms to Know 144
Searching the Internet 152
Internet Safety 153
Summary 155

Table of Contents

Chapter 10: Assessment ... 157
- Competency Descriptive Statements ... 157
- Effective Classroom Assessment ... 157
- Testing Terminology to Know ... 158
- Types of Classwide Assessments ... 161
  - Diagnostic Assessment ... 161
  - Formative Assessment ... 161
  - Summative Assessment ... 162
- K-12 Statewide, Standardized Assessment Program ... 162
- Alternative Classroom Assessment ... 163
- Traditional Assessments ... 165
  - True-False Questions ... 165
  - Multiple-Choice Questions ... 166
  - Matching Questions ... 167
  - Fill-in-the-Blank or Completion Questions ... 168
  - Constructed-Response (or Essay) Questions ... 169
    - Sample Constructed-Response Scoring Guide ... 170
- Homework ... 170
- Correcting Student Errors ... 172
- Study Skills and Test-Taking Strategies ... 173
- Assessment Guidelines ... 174
- Summary ... 176
- Domain III Sample Questions and Answer Explanations ... 176
  - Sample Questions ... 176
  - Answer Explanations ... 178

PART 4 - DOMAIN IV: FULFILLING PROFESSIONAL ROLES AND RESPONSIBILITIES ... 179

Chapter 11: Family Involvement ... 181
- Competency Descriptive Statements ... 181
- Role with Parents ... 181
- Parent-Teacher Conferences ... 183
  - Preparing for the Conference ... 183
  - During the Conference ... 183
  - After the Conference ... 184
- Consequential Texas Statutes Regarding Parents' Rights ... 185
- Summary ... 186

Chapter 12: Professional Knowledge and Skills ... 187
- Competency Descriptive Statements ... 187
- Texas Teacher Standards ... 187
- Teacher Appraisal in Texas ... 190
- Staff Development ... 191
- Collaborative Teams ... 192
- Professional Organizations ... 193
- Reflective Practitioners ... 194
- Summary ... 195

Chapter 13: Professional Conduct ... 197
- Competency Descriptive Statements ... 197
- Code of Ethics and Standard Practices ... 197
  - Professional Ethical Conduct, Practices, and Performance ... 198
  - Ethical Conduct Toward Professional Colleagues ... 199
  - Ethical Conduct Toward Students ... 200

Avoiding Disciplinary Action..201
Professional Responsibility as Advocate for Students.................................203
Professional Conduct with Students Receiving Special Education Services..............207
Texas Statutes Relevant to Teachers..209
Important Legislation and Court Cases..210
Summary..212
Domain IV Sample Questions and Answer Explanations.............................213
    Sample Questions...213
    Answer Explanations..214

PART 5 - TWO FULL-LENGTH MODEL PRACTICE TESTS WITH ANSWER EXPLANATIONS 215

Chapter 14: Practice Test 1..217
Answer Key for Practice Test 1..234
Complete Answers and Explanations for Practice Test 1............................235

Chapter 15: Practice Test 2..249
Answer Key for Practice Test 2..267
Complete Answers and Explanations for Practice Test 2............................268

Appendix A: References and Helpful Resources..............................283

Appendix B: General Educational Terms....................................289

Introduction

General Description

The TExES Pedagogy and Professional Responsibilities EC-12 (160) test (hereafter, abbreviated as TExES PPR EC-12 test) is a computer-administered test (CAT) designed to assess general entry-level knowledge about learning, teaching, and professional conduct.

The test consists of 100 selected-response questions. For each question, you choose one correct answer choice from among four options. You record your answer by clicking the radio button (small open circle) corresponding to your answer choice. No penalty is imposed for wrong answers (i.e., you merely score a zero for that test question). You are given 4 hours and 45 minutes to complete the test. Before you begin the test, you have an additional 15 minutes for a CAT tutorial and compliance agreement.

Question Formats

The questions are presented in two formats: single questions or clustered questions. **Single questions** present a stimulus followed by a single selected-response question. **Clustered questions** present a stimulus followed by two or more selected-response questions that relate to the stimulus. Following are examples of the two question formats.

Note: The example questions in the review chapters and practice tests in this book label each selected-response answer choice with a letter for clarity. These letters do not appear on the computer screen when you take the actual test. Instead, you will click on the radio button next to the answer you choose.

Single Question Format

The following question deals with study skills, a topic that falls under **Competency 010 (Assessment).** Read the stimulus and answer the question.

> **For the following question, select the correct response.**
>
> A social studies teacher asks the students in the class how they could use the word HOMES to help them remember the names of the Great Lakes: Huron, Ontario, Michigan, Erie, and Superior. The students quickly recognize that the first letters of the names of the lakes can be arranged to spell HOMES. This approach to memorizing information best exemplifies using
>
> - an acronym.
> - chunking.
> - rehearsal.
> - rote.

Clustered Questions Format

The first of the following two questions relates to **Competency 008 (Instructional Delivery).** The second question falls under **Competency 007 (Communication).** Read the stimulus and answer the two questions.

Introduction

Read the information below to answer the two questions that follow.

A high school world history studies teacher has observed that during whole-class discussions, the English language learners (ELLs) in the classroom rarely volunteer comments.

In facilitating class discussions, it is important the teacher is aware that

- asking ELLs less challenging questions they can get right will make them more willing to participate in future discussions.
- ELLs who are more willing to speak in class are usually more proficient language users than those who are reluctant to speak.
- cultural factors as well as language ability affect the extent to which ELLs speak out in class.
- probing for further explanation or clarification when ELLs give responses should be avoided, so that they will not be embarrassed in front of their peers.

To encourage all students to think critically and consider a variety of ideas during class discussions, the teacher should ask

- affective domain questions.
- convergent questions.
- divergent questions.
- who, what, where, and when questions.

The TExES PPR EC-12 Test Domains and Competencies

The TExES PPR EC-12 test content is organized into four broad domains. Each domain is defined by a set of competencies that are meant to ensure that entry-level teachers have the necessary professional knowledge to teach effectively in Texas public schools. There is a total of 13 competencies. Each competency is defined by a list of specific skills demonstrating application of that competency. As listed in the TExES PPR EC-12 test preparation manual (www.tx.nesinc.com/Content/Docs/160PrepManual.pdf), the domains and competencies of the TExES PPR EC-12 test (and their approximate percentages of the test) are as follows:

Domain I: Designing Instruction and Assessment to Promote Student Learning

(approximately 34 percent of the test)

- Competency 001: *The teacher understands human developmental processes and applies this knowledge to plan instruction and ongoing assessment that motivate students and are responsive to their developmental characteristics and needs.*
- Competency 002: *The teacher understands student diversity and knows how to plan learning experiences and design assessments that are responsive to differences among students and that promote all students' learning.*
- Competency 003: *The teacher understands procedures for designing effective and coherent instruction and assessment based on appropriate learning goals and objectives.*
- Competency 004: *The teacher understands learning processes and factors that impact student learning and demonstrates this knowledge by planning effective, engaging instruction and appropriate assessments.*

Domain II: Creating a Positive, Productive Classroom Environment

(approximately 13 percent of the test)

- Competency 005: *The teacher knows how to establish a classroom climate that fosters learning, equity, and excellence and uses this knowledge to create a physical and emotional environment that is safe and productive.*
- Competency 006: *The teacher understands strategies for creating an organized and productive learning environment and for managing student behavior.*

Domain III: Implementing Effective, Responsive Instruction and Assessment

(approximately 33 percent of the test)

- Competency 007: *The teacher understands and applies principles and strategies for communicating effectively in varied teaching and learning contexts.*
- Competency 008: *The teacher provides appropriate instruction that actively engages students in the learning process.*
- Competency 009: *The teacher incorporates the effective use of technology to plan, organize, deliver, and evaluate instruction for all students.*
- Competency 010: *The teacher monitors student performance and achievement; provides students with timely, high-quality feedback; and responds flexibly to promote learning for all students.*

Domain IV: Fulfilling Professional Roles and Responsibilities

(approximately 20 percent of the test)

- Competency 011: *The teacher understands the importance of family involvement in children's education and knows how to interact and communicate effectively with families.*
- Competency 012: *The teacher enhances professional knowledge and skills by effectively interacting with other members of the educational community and participating in various types of professional activities.*
- Competency 013: *The teacher understands and adheres to legal and ethical requirements for educators and is knowledgeable of the structure of education in Texas.*

The Role of the TExES PPR EC-12 Test in Teacher Certification

The purpose of the certification program in Texas is to ensure that certified teachers possess sufficient professional knowledge and skills to effectively perform their roles as teachers in Texas schools. To apply for a first-time teaching certificate in Texas, you first must pass the TExES PPR EC-12 test—which is what this book is designed to help you do. In most circumstances, you cannot retake the test more than four times [Texas Education Code (TEC), § 21.048]. You must pass the test to become a Texas teacher. It is the law, so you have no choice but to take it.

Registration and Policies for the TExES PPR EC-12 Test

You can find information about registering for the TExES PPR EC-12 test at www.tx.nesinc.com/PageView.aspx?f=GEN_RegistrationInformation.html. The registration fee in 2019 is $116; the exam must be completed within 170 days of the registration date to avoid forfeiture of the registration fee.

Links for registration policies (for example, payment policies), testing policies (for example, text center rules), and score reporting policies (for example, canceling your scores) can be found at www.tx.nesinc.com/TestView.aspx?f=TXCBT_TestPolicies.html&t=TX160.

Passing Score for the TExES PPR EC-12 Test

The passing score for the TExES PPR EC-12 test is 240 on a scale of 100 to 300. Not all of the 100 questions on the test are used to calculate your score. Your test will likely contain embedded field-test questions, which are being considered for possible inclusion in future versions of the test. These questions, whether you answer them correctly or incorrectly, do not count toward your score; however, you will not know which questions are field-test questions. For each scorable question that you answer correctly, you earn one raw score point. Your scaled score is based on the percentage of raw score points that you obtain.

How to Use This CliffsNotes Book

This book is organized around the 13 competencies of the TExES PPR EC-12 test. It includes a thorough review of the knowledge base related to each competency, study strategies for the test, and two full-length practice tests. The answers to the tests are keyed to the competencies, with explanations supported by educational theory related to effective practice. Upon completion of this book, not only will you be better prepared to take the TExES PPR EC-12 test, but you will also be better prepared to teach in a Texas public school.

When you read through the list of competencies and skills covered on the TExES PPR EC-12 test, you might feel overwhelmed by the task of preparing for the test. Here are some suggestions for developing an effective study program using this book:

- **To help you organize and budget your time, set up a specific schedule of study sessions.** Try to set aside approximately 2 hours for each session. If you complete one session per day (including weekends), it should take you about 5 to 6 weeks to work your way through the review and practice material provided in this book. If your target test date is coming up soon, you may need to increase your study time per day.
- **Choose a place for studying that is free of distractions and undue noise so that you can concentrate.** Make sure you have adequate lighting and a room temperature that is comfortable—neither too warm nor too cold. Be sure you have an ample supply of water to keep your body hydrated; you might also want to have some light snacks available. To improve mental alertness, choose snacks that are high in protein and low in carbohydrates. Try to have all the necessary study aids (paper, pen, note cards, and so on) within easy reach, so that you don't have to interrupt your studying to go get something you need. Ask friends not to call you during your study time. Consider logging out of social media accounts and/or placing your phone on silent during your study sessions.
- **Don't make excuses.** Studying for the TExES PPR EC-12 test must be a priority. It will require a substantial investment of your time and a conscientious commitment on your part. Think of it as a job that you must do. In reality, studying for the TExES PPR EC-12 test is one of the most important jobs you will ever do. The outcome of the test can determine your future career opportunities. Do not avoid studying for it by making excuses or procrastinating.
- **Read through the list of competencies for the TExES PPR EC-12 test to get a general picture of what the test covers; then take Practice Test 1 to help you discover your strengths and weaknesses.** Read the answer explanations for all the questions, not just the ones you missed, because you may have answered some questions correctly by guessing or you may have answered correctly based on a line of thought different from the intent behind the question. Make a list of the competency areas with which you had problems.
- **Carefully study the review chapters, being sure to concentrate as you go through the material.** Don't let yourself be diverted by extraneous thoughts or outside distractions. Monitor yourself by making a check mark on a separate sheet of paper when your concentration wanders. Work on reducing the number of check marks you record each study session.
- **Take notes as you study, using your own words to express ideas.** Leave ample room in the left margin so that you can revise or make comments when you review your notes. Extract key ideas and write them in the left margin to use as study cues later. Make flashcards to aid you in memorizing key ideas and keep them with you at all times. When you have spare time, take out the flashcards and go over the information you've recorded on them.
- **Take several brief 2- to 3-minute breaks during your study sessions to give your mind time to absorb the review material you just read.** According to brain research, you remember the first part and last part of something you've read more easily than you remember the middle part. Taking several breaks will allow you to create more beginnings and endings to maximize the amount of material you remember. The review material is

organized to facilitate taking breaks. The Checkpoint exercises in the review chapters provide a natural way to have more beginnings and endings as you study. It is best not to leave your study area during a break. Try stretching or simply closing your eyes for a few minutes.

- **Set aside certain days to review material you have already studied.** This strategy will allow you to reinforce what you have learned and identify topics you may need to restudy.
- **Plan to master the competencies.** The test is based on these competencies and is designed to ensure that individuals who become teachers in Texas can recognize and apply these "best practices" of classroom instruction. Developing a strong understanding of the TExES PPR EC-12 test competencies is essential to successful performance on the test. Try to relate the competencies to your own experiences so that they will be more meaningful to you.
- **When you complete your review, take Practice Test 2.** Take this test under the same conditions you expect for the actual test, being sure to adhere to the 4 hours and 45 minutes time limit. When you finish taking the test, as you did for Practice Test 1, carefully study the answer explanations for *all* the questions. Analyze the results of the practice test and go back and review competency areas in which you are still weak.
- **Organize a study group, if possible.** A good way of learning and reinforcing the material is to discuss it with others. If possible, set up a regular time to study with one or more classmates or friends. Ask questions among yourselves to discover new insights. Seeing the material from others' perspectives will help you to better formulate your understanding of the content.

After completing your study program, you should find yourself prepared and confident to achieve a passing score on the TExES PPR EC-12 test.

How to Prepare for the Day of the Test

You can do several things to prepare for the day of the test:

- Know where the test center is located and how to get there.
- Make dependable arrangements to get to the test center in plenty of time and know where to park if you plan to go by car.
- Keep all the materials you will need to bring to the test center—especially your admission ticket and two forms of identification—in a secure place so that you can easily find them on the day of the test.
- Get a good night's rest the night before your test. Avoid taking nonprescription drugs or drinking alcohol the day before the test, as the use of these products might impair your mental faculties on test day.
- On the day of the test, plan to get to the testing center early.
- Dress in comfortable clothing and wear comfortable shoes. Even if it is warm outside, wear a light non-outerwear jacket that can be removed or put on, depending on the temperature in the testing room. (*Note:* Heavy jackets, coats, or hoodies are not permitted in the testing room.)
- Eat a light meal. Select foods that you have found usually give you the most energy and stamina.
- Drink plenty of water to make sure your body remains hydrated during the test for optimal thinking.
- Make a copy of this list and post it in a strategic location. Check it over before you leave for the testing center.

What to Do During the Test

Here are some general test-taking strategies to help maximize your score on the test:

- Before you start the test, take several deep, slow breaths, exhaling slowly while mentally visualizing yourself performing successfully on the test. Do not get upset if you feel nervous. Most of the people taking the test with you will be experiencing some measure of anxiety.

Introduction

- During the test, follow all the directions, including the oral directions of the test administrator (TA) and the written directions on the computer screen. If you do not understand something in the directions, ask the TA for clarification. The TA will indicate how you are to ask for assistance.
- Move through the test at a steady pace. The test consists of 100 multiple-choice questions. As you begin the test, make a mental note that question 50 is the halfway point. When you get to question 50, check the on-screen timer to see how much time you have left. If less than 2 hours and 22½ minutes remains, you will need to pick up the pace. Otherwise, continue to work as rapidly as you can without being careless, *but do not rush*.
- Try to answer the questions in order. However, if a question is taking too much time, use the "Flag for Review" button in the upper right corner of the screen to flag the question as one to come back to and move on.
- Read each question entirely. Skimming to save time can cause you to misread a question or miss important information. If the question is complex or wordy, restate it in your own words.
- Try to determine which competency is the primary focus of the question. The answer must relate to that competency.
- Note the students' age/grade level mentioned in the test question so that you can assess whether the answer choices for that question are developmentally appropriate.
- Read all the answer choices before you select an answer. You might find two answer choices that sound good, but one is a better answer to the question. For example, it is better to select answer choices that indicate the benefit to students over those that indicate the benefit to the teacher. *Tip:* Always keep this suggestion in mind as you take the test: Pick the choice that is best for students!
- Try to eliminate at least two answer choices. Be especially watchful for answer choices that express ideas that you agree with but that are too off-topic (not relating to the focus of the question) to apply to the situation being described. Before you make your final choice, reread the question (don't skip doing this!) and select the response that best answers the question and is aligned with the competency that the question is assessing.
- Eliminate answer choices in which teachers appear to give up on students. For example, if the scenario presented involves a student who is struggling to answer a question, the teacher should *not* move on to a different student or switch to an easier question.
- Don't read too much into a question. You should not assume that something is going on or will happen unless it is clearly and plainly stated in the description of the classroom situation.
- Change an answer only if you have a good reason to do so.
- If you are trying to recall information during the test, close your eyes and try to visualize yourself in your study place. This may trigger your memory.
- Remain calm during the test. If you find yourself getting anxious, stop and take several deep, slow breaths and exhale slowly to help you relax. Do not be upset if the person next to you finishes, gets up, and leaves before you do. Keep your mind focused on the task at hand: completing your exam. Trust yourself. You should not expect to know the correct response to every question on the exam. Think only of doing your personal best.
- Before exiting the test, make sure you have marked an answer for every question. Even if you have no clue about the correct answer for a question, make a guess.

Practice these strategies. As you work through the practice tests, consciously use the strategies suggested in this section as preparation for the actual TExES PPR EC-12 test. Try to reach the point that the strategies are automatic for you.

You will benefit greatly from this CliffsNotes book. By using the recommendations provided here as you complete your study program, you will be prepared to walk into the testing room with confidence. Good luck on the test and in your future career as a Texas teacher!

PART 1

DOMAIN I: DESIGNING INSTRUCTION AND ASSESSMENT TO PROMOTE STUDENT LEARNING

- Competency 001: *The teacher understands human developmental processes and applies this knowledge to plan instruction and ongoing assessment that motivate students and are responsive to their developmental characteristics and needs.*
- Competency 002: *The teacher understands student diversity and knows how to plan learning experiences and design assessments that are responsive to differences among students and that promote all students' learning.*
- Competency 003: *The teacher understands procedures for designing effective and coherent instruction and assessment based on appropriate learning goals and objectives.*
- Competency 004: *The teacher understands learning processes and factors that impact student learning and demonstrates this knowledge by planning effective, engaging instruction and appropriate assessments.*

Chapter 1

Developmentally Appropriate Practice

> **Competency 001:** The teacher understands human developmental processes and applies this knowledge to plan instruction and ongoing assessment that motivate students and are responsive to their developmental characteristics and needs.

This chapter provides a general review of knowledge and skills related to Competency 001. Checkpoint exercises are found throughout the review material. These exercises give you an opportunity to practice what you just learned. The answers to the Checkpoint exercises are found immediately following the set of exercises. When doing the Checkpoint exercises, you should cover up the answers. Then check your answers when you've finished the exercises.

Competency Descriptive Statements

The descriptive statements for Competency 001 as given in the TExES PPR EC-12 test preparation manual (www.tx.nesinc.com/Content/Docs/160PrepManual.pdf) specify the following knowledge and skills for beginning teachers in Texas public schools:

- Knows the typical stages of cognitive, social, physical, and emotional development of students in early childhood through grade 12.
- Recognizes the wide range of individual developmental differences that characterizes students in early childhood through grade 12 and the implications of this developmental variation for instructional planning.
- Analyzes ways in which developmental characteristics of students in early childhood through grade 12 impact learning and performance and applies knowledge of students' developmental characteristics and needs to plan effective learning experiences and assessments.
- Demonstrates an understanding of physical changes that occur in early childhood through adolescence, factors that affect students' physical growth and health (e.g., nutrition, sleep, prenatal exposure to drugs, abuse), and ways in which physical development impacts development in other domains (i.e., cognitive, social, emotional).
- Recognizes factors affecting the social and emotional development of students in early childhood through adolescence (e.g., lack of affection and attention, parental divorce, homelessness) and knows that students' social and emotional development impacts their development in other domains (i.e., cognitive, physical).
- Uses knowledge of cognitive changes in students in early childhood through adolescence (e.g., from an emphasis on concrete thinking to the emergence and refinement of abstract thinking and reasoning, increased ability to engage in reflective thinking, increased focus on the world beyond the school setting) to plan developmentally appropriate instruction and assessment that promote learning and development.
- Understands that development in any one domain (i.e., cognitive, social, physical, emotional) impacts development in other domains.
- Recognizes signs of developmental delays or impairments in students in early childhood through grade 4.
- Knows the stages of play development (i.e., from solitary to cooperative) and the important role of play in young children's learning and development.
- Uses knowledge of the developmental characteristics and needs of students in early childhood through grade 4 to plan meaningful, integrated, and active learning and play experiences that promote the development of the whole child.
- Recognizes that positive and productive learning environments involve creating a culture of high academic expectations, equity throughout the learning community, and developmental responsiveness.
- Recognizes the importance of helping students in early childhood through grade 12 learn and apply life skills (e.g., decision-making skills, organizational skills, goal-setting skills, self-direction, workplace skills).

- Knows the rationale for appropriate middle-level education and how middle-level schools are structured to address the characteristics and needs of young adolescents.
- Recognizes typical challenges for students during later childhood, adolescence, and young adulthood (e.g., self-image, physical appearance, eating disorders, feelings of rebelliousness, identity formation, educational and career decisions) and effective ways to help students address these challenges.
- Understands ways in which student involvement in risky behaviors (e.g., drug and alcohol use, gang involvement) impacts development and learning.
- Demonstrates knowledge of the importance of peers, peer acceptance, and conformity to peer group norms and expectations for adolescents and understands the significance of peer-related issues for teaching and learning.

Development and Learning

Teachers enhance students' development and learning by using developmentally appropriate practice. **Developmentally appropriate practice** (DAP) refers to a framework that takes into account the typical patterns of physical, social, and cognitive development of students in order to optimize student learning and to promote social growth. According to the National Association for the Education of Young Children (NAEYC), developmentally appropriate practice should be based on the following elements:

- What is known about child development and learning: Knowledge of age-related human characteristics that permits general predictions within an age range about what activities, materials, interactions, or experiences will best promote learning and development
- What is known about the strengths, interests, and needs of each individual student in the group to be able to adapt to and be responsive to inevitable individual variation
- What is known about the social and cultural contexts in which students live to ensure that learning experiences are meaningful, relevant, and respectful for the students and their families

Further, the NAEYC offers 12 principles of child development and learning that inform developmentally appropriate practice in early childhood (birth through age 8). Following is a simplified version of the 12 principles as they would relate to the TExES PPR EC-12 test:

- Domains of students' development—cognitive, social, physical, and emotional—are interrelated. Development in one domain can limit or facilitate development in others.
- Development occurs in a relatively predictable sequence, with later abilities building on those previously acquired.
- Variation in development occurs among students and within different areas for an individual student. Each student is a unique person with an individual pattern and timing of growth, and this individual variation should be expected and valued.
- Development proceeds in predictable directions toward greater complexity, organization, and internalization.
- Early experiences, either positive or negative, are cumulative in the sense that those that occur most often usually have more impact on the child's learning and/or development.
- Each student's development and learning occur in and are influenced by the sociocultural context of the family, educational setting, community, and broader society.
- The interplay between biological maturation and physical and social experiences impacts development and learning.
- Students are products of both heredity and environment, and these forces are interrelated.
- Most of the time, teachers should give students tasks that, with effort, they can accomplish, and present them with content that is accessible at their level of understanding. At the same time, development advances when, in a supportive context, students experience challenges just beyond their current level of mastery.
- Students exhibit a variety of learning needs. They benefit when teachers select the best strategy to use in a learning situation.

- Play is an important vehicle for young children's social, emotional, and cognitive development. (See the section "Types of Play" that follows for a discussion of play.)
- Students develop and learn best in a learning environment in which they are part of a community where they are safe and valued, their physical needs are met, and they feel psychologically secure. (See Chapter 5, "Classroom Climate," for additional discussion of learning environments.)

Checkpoint

Fill in the blank.

1. Developmentally appropriate practice refers to a framework that takes into account the _____ patterns of physical, social, and cognitive development of students.
2. Development occurs in a relatively _____ sequence.
3. Students learn best when they are part of a nurturing _____.

Mark as True or False.

4. _____ A teacher should never give a student a task above the student's current level of mastery.
5. _____ Play is inappropriate in early-childhood classrooms and should be reserved for the playground.

Checkpoint Answers

1. typical
2. predictable
3. community
4. False
5. False

Types of Play

Carol Gestwicki (1999) characterized **play** as pleasurable, spontaneous, self-motivated, and freely chosen activity. The significant role of play as part of society (Huizinga, 1949) is a long-established factor that is recognized by educators. The NAEYC strongly advocates play as an important component of developmentally appropriate practice in early childhood because play supports children's cognitive, physical, emotional, and social development.

Jean Piaget (in Gestwicki, 1999) identified three categories of increasing sophistication of play:

- **Functional play:** Commonly occurs from birth to age 2 and involves movement and sensory exploration of the environment (for example, a toddler banging on a toy piano)
- **Symbolic play:** Usually begins around age 2 and involves using materials or objects to represent things (for example, a preschooler using a block to represent a telephone) or engaging in imaginary roles (for example, kindergarteners playing store)
- **Games with rules play:** Commonly begins near school age and involves the ability to agree on and abide by rules (for example, children playing "Simon Says")

Note: See "Piaget" later in this chapter for an additional discussion of Piaget's theories.

Mildred Parten (in Gestwicki, 1999) identified five progressive stages of play:

- **Onlooker play:** A child watches other children play, but does not join in.
- **Solitary play:** A child plays alone and does not attempt to get close to or interact with other children.

- **Parallel play:** Children play side by side, engage in similar activities, and might mimic each other, but they do not play together and interact very little.
- **Associative play:** Children play similar activities side by side with interaction such as talking or sharing, but with little joint focus.
- **Cooperative play:** Children play as a group of two or more with more complex social interaction (for example, having conversations, taking turns, and choosing sides) and with a common focus.

Checkpoint

Fill in the blank.

1. Assuming imaginary roles is _____ play.
2. A child works alone on a puzzle. This type of play is _____ play.
3. Two children work together on a puzzle. This type of play is _____ play.

Mark as True or False.

4. _____ Play has an important role in early-childhood classrooms.
5. _____ Making a fort with blocks is symbolic play.

Checkpoint Answers

1. symbolic
2. solitary
3. cooperative
4. True
5. True

Piaget

Jean Piaget (in Slavin, 2008) proposed that learning involves three basic processes: *assimilation, accommodation,* and *equilibration.* **Assimilation** involves fitting new information into existing mental structures, which Piaget called **schemas. Accommodation** requires modifying current schemas or creating new schemas in order to take the new data or information into account. When children encounter new data or information, they experience **disequilibrium,** a cognitive conflict, so to speak, until they can either assimilate or accommodate it and, thus, achieve equilibrium. **Equilibrium** is present when a child's schemas can be relied on to help the child explain or understand the information being encountered. Disequilibrium is a result of insufficient schemas for explaining or making sense of current information. Piaget believed that disequilibrium is an unnatural state and, therefore, all learners seek equilibrium through either assimilation or accommodation when disequilibrium occurs. The process of reaching equilibrium is **equilibration.** Piaget saw the construction of meaning inherent in equilibration as the essence of learning.

Additionally, Piaget asserted that children eventually acquire three types of knowledge:

- **Physical knowledge:** Developed from physical interaction with objects
- **Logical-mathematical knowledge:** Developed from recognizing logical relationships between objects and ideas
- **Social knowledge:** Developed through custom or social convention

Piaget spent a lifetime observing children and the ways they think in learning situations. He concluded that children do not think like adults, nor do they see the world as adults do. According to Piaget, **cognition,** or thinking, is an active and interactive process that develops in stages. The stages of cognitive development are predictable, but the ages of children entering each stage may vary.

The first stage, **sensorimotor,** begins at birth and continues until about age 2. During this stage, children learn through their senses, through motor development, and through trial and error. Children learn to distinguish themselves from the external world. They discover the beginning of independence through cause and effect, learn imitative behavior, and develop **object permanence,** which means they learn that objects continue to exist even when the objects are no longer visible, such as knowing that a ball that rolled behind a piece of furniture did not "disappear."

During the **preoperational** stage, from ages 2 to 6, children are highly imaginative, and they enjoy games of pretend. They see the world from their own points of view **(egocentric),** focus on one aspect of a situation **(centration),** are rapidly developing language, and are beginning to acquire some reasoning ability, although they do not infer beyond what they see. Of particular significance is the development of **symbolic thought**—the ability to mentally represent objects, events, and actions—as evidenced through the use of language and make-believe play. This period is also characterized by what children lack—**reversibility,** the ability to mentally reverse an operation, and **conservation,** the ability to recognize that number, length, quantity, area, mass, weight, and volume of objects have not necessarily changed even though the appearance of these objects might have changed. They also have difficulty distinguishing appearances from reality.

In the **concrete operational** stage, ages 7 to 11, children develop the ability to take another's point of view **(decenter)** and no longer have problems with centration, conservation, reversibility, and distinguishing appearances from reality. They can sort objects into multiple categories and, based on more than one aspect, can think of the whole and its parts simultaneously **(class inclusion),** and can arrange objects in sequential order **(seriation).** They can reason logically to solve concrete problems, can reason and make inferences about reality, and can infer beyond what they see. They are able to logically reason that if A is related to B and B is related to C, then A is related to C **(transitivity).** They acquire the ability to think about and solve problems mentally but still need concrete experiences and physical actions to make mental connections. They can think about their own thinking **(metacognition)** and use metacognitive strategies. Even though they can reason logically (for example, from cause to effect) with concrete objects, they have difficulty with abstract reasoning and hypothetical thinking.

The last stage of development, **formal operational,** begins at about age 12 and continues to adulthood. Adolescents who reach this stage begin to think more easily about **abstract concepts,** things they cannot touch or see. They can develop hypotheses, organize information, test hypotheses, and solve problems. They also can reason both deductively and inductively, make generalizations, and critically analyze the thinking of others. However, for most young adolescents, Piaget's concrete operational stage is predominant, although frequently an adolescent functions at the concrete operational stage for some topics (such as mathematical problem solving) and the formal operational stage for other topics (such as civil rights). Teachers should not assume that all adolescents are at the same stage developmentally or that an individual student functions at the same level in all situations. Whether all people achieve formal operational thinking at this or any other stage is still a major question to which researchers have not provided a definitive answer.

In addition to his stages of cognitive development, Piaget postulated two stages of moral development (Slavin, 2008):

- Younger children are in the **heteronomous morality** stage. In this stage, children see rules as unbreakable and unchangeable—even if everyone agrees to change them. They obey rules for fear of punishment. When very young, they will tattle on rule breakers.
- Older children are in the **autonomous morality** stage. In this stage, children develop autonomy and are willing to challenge rules. They recognize that punishment is not always automatic and that rules exist by mutual agreement and can be changed with the consent of participants.

Checkpoint

Fill in the blank.

1. _____ (Accommodation, Assimilation) involves fitting new information into existing mental structures.
2. A child who recognizes that objects continue to exist even when the objects are no longer visible has acquired _____ (two words).
3. A kindergarten child who tattles on rule breakers is in Piaget's _____ (autonomous, heteronomous) morality stage.

Mark as True or False.

4. _____ Before about age 7, children have difficulty taking the perspective of others.
5. _____ High school teachers should assume that their students have achieved formal operational thinking.

Checkpoint Answers

1. Assimilation
2. object permanence
3. heteronomous
4. True
5. False

Physical Developmental Characteristics of Children

Physical development of children proceeds from head to toe in what is called a **cephalocaudal progression.** This progression means motor ability develops from the top down. Infants are first able to control their heads, then their shoulders, then their arms, and, finally, their legs and feet. While this is taking place, growth and motor ability are also developing in a **proximodistal progression,** from the central axis of the body outward. Trunk and shoulder movements occur before separate arm movements. Hand and finger control develops last. Variations in physical development are to be expected since growth and development are related to heredity, nutrition, and other health factors. Some common (but not absolute) developmental milestones at various ages are shown in the following chart.

Physical Development Chart

Age	Milestones
3	Walk without watching feet; run smoothly; walk up and down stairs with assistance, alternating feet; balance on one foot for 5 to 10 seconds; use a slide without assistance; throw and catch objects; build towers with blocks; manipulate Play-Doh/clay; work simple puzzles; copy circles; push buttons to turn on/off; spread with knife; button and unbutton large buttons; wash hands unassisted
4	Walk heel to toe; walk backward, toe to heel; jump forward 5 to 10 times without falling; gallop smoothly; walk up and down stairs alone, alternating feet; turn somersaults; throw ball overhand; catch bounced ball; cut on line; print some letters; copy squares and rectangles; fold paper and crease it to make objects when shown; make simple drawings; pour well from small pitcher; lace shoes, but not tie bow; wash and dry hands; button, zip, and snap clothes; cut easy foods with knife
5	Run with ease; run on toes; hop a distance on one foot; skip, alternating feet; easily balance on one foot; run and kick moving ball; catch large ball in two hands; print words and numerals; cut with scissors; copy triangles; dress self completely; tie bow; brush teeth independently; grip pencil correctly; use paste and glue appropriately; begin to color within lines

Age	Milestones
6–7	Run, jump, skip, and hop easily (gross-motor skills); view an entire page because eyes can track in a full circle; outgrow farsightedness, which is common up to age 6, but still not ready for sustained close work; draw realistic pictures; improved hand-eye coordination; copy diamonds; can do small printing by age 7; have increased skill in handling tools and materials; lose baby-like contours and features; lose front teeth; grow, mainly in the arms, legs, and face
8–10	Show endurance in physical activities such as running and swimming; perform activities that require control of small muscles of body, hands, feet, and eyes (fine-motor skills); give attention to details; write in cursive; onset of adolescent growth spurt in girls; quiet growth period for boys; by 9, some girls may overtake boys in size; this growth spurt lasts for a few years, and then girls continue to grow more slowly until they are 17 or 18
11–13	Easily perform activities that require fine-motor skills; show improved motor development and coordination; have longer and leaner faces; have most of permanent teeth; pubescent stage for girls; onset of adolescent growth spurt for boys; peak of growth spurt for girls; girls reach puberty before boys; (some) early maturing girls self-conscious; peer recognition becomes important
14–19	Have rapid, but irregular, gain in height and weight, especially boys; might be clumsy because body parts grow at different rates; have high energy; experience restlessness due to hormonal changes; develop secondary sex characteristics; might be completely physically mature before others of the same age have begun puberty; (some) early maturing boys larger and perform better athletically; (some) late maturing boys self-conscious and experience low self-esteem; early maturing girls comfortable with pubertal changes; boys usually begin their growth spurt one to two years after most girls; boys may not finish growing physically until they are 21; boys and girls may experience uncertainty when they do not look similar to other young people their age; peer acceptance and recognition very important

Checkpoint

Fill in the blank.

1. Before about age 6, children's eyesight tends to be _____.
2. In the period from ages 8 to 10, the adolescent growth spurt begins in _____ (girls, boys).
3. In the period from ages 11 to 13, the adolescent growth spurt begins in _____ (girls, boys).

Mark as True or False.

4. _____ By age 4, most children draw realistic pictures.
5. _____ The period from ages 14 to 19 is a time of rapid, but irregular, height and weight gain.

Checkpoint Answers

1. farsighted
2. girls
3. boys
4. False
5. True

Psychosocial Developmental Characteristics of Children

Children enter school with a variety of psychological and social characteristics. Teachers need to be aware that these characteristics have great variability across age groups and cultures. Nevertheless, understanding and dealing with children's and adolescents' behavior can be enhanced when teachers have knowledge of general developmental characteristics. Some common psychosocial characteristics for various age groups are shown in the following chart.

Psychosocial Characteristics of Children and Adolescents

Age	Characteristics
3	Have acquired self-identity; aware of own gender and that of others; will play with other children instead of beside them; beginning to understand that others have feelings, although unable to take the perspective of others; will share toys; learning to take turns; are becoming more self-reliant; need more personal attention; like silly humor; like repetitious activities; might develop irrational fears; have short attention spans
4	Can describe self in simple terms; have developed racial/cultural identity; are self-centered; enjoy group activities; might have imaginary friends; tend to play with same-sex peers and might exclude the other sex; like jokes and silly humor; enjoy the security of repetitious activities; need warm personal attention; have increased attention spans
5	Enjoy the security of repetitious activities; want to be accepted by adults; engage in various forms of play; can play simple board games; will share and take turns but are still very self-centered; are very individualistic; tend to tattle on others (as they become aware of right and wrong); choose own friends; commonly choose same-sex friends with same interests; engage in cooperative play; like practical jokes; have an interest in the world outside their own; very inquisitive about their surroundings; appear to live in a world of make-believe and imagination; are spontaneous and uninhibited
6–7	Can take the perspective of others; tend to overestimate their abilities; are highly competitive (cheating at games common); are highly imaginative and enjoy imitating; like warm personal attention; need encouragement and acceptance from adults; choose same-sex peers as friends at school; neighborhood friends might be mixed; are imaginative in their play; interested in games and rules; show social give-and-take; have a growing social interest; begin to want to "fit in"
8–10	Become more realistic about their abilities; are very curious; have well-established racial/ethnic prejudices, which are resistant to change; are somewhat self-conscious; need encouragement and acceptance from adults; prefer group activities to independent work; are interested in what's happening in the world; have social life focused around family; rely on opinions of family members in forming attitudes; choose same-sex friends; feel pressure to conform to others of same age, especially in terms of dress; might use inappropriate language; might develop hero worship of family member or media/sports figure
11–15 (young adolescents)	Often resistant toward parent/adult authority and will challenge adult authority; need understanding and support from parents and others; have social life shifted in focus from family to friends; are intensely curious; interested in investigating real-life problems; easily offended and sensitive to criticism; concerned about their physical appearance; often preoccupied with self (**adolescent egocentrism**); feel like they are "on stage," others watching and judging them (**imaginary audience**); like to work with peers; have a strong need for approval, especially from peers (**peer pressure**); have a strong desire to belong to a group; want to be different, but "fit in" at same time; very loyal to peer-group values; tend to form cliques; emergence of feelings of sexual desire; choose friends who are like themselves; have both male and female friends; like trends; are generally idealistic; turn to friends for advice and understanding but rely on family when making major decisions; experience mood swings; believe their personal situation is unique (**personal fable**), that no one else understands them; believe that bad things happen to other people, not to them (**invincibility fable**), so will engage in risky behavior; have difficulty coping with being "caught" between childhood and adulthood; may become obsessed with pop culture figures

Age	Characteristics
16–19 (older adolescents)	Show decreased resistance to authority; are beginning to be less influenced by adolescent egocentrism, imaginary audience, and personal fable; need understanding and support from parents and others; interested in opposite sex and dating; are comfortable with their sexuality; still very concerned with their appearance; choose friends who are like themselves; have male and female friends; tend to keep same friends and form cliques; often form a close relationship with a "significant other" and tend to be strongly influenced by this person; have increased personal autonomy; will still test boundaries and engage in risky behavior; turn to trusted friends (male or female) for advice and understanding, but rely on family when making major decisions; interact with their parents as people; interested in investigating real-life problems and topics that are personally meaningful; interested in the future; value support of their families

Checkpoint

Fill in the blank.

1. By age _____, children have acquired gender identity.
2. By no later than age _____, children have well-established racial/ethnic prejudices.
3. Younger adolescents are very susceptible to _____ pressure.

Mark as True or False.

4. _____ A 6-year-old child will tend to overestimate his or her abilities.
5. _____ Younger adolescents tend to be less rebellious than older adolescents.

Checkpoint Answers

1. 3
2. 10
3. peer
4. True
5. False

Kohlberg

Lawrence Kohlberg (1981) studied the ways children (and adults) reason about rules that govern their moral behavior. After conducting a long series of studies with children and adults, Kohlberg concluded that moral development occurs in a specific sequence of stages, regardless of culture. He identified six stages of moral reasoning, which he grouped into the following three levels.

Preconventional Level (Birth to 9 Years)	Conventional Level (10 to 15 Years)	Postconventional Level (16 Years to Adulthood)
Stage 1: Punishment-Obedience Orientation. Rules are obeyed to avoid punishment. Accepts rules, but internalization of moral values is lacking.	**Stage 3: Good Boy–Nice Girl Orientation.** Good behavior is doing what others expect and whatever is approved by them. Accepts and respects authority. Peer acceptance is needed.	**Stage 5: Social Contract Orientation.** What's right is defined in terms of standards that have been agreed on by the whole society. Obeys rules, but might question them. Recognizes that rules are subject to change if outdated. Respects rights of others.
Stage 2: Instrumental-Relativist Orientation. What's right is whatever satisfies one's own needs and occasionally the needs of others. Behaves to get a reward.	**Stage 4: Law-Order Orientation.** Good behavior is doing one's duty, respecting authority, and obeying the laws of society. Regardless of the circumstances, it is wrong to break rules.	**Stage 6: Universal Ethical Principle.** What's right is a decision of one's conscience according to ethical principles. Ethical principles are abstract concepts such as justice, equality, and the dignity of all people.

Checkpoint

Fill in the blank.

1. A person who obeys the rules to avoid punishment is in Kohlberg's _____ stage of moral development.
2. A person who obeys the rules out of a desire to please others is in Kohlberg's _____ stage of moral development.
3. A person who obeys the rules out of a desire to please oneself is in Kohlberg's _____ stage of moral development.

Mark as True or False.

4. _____ Kohlberg believed that moral development occurs in a specific sequence of stages.
5. _____ A person who breaks the rules to follow his or her own conscience is in Kohlberg's law-order orientation of moral development.

Checkpoint Answers

1. punishment-obedience orientation
2. good boy–nice girl orientation
3. instrumental-relativist orientation
4. True
5. False

Erikson

Erik Erikson (1968) developed a life-cycle conception of personality development. According to him, people go through a series of major crises as they proceed through life. At each stage, there is a critical social crisis. How the individual reacts to each future crisis is determined by earlier development and by adjustment to social experiences. The stages are as follows:

- **Trust versus mistrust (birth to 18 months):** During this first stage, an infant whose basic physical needs are met and who feels loved and secure will develop feelings of trust. Otherwise, the seeds of mistrust will be firmly planted.

- **Autonomy versus doubt (18 months to 3 years):** During the second stage, children should be allowed to explore, make simple choices, and learn to control themselves as autonomy is experienced. Otherwise, feelings of self-doubt will prevail.
- **Initiation versus guilt (3 to 6 years):** Children need to develop a confident attitude about their own actions and abilities. It is important that they have opportunities to initiate activities and engage in real and make-believe play. Also, in this period, children need to develop a comfortable sense of their gender identity. Nurturing and reinforcing children's sense of initiative at this stage will help build a firm foundation for the next stages and diminish feelings of guilt for following their own initiatives.
- **Industry versus inferiority (6 to 12 years):** Numerous skills are acquired at this stage, and children seemingly cannot learn fast enough. If they experience satisfaction and success with the completion of tasks they are assigned or initiate, they will feel good about themselves and develop a sense of industry rather than inferiority.
- **Identity versus role confusion (12 to 18 years):** The changes that take place during this stage of adolescence bring about a major shift in personal development. This is the time of transition from childhood to adulthood, when adolescents are developing a sense of identity. They often struggle with self-doubt and question, "Who am I?" When they are able to know themselves, they have a sense of who they are and are comfortable with their own identity. If this does not happen, a sense of role confusion can result.
- **Intimacy versus isolation (young adulthood, 20s to early 40s):** This is the period when young adults are able to make a commitment to another person, to a cause, or to a career. They are able to give a sense of direction to their lives. Otherwise, they feel isolated from the rest of the world.
- **Generativity versus stagnation (middle adulthood, 40s to mid-60s):** Concern with future generations and child rearing is the main focus of this stage. People should continue to grow in this stage and become less selfish; if they don't, stagnation sets in, and they become self-absorbed or self-indulgent, caring for no one.
- **Integrity versus despair (late adulthood, mid-60s through rest of life):** Those who reach the final stage find themselves looking back on their lives with a feeling of satisfaction or with a sense of despair about how life turned out for them—or somewhere in between these two conditions. Coming to terms with one's life and accepting one's failures as well as successes lead to ego integrity. Anguishing over lost opportunities and dreading poor health and death lead to despair.

Checkpoint

Fill in the blank.

1. According to Erikson, an infant whose basic physical needs are met and who feels loved and secure will develop feelings of _____.
2. According to Erikson, between the ages of 3 and 6, children are in the process of developing a sense of _____.
3. According to Erikson, adolescents are in the process of developing a sense of _____.

Mark as True or False.

4. _____ Preschoolers want to take actions that assert themselves.
5. _____ Being successful in school contributes to a child's sense of industry.

Checkpoint Answers

1. trust
2. initiative
3. identity
4. True
5. True

Summary

Effective teachers have a strong understanding of developmentally appropriate practice, and they apply this knowledge to create learning environments in which students engage in active, purposeful, and meaningful learning. They understand that as students mature, they progress through typical cognitive, social, physical, and emotional developmental stages. Moreover, effective teachers recognize that students' developmental characteristics affect their performance in school. Therefore, astute teachers design instruction to accommodate different learning needs and developmental levels.

Chapter 2

Diversity

> **Competency 002:** The teacher understands student diversity and knows how to plan learning experiences and design assessments that are responsive to differences among students and that promote all students' learning.

This chapter provides a general review of knowledge and skills related to Competency 002. Checkpoint exercises are found throughout the review material. These exercises give you an opportunity to practice what you just learned. The answers to the Checkpoint exercises are found immediately following the set of exercises. When doing the Checkpoint exercises, you should cover up the answers. Then check your answers when you've finished the exercises.

Competency Descriptive Statements

The descriptive statements for Competency 002 as given in the TExES PPR EC-12 test preparation manual (www.tx.nesinc.com/Content/Docs/160PrepManual.pdf) specify the following knowledge and skills for beginning teachers in Texas public schools:

- Demonstrates knowledge of students with diverse personal and social characteristics (e.g., those related to ethnicity, gender, language background, exceptionality) and the significance of student diversity for teaching, learning, and assessment.
- Accepts and respects students with diverse backgrounds and needs.
- Knows how to use diversity in the classroom and the community to enrich all students' learning experiences.
- Knows strategies for enhancing one's own understanding of students' diverse backgrounds and needs.
- Knows how to plan and adapt lessons to address students' varied backgrounds, skills, interests, and learning needs, including the needs of English language learners and students with disabilities.
- Understands cultural and socioeconomic differences (including differential access to technology) and knows how to plan instruction that is responsive to cultural and socioeconomic differences among students.
- Understands the instructional significance of varied student learning needs and preferences.
- Knows the ELPS in the domains of listening and speaking in accordance with the proficiency-level descriptors for the beginning, intermediate, advanced, and advanced high levels.
- Knows the ELPS in the domains of reading and writing in accordance with the proficiency-level descriptors for beginning, intermediate, advanced, and advanced high levels.

Learning Styles

Researchers such as Rita and Kenneth Dunn (2006) have suggested that effective teachers should consider their students' learning styles in order to facilitate academic achievement. **Learning style** is the manner in which an individual perceives and processes information in learning situations. Knowledge of learning style theory may help teachers in designing educational conditions in which most students are likely to learn. According to Dunn and Dunn, classrooms can be designed to either stimulate or inhibit learning for students based on their individual learning style needs related to the following:

- The environmental setting in which learning opportunities are presented—includes room temperature, lighting, noise level, and type of seating (for example, desks, chairs, or tables)
- Personal characteristics of the learner—includes motivation, persistence, responsibility, and preference with regard to structure

- The social setting in which learning opportunities are presented—includes grouping arrangement (for example, individual, pairs, small groups, or teams) and teacher interaction patterns
- Physiological factors that impact the learner—includes modality preference (see the section "Modality Preferences" that follows for a discussion of this topic), food/drink intake, time of day, and mobility opportunities

Furthermore, Dunn and Dunn maintained that psychological characteristics of the student influence the student's ability to learn. These psychological characteristics include impulsivity/reflectivity inclination and brain hemisphericity.

Jerome Kagan's (1966) work on **impulsivity/reflectivity inclination** concluded that individuals are consistent in the way they process information and the speed with which they do it. **Impulsive** students tend to work and make decisions quickly. They respond to situations often with the first thought that occurs to them, regularly finishing assignments and tests before everyone else. **Reflective** students ponder all the alternatives carefully before responding, working cautiously and deliberately. Impulsive students tend to concentrate on speed, but reflective students concentrate more on accuracy.

Brain hemisphericity refers to the tendency to be either **right-brain dominant** or **left-brain dominant** in learning style. In theory, each hemisphere of the brain is associated with certain thinking traits and, therefore, certain learning styles. Considerable research has been done that supports the notion that people who are left-brain dominant learn in different ways than do right-brain-dominant people. The terms *left-brained, analytic,* and *deductive* and the terms *right-brained, global,* and *inductive* are often used interchangeably to describe learners based on brain hemispheric orientation. The following table summarizes the characteristics of the different types of learners using these labels.

Type of Learner	Characteristics
Left-brained/analytic/deductive learner	Thinks from part to whole Processes thought logically and analytically Approaches problem solving systematically Is skillful at reasoning deductively Depends on words and language for meaning Readily follows verbal instructions Prefers lessons that proceed in a step-by-step logical order Prefers structured assignments Is independent Prefers quiet, bright lighting, and formal seating when working Might not think of himself/herself as creative
Right-brained/global/inductive learner	Thinks from whole to part Processes thought holistically Approaches problem solving randomly with visual, nonverbal strategies (for example, drawing a picture) Is skillful at reasoning inductively Sees patterns and relationships Prefers to see the big picture before exploring the small details Prefers instructions that are graphically presented or modeled Learns better when images and pictures augment text Can work on several parts of a task at the same time Likes group work and social activities Likes music/sound, dim lighting, and relaxed seating when working Engages in creative activities

Everyone is a whole-brained person but, usually, with a preference for receiving information through either the left or right hemisphere. Neither preference is in any way superior to the other, although instruction in most public schools in the United States has traditionally favored left-brain-dominant students.

Other well-known learning style classifications are *field independence/field dependence, concrete/abstract learning,* and *multiple intelligences.* (See "Field Independence/Field Dependence," "Gregorc's Mind Styles," and "Multiple Intelligences" later in this chapter for discussions of these topics.)

Checkpoint

Fill in the blank.

1. Generally, learners who prefer to see the big picture before engaging in a learning activity are _____ (right-brain-dominant, left-brain-dominant) learners.

2. Learners who approach problem solving systematically are _____ (right-brain-dominant, left-brain-dominant) learners.

3. A brightly lit classroom would appeal to _____ (right-brain-dominant, left-brain-dominant) learners.

Mark as True or False.

4. _____ Impulsive students ponder all the alternatives carefully before responding.

5. _____ Instruction in most public schools in the United States has traditionally favored left-brain-dominant students.

Checkpoint Answers

1. right-brain-dominant
2. left-brain-dominant
3. left-brain-dominant
4. False
5. True

Modality Preferences

Educators usually refer to the predominant way a student takes in information through the five primary senses (sight, hearing, smell, taste, and touch) as **sensory modality strength.** Students who prefer to learn by seeing or reading something are **visual** learners; students who learn best by listening are **auditory** learners; and students who prefer to learn by touching objects, by feeling shapes and textures, and by moving things around are **tactile/kinesthetic** learners. Some students have a single modality strength (visual, auditory, or tactile/kinesthetic), while others have combination, or mixed, modalities. Children with mixed modality strengths usually are able to process information efficiently no matter how it is presented. In contrast, children with single modality strengths might experience difficulties when instruction is presented outside the scope of their modality strength. Most students eventually learn to adjust when the instructional material is not consistent with their modality preference. However, most educators agree that planning for those learners who are visual, auditory, tactile/kinesthetic, or a combination of these is critical if teachers are to help all learners be successful. The following chart describes the three types of learners in regard to modality preferences.

Description of Learners

Auditory Learner	Visual Learner	Kinesthetic/Tactile Learner
Likes to make people laugh	Has good spatial memory	Wants to feel and touch things
Is a good storyteller	Enjoys drawing pictures	Has good motor skills
Enjoys listening activities	Enjoys illustrated books	Enjoys doing things manually
Memorizes easily	Likes to work puzzles	Likes taking things apart

continued

Chapter 2: Diversity

Auditory Learner	Visual Learner	Kinesthetic/Tactile Learner
Can deliver oral messages accurately	Remembers faces	Likes to use concrete objects when learning
Is easily distracted	Has trouble remembering oral instructions	Avoids reading
Enjoys being in charge	Dislikes speaking before a group	Sometimes appears immature in behavior

This next chart contains guidelines for working with auditory, visual, and kinesthetic/tactile learners.

Ways to Accommodate

Auditory Learner	Visual Learner	Kinesthetic/Tactile Learner
Read directions orally.	Use graphic aids (pictures, images, graphs, charts, and so on).	Use hands-on activities.
Use repetition.	Use visual presentations (videos, presentation software, and so on).	Use manipulatives and other tactile materials.
Have learners read aloud.	Use models and demonstrations.	Use outdoor activities.
Use music activities.	Encourage learners to draw or illustrate.	Keep learners physically active.
Use read-alouds.	Use memory and concentration games.	Use role playing and simulations.
Have learners verbalize while reading.	Play "what's missing?" games.	Use dramatic play and puppetry.
Have learners act as peer tutors.	Use puzzles.	Use musical instruments.
Use taped lessons.	Use art activities.	Associate concepts with movement activities.
Use group activities.	Provide time for independent work.	Allow freedom for physical movement by the learner.

Checkpoint

Fill in the blank.

1. Role playing and simulations are most beneficial for _____ (auditory, visual, kinesthetic/tactile) learners.
2. Reading directions aloud will help _____ (auditory, visual, kinesthetic/tactile) learners the most.
3. Students who prefer to learn by seeing or reading something are _____ (auditory, visual, kinesthetic/tactile) learners.

Mark as True or False.

4. _____ Visual learners prefer group activities.
5. _____ Auditory learners are talkative.

Checkpoint Answers

1. kinesthetic/tactile
2. auditory
3. visual
4. False
5. True

Field Independence/Field Dependence

The work of Herman Witkin and Donald Goodenough (1981) on **field independence/field dependence** closely paralleled brain hemisphericity findings. These researchers described learners as **field independent** (having the ability to perceive objects without being influenced by the background) and **field dependent** (having the ability to perceive objects as a whole rather than as individual parts). Characteristics of field-independent and field-dependent learners are summarized in the following chart.

Type of Learner	Characteristics
Field independent	Processes information in parts Might focus on specific parts, rather than see the whole Passive in social situations Tends to be less influenced by peers Likes working alone Chooses fields like math, science, and engineering
Field dependent	Processes information holistically Has difficulty separating specific parts from a situation or pattern Able to see relational concepts Active in social situations Tends to be influenced by suggestions from others Likes to work in groups Chooses fields requiring interpersonal, nonscientific orientation, such as history, art, or social work

Checkpoint

Fill in the blank.

1. Teachers who plan social events for students should keep in mind that _____ (field-independent, field-dependent) learners are likely to be passive during the event.

2. Math and science fields are preferred by _____ (field-independent, field-dependent) learners.

3. Group work appeals to _____ (field-independent, field-dependent) learners.

Mark as True or False.

4. _____ Field-dependent learners process information holistically.

5. _____ Field-independent learners are very susceptible to peer pressure.

Checkpoint Answers

1. field-independent
2. field-independent
3. field-dependent
4. True
5. False

Gregorc's Mind Styles

Anthony Gregorc's (2002) Mind Styles model considers the predominant way learners prefer to process and organize information for learning. To perceive information, **concrete learners** rely on physically experiencing it; in contrast, **abstract learners** are able to process symbolic, abstract representations of information. To organize information, **random organizers** tend to chunk information in no particular order, and **sequential organizers** use a linear, step-by-step organizational approach. These classifications give rise to four types of learners, as described in the following chart.

Type of Learner	Learning Preferences
Concrete-sequential	Enjoys hands-on, linearly sequenced learning
Concrete-random	Enjoys hands-on, exploratory learning
Abstract-sequential	Enjoys abstract, logically sequenced, analytical learning
Abstract-random	Enjoys mentally challenging activities in an informal environment

Checkpoint

Fill in the blank.

1. Using manipulatives would appeal to _____ (concrete, abstract) learners.
2. Solving written abstract equations would appeal to _____ (concrete, abstract) learners.
3. Being given step-by-step directions would appeal to _____ (random, sequential) organizers.

Mark as True or False.

4. _____ Working in an unorganized environment would be difficult for a concrete-sequential learner.
5. _____ Working in a restricted environment would be difficult for an abstract-random learner.

Checkpoint Answers

1. concrete
2. abstract
3. sequential
4. True
5. True

Multiple Intelligences

Howard Gardner proposed the theory of **multiple intelligences** (Davis et al., 2012). In his most recent works, he suggested that humans have nine intelligences:

- **Verbal-linguistic intelligence:** The ability to use and produce words
- **Logical-mathematical intelligence:** The ability to do math, recognize patterns, and problem-solve
- **Visual-spatial intelligence:** The ability to form images and pictures in the mind
- **Bodily-kinesthetic intelligence:** The ability to use the body in physical activities
- **Musical-rhythmic intelligence:** The ability to recognize musical and rhythmic patterns and sounds
- **Intrapersonal intelligence:** The ability to know oneself
- **Interpersonal intelligence:** The ability to work cooperatively with other people
- **Naturalistic intelligence:** The ability to understand and work in the natural world
- **Existential intelligence:** The ability to grapple with issues of human existence

Multiple intelligences inform teachers that students can be smart in many ways. Teachers whose practices reflect the theory of multiple intelligences learn to look at learners from nine different viewpoints. They recognize that students have less anxiety and can learn better when the learning task is congruent with their strengths and abilities. For example, in social studies, verbal-linguistic learners would prefer to debate about a historical event, but bodily-kinesthetic learners would prefer to act it out.

The popularity of Gardner's theory persists among teachers despite criticism of the theory from both psychologists and educators. These detractors contend that Gardner's definition of intelligence is too broad and that some of the so-called intelligences are simply talents or personality traits.

Checkpoint

Fill in the blank.

1. Having students create a human graph will appeal to students with _____ intelligence.
2. Drawing a map of the setting of a story will appeal to students with _____ intelligence.
3. Using a familiar tune to teach math rules will appeal to students with _____ intelligence.

Mark as True or False.

4. _____ Students with strong interpersonal intelligence will enjoy group activities.
5. _____ Students with strong visual-spatial intelligence tend to think in images rather than in words or sounds.

Checkpoint Answers

1. bodily-kinesthetic
2. visual-spatial
3. musical-rhythmic
4. True
5. True

High-Ability Learners

As with all students, high-ability students come to school with unique characteristics and abilities and are from various ethnic, cultural, and socioeconomic backgrounds. Texas's high-ability student population is as diverse as the state itself. According to James Gallagher (1994), teacher identification of high-ability students can be influenced by the erroneous belief that a high-ability student must fit the "perfect" student model (that is, performs well in school, behaves appropriately, turns in work on time, and so forth). However, not all high-ability students perform well in school. Students of high ability might conceal their potential for various reasons, such as peer pressure or cultural norms to "fit in" and not be different. Teachers need to be sensitive to these issues and strive to overcome them by nurturing a climate in the classroom that fosters a positive attitude toward learning.

The Council for Exceptional Children (1990) compiled the following list of general characteristics of high-ability learners:

- shows superior reasoning powers and marked ability to handle ideas; can generalize readily from specific facts and can see subtle relationships; has outstanding problem-solving ability;
- shows persistent intellectual curiosity; asks searching questions; shows exceptional interest in the nature of humanity and the universe;
- has a wide range of interests, often of an intellectual kind; develops one or more interests to considerable depth;

- is markedly superior in quality and quantity of written and/or spoken vocabulary; is interested in the subtleties of words and their uses;
- reads avidly and absorbs books well beyond his/her years;
- learns quickly and easily and retains what is learned; recalls important details, concepts, and principles; comprehends readily;
- shows insight into mathematical problems that require careful reasoning and grasps mathematical concepts readily;
- shows creative ability of imaginative expression in such areas as music, art, dance, drama; shows sensitivity and finesse in rhythm, movement, and bodily control;
- sustains concentration for lengthy periods and shows outstanding responsibility and independence in classroom work;
- sets realistically high standards for self; is self-critical in evaluating and correcting his/her own efforts;
- shows initiative and originality in intellectual work; shows flexibility in thinking and considers problems from a number of viewpoints;
- observes keenly and is responsive to new ideas;
- shows social poise and an ability to communicate with adults in a mature way; and
- gets excitement and pleasure from intellectual challenge; shows an alert and subtle sense of humor.

Traits that often mask high ability in students, but which in some children can actually indicate potential high ability, are listed below.

- questions authority and rules; questions reasons for decisions; may be stubborn; will disagree strongly sometimes;
- sometimes acts without planning; may be sloppy, unorganized; is not bothered by mess and disorder;
- fails to complete homework and classroom assignments; may not pay attention to time limits or deadlines;
- appears bored and withdrawn, yet capable when pressed; may be bashful;
- has extensive knowledge in some out-of-school-oriented topic; may possess a sophisticated collection of models, coins, stamps, etc.;
- is a non-conformist; may not be well-liked by classroom peers; may have odd habits; does not try to act "proper";
- reads a lot and may often choose reading in place of doing classwork;
- is a risk-taker; is willing to take an unpopular stand even if it means losing friends and/or respect;
- is alert to stimuli in environment; is observant; may appear to be "day-dreaming" or distracted; may be stubborn when undertaking difficult tasks;
- likes to be "the best"; may not accept imperfection of any kind; may not take constructive criticism;
- sometimes demonstrates a behavior problem; may be discourteous, unable to accept criticism and/or discipline;
- has high energy; sometimes finds it difficult to sit still; may be impatient; and
- tends to dominate or "take charge" of an activity in which she/he is involved; can be "bossy" with peers.

(From www.coursehero.com/file/p1ono35/CHARACTERISTICS-OF-THE-GIFTED-1Questions-authority-and-rules-questions-reasons/)

Generally, when motivated, high-ability learners are ready for fast-paced, very abstract instruction and learn better in environments in which they are given a measure of control over their learning options. They need learning experiences that are challenging, meaningful, and appropriate to their needs and abilities. In particular, when working with students identified as gifted, effective teachers recognize that gifted students need opportunities to interact and work with the other students in the class, but that they also need time to work alone and with other high-ability students to pursue topics to higher levels of cognitive challenge.

Checkpoint

Mark as True or False.

1. _____ High-ability students are usually very similar in ethnicity, culture, and socioeconomic backgrounds.
2. _____ Not all high-ability students perform well in school.
3. _____ Typically, high-ability learners are avid readers and have extensive vocabularies.
4. _____ High-ability students need time to work alone and with other high-ability students.

Checkpoint Answers

1. False
2. True
3. True
4. True

Struggling Learners

Struggling learners are students who, for a variety of reasons, are at risk of academic failure and might drop out of school at some point. They need high-quality teachers and dramatically different, innovative approaches to teaching and learning. These students are not incapable of learning, but they are (usually) concrete thinkers who need structured environments. Moreover, they need opportunities to experience academic success on assignments they perceive as meaningful and challenging. To make this aim a reality, good teachers differentiate instruction to meet their learning needs (see "Response to Intervention (RtI)" later in this chapter for a discussion of differentiation).

Good teachers are sensitive and caring in their interactions with students of varying abilities. They avoid disparate treatment toward students who are perceived to be high or low achievers, rather aiming to treat all students fairly. In their studies of classrooms, Thomas Good and Jere Brophy (2002) identified the following disparate treatment behaviors by teachers that should be avoided:

- Give high achievers preferential seating.
- Seat low achievers away from the teacher.
- Isolate low achievers from high achievers.
- Use fewer nonverbal cues with low achievers during instruction.
- Call on high achievers more frequently than low achievers.
- Wait longer for responses from high achievers.
- Fail to use probes with low achievers when they attempt a response.
- Criticize low achievers for incorrect responses more often.
- Praise high achievers for correct public responses more often.
- Praise low achievers for inadequate public responses.
- Provide low achievers with less useful feedback.
- Lower standards for low achievers.
- Interrupt low achievers' performances more frequently.
- Talk negatively about low achievers more often.
- Punish off-task behavior of low achievers, but more frequently ignore it in high achievers.

Chapter 2: Diversity

To make instruction effective for all students, teachers need to take into account students' diverse learning needs and must make a conscious effort to avoid disparate treatment based on students' ability levels. It is not unusual for teachers to have a wide range of ability levels in their classrooms. Too much whole-group instruction in such classrooms is likely to be ineffective because the instruction could be too advanced for some students and too easy for others.

Checkpoint

Fill in the blank.

1. Struggling students need _____ teachers.
2. Struggling students need frequent, corrective _____.
3. Struggling students are usually _____ (abstract, concrete) thinkers.
4. Too much whole-group instruction in a mixed-ability classroom is likely to be _____.

Checkpoint Answers

1. high-quality
2. feedback
3. concrete
4. ineffective

Gender Patterns

Gender equity is an important initiative in the nation and in the state of Texas. In planning for instruction, teachers need to recognize that although male and female students are equally capable of academic achievement, learned patterns of gender differences might be exhibited in their classrooms. To counteract such patterns, teachers should first check themselves to make sure they are not exhibiting stereotypical behavior toward students and then build safeguards into their lessons that include the following actions:

- monitoring group activities to make sure both male and female students assume various roles during activities.
- using inclusive language such as "class" instead of "boys and girls."
- modeling acceptance of nonstereotypical behaviors and attitudes.
- bringing in both male and female guest speakers who have what once were considered "nontraditional" careers.
- openly discussing gender stereotyping with students, when necessary.
- encouraging students to strive for excellence in all subject areas.
- consciously endeavoring to provide equitable opportunities for boys and girls alike.

Checkpoint

Fill in the blank.

1. Male and female students are _____ capable of academic achievement.
2. Teachers should encourage students to strive for excellence in _____ subject areas.
3. Teachers should consciously endeavor to provide _____ opportunities for male and female students alike.

Mark as True or False.

4. _____ Gender equity is an important issue in Texas.
5. _____ High school teachers should encourage students to consider careers traditionally associated with their gender roles.

30

Checkpoint Answers

1. equally
2. all
3. equitable
4. True
5. False

Response to Intervention (RtI)

Response to intervention (RtI) is used by schools in Texas to help all students, including struggling learners, to have opportunities to learn and work at their grade level. RtI focuses on identifying and addressing problems early with students who exhibit academic weakness. It is a data-based, decision-making model that enables educators to match instruction and/or intervention to learners' areas of specific need as soon as those needs become apparent. RtI is implemented through multi-tiered systems of supports (sometimes referred to as **RtI/MTSS—response to intervention/multi-tiered systems of supports**). The basic premise of RtI is for students to receive an array of high-quality, research-based instruction and/or interventions in multi-tiered learning situations (all students, small-group, or one-on-one) to increase the expectation that they will achieve district grade-level/subject area proficiency levels. Differentiating instruction in a three-tiered model that uses increasingly "intense" (increased time, smaller group size, narrower focus) instruction and support based on student screening, progress monitoring, and data analysis is the framework for RtI.

Tier 1 (universal) instruction provides general core academic instruction to all students in whole-group or small-group settings in the general education classroom. Differentiated instruction occurs based on students' diverse learning abilities. Instructional time for a particular content/subject area is based on district standards, which must comply with state guidelines/regulations. On average, roughly 80 percent of students are expected to achieve academic success (that is, achieve district grade-level/subject area expectations) with Tier 1 instruction.

Tier 2 (targeted) instruction is targeted, supplemental skills-focused instruction that uses evidence-based interventions. It is delivered to small groups of only three to five students. Students are grouped for this supplemental instruction based on common academic needs identified through the use of formative assessment, observation, and other relevant data. They receive Tier 2 instruction (in addition to their Tier 1 instruction) to help them catch up. It must be integrated with Tier 1 content and grade-level expectations. Tier 2 instruction can be provided in the general education classroom by the general education teacher or by a supplemental instruction teacher, or it can be provided outside of the general education classroom. The number of minutes of instruction should be greater than the number of minutes typically provided to students for that skill focus. On average, around 15 percent of students might need Tier 2 interventions.

Tier 3 (intensive) instruction uses the most intensive, evidence-based interventions and support. Usually, Tier 3 instruction is provided to students individually. The interventions for these students focus on skills that assessment data indicate are the greatest barriers to their learning. Candidates for Tier 3 instruction are students who are most at risk of failure and need concentrated, individualized help. Compared to Tiers 1 and 2, Tier 3 instruction has the most instructional time, smallest group size (most often, one student), and narrowest skills focus. It also provides extensive opportunities for practice, error correction, and feedback. On average, around 5 percent of students might need Tier 3 interventions when data from progress monitoring show that Tier 1 instruction and Tier 2 instruction have not resulted in the student achieving desired learning goals.

Teachers should be aware that the three tiers describe different instructional levels of help that students may need at a particular time. These are not instructional categories that students are locked into. Instead, the levels of support a student receives will increase or decrease as the student's level of need changes.

A principal idea behind RtI is that proactive continuous progress monitoring of students' performance and delivery of appropriate support and interventions should be an ongoing part of the educational experience of all Texas students, from kindergarten through graduation. Instead of waiting until students fail when they are typically too far behind to reach grade-level expectations through interventions normally available in public schools, RtI procedures identify and begin interventions early, monitor frequently, and modify based on student response to intervention. A data collection and assessment system is used to inform decisions at the different tier levels. The goal of the process is to improve the effectiveness of instruction/interventions to maximize achievement of positive outcomes for students.

Checkpoint

Fill in the blank.

1. RtI involves _____ instruction and/or interventions to meet the diverse needs of learners.
2. The basic premise of RtI is that all students must receive high-quality, _____ instruction in multi-tiered learner situations.
3. RtI uses _____ (number) tiers for instruction differentiation.

Mark as True or False.

4. _____ A principal idea behind RtI is that waiting until students fail is the most effective way to determine appropriate interventions.
5. _____ RtI is only for students with disabilities.

Checkpoint Answers

1. matching
2. research-based
3. three
4. False
5. False

Accommodations for Eligible Students with Disabilities

The Individuals with Disabilities Education Act (IDEA) and Texas state law require teachers in Texas to provide needed modifications and accommodations to eligible students with disabilities. **Modifications** are changes in what a student is expected to learn and may include changes to content, requirements, and expected level of mastery, which might, at graduation, result in the awarding of a special diploma to the student receiving the modifications. **Accommodations** are changes that are made in how the student accesses information and demonstrates performance. Accommodations are the adaptations that need to be made so that students with disabilities can participate in the general curriculum as fully as possible and, thus, be eligible for a standard diploma. When providing accommodations, teachers should avoid making learners with disabilities feel singled out or stigmatized. (See "Professional Conduct with Students Receiving Special Education Services" in Chapter 13 for further discussion of this topic.)

The focus here is on accommodations. Students eligible for accommodations are those with physical or mental disabilities who are identified as needing special education and have an Individualized Educational Program (IEP; also commonly referred to as an Individual Educational Plan) or who qualify under Section 504 of the Rehabilitation Act of 1973 and have 504 plans. IDEA specifies the following categories under which 3- through 21-year-olds are eligible for services:

- **Autism.** A developmental disability significantly affecting verbal and nonverbal communication and social interaction, generally evident before age 3, that adversely affects a child's educational performance. Other characteristics often associated with autism are engagement in repetitive activities and stereotyped movements, resistance to environmental change or change in daily routines, and unusual responses to sensory experiences.

- **Deaf-blindness.** Concomitant hearing and visual impairments, the combination of which causes such severe communication and other developmental and educational needs that they cannot be accommodated in special education programs solely for children with deafness or children with blindness.
- **Deafness.** A hearing impairment that is so severe that the child is impaired in processing linguistic information through hearing, with or without amplification, that adversely affects a child's educational performance.
- **Emotional disturbance.** A condition exhibiting one or more of the following characteristics over a long period of time and to a marked degree that adversely affects a child's educational performance: an inability to learn that cannot be explained by intellectual, sensory, or health factors; an inability to build or maintain satisfactory interpersonal relationships with peers and teachers; inappropriate types of behavior or feelings under normal circumstances; a general pervasive mood of unhappiness or depression; a tendency to develop physical symptoms or fears associated with personal or school problems. Emotional disturbance includes schizophrenia.
- **Hearing impairment.** An impairment in hearing, whether permanent or fluctuating, that adversely affects a child's educational performance but that is not included under the definition of deafness in this section.
- **Intellectual disability.** Significantly subaverage general intellectual functioning, existing concurrently with deficits in adaptive behavior and manifested during the developmental period, that adversely affects a child's educational performance.
- **Multiple disabilities.** Concomitant impairments (such as intellectual disability-blindness or intellectual disability-orthopedic impairment), the combination of which causes such severe educational needs that they cannot be accommodated in special education programs solely for one of the impairments. Multiple disabilities does not include deaf-blindness.
- **Orthopedic impairment.** A severe orthopedic impairment that adversely affects a child's educational performance. The term includes impairments caused by a congenital anomaly, impairments caused by disease (e.g., poliomyelitis, bone tuberculosis), and impairments from other causes (e.g., cerebral palsy, amputations, and fractures or burns that cause contractures).
- **Other health impairment.** Having limited strength, vitality, or alertness, including a heightened alertness to environmental stimuli, that results in limited alertness with respect to the educational environment, that is due to chronic or acute health problems such as asthma, attention deficit disorder or attention deficit hyperactivity disorder, diabetes, epilepsy, a heart condition, hemophilia, lead poisoning, leukemia, nephritis, rheumatic fever, sickle cell anemia, and Tourette syndrome; and adversely affects a child's educational performance.
- **Specific learning disability.** A disorder in one or more of the basic psychological processes involved in understanding or in using language, spoken or written, that may manifest itself in the imperfect ability to listen, think, speak, read, write, spell, or to do mathematical calculations, including conditions such as perceptual disabilities, brain injury, minimal brain dysfunction, dyslexia, and developmental aphasia.
- **Speech or language impairment.** A communication disorder, such as stuttering, impaired articulation, a language impairment, or a voice impairment, that adversely affects a child's educational performance.
- **Traumatic brain injury.** An acquired injury to the brain caused by an external physical force, resulting in total or partial functional disability or psychosocial impairment, or both, that adversely affects a child's educational performance. Traumatic brain injury applies to open or closed head injuries resulting in impairments in one or more areas, such as cognition; language; memory; attention; reasoning; abstract thinking; judgment; problem-solving; sensory, perceptual, and motor abilities; psychosocial behavior; physical functions; information processing; and speech. Traumatic brain injury does not apply to brain injuries that are congenital or degenerative, or to brain injuries induced by birth trauma.
- **Visual impairment, including blindness.** An impairment in vision that, even with correction, adversely affects a child's educational performance. The term includes both partial sight and blindness.

According to the *Accommodations Manual: How to Select, Administer, and Evaluate Use of Accommodations for Instruction and Assessment of Students with Disabilities,* 2nd Edition (Thompson, Morse, Sharpe, and Hall, 2005), accommodations may be made in four general ways:

- **Presentation accommodations:** The adaptive ways information and tests are presented to students. For example, for learners with visual impairments, use large print; books, text, or notes on tape; peer or adult readers; note-takers; preferential seating; magnifying devices; color contrast/color overlays; large-key calculators; or devices that use synthesized speech (for example, "talking" calculators, text-to-speech technology). For learners who are deaf or hard of hearing, use visuals and graphics, gestures and visual cues, note-takers, sign language interpreters, audio amplifying devices, and/or speech-to-text technology. For learners who are easily distracted, use prearranged cues and signals, checklists and agendas, highlighters, and written step-by-step instructions. For learners who have trouble comprehending material, provide graphic organizers and overviews, vocabulary lists, and checklists; use repetition, paraphrasing, and summarizing; use concrete materials and hands-on activities; and use peer helpers and cooperative learning groups.

- **Response accommodations:** The adaptive ways students are allowed to complete assignments and tests. For example, for learners with visual impairments, allow the use of personal note-takers, Braillers, large-key calculators, and devices with an audio component (for example, talking calculators or thermometers), and accept oral responses, as well as responses through a scribe, on tape, and/or through speech-to-text technology. For learners who are deaf or hard of hearing, allow the use of sign language interpreters, word processors, visual organizers, and/or spelling and grammar assistive devices. For learners who have physical impairments and those who have speech and language impairments, allow the use of scribes, assistive communication devices, and/or tape recorders. For learners who have specific learning disabilities, allow the use of word processors, spelling and grammar assistive devices, word prediction software, written notes, math tables and formula sheets, and/or calculators.

- **Setting accommodations:** The adaptive ways to change the setting to make completion of assignments and tests more appropriate for the student. For example, for learners with visual impairments and those who are deaf or hard of hearing, change location to reduce distractions to the student and to surrounding students or to provide access to special equipment. For learners who have physical impairments, change location to provide access to special equipment. For learners who are easily distracted, change location to reduce distractions and/or use white noise or music to mask sounds in the environment.

- **Timing and scheduling accommodations:** The adaptive ways to alter time constraints and scheduling to be more appropriate for the student. For most categories, give extended time based on the needs of the student. For learners who have trouble concentrating, build in frequent breaks and/or split assignments or tests into subparts and give at different times or on different days.

It is important to note that in order for an accommodation to be allowed on a statewide assessment, the accommodation must be specified in the IEP or 504 plan and used regularly in classroom instruction and assessment. Furthermore, parents must be informed about and their permission obtained for any accommodation not allowed on statewide assessments. For example, students cannot use spell checkers or grammar checkers when taking the statewide assessments.

Note: See "Learning Environment Accommodations for Learners with Special Educational Needs" in Chapter 5 for a discussion of accommodations for students with disabilities that affect their behavior in the classroom.

Checkpoint

Fill in the blank.

1. Modifications are changes in _____ a student is expected to learn.

2. Accommodations are changes in _____ a student accesses information and demonstrates performance.

3. In order for an accommodation to be allowed on a statewide assessment, the accommodation must be specified in the IEP or 504 plan and used _____ in classroom instruction and assessment.

Mark as True or False.

4. _____ Teachers are required by law to make accommodations for students with disabilities.

5. _____ Giving students extended time is an example of an accommodation.

Checkpoint Answers

1. what
2. how
3. regularly
4. True
5. True

English Language Proficiency Levels

In Texas, the English language proficiency of English language learners (ELLs) in kindergarten through grade 12 is determined based on four proficiency levels—*beginning, intermediate, advanced, and advanced high*—in four language domains—*listening, speaking, reading,* and *writing*.

ELLs are at different stages of language acquisition. The proficiency levels are not grade or domain specific. ELLs might exhibit different proficiency levels within the four language components: listening, speaking, reading, and writing. A student may exhibit oral skills at the advanced level, reading skills at the intermediate level, and writing skills at the beginning level. Understanding the level of English language proficiency of the student is critical in order for the student to have access to the curriculum. Any combination of the language components is possible and is affected by opportunities for interaction in and outside of school.

Here are general descriptors of the four proficiency levels:

- **Beginning.** These students associate utterances with meaning as they make inferences based on actions, visuals, text, tone of voice, and inflections. Receptive language with some comprehension is acquired earlier than oral production. Beginning ELLs produce spoken English with increasing accuracy and fluency to convey appropriate meaning. They read English using letter-sound cues, syntax, visuals, the context of the text, and their prior knowledge of language and structure of text.
- **Intermediate.** These students use the listening process to improve comprehension and oral skills in English. Through listening and speaking in meaningful interactions, they clarify, distinguish, and evaluate ideas and responses in a variety of situations. Intermediate ELLs participate successfully in academic, social, and work contexts in English using the process of speaking to create, clarify, critique, and evaluate ideas and responses. Intermediate ELLs read English using and applying developmental vocabulary to increase comprehension and produce written text to address a variety of audiences and purposes.
- **Advanced.** These students, through developmental listening skills, actively expand their vocabulary to evaluate and analyze spoken English for a variety of situations and purposes. These ELLs participate in a variety of situations using spoken English to create, clarify, critique, and evaluate ideas and responses. Advanced ELLs continually develop reading skills for increasing reading proficiency in content area texts for a variety of purposes and generate written text for different audiences in a variety of modes to convey appropriate meaning according to their level of proficiency.
- **Advanced High.** These students' reading, speaking, and writing abilities are comparable to those of their native English-speaking peers. They understand grade-appropriate English as it is used in academic and social settings. Advanced high ELLs use language skills on their grade level in the academic subject areas with minimal interruptions, and they use abstract and content-based vocabulary effectively. These ELLs continually use the English language to build additional foundational reading skills such as fluency and prosody, as well as higher-order comprehension skills. They have a strong command of English language structures necessary to address writing at appropriate grade levels.

[Source: adapted from 19 TAC § 128.31 (a)(10)]

The ELPS **proficiency level descriptors (PLDs)** specify the main characteristics of each language proficiency level for each language domain and define how well ELLs at the four proficiency levels are able to understand and use English in academic and social settings. The PLDs are a component of the Texas English Language Proficiency

Standards (ELPS; see Chapter 8 for a further discussion of the ELPS), which, in turn, are part of the Texas Essential Knowledge and Skills (TEKS; see Chapter 3 for a discussion of the TEKS). Student performance in each domain is reported in terms of the four English language proficiency levels described in the ELPS. Below are the descriptors for the proficiency levels for each of the four domains.

Listening, Kindergarten-Grade 12. ELLs may be at the beginning, intermediate, advanced, or advanced high stage of English language acquisition in listening. The following proficiency level descriptors for listening are sufficient to describe the overall English language proficiency levels of ELLs in this language domain in order to linguistically accommodate their instruction.

Beginning. Beginning ELLs have little or no ability to understand spoken English in academic and social settings.

These students:

- struggle to understand simple conversations and simple discussions even when the topics are familiar and the speaker uses linguistic supports such as visuals, slower speech and other verbal cues, and gestures;
- struggle to identify and distinguish individual words and phrases during social and instructional interactions that have not been intentionally modified for ELLs; and
- may not seek clarification in English when failing to comprehend the English they hear; frequently remain silent, watching others for cues.

Intermediate. Intermediate ELLs have the ability to understand simple, high-frequency spoken English used in routine academic and social settings.

These students:

- usually understand simple or routine directions, as well as short, simple conversations and short, simple discussions on familiar topics; when topics are unfamiliar, require extensive linguistic supports and adaptations such as visuals, slower speech and other verbal cues, simplified language, gestures, and preteaching to preview or build topic-related vocabulary;
- often identify and distinguish key words and phrases necessary to understand the general meaning during social and basic instructional interactions that have not been intentionally modified for ELLs; and
- have the ability to seek clarification in English when failing to comprehend the English they hear by requiring/requesting the speaker to repeat, slow down, or rephrase speech.

Advanced. Advanced ELLs have the ability to understand, with second language acquisition support, grade-appropriate spoken English used in academic and social settings.

These students:

- usually understand longer, more elaborated directions, conversations, and discussions on familiar and some unfamiliar topics, but sometimes need processing time and sometimes depend on visuals, verbal cues, and gestures to support understanding;
- understand most main points, most important details, and some implicit information during social and basic instructional interactions that have not been intentionally modified for ELLs; and
- occasionally require/request the speaker to repeat, slow down, or rephrase to clarify the meaning of the English they hear.

Advanced high. Advanced high ELLs have the ability to understand, with minimal second language acquisition support, grade-appropriate spoken English used in academic and social settings.

These students:

- understand longer, elaborated directions, conversations, and discussions on familiar and unfamiliar topics with occasional need for processing time and with little dependence on visuals, verbal cues, and gestures; demonstrate some exceptions when complex academic or highly specialized language is used;

- understand main points, important details, and implicit information at a level nearly comparable to native English-speaking peers during social and instructional interactions; and
- rarely require/request the speaker to repeat, slow down, or rephrase to clarify the meaning of the English they hear.

Speaking, Kindergarten-Grade 12. ELLs may be at the beginning, intermediate, advanced, or advanced high stage of English language acquisition in speaking. The following proficiency level descriptors for speaking are sufficient to describe the overall English language proficiency levels of ELLs in this language domain in order to linguistically accommodate their instruction.

Beginning. Beginning ELLs have little or no ability to speak English in academic and social settings.

These students:

- mainly speak using single words and short phrases consisting of recently practiced, memorized, or highly familiar material to get immediate needs met; may be hesitant to speak and often give up in their attempts to communicate;
- speak using a very limited bank of high-frequency, high-need, concrete vocabulary, including key words and expressions needed for basic communication in academic and social contexts;
- lack the knowledge of English grammar necessary to connect ideas and speak in sentences; can sometimes produce sentences using recently practiced, memorized, or highly familiar material;
- exhibit second language acquisition errors that may hinder overall communication, particularly when trying to convey information beyond memorized, practiced, or highly familiar material; and
- typically use pronunciation that significantly inhibits communication.

Intermediate. Intermediate ELLs have the ability to speak in a simple manner using English commonly heard in routine academic and social settings.

These students:

- are able to express simple, original messages, speak using sentences, and participate in short conversations and classroom interactions; may hesitate frequently and for long periods to think about how to communicate desired meaning;
- speak simply using basic vocabulary needed in everyday social interactions and routine academic contexts; rarely have vocabulary to speak in detail;
- exhibit an emerging awareness of English grammar and speak using mostly simple sentence structures and simple tenses; are most comfortable speaking in present tense;
- exhibit second language acquisition errors that may hinder overall communication when trying to use complex or less familiar English; and
- use pronunciation that can usually be understood by people accustomed to interacting with ELLs.

Advanced. Advanced ELLs have the ability to speak using grade-appropriate English, with second language acquisition support, in academic and social settings.

These students:

- are able to participate comfortably in most conversations and academic discussions on familiar topics, with some pauses to restate, repeat, or search for words and phrases to clarify meaning;
- discuss familiar academic topics using content-based terms and common abstract vocabulary; can usually speak in some detail on familiar topics;
- have a grasp of basic grammar features, including a basic ability to narrate and describe in present, past, and future tenses; have an emerging ability to use complex sentences and complex grammar features;

Chapter 2: Diversity

- make errors that interfere somewhat with communication when using complex grammar structures, long sentences, and less familiar words and expressions; and
- may mispronounce words, but use pronunciation that can usually be understood by people not accustomed to interacting with ELLs.

Advanced high. Advanced high ELLs have the ability to speak using grade-appropriate English, with minimal second language acquisition support, in academic and social settings.

These students:

- are able to participate in extended discussions on a variety of social and grade-appropriate academic topics with only occasional disruptions, hesitations, or pauses;
- communicate effectively using abstract and content-based vocabulary during classroom instructional tasks, with some exceptions when low-frequency or academically demanding vocabulary is needed; use many of the same idioms and colloquialisms as their native English-speaking peers;
- can use English grammar structures and complex sentences to narrate and describe at a level nearly comparable to native English-speaking peers;
- make few second language acquisition errors that interfere with overall communication; and
- may mispronounce words, but rarely use pronunciation that interferes with overall communication.

Reading, Kindergarten-Grade 1. ELLs in Kindergarten and Grade 1 may be at the beginning, intermediate, advanced, or advanced high stage of English language acquisition in reading. The following proficiency level descriptors for reading are sufficient to describe the overall English language proficiency levels of ELLs in this language domain in order to linguistically accommodate their instruction and should take into account developmental stages of emergent readers.

Beginning. Beginning ELLs have little or no ability to use the English language to build foundational reading skills.

These students:

- derive little or no meaning from grade-appropriate stories read aloud in English, unless the stories are read in short "chunks"; controlled to include the little English they know such as language that is high frequency, concrete, and recently practiced; and accompanied by ample visual supports such as illustrations, gestures, pantomime, and objects and by linguistic supports such as careful enunciation and slower speech;
- begin to recognize and understand environmental print in English such as signs, labeled items, names of peers, and logos; and
- have difficulty decoding most grade-appropriate English text because they understand the meaning of very few words in English; and struggle significantly with sounds in spoken English words and with sound-symbol relationships due to differences between their primary language and English.

Intermediate. Intermediate ELLs have a limited ability to use the English language to build foundational reading skills.

These students:

- demonstrate limited comprehension (key words and general meaning) of grade-appropriate stories read aloud in English, unless the stories include predictable story lines; highly familiar topics; primarily high-frequency, concrete vocabulary; short, simple sentences; and visual and linguistic supports;
- regularly recognize and understand common environmental print in English such as signs, labeled items, names of peers, or logos; and
- have difficulty decoding grade-appropriate English text because they understand the meaning of only those English words they hear frequently; and struggle with some sounds in English words and some sound-symbol relationships due to differences between their primary language and English.

Advanced. Advanced ELLs have the ability to use the English language, with second language acquisition support, to build foundational reading skills.

These students:

- demonstrate comprehension of most main points and most supporting ideas in grade-appropriate stories read aloud in English, although they may still depend on visual and linguistic supports to gain or confirm meaning;
- recognize some basic English vocabulary and high-frequency words in isolated print; and
- with second language acquisition support, are able to decode most grade-appropriate English text because they understand the meaning of most grade-appropriate English words; and have little difficulty with English sounds and sound-symbol relationships that result from differences between their primary language and English.

Advanced high. Advanced high ELLs have the ability to use the English language, with minimal second language acquisition support, to build foundational reading skills.

These students:

- demonstrate, with minimal second language acquisition support and at a level nearly comparable to native English-speaking peers, comprehension of main points and supporting ideas (explicit and implicit) in grade-appropriate stories read aloud in English;
- with some exceptions, recognize sight vocabulary and high-frequency words to a degree nearly comparable to that of native English-speaking peers; and
- with minimal second language acquisition support, are able to decode and understand grade-appropriate English text at a level nearly comparable to native English-speaking peers.

<u>**Reading, Grades 2-12.**</u> ELLs in Grades 2-12 may be at the beginning, intermediate, advanced, or advanced high stage of English language acquisition in reading. The following proficiency level descriptors for reading are sufficient to describe the overall English language proficiency levels of ELLs in this language domain in order to linguistically accommodate their instruction.

Beginning. Beginning ELLs have little or no ability to read and understand English used in academic and social contexts.

These students:

- read and understand the very limited recently practiced, memorized, or highly familiar English they have learned; vocabulary predominantly includes environmental print, some very high-frequency words, and concrete words that can be represented by pictures;
- read slowly, word by word;
- have a very limited sense of English language structures;
- comprehend predominantly isolated familiar words and phrases; comprehend some sentences in highly routine contexts or recently practiced, highly familiar text;
- are highly dependent on visuals and prior knowledge to derive meaning from text in English; and
- are able to apply reading comprehension skills in English only when reading texts written for this level.

Intermediate. Intermediate ELLs have the ability to read and understand simple, high-frequency English used in routine academic and social contexts.

These students:

- read and understand English vocabulary on a somewhat wider range of topics and with increased depth; vocabulary predominantly includes everyday oral language, literal meanings of common words, routine academic language and terms, and commonly used abstract language such as terms used to describe basic feelings;

- often read slowly and in short phrases; may re-read to clarify meaning;
- have a growing understanding of basic, routinely used English language structures;
- understand simple sentences in short, connected texts, but are dependent on visual cues, topic familiarity, prior knowledge, pretaught topic-related vocabulary, story predictability, and teacher/peer assistance to sustain comprehension;
- struggle to independently read and understand grade-level texts; and
- are able to apply basic and some higher-order comprehension skills when reading texts that are linguistically accommodated and/or simplified for this level.

Advanced. Advanced ELLs have the ability to read and understand, with second language acquisition support, grade-appropriate English used in academic and social contexts.

These students:

- read and understand, with second language acquisition support, a variety of grade-appropriate English vocabulary used in social and academic contexts with second language acquisition support; read and understand grade-appropriate concrete and abstract vocabulary, but have difficulty with less commonly encountered words; demonstrate an emerging ability to understand words and phrases beyond their literal meaning; and understand multiple meanings of commonly used words;
- read longer phrases and simple sentences from familiar text with appropriate rate and speed;
- are developing skill in using their growing familiarity with English language structures to construct meaning of grade-appropriate text; and
- are able to apply basic and higher-order comprehension skills when reading grade-appropriate text, but are still occasionally dependent on visuals, teacher/peer assistance, and other linguistically accommodated text features to determine or clarify meaning, particularly with unfamiliar topics.

Advanced high. Advanced high ELLs have the ability to read and understand, with minimal second language acquisition support, grade-appropriate English used in academic and social contexts.

These students:

- read and understand vocabulary at a level nearly comparable to that of their native English-speaking peers, with some exceptions when low-frequency or specialized vocabulary is used;
- generally, read grade-appropriate, familiar text with appropriate rate, speed, intonation, and expression;
- are able to, at a level nearly comparable to native English-speaking peers, use their familiarity with English language structures to construct meaning of grade-appropriate text; and
- are able to apply, with minimal second language acquisition support and at a level nearly comparable to native English-speaking peers, basic and higher-order comprehension skills when reading grade-appropriate text.

<u>Writing, Kindergarten-Grade 1.</u> ELLs in Kindergarten and Grade 1 may be at the beginning, intermediate, advanced, or advanced high stage of English language acquisition in writing. The following proficiency level descriptors for writing are sufficient to describe the overall English language proficiency levels of ELLs in this language domain in order to linguistically accommodate their instruction and should take into account developmental stages of emergent writers.

Beginning. Beginning ELLs have little or no ability to use the English language to build foundational writing skills.

These students:

- are unable to use English to explain self-generated writing such as stories they have created or other personal expressions, including emergent forms of writing (pictures, letter-like forms, mock words, scribbling, etc.);
- know too little English to participate meaningfully in grade-appropriate shared writing activities using the English language;

- cannot express themselves meaningfully in self-generated, connected written text in English beyond the level of high-frequency, concrete words, phrases, or short sentences that have been recently practiced and/or memorized; and
- may demonstrate little or no awareness of English print conventions.

Intermediate. Intermediate ELLs have a limited ability to use the English language to build foundational writing skills.

These students:

- know enough English to explain briefly and simply self-generated writing, including emergent forms of writing, as long as the topic is highly familiar and concrete and requires very high-frequency English;
- can participate meaningfully in grade-appropriate shared writing activities using the English language only when the writing topic is highly familiar and concrete and requires very high-frequency English;
- express themselves meaningfully in self-generated, connected written text in English when their writing is limited to short sentences featuring simple, concrete English used frequently in class; and
- frequently exhibit features of their primary language when writing in English such as primary language words, spelling patterns, word order, and literal translating.

Advanced. Advanced ELLs have the ability to use the English language to build, with second language acquisition support, foundational writing skills.

These students:

- use predominantly grade-appropriate English to explain, in some detail, most self-generated writing, including emergent forms of writing;
- can participate meaningfully, with second language acquisition support, in most grade-appropriate shared writing activities using the English language;
- although second language acquisition support is needed, have an emerging ability to express themselves in self-generated, connected written text in English in a grade-appropriate manner; and
- occasionally exhibit second language acquisition errors when writing in English.

Advanced high. Advanced high ELLs have the ability to use the English language to build, with minimal second language acquisition support, foundational writing skills.

These students:

- use English at a level of complexity and detail nearly comparable to that of native English-speaking peers when explaining self-generated writing, including emergent forms of writing;
- can participate meaningfully in most grade-appropriate shared writing activities using the English language; and
- although minimal second language acquisition support may be needed, can express themselves in self-generated, connected written text in English in a manner nearly comparable to their native English-speaking peers.

<u>**Writing, Grades 2-12.**</u> ELLs in Grades 2-12 may be at the beginning, intermediate, advanced, or advanced high stage of English language acquisition in writing. The following proficiency level descriptors for writing are sufficient to describe the overall English language proficiency levels of ELLs in this language domain in order to linguistically accommodate their instruction.

Beginning. Beginning ELLs lack the English vocabulary and grasp of English language structures necessary to address grade-appropriate writing tasks meaningfully.

These students:

- have little or no ability to use the English language to express ideas in writing and engage meaningfully in grade-appropriate writing assignments in content area instruction;
- lack the English necessary to develop or demonstrate elements of grade-appropriate writing such as focus and coherence, conventions, organization, voice, and development of ideas in English; and
- exhibit writing features typical at this level, including ability to label, list, and copy high-frequency words/phrases and short, simple sentences (or even short paragraphs) based primarily on recently practiced, memorized, or highly familiar material; may write recently practiced, memorized, or highly familiar material quite accurately; primarily use present tense; and have frequent primary language features (spelling patterns, word order, literal translations, and words from the student's primary language) and other errors associated with second language acquisition that may significantly hinder or prevent understanding, even for individuals accustomed to the writing of ELLs.

Intermediate. Intermediate ELLs have enough English vocabulary and enough grasp of English language structures to address grade-appropriate writing tasks in a limited way.

These students:

- have a limited ability to use the English language to express ideas in writing and engage meaningfully in grade-appropriate writing assignments in content area instruction;
- are limited in their ability to develop or demonstrate elements of grade-appropriate writing in English; communicate best when topics are highly familiar and concrete, and require simple, high-frequency English; and
- exhibit writing features typical at this level, including simple, original messages consisting of short, simple sentences; have frequent inaccuracies when creating or taking risks beyond familiar English and high-frequency vocabulary; use an oral tone in academic writing, loosely connected text with limited use of cohesive devices or repetitive use, which may cause gaps in meaning, and repetition of ideas due to lack of vocabulary and language structures; use present tense most accurately; if attempted, use simple future and past tenses inconsistently or with frequent inaccuracies; have undetailed descriptions, explanations, and narrations; have difficulty expressing abstract ideas; may have frequent primary language features and errors associated with second language acquisition, with some writing understood only by individuals accustomed to the writing of ELLs; may have parts of the writing that is hard to understand, even for individuals accustomed to ELL writing.

Advanced. Advanced ELLs have enough English vocabulary and command of English language structures to address grade-appropriate writing tasks, although second language acquisition support is needed.

These students:

- are able to use the English language, with second language acquisition support, to express ideas in writing and engage meaningfully in grade-appropriate writing assignments in content area instruction;
- know enough English to be able to develop or demonstrate elements of grade-appropriate writing in English, although second language acquisition support is particularly needed when topics are abstract, academically challenging, or unfamiliar; and
- exhibit writing features typical at this level, including grasp of basic verbs, tenses, grammar features, and sentence patterns; have a partial grasp of more complex verbs, tenses, grammar features, and sentence patterns; demonstrate use of emerging grade-appropriate vocabulary; have a more academic tone in their academic writing; use a variety of common cohesive devices, although some redundancy may occur; develop narrations, explanations, and descriptions in some detail with emerging clarity; show a decline in quality or quantity when abstract ideas are expressed, academic demands are high, or low-frequency vocabulary is required; have occasional second language acquisition errors; and have communications that are usually understood by individuals not accustomed to the writing of ELLs.

Advanced high. Advanced high ELLs have acquired the English vocabulary and command of English language structures necessary to address grade-appropriate writing tasks with minimal second language acquisition support.

These students:

- are able to use the English language, with minimal second language acquisition support, to express ideas in writing and engage meaningfully in grade-appropriate writing assignments in content area instruction;
- know enough English to be able to develop or demonstrate, with minimal second language acquisition support, elements of grade-appropriate writing in English; and
- exhibit writing features typical at this level, including nearly comparable to writing of native English-speaking peers in clarity and precision with regard to English vocabulary and language structures, with occasional exceptions when writing about academically complex ideas, abstract ideas, or topics requiring low-frequency vocabulary; have occasional difficulty with naturalness of phrasing and expression, and errors associated with second language acquisition are minor and usually limited to low-frequency words and structures and rarely interfere with communication.

[Source: Adapted from 19 Texas Administrative Code (TAC) § 149.74.4 (d)]

Checkpoint

Fill in the blank.

1. In Texas, the English language proficiency of English language learners (ELLs) is assessed in four language domains: _____, _____, _____, and _____.
2. The four English language proficiency levels described in the ELPS are _____, _____, _____, and _____ (two words).

Mark as True or False.

3. _____ Beginning ELLs frequently remain silent in academic settings.
4. _____ Advanced high ELLs exhibit writing features nearly comparable to writing of native English-speaking peers.

Checkpoint Answers

1. listening; speaking; reading; writing
2. beginning; intermediate; advanced; advanced high
3. True
4. True

Embracing Diversity

Teachers should be careful not to view students whose behaviors are different from those of the predominant social or cultural group as less worthy or less capable. The first step teachers should take is to examine their own views and feelings about cultural differences. Having biases is common, so it takes a concentrated effort to avoid stereotypical expectations. To meet this challenge, teachers can begin by developing good teacher-student relationships. Teachers need to develop an awareness of practices common in various cultures so that when children behave in a manner consistent with their culture, the behavior will not be misinterpreted. For example, in some cultures a person in a subordinate position would not make eye contact with a superior because doing so would be disrespectful. Therefore, a student may avoid making eye contact with a teacher for this reason. However, the teacher may view this student's actions as disrespectful if he or she is unfamiliar with the cultural expectation that has influenced the student's behavior. Nevertheless, teachers should discuss with students that some behaviors that are acceptable at home are not acceptable at school.

Teachers must realize that they themselves are the essential factor in creating a welcoming environment because they set the climate for learning. It is of paramount importance for teachers to embrace the attitude that if the materials are suitable and presented on the appropriate level, all students can learn. Children's academic achievements are contingent on whether they have self-esteem and are confident in their own abilities and on whether their teachers believe they can succeed. Creating an environment that respects and confirms the dignity of students as human beings is essential in meeting the needs of diverse students. Teachers must be aware of cultural and sexual stereotypes and should avoid behavior that pigeonholes students. Rather, teachers must promote learning for all students.

In her review of the research, Kathleen Cotton (1993) found that effective teachers of culturally diverse classes

- reflect on their own values, stereotypes, and prejudices and how these might be affecting their interactions with children and parents.
- engage in staff development activities that can expose and reduce biases and increase skill in working with diverse populations.
- arrange their classrooms for movement and active learning.
- interact one-on-one with each child at least once daily.
- communicate high expectations for the performance of all students.
- give praise and encouragement.
- communicate affection for and closeness with students through verbal and nonverbal means, such as humor, soliciting student opinion, self-disclosure, eye contact, close proximity, and smiling.
- avoid public charting of achievement data.
- give children responsibility for taking care of materials, decorating, greeting visitors, and so on.
- treat all students equitably and fairly.
- have classrooms that reflect the ethnic heritage and background of all the children in the classroom.
- form flexible reading groups.
- make use of cooperative learning groups that are culturally heterogeneous and teach students skills for working in these groups.
- offer learning activities congruent with the cultural and individual learning styles and strengths of students.
- explicitly teach students social skills related to getting along well together.
- conduct many learning activities that are not graded.
- include student-selected activities.
- provide accurate information about cultural groups through straightforward discussions of race, ethnicity, and other cultural differences.
- teach about both cross-cultural similarities and cross-cultural differences.
- learn a few words of the language and general information about the backgrounds, customs, traditions, holidays, festivals, practices, and so on of students and incorporate this information into learning experiences for them.
- use a variety of materials rather than relying only on the information in textbooks.
- review materials for cultural biases and stereotypes and remove biased items from the curriculum.
- take issue with culturally demeaning statements, jokes, graffiti, and so on.
- use gender, racial, or other intercultural conflicts as a springboard for providing information and skills to avoid such incidents.
- encourage parental involvement.
- demonstrate interest in and respect for the family's culture when interacting with parents.
- find out as much as they can about each child's experiences and family situation to help them to understand and meet the child's needs.

Some suggestions for teachers are the following:

- Remember that diversity in our schools and society should be recognized and appreciated.
- Be prepared to expect differences within a group as well as between groups.
- Remember there is a positive correlation between teacher expectations and student success.

- Remember to hold high expectations for all students, regardless of ethnicity, gender, or other student characteristics.
- Remember that self-esteem and academic achievement are closely linked.
- Remember there is no one-size-fits-all approach to meeting the educational needs of all children in a diverse classroom.

Furthermore, numerous research studies consistently support the idea that each student learns differently. When each student is taught through the method that he or she prefers, students do better. Teachers should be aware of student differences and be willing to examine their own teaching styles in order to modify classroom practices and procedures to optimize the learning situation for all students. Considering the diverse demographic characteristics of the students in most Texas classrooms, this recommended strategy might be particularly useful in spotting learning problems and enhancing the overall performance of Texas schoolchildren. Teachers should respond flexibly and creatively to students' needs. They should provide varied environments within the classroom and use multisensory resources in the delivery of instruction.

Checkpoint

Fill in the blank.

1. Teachers must embrace the attitude that _____ students can learn.
2. In diverse classrooms, teachers should explicitly teach students _____ skills related to getting along well together.
3. Teachers should be prepared to expect differences _____ a group as well as between groups.

Mark as True or False.

4. _____ Teachers are the essential factor in creating a welcoming environment in their classrooms.

Checkpoint Answers

1. all
2. social
3. within
4. True

Summary

Teachers should be mindful of student differences and be willing to examine their own teaching styles in order to modify classroom practices and procedures to optimize the learning situation for all students. Considering the diverse demographic characteristics of the students in most Texas classrooms, this recommended strategy might be particularly useful in spotting learning problems and enhancing the overall performance of Texas schoolchildren. Teachers should respond flexibly and creatively to students' needs. They should provide varied environments within the classroom and use multisensory resources in the delivery of instruction. Furthermore, classroom teachers need to be aware of their responsibilities toward students with special needs and ELLs so that all students in Texas will have opportunities to achieve success.

Chapter 3

Instructional Design and Planning

> **Competency 003:** The teacher understands procedures for designing effective and coherent instruction and assessment based on appropriate learning goals and objectives.

This chapter provides a general review of knowledge and skills related to Competency 003. Checkpoint exercises are found throughout the review material. These exercises give you an opportunity to practice what you just learned. The answers to the Checkpoint exercises are found immediately following the set of exercises. When doing the Checkpoint exercises, you should cover up the answers. Then check your answers when you've finished the exercises.

Competency Descriptive Statements

The descriptive statements for Competency 003 as given in the TExES PPR EC-12 test preparation manual (www.tx.nesinc.com/Content/Docs/160PrepManual.pdf) specify the following knowledge and skills for beginning teachers in Texas public schools:

- Understands the significance of the Texas Essential Knowledge and Skills (TEKS) and of prerequisite knowledge and skills in determining instructional goals and objectives.
- Uses appropriate criteria to evaluate the appropriateness of learning goals and objectives (e.g., clarity; relevance; significance; age-appropriateness; ability to be assessed; responsiveness to students' current skills and knowledge, background, needs, and interests; alignment with campus and district goals).
- Uses assessment to analyze students' strengths and needs, evaluate teacher effectiveness, and guide instructional planning for individuals and groups.
- Understands the connection between various components of the Texas statewide assessment program, the TEKS, and instruction and analyzes data from state and other assessments using common statistical measures to help identify students' strengths and needs.
- Demonstrates knowledge of various types of materials and resources (including technological resources and resources outside the school) that may be used to enhance student learning and engagement and evaluates the appropriateness of specific materials and resources for use in particular situations, to address specific purposes, and to meet varied student needs.
- Plans lessons and structures units so that activities progress in a logical sequence and support stated instructional goals.
- Plans learning experiences that provide students with developmentally appropriate opportunities to explore content from integrated and varied perspectives (e.g., by presenting thematic units that incorporate different disciplines, providing intradisciplinary and interdisciplinary instruction, designing instruction that enables students to work cooperatively, providing multicultural learning experiences, prompting students to consider ideas from multiple viewpoints, encouraging students' application of knowledge and skills to the world beyond the school).
- Allocates time appropriately within lessons and units, including providing adequate opportunities for students to engage in reflection, self-assessment, and closure.

Effective Planning

Planning is the decision-making process in which a teacher decides what, why, when, and how to teach. Effective planning is an important component of effective instruction (Reinhartz and Beach, 1996). Furthermore, planning is critical to successful alignment of curriculum, instruction, and assessment. Effective teachers use progress monitoring, including observation and formative assessment data, to inform their instructional planning so that instruction is matched to students' academic needs. In addition, they take into account the diverse ways students learn, their developmental levels, linguistic development, and the various backgrounds, cultural heritage, interests, and experiences they bring to the classroom. They work within the framework of the RtI process with the goal of maximizing achievement for all students (see "Response to Intervention (RtI)" in Chapter 2 for a discussion of this topic).

Effective planners design their lessons around research- and/or evidence-based instruction that will promote student achievement. They proceed thoughtfully and deliberately. They write out what they are planning to do, how they are going to do it, and how they will determine whether it worked.

Before planning a lesson, a teacher must first determine instructional long-term goals appropriate to students' grade level and individual needs. The goals must be aligned with the Texas Essential Knowledge and Skills (TEKS). (See the section "TEKS" that follows for a discussion of these standards.)

A teacher's first step in planning a lesson is to identify, within the framework of the state-adopted standards, the instructional objective(s) for the lesson. To do this, the teacher must answer the following questions: What do I want students to learn and be able to do at the end of this lesson? Which specific benchmark(s) will this lesson address? (See "Instructional Objectives" later in this chapter for a discussion of instructional objectives.) This approach to planning that begins with a consideration of the end goal of a lesson is the **backward design approach.** It is considered the most effective approach to lesson design (Wiggins and McTighe, 2005).

The next step in planning the lesson is deciding on the research- and/or evidence-based instructional methods that will best support the instructional objective and result in student achievement. (See "Instructional Methods" in Chapter 8 for descriptions of various instructional methods.) When designing instruction, the teacher should focus on the desired instructional objective while considering appropriate differentiated strategies and grouping arrangements. At the same time, the teacher should take into account input from students; students' learning preferences, backgrounds, interests, experiences, and prior knowledge; the content of instruction; available materials and resources; time and space constraints; and assessment issues. When planning what to do in the lesson to engage students in learning, teachers should do the following:

- Use developmentally appropriate activities and strategies.
- Apply knowledge of learning theories to classroom practices.
- Routinely involve students in choosing and planning their own learning activities.
- Activate students' prior knowledge related to the concepts to be learned.
- Provide challenging experiences that actively engage students.
- Incorporate Marzano's High Yield Instructional Strategies into lesson planning (see Chapter 8 for a discussion of this topic).
- Use a variety of materials and/or technologies.
- Provide meaningful experiences that reflect students' own interests and experiences.
- Routinely use hands-on, minds-on activities.
- Use activities that address students' individual needs and abilities.
- Provide opportunities for whole-group, small-group, and individual work.
- Allow opportunities for students to talk and discuss their learning among themselves and with the teacher.
- Make the learning student-centered, not teacher-focused.
- Avoid relying solely on the textbook when planning or providing limited options for students.
- Avoid using worksheets or workbooks; meaningless drills; or excessive, quiet seatwork.
- Make sure that students with special needs—for example, students receiving special education services or English language learners (ELLs)—participate in the lesson to the fullest extent possible.
- Offer learning activities congruent with the cultural and individual learning preferences and strengths of students (see "Embracing Diversity" in Chapter 2 for a discussion of this topic).

A critical step in planning a lesson is to decide on the assessment method: how to determine that the students "got it." Good assessment reflects what is taught—it's aligned with the curriculum and how it is taught; that is, it matches the instructional objective and the method of instruction. For best results, the teacher should plan to use multiple assessment approaches and ensure that assessment is ongoing and an integral part of the lesson. There are many ways to find out how well students know, understand, and are able to apply the curriculum. One very effective way is to use informal observation and questioning—in other words, watching the students when they are working to see whether they are "getting it" and asking questions about what they are doing and what they are thinking as they work. This approach will give much insight into the effectiveness of a lesson. Other assessment strategies include formal interviews, collections of students' work over time (portfolios), self-assessment, peer assessment, formal performance assessments, and traditional tests. The teacher's assessment strategies will be most useful when they aim to help the students by identifying their unique strengths and needs so as to inform planning. (See Chapter 10 for a full discussion of assessment.)

After developing a lesson plan, teachers **preplan.** That is, they go through the lesson mentally from a student's point of view and anticipate explanations, information, directions, additional instruction, and so on that they will need in order to carry out the lesson successfully.

Checkpoint

Fill in the blank.

1. Planning is critical to successful _____ of curriculum, instruction, and assessment.
2. When designing instruction, teachers should focus on the desired instructional _____.
3. Good assessment reflects what is _____.

Mark as True or False.

4. _____ When planning lessons, teachers should rely solely on their textbooks.
5. _____ Worksheets and drills are the hallmarks of effective instruction.

Checkpoint Answers

1. alignment
2. objectives
3. taught
4. False
5. False

TEKS

The **TEKS** (Texas Essential Knowledge and Skills) are the foundation of the Texas curriculum. They establish the core content knowledge and skills that K-12 public school students are expected to acquire for English language arts and reading, mathematics, science, social studies, languages other than English, health education, physical education, fine arts, economics with emphasis on the free enterprise system and its benefits, technology applications, career development, Spanish language arts and English as a second language, and career and technical education. The standards outlined in the TEKS are relevant, rigorous, and logically sequential. The Texas Education Agency (TEA) is the official source for information about the TEKS (https://tea.texas.gov/curriculum/teks/).

The TEKS specify, in clear, precise language, what students are expected to know, understand, and be able to do. Teachers in Texas schools must design instruction that addresses the TEKS for their grade levels. State law requires that the TEKS be the focus of the learning in classrooms. Instructional strategies must help students develop the knowledge and skills embodied in the TEKS (see Chapter 8 for a discussion of instructional strategies). Instructional materials must be selected to support the important ideas identified in the TEKS.

Assessment data must inform as to whether learners have met the TEKS standards (see Chapter 10 for a discussion of assessment). The idea is simple—the TEKS must be the primary focus of K-12 education in Texas. What is to be learned, must be taught. By following this directive, Texas teachers can ensure that learners will achieve the standards identified in the TEKS.

State-mandated standardized tests assess students' acquisition of specific knowledge and skills outlined in the TEKS curriculum. The State of Texas Assessments of Academic Readiness (STAAR) program, which was implemented in spring 2012, includes annual TEKS-congruent assessments.

Checkpoint

Fill in the blank.

1. The TEKS are the _____ of the Texas curriculum.
2. The standards are relevant, _____, and logically sequential.
3. The _____ program includes annual assessments based on the TEKS.
4. _____ is the State of Texas's official source for information about the TEKS.

Checkpoint Answers

1. foundation
2. rigorous
3. STAAR
4. TEA

Instructional Objectives

An **instructional objective** is a clearly written statement of what students are expected to know and be able to do as a result of an instructional learning experience. Instructional objectives are the cornerstone of effective teaching. They "become the criteria by which materials are selected, content is outlined, instructional procedures are developed, and tests and examinations are prepared" (Tyler, 1949, p. 1).

A well-written instructional objective consists of three elements: **action,** what the student will do; **conditions,** the circumstances in which the action will take place; and **level of mastery,** the level of proficiency expected for the action (Houston and Beech, 2002). Additionally, although the grading criteria are not part of an instructional objective, the objective should be aligned with the assessment procedure. With this requirement in mind, teachers need to be sure that instructional objectives are written as measurable behaviors, that is, as behaviors that can be observed, recorded, and assessed. The best way to write measurable objectives is to use action verbs such as *analyze, arrange, assess, classify, compare, compose, contrast, create, define, discuss, identify, judge, list, predict, recite, show, solve,* and *summarize* to describe exactly what the student is expected to do to achieve the objective.

To determine whether a lesson objective is at an appropriate level of difficulty, a task analysis should be conducted for each instructional objective. **Task analysis** is the process of identifying the prerequisite skills and prior knowledge that students must have in order to achieve the instructional objective with a high degree of success.

Instructional objectives differ in both the types of learning involved and the level of learning involved. Teachers need to write objectives that result in the types and levels of learning desired for students. A classic and widely used guide in identifying and writing instructional objectives is the *Taxonomy of Educational Objectives Handbook* by Benjamin Bloom and colleagues (1956), commonly known as **Bloom's Taxonomy.** The classification system was developed by psychologists, teachers, and test experts for use in curriculum development, teaching, and testing, and consists of three general categories called **domains** that encompass the possibilities of learning outcomes that might be expected from instruction:

- The **cognitive domain** is the category for learning that involves thinking capabilities, from recalling simple facts to judging the quality of an argument. (See "Skillful Questioning" in Chapter 7 for additional discussion of the cognitive domain of Bloom's Taxonomy.)
- The **affective domain** is the category for learning that involves feelings, values, and dispositions.
- The **psychomotor domain** is the category for learning that involves manual, athletic, and other physical skills.

Each domain consists of a set of subcategories that have a hierarchical relationship going from the simplest outcomes to the most complex, as shown in the following table.

Cognitive Domain	Affective Domain	Psychomotor Domain
Knowledge: Involves remembering, memorizing, recognizing, recalling, and so on.	**Receiving:** Involves the willingness to be open to stimuli and messages in the environment, willingness to receive a message or to acknowledge that a phenomenon is taking place.	**Generic movement:** Includes the perception of body positions and motor acts and the arrangement of movement to achieve a skill.
Comprehension: Involves interpreting and understanding meaning, stating or describing in one's own words.	**Responding:** Involves attending to and reacting to a stimulus or replying to a message.	**Ordinate movement:** Includes organizing, refining, and performing movement skillfully; achieving precision in motor performance.
Application: Involves applying information to produce results, transferring learning to a new context, or problem solving.	**Valuing:** Involves accepting an idea, phenomenon, or stimulus and internalizing it.	**Creative movement:** Includes the invention or creation of movement personally unique to the performer.
Analysis: Involves the subdividing or breaking down of a stimulus or concept to show how it's put together.	**Organizing:** Involves classifying and ordering values, ranking by priorities.	
Synthesis: Involves the creation of a unique product that might be verbal, abstract, or physical in form; putting together concepts to form a whole.	**Internalizing:** Involves committing totally to certain attitudes, beliefs, or dispositions; "buying in" to the point that values are reflected in one's behavior.	
Evaluation: Involves making value decisions about a phenomenon, an idea, or a stimulus.		

Examples of instructional objectives for each domain are shown in the following chart.

Domain	Sample Instructional Objective
Cognitive	Given a list of 10 animals, the student will classify the animals as herbivores, carnivores, or omnivores with 90 percent accuracy.
Affective	While participating in a whole-class discussion, the student will show respect for others by not interrupting when others are talking for 100 percent of the discussion time.
Psychomotor	Given a set of 10 functions, the student will graph the functions on a graphing calculator with 90 percent accuracy.

Checkpoint

Fill in the blank.

1. The circumstances in which the action of an instructional objective will take place are called the _____.

2. "The student will catch the ball" is an action that falls in the _____ domain of instructional objectives.

3. The process of identifying the prerequisite skills and prior knowledge that students must have in order to achieve an instructional objective is called _____ (two words).

Mark as True or False.

4. _____ The cognitive domain is the category for learning that involves thinking capabilities.

5. _____ The action in an instructional objective must be observable.

Checkpoint Answers

1. conditions
2. psychomotor
3. task analysis
4. True
5. True

Levels of Content Complexity

Content complexity refers to the level of cognitive demand that standards and curriculum place on learners. Texas uses Norman Webb's (2002) depth of knowledge (DOK) model of content complexity as a means of classifying the cognitive demand presented by standards and curriculum. The DOK model consists of four levels, as shown in the following chart.

Level of Complexity	Student Expectations	Examples
Level 1: Recall	Recall, identify, locate, or recognize facts or information and demonstrate simple skills or abilities.	• In reading, locate details in a passage. • In writing, identify incorrect punctuation. • In math, identify a number as prime. • In science, retrieve information from a chart.
Level 2: Basic Application of Concepts and Skills	Demonstrate comprehension and processing of information.	• In reading, determine the main idea of a passage. • In writing, write a summary of a passage. • In math, solve a multiple-step but routine-type problem. • In science, give examples and nonexamples of a concept.
Level 3: Strategic Thinking and Complex Reasoning	Demonstrate the use of higher-order thinking skills, including abstract reasoning.	• In reading, identify cause-and-effect relationships. • In writing, develop a constructed response to a prompt. • In math, determine a formula for the general term of a sequenced numerical pattern. • In science, draw a conclusion based on data.

Level of Complexity	Student Expectations	Examples
Level 4: Extended Thinking and Complex Reasoning	Demonstrate significant conceptual understanding and higher-order thinking extended over time and multiple resources.	• In reading, analyze and synthesize common themes in several authors' works. • In writing, write a research paper on a multifaceted topic. • In math, model the relationship between two variables by collecting and analyzing data. • In science, conduct a scientific investigation of a hypothesis.

Checkpoint

Fill in the blank.

1. Content complexity refers to the level of cognitive demand associated with _____ and curriculum.
2. In reading, determining the author's purpose is level _____ (1, 2, 3, or 4) complexity.
3. In social studies, conducting a study of local natural resources is level _____ (1, 2, 3, or 4) complexity.
4. In math, solving a simple linear equation is level _____ (1, 2, 3, or 4) complexity.

Checkpoint Answers

1. standards
2. 3
3. 4
4. 2

Lesson Cycle Model

The **lesson cycle model** follows the adage: "Tell them what you're going to say, say it, and then tell them what you said" (Kizlik, 2014). Although there are variations of the model, basically, it consists of the following components:

- **Focus (or anticipatory set):** The teacher gains students' attention, explains the instructional objective(s) of the lesson, communicates the expectations for the lesson, and links the lesson objective to students' prior knowledge.
- **Explanation:** The teacher presents new information related to the lesson's instructional objective using various techniques such as demonstrating and modeling skills, giving examples and nonexamples of concepts, and stating and applying academic rules.
- **Check for understanding:** The teacher observes and questions students to determine the degree to which they understand the concepts and essential information presented in the explanation component of the lesson. Checking for understanding is frequent and ongoing throughout the lesson. The teacher provides clarification and specific feedback to reinforce learning and to avert misunderstandings.
- **Guided practice:** The teacher monitors and scaffolds students' learning as they apply the new knowledge or skills.
- **Closure:** The teacher "wraps up" the lesson by reviewing with the students the instructional content that was presented in the lesson.
- **Independent practice:** The students apply the new knowledge or skills without assistance from the teacher. Independent practice is usually given as homework.
- **Reteach and extend:** The teacher has planned (1) additional instruction using an alternative strategy for students who fail to achieve the instructional objective, and (2) new learning experiences for students who are ready to extend their learning.

Chapter 3: Instructional Design and Planning

Checkpoint

Fill in the blank.

1. One purpose of the focus component of the lesson cycle model is to gain students' _____.
2. Checking for understanding is _____ throughout the lesson.
3. During guided practice, the teacher _____ and scaffolds students' learning as they apply the new knowledge or skills.

Mark as True or False.

4. _____ Giving examples and nonexamples is an appropriate teacher action during the explanation component of the lesson cycle model.
5. _____ During guided practice, students work alone, without teacher assistance.

Checkpoint Answers

1. attention
2. ongoing
3. monitors
4. True
5. False

5E Model

The **5E model** (also called the **learning cycle model**) follows the principle that students learn best when they are provided opportunities to construct their own understandings of concepts by building on prior knowledge and by actively engaging in the learning experience. The five *E*s are as follows:

- **Engage:** The teacher engages students' attention and stimulates motivation to learn by helping students relate the content to their prior knowledge and to their own personal interests and experiences.
- **Explore:** Students work together, usually in pairs or small groups, to get directly involved with the phenomena and materials. The teacher becomes a facilitator, providing support as the students engage in active inquiry.
- **Explain:** Students support each other's understandings as they communicate their findings and discuss their ideas, observations, questions, and predictions.
- **Extend/Elaborate:** Students expand on the concepts learned, make connections to other related concepts, and apply their understandings to real-world settings.
- **Evaluate:** In Texas, the last *E* is more directly about assessment than evaluation.

The 5E model is compatible with the lesson cycle model. The two models overlap (for example, engage and focus are essentially the same in both models), and both models are designed to accomplish learning objectives.

Checkpoint

Fill in the blank.

1. The 5E model is designed to help students _____ their own understandings of concepts.
2. One purpose of the engage component of the 5E model is to gain students' _____.
3. During the explore component of a 5E lesson, the teacher's role is as a _____.

Mark as True or False.

4. ____ During the explain component of a 5E lesson, the teacher is doing most of the explaining.

5. ____ The 5E model is most consistent with a behaviorist point of view.

Checkpoint Answers

1. construct
2. attention
3. facilitator
4. False
5. False

Interdisciplinary Units

An **interdisciplinary unit** combines lessons around a major issue or overarching **theme** that is related to two or more subject disciplines. This issue becomes the question around which participating teachers from the involved subject disciplines collaborate to develop a thematic unit. Although the theme acts as a central organizer, each subject discipline teacher contributes from his or her own content area. Students remain engaged in learning the knowledge and skills of the separate disciplines because a sense of meaningfulness or wholeness is generally a goal of the teachers. By relating content and skills from each of their separate disciplines to the central concept of the theme, the learning is more relevant, connected, and meaningful to students.

Since this approach is rewarding to students and teachers alike, strategies should be in place to encourage teachers to become involved in planning interdisciplinary units. The strategies to consider when implementing this approach are the following:

- Integrate information and activities from different subject domains.
- Use reading, writing, art, and mathematics across disciplines.
- Work collaboratively with other teachers to plan the unit.
- Implement each subject-specific component of the unit separately in each teacher's own classroom.

Checkpoint

Fill in the blank.

1. _____ units involve integrating academic fields of study.
2. The central concept of a _____ makes the learning in interdisciplinary units more meaningful to students.

Mark as True or False.

3. ____ In an interdisciplinary unit, mathematics is excluded.
4. ____ Problem solving is discouraged in interdisciplinary units.

Checkpoint Answers

1. Interdisciplinary
2. theme
3. False
4. False

Selecting Technology

Technology includes projectors, interactive whiteboards, computers/laptops/tablets, scanners, printers/copiers (including 3D printers), sophisticated calculators, digital gaming, social networking technologies, e-readers, webcams, smartphones, iPads, software/apps, DVDs, CDs, TV, and the Internet. Teachers must learn to use these tools effectively. They should be knowledgeable and selective in choosing the appropriate technology for instructional purposes. (See Chapter 9 for a full discussion of technology.)

Advanced technology adds new dimensions to teaching and learning. Instead of writing with pen and paper, students can use word processors with spell checkers, grammar checkers, and thesauruses to create written documents such as letters, themes, essays, and research papers. An advantage of word processing is that corrections and revisions can be made without retyping the entire document; collaborative word processing tools also allow students to synchronously or asynchronously work together on a shared assignment. Simulation software and virtual reality create interactive, reality-based environments. They allow the user to explore, investigate, and problem-solve in simulated real-life settings. Spreadsheets can perform mathematical or statistical calculations on data and create graphs, charts, and other data summaries. They can be used by teachers for making grade books and by students for recording data from experiments or inventory for a make-believe company. Scanners can convert graphics into digitized images. Students can access resource material like multimedia encyclopedias on CDs or use interactive apps and software packages. They also can link up to other resources and to students at other schools in the state, country, and world via the Internet; this level of connectivity allows for the creation of transnational youth communities focused on shared interests.

Technology can help teachers create learning environments that change and interact with students' needs. **Assistive technology** (any item, piece of equipment, or product system, whether acquired commercially off the shelf, modified, or customized) can be used to increase, maintain, or improve the functional capabilities of children with disabilities (Section 34, Code of Federal Regulations). **Computer-assisted instruction (CAI)** can be used for individualized instruction. CAI sequences content into small units of information and provides immediate feedback to the student on the student's grasp of the content, thereby allowing the student to monitor progress while proceeding through the program. **Blended learning** is a term applied to an education program in which students learn in part in a traditional school setting and in part through online learning. **Hybrid learning** refers to learning that takes place mainly online, although some aspects may be conducted in school settings. Although blended learning and hybrid learning are often used synonymously, with hybrid learning, much of the student-teacher interaction takes place via online discussion forums or through other digital tools, rather than face-to-face. The **flipped classroom** approach is a form of blended learning that involves students first encountering new information through videos or online content delivered outside of class time; then the following class session is structured to focus on practicing or applying the content that was presented digitally. **Information and communications technologies (ICTs)** can be used to provide access to information through telecommunications.

Technology in the classroom can benefit students by

- offering more control and involvement in the learning process.
- making learning more interesting.
- promoting investigative skills.
- allowing access to almost unlimited sources of information.
- developing skills to measure, monitor, and improve performance.
- enabling communication with people from many parts of the world, bringing the sights, sounds, and thoughts of another language and culture into the classroom.
- providing opportunities to apply knowledge to simulated or real-life projects.
- developing readiness for a high-tech world of work.

(Source: Secondary Physical Education Curriculum Guide, 2003–2004, Brevard Public Schools)

Checkpoint

Fill in the blank.

1. Teachers should be knowledgeable and selective in choosing _____ technology.
2. An advantage of using word processing in writing is that corrections and revisions can be made without _____ the entire document.
3. Technology can help teachers create a learning environment that changes and interacts with students' _____.
4. In blended learning, students learn in part in a traditional school setting and in part through _____ learning.

Checkpoint Answers

1. appropriate
2. retyping
3. needs
4. online

Summary

Effective planning is a thoughtful, decision-making process. Effective teachers know that well-designed instructional plans are the key to improved student learning. Based on progress monitoring data and with the guidance of the TEKS, they identify appropriate goals and objectives for their students and then design developmentally appropriate learning opportunities that will move students toward achievement of those goals and objectives. Lessons are carefully planned and differentiated according to the RtI process in Texas, using a mixture of instructional strategies and supports of varying intensity levels in varied learning settings: whole class, small group, or individual.

Chapter 4

Learning Principles

> **Competency 004:** The teacher understands learning processes and factors that impact student learning and demonstrates this knowledge by planning effective, engaging instruction and appropriate assessments.

This chapter provides a general review of knowledge and skills related to Competency 004. Checkpoint exercises are found throughout the review material. These exercises give you an opportunity to practice what you just learned. The answers to the Checkpoint exercises are found immediately following the set of exercises. When doing the Checkpoint exercises, you should cover up the answers. Then check your answers when you've finished the exercises.

Competency Descriptive Statements

The descriptive statements for Competency 004 as given in the TExES PPR EC-12 test preparation manual (www.tx.nesinc.com/Content/Docs/160PrepManual.pdf) specify the following knowledge and skills for beginning teachers in Texas public schools:

- Understands the role of learning theory in the instructional process and uses instructional strategies and appropriate technologies to facilitate student learning (e.g., connecting new information and ideas to prior knowledge, making learning meaningful and relevant to students).

- Understands that young children think concretely and rely primarily on motor and sensory input and direct experience for development of skills and knowledge and uses this understanding to plan effective, developmentally appropriate learning experiences and assessments.

- Understands that the middle-level years are a transitional stage in which students may exhibit characteristics of both older and younger children and that these are critical years for developing important skills and attitudes (e.g., working and getting along with others, appreciating diversity, making a commitment to continued schooling).

- Recognizes how characteristics of students at different developmental levels (e.g., limited attention span and need for physical activity and movement for younger children; importance of peers, search for identity, questioning of values and exploration of long-term career and life goals for older students) impact teaching and learning.

- Stimulates reflection, critical thinking, and inquiry among students (e.g., supports the concept of play as a valid vehicle for young children's learning; provides opportunities for young children to manipulate materials and to test ideas and hypotheses; engages students in structured, hands-on problem-solving activities that are challenging; encourages exploration and risk taking; creates a learning community that promotes positive contributions, effective communication, and the respectful exchange of ideas).

- Enhances learning for students by providing age-appropriate instruction that encourages the use and refinement of higher-order thinking skills (e.g., prompting students to explore ideas from diverse perspectives; structuring active learning experiences involving cooperative learning, problem solving, open-ended questioning, and inquiry; promoting students' development of research skills).

- Teaches, models, and monitors organizational and time-management skills at an age-appropriate level (e.g., establishing regular places for classroom toys and materials for young children, keeping related materials together, using organizational tools, using effective strategies for locating information, and organizing information systematically).

- Teaches, models, and monitors age-appropriate study skills (e.g., using graphic organizers, outlining, note-taking, summarizing, test-taking) and structures research projects appropriately (e.g., teaches students the steps in research, establishes checkpoints during research projects, helps students use time-management tools).

- Analyzes ways in which teacher behaviors (e.g., teacher expectations, student grouping practices, teacher-student interactions) impact student learning and plans instruction and assessment that minimize the effects of negative factors and enhance all students' learning.
- Analyzes ways in which factors in the home and community (e.g., parent expectations, availability of community resources, community problems) impact student learning and plans instruction and assessment with awareness of social and cultural factors to enhance all students' learning.
- Understands the importance of self-directed learning and plans instruction and assessment that promote students' motivation and their sense of ownership of and responsibility for their learning.
- Analyzes ways in which various teacher roles (e.g., facilitator, lecturer) and student roles (e.g., active learner, observer, group participant) impact student learning.
- Incorporates students' different approaches to learning (e.g., auditory, visual, tactile, kinesthetic) into instructional practices.
- Provides instruction to ensure that students can apply various learning strategies (e.g., using prior knowledge, metacognition, graphic organizers) across content areas, in accordance with the ELPS.
- Provides instruction in a manner that is linguistically accommodated (communicated, sequenced, and scaffolded) to the student's level of English-language proficiency to ensure that the student learns the knowledge and skills across content areas, in accordance with the ELPS.
- Applies knowledge of the implications for learning and instruction of the range of thinking abilities found among students in any one grade level and students' increasing ability over time to engage in abstract thinking and reasoning.

Motivational Strategies

All human beings are born with a natural curiosity and desire to learn (Gestwicki, 1999). Unfortunately, many students show little or no excitement about school learning. A primary intention of an effective teacher is to evoke in pupils the desire, or motivation, to learn. **Motivation** is the willingness or desire of a student to exhibit a behavior such as productively engaging in a learning experience. Teachers are challenged to tap into students' innate urges to learn by using teaching strategies that influence students' motivation. Research on motivation has focused on topics such as intrinsic and extrinsic motivation, reinforcement, and achievement motivation.

Sometimes, a student wants to learn something just for the sake of learning it. We say this student wants to learn because of **intrinsic motivation.** The desire to learn originates within the student and stems from the student's intellectual curiosity, attitudes, beliefs, and needs regarding the learning task. Brain research indicates that teachers who make learning relevant and personally meaningful to students, give them choices in what they learn and how they learn it, and provide learning experiences in which students are actively engaged often will find that students become intrinsically motivated to learn.

If a desire to learn does not arise from within a student, the teacher may need to stimulate **extrinsic motivation** by using external reinforcement (see "Behaviorism and Constructivism" later in this chapter for a discussion of reinforcement) in the form of rewards or incentives to engage the student in learning. In extrinsic motivation, the emphasis is on external factors that students find desirable. Teachers who reward students with stickers or stars, public recognition, privileges, or special treats are capitalizing on extrinsic motivation.

However, teachers should be aware that a great deal of reinforcement occurs in students when they do something well, regardless of whether they receive tangible rewards or incentives from the teacher. The satisfaction and accomplishment that students feel for success in school and gaining the respect of their teachers and peers are potent reinforcers. Eric Jensen (1998) pointed out that, biologically, "the limbic system ordinarily rewards cerebral learning with good feelings on a daily basis" (p. 65). In light of this internal reward system, some experts suggest tangible rewards can negatively impact intrinsic motivation when the reinforcement is given for tasks that students have a high interest in doing anyway. Moreover, students' reactions to external rewards vary from student to student, depending on the personal characteristics and previous experiences of the student. Jensen argued that external rewards are unfair because an external reward that motivates one student will not necessarily motivate another student. However, when students are successful in a learning task, "nearly all students will respond positively in their unique biological ways" (Jensen, 1998, p. 65). Given these concerns, experts (e.g., Gersten et al., 2009) suggest that when tangible rewards are used to stimulate student learning, teachers can gradually discontinue the use of rewards because students' successes will trigger intrinsic rewards.

A noteworthy exception to the cautions given here about external rewards or incentives is Robert Marzano's evidence-based strategy of **reinforcing effort and providing recognition,** which research indicates positively affects students' level of engagement in learning tasks (see "Marzano's High Yield Instructional Strategies" in Chapter 8 for a discussion of this topic). Teachers should be purposeful in helping students relate their successes to their efforts in achieving those successes (see "Attributions and Locus of Control" and "Mindset" later in this chapter for further discussion of this topic). Marzano et al. (2000) stated that "Believing that effort will affect level of achievement can serve as a powerful motivational tool that students can apply to any situation" (p. 54). Recognition, particularly verbal praise that is specific, honest, and credible to the student, is an external reinforcer that has been shown to increase intrinsic motivation—even after giving praise is discontinued (see "Praise" in Chapter 5 for guidelines on effective praise). Also, timely feedback—even when it is self-managed, as in interactive computer instructional programs—that informs students about what they are doing correctly and what they still need to work on strongly increases intrinsic motivation.

Achievement motivation is the tendency to strive for success and choose goal-oriented, success/failure activities. Students high in achievement motivation want and expect to succeed, and when they fail, they try harder. In some cases, students may have a strong desire to achieve, but they may be more controlled by the need to maintain a positive self-image, so they seek achievement by avoiding failure. Failure avoiders tend to choose either very easy or very difficult tasks, the reasoning being that they will likely succeed at the easy task, and if they fail at the difficult task, they can attribute the failure to the difficulty level of the task, rather than to their own lack of ability. This attribution of failure to the task itself, rather than considering the failure as a personal lack of ability, relates to the social learning concept of having an **external locus of control** (Rotter, 1966). On the other hand, students who have an **internal locus of control** tend to take ownership of the personal factors related to their successes and shortcomings. Students with an internal locus of control tend to be intrinsically motivated. Students with an external locus of control tend to rely more on extrinsic reinforcement for their actions (see "Attributions and Locus of Control" later in this chapter for a fuller discussion of locus of control).

Teachers' behavior and demeanor in the classroom can also affect student motivation. Highly motivating teachers are enthusiastic, energetic, exciting, and stimulating (Kindsvatter et al., 1996). When such teachers introduce lessons, they focus students' attention on the learning activity, clearly communicate the purposes of activities, and stimulate students to get involved. During lessons, they move around the classroom, vary voice level and quality, use instructional variety, change pace during the lesson, and use gestures (such as thumbs up signs), facial expressions (such as smiles), body movements (such as nods), and other nonverbal signals to create a presence in the classroom that excites students to learn. In addition, their questioning techniques are student-oriented and nonjudgmental.

Here are some guidelines based on ideas of experts, particularly the work of Jensen (1998), for intrinsically motivating students to learn:

- Remove obstacles—such as lack of resources, language barriers, text difficulty, and uncomfortable environmental conditions—that discourage engagement in learning.
- Make sure students have sufficient background knowledge for the content presented.
- Relate subject content to students' interest and experiences.
- Appeal to students' natural curiosity, desire for fun, and need for social interaction.
- Be alert to an increase in student interest or curiosity and capitalize on it.
- Involve students in choosing and planning their learning activities.
- Help students set goals for learning that are achievable with effort.
- Use a variety of instructional strategies that address various learning preferences.
- Use hands-on, minds-on activities in which students are actively engaged in learning.
- Use role playing, simulation, drama, debate, games, rituals, celebrations, and so on to evoke positive emotional involvement of students.

- Be sure students understand your expectations and how to meet those expectations.
- Affirm and encourage students' efforts and involvement.
- Build frequent, constructive feedback into learning activities.
- Maintain a warm, supportive atmosphere.
- Model desired behavior (enthusiasm, interest, curiosity, and so on).

Note: See "Maslow's Hierarchy of Needs" in Chapter 5 for a discussion of understanding motivation from the standpoint of a hierarchy of needs.

Checkpoint

Fill in the blank.

1. In intrinsic motivation, the desire to learn is based on factors that are _____ (external, internal) to the learner.
2. In extrinsic motivation, the emphasis is on _____ (external, internal) factors that students find desirable.
3. Relating content to students' interest and experiences is a way to stimulate _____ (extrinsic, intrinsic) motivation.

Mark as True or False.

4. _____ Students high in achievement motivation want and expect to succeed.
5. _____ Teachers' behavior and demeanor in the classroom have little impact on student motivation.

Checkpoint Answers

1. internal
2. external
3. intrinsic
4. True
5. False

Teacher Expectations

Teacher expectations is a term that describes a teacher's opinion of the likelihood that students will be successful. Research suggests that a teacher's attitude about students' abilities is an important classroom climate variable that is significantly related to student success. Teachers who exhibit high expectations toward their students have students who actually perform better. This phenomenon is often referred to as a **self-fulfilling prophecy,** which simply means that teachers get what they expect from students. Teachers who expect students to be successful have confidence in their students' abilities and treat them accordingly. This positive climate fosters students' belief in themselves and increases their ability to achieve.

Sometimes teachers unconsciously, rather than explicitly, convey low expectations to students. For example, a teacher might ask lower-level questions to at-risk students or minority students. This teacher behavior can send the message that the teacher believes these students are not capable of answering higher-level questions. Researchers have found a number of factors that influence how teachers perceive students. They warn that these potential sources of bias might result in disparate teacher expectations—for example:

- Socioeconomic status (SES)—lower expectations for lower-SES students
- Gender—lower expectations for elementary boys because of their slower maturation; lower expectations for girls in upper grades because of sex-role stereotyping

- Ethnicity—lower expectations for minorities
- Previous academic performance/standardized test scores—lower expectations for low performers

Teachers should monitor their interactions with students to make sure that they are communicating high expectations for all their students. Some ways to communicate high expectations are to

- promote the importance of education and each student's capacity for academic achievement.
- set realistic goals for students that can be achieved with effort, and recognize students when they are successful.
- adopt incentives that encourage individual progress toward a high, challenging, yet attainable, standard of performance, instead of emphasizing competition.
- clearly communicate goals and objectives to students and their responsibilities for attainment.
- be explicit about expectations for learning and behavior and reiterate these expectations throughout the school year.
- provide regular, constructive feedback to students and information about grading criteria.
- engage all students in thought-provoking, challenging activities while avoiding diluted instruction for lower achievers.
- base academic grades on the measurement of students' performance according to established learning criteria (that is, the TEKS).
- adopt flexible behavior standards that allow students to interact when engaged in learning.
- for cooperative learning, use heterogeneous grouping practices, instead of separating high-achieving students from low achievers.

Checkpoint

Fill in the blank.

1. Teacher expectations are significantly related to student _____.
2. Teachers should adopt incentives that encourage individual progress rather than emphasize _____.
3. For cooperative learning, teachers should use _____ (heterogeneous, homogeneous) grouping practices.

Mark as True or False.

4. _____ A self-fulfilling prophecy means that if a teacher expects little from students, the teacher is likely to get little.
5. _____ To convey high expectations to low achievers, a teacher should set challenging, but attainable, performance standards.
6. _____ Grouping low-ability students together provides a risk-free environment that makes them feel like they can succeed.

Checkpoint Answers

1. success
2. competition
3. heterogeneous
4. True
5. True
6. False

Attributions and Locus of Control

Attributions are the causes students assign to their successes or failures. The following four attributions are used most frequently:

- **Ability:** For example, the student might say/think, "I failed because I'm just not smart."
- **Effort:** For example, the student might say/think, "I succeeded because I tried really hard."
- **Task difficulty:** For example, the student might say/think, "I failed because the test was too hard."
- **Luck:** For example, the student might say/think, "I passed the test because I guessed right."

Locus of control reflects the degree to which students feel they have power over forces in their lives (Rotter, 1966). Students with an **internal locus of control** believe that events they experience are under their own control. These students attribute their successes to their own effort or ability. When students have an **external locus of control,** they believe that they are under the control of other people or forces outside themselves. These students attribute their successes to luck and their failures to factors that they have no control over (for example, task difficulty). Researchers believe that students will be more likely to engage in learning activities when they attribute success or failure to things they can control, like their own effort or lack of it, rather than to forces over which they have little or no control, such as luck or outside forces. Teachers should help students, especially at-risk learners, link their successes to something they did to contribute to their success. When this occurs, the students develop **self-efficacy,** meaning they believe in their own ability to be successful.

Checkpoint

Fill in the blank.

1. Attributions are the _____ students assign to their successes or failures.
2. Locus of control reflects the degree to which students feel they have _____ over forces in their lives.
3. A student who says, "I failed the test because there were a lot of trick questions on it," likely has an _____ (external, internal) locus of control.

Mark as True or False.

4. _____ Internal locus of control is linked to self-confidence.
5. _____ A teacher should be concerned if a student attributes failure on a test to bad luck.

Checkpoint Answers

1. causes
2. power
3. external
4. True
5. True

Mindset

According to Carol Dweck, students who have a **fixed mindset** believe intelligence is static and cannot change, while students with a growth mindset believe their intelligence can grow and improve. Students who possess a fixed mindset seek opportunities where they can prove their skills while avoiding situations where they might fail. They do not respond well to failure because it negatively impacts their self-image. Thus, they give up easily, see effort as futile, ignore useful negative feedback, and downplay the success of others by suggesting the success was due to luck.

On the other hand, students who possess a **growth mindset** believe that their abilities can develop. Students who take this approach seek out opportunities to learn new things and expand their skills. They welcome challenges, persist in the face of obstacles, and attribute success to their effort and abilities.

(Source: www.aacu.org/sites/default/files/files/ild/symonette.makeassessmentwork.dweck_.pdf)

Checkpoint

Mark as True or False.

1. _____ Students who have a fixed mindset believe they are either smart or not.
2. _____ Students who have a fixed mindset avoid failure.
3. _____ Students who have a growth mindset believe intelligence is static.
4. _____ Students who have a growth mindset persist in the face of obstacles.

Checkpoint Answers

1. True
2. True
3. False
4. True

Bruner

Like Piaget, Jerome Bruner (in Reinhartz and Beach, 1996) viewed learning as a process of constructing meaning by building on prior understandings. He believed that children learn best when tasks are presented to them at their appropriate level of development through a discovery-oriented approach. He proposed three modes through which children can learn based on their level of cognitive development:

- Up to about age 6, children primarily learn through the **enactive mode,** which involves interacting with objects in their environment.
- Elementary children (ages 6 through 11) can learn through the **iconic mode,** which involves the use of images or graphic illustrations to convey concepts.
- Older students and adults (ages 11 and above) can learn through the **symbolic mode,** which involves using symbols and words to represent concepts.

According to Bruner, when a concept is first introduced to students, teachers should structure the presentation of the concept so that it proceeds from enactive to iconic to symbolic mode. For example, in science, students might first build models of simple molecules, next draw pictures of molecules, and finally, write the symbolic representation of molecules.

Checkpoint

Fill in the blank.

1. Bruner viewed learning as a process of _____ meaning by building on prior understandings.
2. Up to about age 6, children primarily learn through the _____ (enactive, iconic, symbolic) mode.
3. The _____ (enactive, iconic, symbolic) mode involves using symbols and words to represent concepts.

Mark as True or False.

4. ____ Bruner was an advocate of discovery learning.

5. ____ According to Bruner, when introducing concepts, teachers should start with the symbolic representation of the concept.

Checkpoint Answers
1. constructing
2. enactive
3. symbolic
4. True
5. False

Vygotsky

Lev Vygotsky's 1978 work is based on the premise that learning cannot be understood without consideration of its cultural and social context. Carol Gestwicki (1999) expressed Vygotsky's view of learning by saying, "Social engagement and collaboration with others is [sic] the powerful force that transforms children's thinking" (p. 39). Terms associated with Vygotsky's theory of cognitive development are *self-regulation, private speech, zone of proximal development,* and *scaffolding* (Slavin, 2008).

Self-regulation is the ability to learn and solve problems on one's own without assistance.

Private speech is the self-talk learners use to monitor and guide themselves as they work through a problem or complete a learning task.

The **zone of proximal development** is the gap between a student's independent level of problem-solving ability and the student's potential level of problem-solving ability that can be achieved with assistance from an adult or more capable peer (Gestwicki, 1999).

When students are learning in their zone of proximal development, **scaffolding** is the support and assistance provided for learning and problem solving, such as verbal cues or prompts, visual highlighting, diagrams, checklists, reminders, modeling, partially completed learning charts or tasks, and examples. Scaffolding is more intense and frequent at first but should be diminished as learners become self-regulated.

Checkpoint
Fill in the blank.

1. The self-talk learners use to monitor and guide themselves as they work through a problem is _____ (two words).

2. The zone of proximal development is the gap between a student's independent level of problem-solving ability and the student's _____ level of problem-solving ability that can be achieved with assistance.

3. Vygotsky described the support and assistance provided for learning and problem solving as _____.

Mark as True or False.

4. ____ According to Vygotsky, learning is enhanced by social interaction.

5. ____ Scaffolding should be diminished as learners become self-regulated.

Checkpoint Answers
1. private speech
2. potential
3. scaffolding
4. True
5. True

Behaviorism and Constructivism

Behaviorism is a learning theory based on using immediate consequences to either weaken or strengthen a learner's observable response. A **consequence** is a pleasant or unpleasant effect that follows a behavior and influences whether the behavior will occur again. Other key ideas associated with behaviorism include *positive* and *negative reinforcement, intrinsic* and *extrinsic reinforcers, extinction, reinforcement schedule,* and *shaping.*

The appropriate use of **reinforcement,** which is a pleasant consequence that follows a behavior, is an essential strategy associated with a behavioristic approach to learning. The idea is that students' accomplishments and appropriate behavior should be rewarded not only with good grades but also with other rewards and incentives: attention, public recognition (such as public displays of good work), tangible rewards (such as stickers, stars, and stamps), extra privileges, and so forth. The basic principle of reinforcement is that students will continue good behaviors that are reinforced and discontinue undesirable behaviors when they are not reinforced.

Reinforcers are either **extrinsic reinforcers,** which are reinforcers that are external to a student such as tangible rewards or grades, or **intrinsic reinforcers,** which are reinforcers that come from within a student such as a personal enjoyment of problem solving. When using extrinsic reinforcement, most teachers prefer to use **positive reinforcement,** in the form of things given to students (such as tangible rewards or special privileges), rather than **negative reinforcement,** which is removal from a situation perceived by the student to be unpleasant (such as a night off from doing homework). In either case, teachers need to use reinforcers that are perceived as desirable by students. For example, elementary students might enjoy getting stickers as rewards, but high school students would prefer the reward of free time or getting to see a movie for their good behavior. Teachers should use reinforcement to inform students about what they are doing right. Reinforcement should be given contingent on specific student behaviors and should be awarded in such a way that it helps to develop intrinsic motivation and other natural reinforcers of desirable student performance. (See "Motivational Strategies" earlier in this chapter for a discussion of intrinsic motivation.)

Extinction is the process of weakening and eventually eliminating the occurrence of a behavior, usually through the removal or withholding of reinforcement. The **schedule of reinforcement,** which is the frequency with which reinforcement is given, influences the response rate of a behavior and, furthermore, its resistance to extinction. Slavin (2008) explained that behaviors that are reinforced on a **variable, unpredictable schedule** tend to have steady, high response rates and be resistant to extinction, while behaviors that are reinforced on a **fixed, predictable schedule** have uneven response rates and drop off quickly after reinforcement is removed.

Shaping uses positive reinforcement upon successful completion of incremental steps along the way toward a desired learning goal or behavior to change a student's behavior. Teachers might use shaping to teach a complex skill by using reinforcement of step-by-step procedures.

Punishment is characterized as positive or negative. **Positive punishment** involves giving an undesirable consequence (for example, extra work) in order to deter undesirable behavior. **Negative punishment** involves taking away a desirable reward (for example, free time) in order to deter undesirable behavior. Do not confuse punishment, which penalizes students and, is, thus, perceived negatively by them, with negative reinforcement, which is a type of reward that is perceived positively by students. Teachers should avoid using punishment in their classrooms because it puts in jeopardy the safe, supportive learning environment that is essential for facilitating student learning. (See Chapter 5 for additional discussion of learning environments.)

Behavioristic lessons often involve direct instruction. Teachers gain attention, activate prior knowledge, and present explicit information about the lesson content and structured models that demonstrate the knowledge or skill. They scaffold students' understanding, often with examples and nonexamples, and provide clarification and immediate feedback. (See "Instructional Methods" in Chapter 8 for further discussion of direct instruction.) It should be noted that, according to research, the most effective approach to help students learn to read, especially students at risk for reading difficulties, is systematic and explicit direct instruction.

Evolving from the works of John Dewey, Jean Piaget, Lev Vygotsky, and other proponents of child-centered methods, **constructivism** is a learner-centered approach to teaching that emphasizes teaching for understanding, predicated on the concept that students construct knowledge by making connections between present learning experiences and the existing knowledge they already possess. Teachers must establish learning environments that provide experiences from which learners can construct meaning based on what they already know. Constructivist teachers help learners to reinvent their knowledge, thus creating new understandings. To develop understanding about a concept, students need to see the whole picture and also need to be able to break it down into its various parts. Constructivist teachers take a whole-to-parts approach, with the content organized around broad concepts. When students break down a concept into parts, they can understand how the parts fit together because they know what the whole looks like.

In constructivist lessons, teachers intentionally help students connect new learning to prior understandings, foster a view of learning as a personally meaningful pursuit, promote a sense of responsibility for one's own learning, and encourage exploration, problem solving, inquiry, and discovery in individual and collaborative settings.

Constructivist teachers recognize the power of group dynamics and the key role of social groups in promoting understanding. They use a variety of collaborative strategies such as cooperative learning groups, teaming, and pairing, along with class discussions to create a rich environment of productive communication and interactive problem solving and inquiry.

Constructivist learning encourages students to think creatively and critically, to consider carefully, to make decisions, and to reflect. Teachers seek out and value students' input. Students are actively engaged—either independently, in pairs, or in collaborative groups—in seeking answers to questions and solutions to actual or authentic problems. They reflect on their ideas and communicate them as a regular part of instruction and are provided with opportunities to discover principles on their own. Student autonomy and initiative are encouraged. Learning is negotiated between the teacher and the students. This practice results in decreasing the number of activities controlled by the teacher, thus empowering the students to assume responsibility for their own learning.

Checkpoint

Fill in the blank.

1. The appropriate use of _____, which is a pleasant consequence that follows a behavior, is an essential strategy associated with behaviorism.
2. Giving gold star stickers is an example of using _____ (intrinsic, extrinsic) reinforcers.
3. Taking away a desirable reward is an example of _____ (positive, negative) punishment.
4. Constructivist teachers establish learning environments that provide experiences from which the learner can _____ meaning based on what the learner already knows.
5. In constructivist classrooms, students are encouraged to assume _____ for their own learning.

Mark as True or False.

6. _____ Detention is an example of negative reinforcement.
7. _____ Constructivist approaches are mainly teacher-centered.

Checkpoint Answers

1. reinforcement
2. extrinsic
3. negative
4. construct
5. responsibility
6. False
7. False

Summary

Effective teachers have a strong foundational knowledge of learning theories, and they apply this knowledge to facilitate student learning. To further enhance their practice, they use motivational strategies to encourage students to be achievement-oriented and have growth mindsets. By understanding important principles of human development and learning, effective teachers are able to use developmentally appropriate practices that enhance the social and academic development of students.

Domain I Sample Questions and Answer Explanations

Sample Questions

1. A second-grade student behaves in school to avoid getting into trouble. The student is probably in which of Kohlberg's stages of moral development?

   A. punishment-obedience orientation
   B. instrumental-relativist orientation
   C. good boy–nice girl orientation
   D. law-order orientation

2. A teacher can convey high expectations to a low-achieving student by

   A. accepting and praising all work.
   B. setting challenging but attainable performance standards that can be achieved with effort.
   C. using a lower grading standard that better reflects the student's abilities.
   D. modeling creative and critical thinking when working with the student.

3. Which of the following would be the most appropriate way to express the action element of an instructional objective?

   A. The student will understand the solar system.
   B. The student will be aware of the solar system.
   C. The student will recite the names of the planets.
   D. The student will know the names of the planets.

4. "Given examples of 10 mammals, the student will be able to classify 9 out of 10 correctly as herbivore, carnivore, or omnivore." This statement is an example of a(n)

   A. affective objective.
   B. cognitive objective.
   C. psychomotor objective.
   D. reflective objective.

5. Which of the following instructional strategies is most compatible with a behaviorist point of view?

   A. discovery learning
   B. project-based learning
   C. inquiry learning
   D. direct instruction

6. A teacher makes a student remain in the classroom during a school pep rally as a consequence for inappropriate behavior. This measure is an example of which of the following?

   A. positive reinforcement
   B. negative reinforcement
   C. positive punishment
   D. negative punishment

7. Of the following instructional methods, which is best for teaching reading?

   A. direct instruction
   B. inquiry-based learning
   C. discovery learning
   D. traditional lecture

8. A science teacher is participating in a cross-discipline unit on surviving in the wilderness. The teacher is working collaboratively with teachers from other disciplines to plan the unit, which will include lessons on edible plant life, physical fitness, calculating caloric intake, and problem solving. Planning across disciplines as in this team effort is best characterized as which of the following?

   A. intersected
   B. multifaceted
   C. interdisciplinary
   D. intradisciplinary

Answer Explanations

1. **A.** Choice A is the correct response. When children are in the stage of punishment-obedience orientation, they obey rules to avoid punishment. Eliminate choices B, C, and D because these stages are higher levels of moral development than what is indicated by the situation described in the question.

2. **B.** Eliminate choices A and C because these practices would convey low expectations to the student. Eliminate choice D because it is not aligned with the question. Setting challenging but attainable performance standards that can be achieved with effort is an effective way for a teacher to convey high expectations to a low-achieving student. Thus, choice B is the correct response.

3. **C.** Notice that you must select the answer choice that is the *most* appropriate way to express the action element of an instructional objective. Choice C is the correct response. The statement in choice C contains the action verb *recite,* so it is the most appropriate way to express the action element of an instructional objective. Eliminate choices A, B, and D because these statements do not contain action verbs.

4. **B.** The statement in the question is an example of an instructional objective. Instructional objectives are classified as affective, cognitive, or psychomotor. Eliminate choice D because reflective objective is not a type of lesson objective. Eliminate choice A because affective objectives involve feelings and dispositions. Eliminate choice C because psychomotor objectives involve physical activity on the part of the student. Cognitive objectives involve thinking capabilities such as classifying mammals as herbivores, carnivores, or omnivores. Therefore, choice B is the correct response.

5. **D.** Notice that you must select the answer choice that is *most* compatible with a behaviorist point of view. Of the instructional strategies given in the answer choices, direct instruction is the one that is most compatible with a behaviorist point of view. Thus, choice D is the correct response. The instructional strategies given in the other answer choices are compatible with a constructivist point of view.

6. **D.** Staying in the classroom instead of going to a pep rally is an undesirable consequence, so eliminate choices A and B because reinforcement is a desirable consequence. Eliminate choice C because positive punishment involves giving an undesirable consequence (for example, extra work). Choice D is the correct response because negative punishment involves taking away a desirable reward (for example, going to a pep rally) in order to deter undesirable behavior.

7. **A.** Choice A is the correct response. Research consistently points to direct instruction as a highly effective instructional method for teaching reading. The methods in the other answer choices are not as effective.

8. **C.** Choice C is the correct response. *Interdisciplinary* correctly characterizes planning across disciplines. Eliminate choices A, B, and D because the terms given in these answer choices do not accurately characterize the planning approach reflected by the use of a cross-discipline unit.

PART 2

DOMAIN II: CREATING A POSITIVE, PRODUCTIVE CLASSROOM ENVIRONMENT

- Competency 005: *The teacher knows how to establish a classroom climate that fosters learning, equity, and excellence and uses this knowledge to create a physical and emotional environment that is safe and productive.*
- Competency 006: *The teacher understands strategies for creating an organized and productive learning environment and for managing student behavior.*

Chapter 5

Classroom Climate

> **Competency 005:** The teacher knows how to establish a classroom climate that fosters learning, equity, and excellence and uses this knowledge to create a physical and emotional environment that is safe and productive.

This chapter provides a general review of knowledge and skills related to Competency 005. Checkpoint exercises are found throughout the review material. These exercises give you an opportunity to practice what you just learned. The answers to the Checkpoint exercises are found immediately following the set of exercises. When doing the Checkpoint exercises, you should cover up the answers. Then check your answers when you've finished the exercises.

Competency Descriptive Statements

The descriptive statements for Competency 005 as given in the TExES PPR EC-12 test preparation manual (www.tx.nesinc.com/Content/Docs/160PrepManual.pdf) specify the following knowledge and skills for beginning teachers in Texas public schools:

- Uses knowledge of the unique characteristics and needs of students at different developmental levels to establish a positive, productive classroom environment (e.g., encourages cooperation and sharing among younger students; provides middle-level students with opportunities to collaborate with peers; encourages older students' respect for the community and the people in it).
- Establishes a classroom climate that emphasizes collaboration and supportive interactions, respect for diversity and individual differences, and active engagement in learning by all students.
- Analyzes ways in which teacher-student interactions and interactions among students impact classroom climate and student learning and development.
- Presents instruction in ways that communicate the teacher's enthusiasm for learning.
- Uses a variety of means to convey high expectations for all students.
- Knows characteristics of physical spaces that are safe and productive for learning, recognizes the benefits and limitations of various arrangements of furniture in the classroom, and applies strategies for organizing the physical environment to ensure physical accessibility and facilitate learning in various instructional contexts.
- Creates a safe, nurturing, and inclusive classroom environment that addresses students' emotional needs and respects students' rights and dignity.

Creating Supportive Classroom Climates

Classrooms should be inviting, attractive places where students feel welcome, connected, secure, and safe. A teacher who creates such a climate is providing a learning environment that encourages and motivates students to be successful, thus creating good feelings of self-worth.

In particular, supportive classroom climates contribute to the following outcomes for students:

- They do better academically.
- They attend school more regularly, which leads to higher graduation rates.
- They feel better about themselves and have better relationships with their teachers and with one another.
- They engage in fewer risky behaviors such as drinking alcohol or using drugs.
- They engage less in bullying and in other problem behaviors.

(Source: Diamanti, K., Duffey, T., and Fisher, D., 2018)

Chapter 5: Classroom Climate

Diamanti, Duffey, and Fisher (2018) postulated that engagement, safety, and environment are central to a supportive classroom climate. Key features of these three aspects are the following:

Engagement: Characterized by strong relationships among students, teachers, families, and schools; positive emotions and a sense of belonging conveyed by students toward school; and respect for diversity.

Safety: Includes supporting students to feel secure when expressing emotions, to feel confident when taking healthy risks and embracing challenges, and to feel excited to try something new; and protecting students from violence, theft, bullying, harassment, substance abuse, and exposure to threats and weapons.

Environment: Includes the physical setting; instructional, behavioral, and personal aspects of the classroom experience; and the discipline, rules, and strategies applied to manage student behavior and the practices used to encourage self-discipline.

The following table summarizes ways to build supportive classroom climates in the context of these three core concepts:

Engagement	Safety	Environment
Be a role model.	Intervene in problematic situations.	Walk your talk.
Be proactive.	Make a safe culture the norm.	Set a positive tone of respect in your classroom.
Be available.	Encourage students' individual aptitudes and passions.	Examine your own beliefs.
Actively listen.	Keep communication open.	Treat students fairly.
Encourage and model positive thinking.	Stay on top of things.	Establish a culture of respect for differences.
Have a sense of humor.	Use positive terms and language.	Work together with parents.
Teach inclusively.	Teach positive relationship skills.	Create a safe environment.

Checkpoint

Fill in the blank(s).

1. Positive classroom climates help students do better _____, and attend school more _____.

2. Diamanti, Duffey, and Fisher postulated that _____, _____, and _____ are central to a supportive classroom climate.

3. Which aspect of a supportive classroom climate is characterized by a sense of belonging? _____

Mark as True or False.

4. _____ Teachers can build supportive classroom climates by listening to students' concerns.

5. _____ Avoiding the use of humor is a recommended way to build supportive classroom climates.

Checkpoint Answers

1. academically; regularly
2. engagement; safety; environment
3. Engagement
4. True
5. False

Physical Layout

Successful classroom managers arrange the physical layout of their classrooms so that they can see each student from anywhere in the classroom. They know that the physical arrangement of the classroom influences the way teachers and students feel, think, and behave. Classroom furniture might consist of desks or tables and chairs. The seating arrangement can determine the kind and extent of interactions that will take place in the classroom.

Clusters of three to five desks or students seated at small tables promote social contact and interaction. Students can easily share materials, have group discussions, and work together on assignments. This arrangement is particularly appropriate when teachers want to use cooperative learning activities (see "Cooperative Learning" in Chapter 8 for a discussion of this topic).

Teachers who want their students to exchange ideas know that the more the students see each other, the more they will be involved in discussions. Thus, for whole-group settings, circles and U-shaped designs promote discussion. Teachers who use these arrangements usually place their own desks in an out-of-the-way place or in a corner.

Arranging desks in rows is particularly appropriate for teacher-centered instruction. Rows tend to reduce the interaction among students and make it easier for them to work individually. Rows also direct the students' attention toward the teacher. Teachers who use this type of physical arrangement typically place their desks in the front of the room where they are easily visible.

Where students are seated in the classroom can also influence participation patterns. Planned seating is better than random seating. When desks are arranged in rows, students who are seated in the front and center are in the **action zone.** These students interact most frequently with the teacher. Students who are seated in the back and corners tend to participate less. Some evidence indicates that teachers might communicate differently with students, depending on where the students are seated. Students in the action zone receive a more permissive and interactive style of communication, while students in the back and corners receive more lecturing and one-way communication.

Effective teachers arrange and change the environment as needed to encourage learning. They make sure that movement in the classroom and acquisition of materials can occur with little disruption; that students can see and be seen by the teacher; and that students can see the whiteboard/SMART Board, projector screen or display screen, and so forth, when necessary. They are also aware that an accessible and barrier-free environment is necessary for students with physical disabilities.

Checkpoint

Fill in the blank.

1. The seating arrangement can determine the kind and extent of _____ that will take place in the classroom.

2. Social contact and interaction are promoted by _____ arrangements.

3. Seating students in rows directs the students' attention toward the _____.

Mark as True or False.

4. _____ Putting desks in a U-shaped design minimizes interaction.

5. _____ Students in the action zone usually get most of the teacher's attention.

Checkpoint Answers

1. interactions
2. cluster
3. teacher
4. False
5. True

Maslow's Hierarchy of Needs

According to Abraham Maslow (1954), all human beings have certain needs that must be met. These needs are listed in a hierarchy, with the primary needs requiring attention before the other needs can be achieved, as follows:

- **Physiological needs,** such as food and shelter
- **Safety needs,** such as a predictable environment and security from harm
- **Belongingness and love needs,** such as affection and affiliation with others
- **Esteem needs,** such as self-respect, worthiness, and gaining approval and recognition
- **Self-actualization needs,** such as self-fulfillment and personal achievement

Maslow explained that everyone has an innate desire to achieve self-actualization, the highest level of needs; however, lower-level needs must be satisfied before higher-level needs can be met. He described physiological, safety, belongingness and love, and esteem needs as **deficiency needs** and contended that motivation to learn is hampered when these needs are not satisfied. The implication is that a hungry child or a child who is worried about a family problem such as divorce or illness likely will not be interested in the lesson topic, or even be attentive in the classroom, for that matter. The charge for teachers is to strive to keep the learning environment conducive to student learning by being on the alert for situations where deficiency needs are not being met and to do what they can to assist the student or students in satisfying those needs.

Checkpoint

Fill in the blank.

1. Food and shelter are examples of _____ needs, which fall under deficiency needs.
2. Self-respect is an example of _____ needs, which fall under deficiency needs.
3. Personal achievement is an example of _____ needs.

Mark as True or False.

4. _____ According to Maslow, a student will have difficulty learning if deficiency needs have not been satisfied.
5. _____ According to Maslow, everyone has an innate desire to achieve self-actualization.

Checkpoint Answers

1. physiological
2. esteem
3. self-actualization
4. True
5. True

Praise

Praise, if used appropriately, can be a valuable tool for teachers. It is a way for teachers to inform students about what the students are doing right. Teachers should praise students frequently, especially students in early-childhood classrooms and low-performing students who are struggling. However, some experts contend that indiscriminate praise can have undesirable effects in the classroom. They assert that some teachers overuse global, nonspecific praise (for example, "Good job" or "Great") to the point that it becomes meaningless to students. Specific praise for desired performance and behavior is more powerful. Here are some guidelines for effectively using praise in the classroom.

Effective Praise

- Specifies the behavior or accomplishment that is worthy of praise—for example, "Jisela, you did a very good job punctuating the sentences correctly on the quiz."
- Is genuine, honest, and not given randomly.
- Is given in a natural, not exaggerated, voice.
- Is most effective when done privately and paired with students' names, rather than publicly in front of the whole class.
- Is given for effort and persistence as well as for accomplishments.
- Is given for risk taking and bold thinking, regardless of the "correctness" of the ideas—for example, "That is very good thinking about this issue, Dante."
- Is done in a way that encourages intrinsic motivation—for example, "You must feel pleased that you were able to name the planets from memory, Josephine."
- Attributes success to effort (rather than to ability or luck).
- Implies that present success leads to high expectations for future successes.

Ineffective Praise

- Is global ("Good job," "Nice work") rather than specific.
- Is given indiscriminately, with little thought to meaning.
- Is reserved for only strong or correct responses from students.
- Rewards participation rather than the value of the effort or accomplishment.
- Attributes success to external forces rather than to the student's ability—for example, "You were lucky to get so many questions correct. Good job!"
- Is used publicly as a control technique—for example, "I like the way that Kelsey is paying attention while I'm talking."
- Suggests that the behavior or performance deserves praise because it pleases the teacher—for example, "I'm so happy that you finished your assignment on time."
- Fosters a climate in which students feel manipulated by the teacher.
- Creates a competitive climate in which students compare themselves to others in the classroom.
- Is overused to the point of being meaningless.

The amount of praise that teachers give students for appropriate behavior should substantially exceed the amount of reprimands they give to students. Research indicates that a ratio of about four to one for positive over corrective statements can improve students' academic and behavioral outcomes (Epstein et al., 2008). It is also a good idea to use the "Pause, Prompt, Praise" technique. If a student is struggling, *pause* (instead of assisting right away) to give him or her "think time" to figure out a correct response or to correct an error. If the student continues to struggle, then *prompt* with suggestions/hints or helpful questions to scaffold successful performance. When the student responds correctly, recognize his or her effort and achievement by offering meaningful, specific *praise*.

Checkpoint

Fill in the blank.

1. Praise should be _____, not global.
2. Teachers should avoid overusing global, nonspecific praise because it can become _____ to students.
3. Using praise to foster competition among students is a _____ (good, poor) practice.
4. "Good job" is an example of _____ (effective, ineffective) praise.

Checkpoint Answers
1. specific
2. meaningless
3. poor
4. ineffective

Learning Environment Accommodations for Learners with Special Educational Needs

Teachers need to use appropriate management strategies for learners who have disabilities, are easily distracted, have difficulty completing work, or have difficulty controlling their behavior. The publication *Accommodations, Assisting Students with Disabilities*, Third Edition (Beech, 2010) offers guidelines for making accommodations to the learning environment for these students. The following chart summarizes the guidelines.

Learner Difficulty	Suggested Accommodations
Short attention span	Minimize classroom distractions; seat away from windows, doors, materials center, and noisy machinery; use white noise or soft music to neutralize distracting noise; provide planned opportunities for physical movement (for example, running errands, erasing the board, or passing out materials); break tasks into smaller chunks; have a private area where the student can voluntarily go when needed.
Working in large groups	Preview activities so the student will know what to expect; recruit and train a peer helper to sit next to the student to help him or her know what to do and stay on-task.
Working in small groups	Spend time explicitly teaching the student (through modeling and role playing) how to share responsibility, how to plan with others, and so on; assign roles to the students in the group, including the learner with special needs; recruit and train a peer helper to join the student's group and help the student stay on-task.
Working independently	Make sure the task is one the student wants to do and understands how to do; offer a choice of tasks and use hands-on activities frequently; use computer-assisted instruction or learning centers with easy-to-follow directions (which are illustrated for younger students); recruit and train a peer helper to repeat and explain directions and give assistance when the teacher is unavailable.
Controlling his/her own behavior	Provide a structured environment with predictable routines; use a cueing system, agreed upon with the student, to signal transitions; make sure the student understands the class rules and consequences by having the student role-play (on a regular basis) examples of appropriate and inappropriate behaviors; as with other students, use meaningful consequences that escalate in severity depending on the seriousness of the infraction and/or the number of times it is repeated; monitor the student's compliance with the rules and provide constructive feedback and positive reinforcement; communicate regularly with the student's parents/guardians and elicit their support of positive behavior; if ordinary measures fail to yield success, contact the special education teacher for assistance.

Checkpoint

Fill in the blank.

1. A student who has a short attention span will be helped by minimizing classroom _____.
2. Providing a learning center is a way to accommodate a student who has difficultly working _____.
3. A student who has difficulty controlling his or her own behavior needs _____ routines.

Mark as True or False.

4. _____ When a student has difficulty working in a small group, the teacher should teach the student group process skills.
5. _____ Peer helpers do not need to be trained.

Checkpoint Answers

1. distractions
2. independently
3. predictable
4. True
5. False

Summary

Successful classroom managers understand their responsibilities in regard to the learning environment. They strive to build positive, organized, and safe physical, social, and intellectual environments that are equitable, flexible, and inclusive. They create classroom climates that are conducive to learning and responsive to students' needs and characteristics. And they value and respect all students and treat them with dignity and respect at all times.

Chapter 6

Classroom Management

> **Competency 006:** The teacher understands strategies for creating an organized and productive learning environment and for managing student behavior.

This chapter provides a general review of knowledge and skills related to Competency 006. Checkpoint exercises are found throughout the review material. These exercises give you an opportunity to practice what you just learned. The answers to the Checkpoint exercises are found immediately following the set of exercises. When doing the Checkpoint exercises, you should cover up the answers. Then check your answers when you've finished the exercises.

Competency Descriptive Statements

The descriptive statements for Competency 006 as given in the TExES PPR EC-12 test preparation manual (www.tx.nesinc.com/Content/Docs/160PrepManual.pdf) specify the following knowledge and skills for beginning teachers in Texas public schools:

- Analyzes the effects of classroom routines and procedures on student learning, and knows how to establish and implement age-appropriate routines and procedures to promote an organized and productive learning environment.
- Demonstrates an understanding of how young children function in groups and designs group activities that reflect a realistic understanding of the extent of young children's ability to collaborate with others.
- Organizes and manages group activities that promote students' ability to work together cooperatively and productively, assume responsible roles, and develop collaborative skills and individual accountability.
- Recognizes the importance of creating a schedule for young children that balances restful and active movement activities and that provides large blocks of time for play, projects, and learning centers.
- Schedules activities and manages time in ways that maximize student learning, including using effective procedures to manage transitions; to manage materials, supplies, and technology; and to coordinate the performance of noninstructional duties (e.g., taking attendance) with instructional activities.
- Uses technological tools to perform administrative tasks such as taking attendance, maintaining grade books, and facilitating communication.
- Works with volunteers and paraprofessionals to enhance and enrich instruction and applies procedures for monitoring the performance of volunteers and paraprofessionals in the classroom.
- Applies theories and techniques related to managing and monitoring student behavior.
- Demonstrates awareness of appropriate behavior standards and expectations for students at various developmental levels.
- Applies effective procedures for managing student behavior and for promoting appropriate behavior and ethical work habits (e.g., academic integrity) in the classroom (e.g., communicating high and realistic behavior expectations, involving students in developing rules and procedures, establishing clear consequences for inappropriate behavior, enforcing behavior standards consistently, encouraging students to monitor their own behavior and to use conflict resolution skills, responding appropriately to various types of behavior).

Effective Classroom Management

An important key to being a successful classroom manager is planning effective lessons. Planning means being prepared each day with lesson plans and everything needed to implement those plans. Planning also includes going through each lesson mentally beforehand, from a student's point of view, and anticipating explanations, information, and directions needed in order to carry out the lesson successfully. Teaching well-planned lessons using evidence-based instructional strategies that actively engage students in learning is a powerful way to deter undesirable student behavior.

Effective managers are able to secure the cooperation of students, maintain their involvement in instructional tasks, and attend to the clerical or business duties of the classroom quickly and smoothly. They move around the room, monitoring and interacting with students. They are courteous and respectful and expect students to be courteous and respectful as well. Furthermore, the classroom environment is organized and predictable, providing an overall secure structure in which maximum student learning can take place.

Successful classroom managers are skillful in anticipating problem behavior and addressing it before it occurs. They often use antecedent **precorrective** prompts to cue students as to expected appropriate behavior; for example, at the beginning of an activity or transition (such as "Before we begin the class discussion, let's review the ground rules."). When problem behavior does arise, they deal with it appropriately.

In handling discipline situations, they ensure at all times that the dignity of students, even that of a seriously disruptive student, is preserved. They listen to and acknowledge students' feelings and frustrations and respond with respect. They guide students to resolve conflicts and model skills that encourage students to solve problems constructively. They help students to come to the realization that conflict can be positive and, when handled appropriately, can promote improved relationships among students. Moreover, they encourage parents[*] to become active partners in promoting and reinforcing appropriate behavior.

> **Note: By state law, a *parent* is either or both parents, a guardian, or any person standing in parental relation to a child, or who has legal charge over a child in place of the parent. Throughout this book, any use of the word "parent" means *parent* in the sense given here.**

Creating and managing smoothly functioning learning communities is central to the work of teachers. Effective teachers use a variety of ways of flexibly grouping students for instruction and interventions that support collaboration and interaction among students. At appropriate times, students have opportunities to work as a whole class, in small groups, and individually. When teachers are working with small groups, they need to be clear about directions and expectations. Additionally, they need to spend time moving through the room and checking on the groups so that they can offer reinforcement and feedback to students about their academic work as well as their group process skills.

The following guidelines for classroom management have been gleaned from USDOE (www.ed.gov/) and the works of Brophy (1983), Cotton (1993), Borgmeier (2006), Slavin (2008), and Bindreiff (2017):

- Be available and show interest and care about students' lives.
- Be a physical presence. Move around the room while monitoring and interacting with students.
- Be a good listener. Listening demonstrates respect and empathy.
- Be genuine, not phony.
- Be warm and friendly toward students.
- Be sensitive to the impact of sociocultural factors on students' behavior and ways of communicating.
- Make sure your nonverbal behavior is consistent with students' cultural backgrounds, and be aware of their nonverbal behavior as well.
- Encourage and model positive thinking.
- Show students you have a sense of humor, but do not use sarcasm or make fun of students. Avoid humor that shows racial/ethnic, political, religious, or gender bias.
- Communicate high expectations to all students.
- Learn students' names by the end of the first day and use their names regularly.
- Align classroom procedures and rules with schoolwide expectations.

- Involve students in creating age-appropriate classroom rules and fair, meaningful consequences for infractions.
- Teach classroom rules and procedures at the beginning of the year.
- Give reasons for consequences when going over the rules.
- Set clear standards and limits for classroom behavior.
- Use precorrection to prompt students for expected appropriate behavior, without pointing out undesirable student behavior.
- Apply the established rules and standards for behavior consistently and equitably.
- Establish norms for everyday activities so that students know, for example, the appropriate voice level for various situations, how to make transitions, how to get help, and how to turn in homework.
- Initially, work with the whole class and use activities with low content demand and high emphasis on procedures while students are adjusting to classroom rules and procedures.
- Use well-planned lessons and a variety of teaching strategies in varied learning settings—whole class, small group, or individual.
- Adapt instruction to meet students' needs and special characteristics (for example, learning style, modality, and strength).
- Begin lessons promptly and provide transitions between activities.
- Use signals (bell, clapping pattern) for transitions.
- Give explicit directions so that students know what to do and how to do it.
- Anticipate problems and try to prevent or minimize the effect of their occurrence.
- Make sure that all students have access to instructional materials.
- Maintain instructional momentum at a brisk, but appropriate, pace.
- Include all students in class discussions, showing respect and sensitivity to each student.
- Elicit students' cooperation, and give genuine praise when they comply.
- Promote students' development of internal locus of control.
- Monitor student behavior and provide feedback to students about what they are doing correctly and what they still need to work on.
- Approach off-task students promptly and privately to avoid power struggles and possible negative impact on the classroom learning environment.
- Be quick to stop or redirect misconduct.
- Whenever possible, begin with the least intrusive intervention to stop or redirect misconduct.
- Use a variety of verbal and nonverbal signals to stop misconduct.
- Avoid framing requests for compliance as a question (which implies students have a choice about whether to comply). Say, "I need you to . . . ," not "Will you please . . . ?".
- Make requests for compliance from up close and in a non-emotional, soft, but firm voice; rather than from across the room in a loud voice.
- Formulate compliance requests as positive statements (e.g., "Please start working on your assignment.") rather than negative statements (e.g., "Stop playing around.").
- Formulate compliance requests that are specific and descriptive, rather than global and vague. Say, "Face the speaker with your feet on the floor and hands in your lap" instead of "Pay attention to the speaker."
- If a discipline situation involving a "perpetrator" and a "victim" occurs, immediately stop the perpetrator's actions, but then do what is necessary to take care of the victim.
- When a student misbehaves, focus on the misconduct, not on the student.
- Make sure that students who misbehave know what they did wrong, why the behavior is unacceptable, and what appropriate behavior should have occurred in place of the misbehavior.
- Use incidences of misconduct to teach appropriate behavior.

- If discipline in a student's home is inconsistent with classroom rules, explain to the student that obeying the rules at school is necessary, but do so with sensitivity and respect for the student's home culture.
- Consider placing students with behavior problems in peer tutoring arrangements, either as tutors or tutees, as appropriate.
- Model positive behavior and constructive conflict resolution.
- Encourage students to assume responsibility for their own behavior.
- Explicitly teach (for example, through modeling and role playing) self-monitoring and self-regulating behaviors.
- Elicit ideas from students on how to prevent and stop misconduct.
- Contact parents and elicit their help and support for appropriate classroom behavior.
- Make sure that the classroom is physically comfortable.
- Make appropriate accommodations in the learning environment for learners with special needs. (See "Learning Environment Accommodations for Learners with Special Educational Needs" in Chapter 5 for a discussion of this topic.)
- Avoid punitive discipline measures such as writing students' names on the board or other public display, taking away privileges, or assigning extra work.
- Avoid using threats, bribes, or coaxing to elicit appropriate behavior.
- Avoid sarcasm and put-downs.
- Avoid giving long lectures to students who misbehave.
- Never react to student misbehavior in anger.
- Never embarrass, humiliate, or disparage a student.
- Never harass or discriminate against a student.
- Be on the alert for bullying, intimidation, sexual harassment, alcohol or tobacco use, or other behaviors that threaten school safety. (See Chapter 13 for a discussion of laws related to bullying.)
- Make students aware of building procedures to follow in case of an emergency.
- Maintain a safe and orderly environment in a manner consistent with district policies.

Checkpoint

Fill in the blank.

1. Good classroom managers facilitate the development of _____ and self-regulation in students.
2. Teachers' responses to student misconduct should be fair and _____ without regard to students' personal characteristics.
3. Good teachers never react to student misbehavior in _____.

Mark as True or False.

4. _____ A well-planned lesson is a deterrent to misconduct.
5. _____ Teachers should make a practice of giving long lectures to students who misbehave.

Checkpoint Answers

1. responsibility
2. equitable
3. anger
4. True
5. False

Kounin

Based on an observational study of 80 elementary classrooms, Jacob Kounin (1970) determined that the responses to classroom disruptions of unsuccessful classroom managers compared to those of successful classroom managers were not dramatically different. Instead, asserted Kounin, the difference between the two groups was that successful classroom managers, unlike unsuccessful classroom managers, were proactive in preventing disruptions before they occurred. He went on to identify specific classroom management skills associated with effective prevention of classroom disruptions:

- **Withitness:** Being aware of what is happening in the classroom at all times
- **Overlapping:** Being able to do more than one thing at a time, such as moving to stand beside a student who is off-task, answering a question from another student, and monitoring cooperative learning groups, all simultaneously
- **Group alerting:** Being able to keep students' attention on the learning task
- **Momentum:** Being able to keep instruction moving at a brisk pace
- **Smoothness:** Being able to effect smooth transitions between activities
- **Exploiting the ripple effect:** Skillfully using the phenomenon that occurs; for example, when a teacher reminds an off-task student to get back to work and all other off-task students also return to their assigned task

(Source: http://universityofhullscitts.org.uk/scitts/site/pt/behaviour/kounin.html)

Checkpoint

Fill in the blank.

1. According to Kounin, the main difference between successful and unsuccessful classroom managers is that successful classroom managers are _____ in preventing disruptions before they occur.

2. A teacher who is able to give instructions and distribute materials at the same time is exhibiting _____.

3. A teacher who redirects an off-task student when the teacher's attention appears to be focused elsewhere is exhibiting _____.

Mark as True or False.

4. _____ Kounin found that successful classroom managers were significantly better at handling disruptions than unsuccessful classroom managers.

5. _____ Successful classroom managers know how to stop misconduct before it starts.

Checkpoint Answers

1. proactive
2. overlapping
3. withitness
4. False
5. True

Chapter 6: Classroom Management

Procedures and Rules

Procedures are guidelines for regular daily routines (transitions, homework policy, turning in papers, bathroom policy, and so on). **Rules** specify behavior expectations (be respectful, be responsible, be safe). When developing their classroom procedures and rules, it is imperative that teachers use their school's universal (schoolwide) behavior expectations. Students need to understand and experience that the entire school community is working together to create a positive, safe, and productive learning environment.

Good classroom managers facilitate the development of responsibility and self-regulation in students. They welcome student participation in developing classroom rules and procedures and engage students' assistance in resolving problems and conflicts in the classroom (for example, through class meetings and other conflict resolution skills; see "Conflict Resolution Strategies" later in this chapter for a discussion of this topic). The feeling is cultivated that the classroom is the students' classroom and that each student has a definite responsibility in helping determine and maintain the standards by which it functions. Within this collaborative context, clear, appropriate, consistent, and fair expectations for student behavior are established, and students are held accountable to age-appropriate standards of acceptable behavior. The classroom incentives/rewards and consequences system is fair, equitable, and aligned with schoolwide standards. Meaningful consequences for inappropriate behavior are decided upon and adhered to.

Effective teachers spend time at the beginning of the school year teaching students procedures and rules of the classroom and school. Procedures and rules should be explicitly taught using, for example, modeling, role playing, and practicing with monitoring and feedback. Thereafter, teachers should monitor student compliance and, at the same time, reinforce rules by modeling expected behaviors. They should regularly review procedures and rules with students to keep them fresh in their minds (i.e., after breaks/holidays). In grades 5 through 10, disciplinary aspects of classroom management become more pronounced, so consistent enforcement of behavior standards is critical. In grades 11 and 12, most students have passed through the oppositional phase of adolescence, although the teacher still will need to reinforce expected appropriate behavior. Students at risk of academic failure, regardless of grade level, need explicit orientation to and frequent review of classroom rules and procedures.

Students want structure and need limits. They also expect teachers to treat them with dignity and be consistent and fair in enforcing classroom rules. Effective teachers post classroom rules that are fair and appropriate for the grade level. For the rules to be effective, the students must know the rules and their consequences, and the teacher must enforce the rules consistently and impartially. Consequences should be **logical** (that is, clearly related to the behavior violation) and **proportional** (that is, matched to the severity of the infraction). In general, rules should be positively stated (that is, tell students what they *should* do, rather than what they *should not* do). To foster retention by students, there should be no more than five classroom rules.

At the building level, teachers need to know the specific codes and procedures that are used on their particular campuses for emergencies. It is important that they make sure their students know and practice building-level procedures that should be followed for campus emergencies, including life-threatening emergencies such as weapon use and hostage situations. (By state law, Texas Education Code, Section 37.108, the district school board must adopt and implement a multihazard emergency operations plan (EOP) for use in the district's facilities.)

Checkpoint

Fill in the blank.

1. Procedures and rules should be _____ taught to students.

2. Students at risk of academic failure need _____ orientation to classroom rules and procedures.

3. Rules specify behavior _____.

4. Rules should be stated _____ (negatively, positively).

Mark as True or False.

5. _____ Consequences should be logical and proportional.

Checkpoint Answers

1. explicitly
2. explicit
3. expectations
4. positively
5. True

Discipline Management

With regard to discipline, effective teachers are proactive rather than reactive. They anticipate when misconduct is likely to occur and take action beforehand to prevent or limit its occurrence. When a discipline situation does arise, effective classroom managers are quick to stop or redirect off-task or inappropriate behavior. They use the least intrusive means—for example, dealing with potentially serious disruptions early by using eye contact, moving around the room, or providing short, quiet comments to a disruptive student, and talking privately with students who misbehave to avoid power struggles and to prevent face-saving gestures from students. Stronger measures are used only when the teacher has exhausted all other options to curtail misbehavior. Nevertheless, when a disruption or behavior threatens the maintenance of a safe and orderly classroom environment, a teacher should refer the student to an appropriate administrator along with a referral form that contains a written description of the incident.

Teachers should avoid using harsh or punitive discipline measures. Epstein et al. (2008) recommended that "teachers adopt an overall positive and problem-solving approach . . . because harsh or punitive discipline is not effective in increasing the likelihood of appropriate behavior and tends to elicit student resentment and resistance" (p. 34). Furthermore, teachers' responses to student misconduct should be fair and equitable without regard to students' personal characteristics such as race, ethnicity, sex, English language learner (ELL) or exceptionality status, migrant or homeless status, national origin, sexual orientation, or religion.

When talking with a student who has misbehaved, teachers need to make sure that the student knows that he or she has done something that is unacceptable, and they should ask for an explanation from the student. It is important that the student understands why the behavior is unacceptable and cannot be tolerated. Teachers should be careful to talk about the behavior, not the student. Effective teachers describe what they saw, how they feel about it, how it affects others, and what needs to be done. They try to get the student to accept responsibility for the misbehavior and to agree not to commit the offense again. In some cases, the teacher might need to help the student develop a plan for changing his or her behavior so that it becomes acceptable. In other words, good teachers use students' mistakes as learning opportunities in the caring atmosphere of a warm, supportive classroom environment.

Checkpoint

Fill in the blank.

1. With regard to discipline, effective teachers are _____ rather than reactive.
2. Harsh or punitive discipline tends to elicit student resentment and _____.

Mark as True or False.

3. _____ When a discipline situation arises, effective classroom managers wait to see what is going to happen before intervening.
4. _____ Good teachers use students' mistakes as learning opportunities.

Checkpoint Answers

1. proactive
2. resistance
3. False
4. True

Conflict Resolution Strategies

Conflicts, disagreements or arguments between perceived equals, are a natural part of classroom interactions. Teachers use **conflict resolution** strategies to engage students in collaboratively de-escalating and resolving conflicts. For example, if two third-graders are arguing over who gets to type on the keyboard of a shared computer, the teacher mediates the conflict resolution process by having each child, in turn, express their perspective to the other child. Thereafter, the teacher summarizes what he or she heard, while acknowledging the children's feelings about the issue. After making sure both sides agree on what the problem is, the teacher prompts the children to decide for themselves how they will resolve the conflict (e.g., take turns, use a coin toss to decide who goes first). If the two children cannot reach an agreement, the teacher asks the class to assist in coming up with a resolution. Throughout the process, the teacher keeps in mind that young children may need help in communicating their feelings and ideas. The process is similar with older students. However, rather than the teacher acting as the mediator, peer mediators might help their classmates work through a conflict situation.

Before conflicts emerge, the teacher and students establish ground rules for the conflict resolution process. Typical ground rules are as follows:

- Accept that only one person speaks at a time.
- Use I-statements ("I feel . . .") and avoid personal attacks on others.
- Listen actively to one another and make a commitment to try to understand the other person's viewpoint.
- Stay calm and respectful.
- Be willing to work toward a mutually agreeable solution.

Effective teachers give students opportunities to internalize the ground rules using role play, discussing examples and nonexamples of rules, and expressing rules in their own words. They model the behaviors they want students to emulate. They avoid being judgmental and keep their own suggestions and advice about the issue at hand to a minimum. They avoid forcing apologies from students who are not remorseful. Rather, they encourage students to empathize with one another. They praise students for participating sincerely and peacefully in the conflict resolution process.

Checkpoint

Fill in the blank.

1. In the conflict resolution process, teachers want students to _____ how they will resolve the conflict.
2. _____ children may need help in communicating their feelings and ideas.
3. A typical ground rule for the conflict resolution process is to stay calm and _____.

Mark as True or False.

4. _____ During the conflict resolution process, you-statements are preferred over I-statements.
5. _____ When mediating conflicts, teachers should rush students to apologize right away.

Checkpoint Answers

1. decide
2. Young
3. respectful
4. False
5. False

Positive Behavioral Interventions and Supports (PBIS)

Positive behavioral interventions and supports (PBIS) is a multi-tiered initiative to create and sustain positive, safe, and productive learning environments in schools. Schoolwide, PBIS is a three-tiered prevention-based framework that uses data, problem solving, and decision making to provide a continuum of evidence-based interventions based on students' behavioral needs. Schoolwide PBIS includes the following defining features:

- explicit teaching of appropriate school behaviors.
- adequate time for students to practice appropriate school behaviors.
- progress assessment and program decisions based on data collected about student behavior.
- appropriate interventions validated by research.
- systematic monitoring of student progress; using data to guide decisions to help maximize responsiveness to students' and educators' needs.
- collaborative cooperation among school staff, families, and community members.

(Source: www.usccr.gov/pubs/docs/FLSchoolDisciplineReport.pdf)

At Tier 1 (universal), supports are applied to all students and are designed to promote positive behavior and prevent behavioral problems. Teachers' classroom management plans should be built on and support the Tier 1 (schoolwide) behavior expectations. For example, teaching students the schoolwide expectations and reinforcing students for displaying appropriate behaviors is a Tier 1 intervention that occurs at the whole-class level.

At Tier 2 (group), research-based interventions are provided to small groups of students who need additional support beyond that provided in Tier 1. Tier 2 support provides intensive or targeted interventions to students who are not responding to Tier 1 support efforts. These students are at risk of exhibiting chronic problem behavior. Tier 2 interventions should be easy to administer to small groups of students, with minimal time and staff involvement. For example, social skills training in a small group setting is a Tier 2 intervention.

At Tier 3 (individual student), focused, high-intensity interventions are provided to individual students. Tier 3 supports include the implementation of a **behavior intervention plan (BIP),** routinely based on a **functional behavioral assessment (FBA).** An FBA focuses on identifying the purpose or function behind a child's problem behavior. Typically, the process involves scrutinizing a wide range of child-specific factors, such as social, affective, or environmental influences. The BIP is composed of individualized, assessment-based intervention strategies and requires more resources and staff time than is customary. Consequently, it provides a means for addressing the needs of individual students in a more comprehensive manner.

Research indicates that implementation of PBIS results in positive student outcomes (for example, decreased problem behavior, decreased bullying, and increased positive school climate).

(Source: https://www.pbis.org/pbis-network/texas)

Checkpoint

Fill in the blank.

1. PBIS is a _____-tiered framework.
2. PBIS includes _____ teaching of appropriate school behaviors.
3. PBIS Tier 1 supports are designed to promote positive behavior and _____ behavioral problems.

Mark as True or False.

4. _____ Tier 1 supports are applied to all students.
5. _____ Teachers' classroom management plans should be built on and support the Tier 1 behavior expectations.

Checkpoint Answers

1. three
2. explicit
3. prevent
4. True
5. True

Summary

Effective teachers understand that the goal of classroom management is to maximize student achievement. They use developmentally appropriate, culturally sensitive strategies and procedures to manage group dynamics and individual student behavior. They involve students in determining expectations for student behavior in the classroom. Most important, they are aware that a good classroom management system exploits the close relationship between effective instruction and appropriate student behavior. Therefore, they plan high-quality instruction that provides ample opportunities for student engagement and time on task.

Domain II Sample Questions and Answer Explanations

Sample Questions

1. A middle school teacher has been assigned to a class that has a wide range of socioeconomic and cultural backgrounds. Most of the students have had varied school experiences with little or no success. Which of the following approaches at the beginning of the school year would best promote a productive learning environment in the classroom?

   A. Initially have students work independently and then incorporate group activities after students have adjusted to classroom routines.
   B. Select one or two students who will take responsibility for monitoring the behavior of peers and helping to maintain order in the classroom.
   C. Adopt a punitive-based discipline plan and enforce it consistently and fairly.
   D. Explicitly teach classroom procedures and rules, including those that seem self-evident (for example, how to disagree with peers).

2. A newly hired third-grade teacher wants the students to work in cooperative learning groups, but the teacher is reluctant to use group activities because the students are too noisy when it's time to transition from whole-class to group instruction. The best way for the teacher to improve the situation is to

   A. give free time to students who move into groups quietly.
   B. spend time teaching students how to transition from whole-class to group activities.
   C. assign roles to the members of the groups.
   D. hold a class meeting to discuss the importance of keeping the noise in the classroom at a reasonable level.

3. A ninth-grade student is worried because his father just got laid off from work. This situation is most closely related to which of the following types of needs?

   A. physiological needs
   B. safety needs
   C. belongingness and love needs
   D. esteem needs

4. A first-year fifth-grade teacher has received the class roster for the upcoming school year. The teacher notes that the 19 students in the class are culturally diverse and that two students are receiving special education services—one is visually impaired and the other has mild hearing loss. In planning the classroom layout, it is most important for the teacher to consider the

   A. materials and resources available in the classroom.
   B. availability of assistive technology equipment in the school.
   C. potential discipline problems that might occur with such a varied group of students.
   D. instructional approaches the teacher plans to use in the classroom.

Answer Explanations

1. **D.** Eliminate choice B because students should not be put in charge of classroom discipline. Eliminate choice C because teachers should use positive discipline approaches. Now you must choose between choices A and D. Choice A is a tempting response because students should not work in groups until they have learned appropriate group behaviors; however, the teacher is usually working with the class as a whole rather than having the students work independently, before group activities begin. At the beginning of the school year, teachers should explicitly teach classroom and school procedures and rules to all students. In particular, students at risk for academic failure benefit from explicit instruction in classroom procedures and rules. Thus, choice D is the correct response.

2. **B.** Eliminate choice C because this measure has impact only after students are in groups, not when they are transitioning into group work. Eliminate choices A and D because while these measures might result in quieter transitioning, neither would be as effective as explicitly teaching students how to transition from whole-class to group activities. Thus, choice B is the correct response. At the beginning of the school year, successful classroom managers establish and teach classroom procedures (including how to make transitions) to create smoothly functioning learning communities.

3. **B.** The student's sense of security about his home situation is threatened, so his safety needs are not being met. Thus, choice B is the correct response. Eliminate choices A, C, and D because none of the needs in these answer choices is as closely aligned with the situation given in the question stem as is the need in choice B.

4. **D.** Eliminate choices A and B because materials, resources, and technology should not be limiting factors for teachers. In other words, the teacher should decide on a spatial arrangement based on what the teacher thinks would provide the most effective learning environment for the students, not on what materials, resources, and technology are available. Eliminate choice C because although this aspect might be a factor for the teacher to consider, it is not as important as considering the instructional approaches the teacher plans to use with this group of diverse learners. Thus, choice D is the correct response.

PART 3

DOMAIN III: IMPLEMENTING EFFECTIVE, RESPONSIVE INSTRUCTION AND ASSESSMENT

- Competency 007: *The teacher understands and applies principles and strategies for communicating effectively in varied teaching and learning contexts.*
- Competency 008: *The teacher provides appropriate instruction that actively engages students in the learning process.*
- Competency 009: *The teacher incorporates the effective use of technology to plan, organize, deliver, and evaluate instruction for all students.*
- Competency 010: *The teacher monitors student performance and achievement; provides students with timely, high-quality feedback; and responds flexibly to promote learning for all students.*

Chapter 7

Communication

> **Competency 007:** The teacher understands and applies principles and strategies for communicating effectively in varied teaching and learning contexts.

This chapter provides a general review of knowledge and skills related to Competency 007. Checkpoint exercises are found throughout the review material. These exercises give you an opportunity to practice what you just learned. The answers to the Checkpoint exercises are found immediately following the set of exercises. When doing the Checkpoint exercises, you should cover up the answers. Then check your answers when you've finished the exercises.

Competency Descriptive Statements

The descriptive statements for Competency 007 as given in the TExES PPR EC-12 test preparation manual (www.tx.nesinc.com/Content/Docs/160PrepManual.pdf) specify the following knowledge and skills for beginning teachers in Texas public schools:

- Demonstrates clear, accurate communication in the teaching and learning process and uses language that is appropriate to students' ages, interests, and backgrounds.
- Engages in skilled questioning and leads effective student discussions, including using questioning and discussion to engage all students in exploring content; extends students' knowledge; and fosters active student inquiry, higher-order thinking, problem solving, and productive, supportive interactions, including appropriate wait time.
- Communicates directions, explanations, and procedures effectively and uses strategies for adjusting communication to enhance student understanding (e.g., by providing examples, simplifying complex ideas, using appropriate communication tools).
- Practices effective communication techniques and interpersonal skills (including both verbal and nonverbal skills and electronic communication) for meeting specified goals in various contexts.

Verbal and Written Communication

"Teachers communicate clearly and accurately and engage students in a manner that encourages students' persistence and best efforts" [19 Texas TAC § 149.1001 (b)(1)(D)]. They model and emphasize to students that the critical elements of effective verbal communication are

- accuracy of language.
- accuracy of information.
- standardization of language.
- clearly defined expectations.

Because communication is vital to the learning process, teachers need to be effective speakers. Not only are the words themselves important, but also of importance is the way in which the words are said. Effective teachers speak to students using a firm, respectful, calm voice. They are aware that changes in voice loudness, rate, tone, inflection, and pitch can change the meaning of words and the emphasis of the message. Projection of the voice so it can be heard by all students is also necessary.

Asking questions is a key component of verbal communication. Questions should be determined by the lesson objectives. Questions should be clear and should yield student responses—even though students' answers might not always be correct. Effective teachers provide supportive feedback to incorrect student responses. Questions can be categorized as **convergent** (closed-ended) or **divergent** (open-ended), depending on whether the teacher is seeking knowledge of information or is trying to generate ideas and stimulate thinking, respectively. If a teacher wants to determine the level of student learning, a **focusing question** is appropriate. To increase student interaction, a teacher might ask a **prompting question.** To elicit clarification or justification of an answer, a **probing question** is suitable. (See "Facilitating Class Discussions" and "Skillful Questioning" later in this chapter for additional discussion of questioning.)

Written communication of teachers should be coherent and understandable with proper grammar, spelling, and sentence structure. This standard should be reflected in all written communications with students, parents, administrators, community members, and others. For example, when teachers prepare written instructions for students, the instructions should be clear and easy to follow. Performing or visualizing what students are expected to do is an effective way to make sure that all necessary details are included.

Whenever written instructions are presented to students, they should be communicated orally as well. This approach accommodates different learning styles in the classroom, while providing the written instructions to which the students can refer as they complete the assigned task. Asking students to repeat directions or to chorus important steps or cautions helps to ensure that the instructions are communicated effectively. If students are working in groups, giving the group leader the task of reading the instructions aloud before students begin is another effective way to communicate the instructions orally. When appropriate, graphic representation, modeling, or demonstration should be included to enhance understanding. In particular, previewing centers and modeling the instructions for centers is imperative for centers in early-childhood classrooms. Early-childhood teachers commonly use pictograms (pictorial representations of instructions), which are an effective way to provide directions for centers. Finally, students should be given an opportunity to ask questions about the instructions for clarification.

Checkpoint

Fill in the blank.

1. The critical elements of effective verbal communication are accuracy of language, accuracy of information, standardization of language, and clearly defined _____.
2. Effective teachers speak to students using a _____, respectful, calm voice.
3. Teachers should use proper _____, _____, and sentence structure.
4. Questions should be determined by the lesson _____.
5. To elicit clarification or justification of an answer, teachers use _____ questions.

Checkpoint Answers

1. expectations
2. firm
3. grammar; spelling
4. objectives
5. probing

Nonverbal Communication

The importance of nonverbal communication should not be underestimated. Most experts contend that nonverbal communication "speaks" louder than words. **Nonverbal communication** includes vocal cues, eye contact, facial expressions, gestures, body language and posture, proximity, and appearance and dress.

Vocal cues include such vocal elements as tone, pitch, tempo, loudness, and inflection. Teachers who speak in a monotone are often perceived as boring and uninteresting. When teachers modulate their voices and speak in an animated manner, students are more likely to listen and be interested in the teacher's message. Research suggests that people who use a fast tempo in speech are perceived as intelligent and dynamic, while those who use a slow tempo are perceived as kind and people-oriented. However, listeners usually prefer a tempo that is similar to their own, so adopting a moderate tempo would be a safe course for a teacher.

Eye contact is an indication of a person's openness to communication. During a conversation, a speaker will make direct eye contact to signal that another person can speak. When a teacher is asking questions, as a general rule, students who know the answers look at the teacher; those who don't, avoid eye contact. Furthermore, in "Six Ways to Improve Your Nonverbal Communications," Ritts and Stein (2011) maintained that eye contact with students increases a teacher's credibility and conveys warmth and concern. In some cultures, eye contact is used as an indicator of a person's veracity, with a direct gaze indicating truthfulness and an averted gaze, dishonesty. Research does not support this view; furthermore, a direct gaze is considered disrespectful in some cultures. Notwithstanding, teachers often use a stern look as a nonverbal cue to signal students to stop inappropriate behaviors.

Facial expressions can send positive or negative nonverbal messages. Smiling is a powerful nonverbal cue that conveys approval, warmth, friendliness, and approachability. When students are confused or don't understand, they might frown or look perplexed. A raised eyebrow might signal skepticism. A sneer might mean hostility.

Gestures such as pointing and illustrating with limbs and other body parts are forms of nonverbal communication. Speakers who fail to use gestures often appear wooden and boring. But, as a caution, teachers need to be aware that physical gestures can have rude or even vulgar meanings in different cultures.

Body language and posture indicate the listener's respect for the speaker and interest in the speaker's message. Head nodding and leaning slightly forward convey respect and attention, but turning away or slouching shows disrespect and lack of interest.

Proximity refers to the physical distance separating individuals. Teachers can use closeness to increase student interaction or discourage inappropriate student behavior. At the same time, teachers should be aware of cultural norms of personal space and should be on the alert for signals (such as leaning back or backing away) that students are being made to feel uneasy because the teacher is invading their personal space. Another aspect of proximity is vertical distance, with a higher level conveying more authority than a lower level. Generally, teachers improve communication with students, especially younger students, by making an effort to get on eye level with the student (for example, getting on one knee to talk with a young child).

Appearance and dress are often overlooked forms of nonverbal communication. During the first weeks of school, when students are forming their first impressions of teachers, it is particularly important that teachers dress appropriately. Teachers who dress professionally are perceived as competent and capable. Moreover, to establish credibility, teachers should avoid dressing like their students.

Teachers' relationships with their students are affected by nonverbal communication. Negative nonverbal signals or misunderstood nonverbal communication can lead to conflict between teachers and students. Therefore, teachers' nonverbal communication should promote positive interactions and be congruent with students' cultural backgrounds.

Students as well as teachers communicate nonverbally. Teachers need to "hear" the messages students are sending them by nonverbal communication. If there is a discrepancy between the verbal and nonverbal message, teachers should pay closer attention to the nonverbal message because it is usually more valid. Using these cues, instruction can be adjusted as needed.

Checkpoint

Fill in the blank.

1. In general, nonverbal messages are _____ (less, more) powerful than verbal messages.
2. Teachers who speak in a _____ are often perceived as boring and uninteresting.
3. Eye contact with students _____ (decreases, increases) a teacher's credibility.

4. When speaking with a preschooler, a teacher could improve communication by getting on _____ (two words) with the student.

Checkpoint Answers

1. more
2. monotone
3. increases
4. eye level

Facilitating Class Discussions

Teachers need to take advantage of what students can learn in social situations such as class discussions and, in so doing, focus on developing communities of learners in their classrooms. Teachers who intend to make frequent use of class discussion can promote effective use of the discussion format by establishing rules and directly teaching procedures for proper discussion behavior and turn-taking to students.

In classrooms, most discussions and conversations are spontaneous and informal. However, sometimes teachers need to bring students together to process information, discuss an activity, brainstorm ideas, resolve a conflict, and so on. Teachers can use these occasions as opportunities to assess student learning and evaluate students' thinking. Class discussions also provide students with an opportunity to learn how to share and disagree about ideas in an intellectually productive way.

When a formal discussion is warranted, the discussion must have a purpose that is aligned with the teacher's goals and objectives for the subject at hand. The discussion needs to be well planned without being scripted. The teacher should have in mind questions and prompts that will elicit critical thinking from the students about the topic of discussion. However, this preparation does not mean that the teacher does most of the talking. Teachers should avoid the initiation-response-evaluation (IRE; Mehan, 1979) pattern in which the teacher asks a question and then provides an evaluation (such as "Yes, that's correct") of a student's response. On the contrary, teachers should aim to facilitate discussions that are sustained by student-initiated questions and ideas and that allow students to assume ownership of the classroom discourse.

Teachers play key roles as facilitators of classroom discussions, with the goal being to excite teacher-student interactions and interactions among students in ways that actively engage students in the discussion topic and allow them to use critical thinking skills. In other words, teachers set the stage for interactions without dominating the discussion. Appropriate techniques for facilitating class discussions are posing questions, active listening, identifying relevant information, probing, prompting or asking leading questions, redirecting, and drawing inferences.

During class discussions, **posing questions** is a crucial skill that teachers use to provide focus to the discussion and elicit and extend students' reasoning and critical thinking. Skilled facilitators use divergent questions (open-ended questions that allow many correct responses) to engage students in higher-level thinking and generate ideas, reactions, or opinions (for example, "What would our world be like without paper?"). Facilitators employ convergent questions (closed-ended questions that have a limited number of correct responses) to obtain facts, obtain specific information, check for understanding, ask for a different opinion, or, when appropriate, direct the discussion toward consensus (for example, "Does everyone agree with that solution?"). In general, active classroom discourse is best promoted by the use of open-ended questions. Asking too many closed-ended questions tends to make the discussion overly teacher-centered and stifles creative and critical thinking on the part of students. Artful teachers are purposeful in their questioning to ensure an appropriate mixture of convergent and divergent thinking.

Active listening is listening behavior that indicates to the speaker you are paying attention and hearing the speaker's message. Active listening skills include **repetition** (repeating the speaker's message), **paraphrasing** (putting the speaker's message in your own words to check for understanding), **summarizing** (stating key points of the speaker's message), and **asking questions** to clarify the content of the message or the speaker's intent. Additionally, active listeners use tone, voice level, and nonverbal behaviors such as eye contact, facial expressions, attentive body language, and proximity to indicate respect and interest in the responses and contributions of others. Teachers should foster active listening skills in students by modeling those skills when listening to others.

Identifying relevant information is extracting major ideas or themes from the statements of others. During classroom discussions, teachers should periodically point out key ideas and relevant information that have been brought forth. Sometimes, writing/displaying major ideas or themes on the whiteboard/SMART Board is an effective way to accomplish this task. Besides helping students recognize the main ideas that have been generated, this practice sends the message to students that their ideas are valued and important to their learning.

Probing is the technique of eliciting more information from students, often for the purpose of clarifying students' contributions or obtaining justification for their answers. Probing is a device that teachers use to help students clarify their own understandings. When students make errors, probing can be used to help them self-correct their mistakes. (See "Correcting Student Errors" in Chapter 10 for additional discussion of this topic.) Probing can be verbal (for example, "Please elaborate on what you mean by that") or nonverbal (for example, head nodding, direct eye contact). Creating a climate of trust and respect is essential when teachers use probing. Otherwise, students might become defensive or feel interrogated. Modeling respect for students' ideas and conveying an expectation that students are obliged to state their ideas clearly and defend them, when necessary, is crucial.

Prompting or asking leading questions is the technique of providing hints or suggestions to encourage students to keep trying and not give up. Deciding when to let a student struggle and when to offer assistance is based on the teacher's judgment of the student. Regardless, the teacher should not move on to a different student or switch to an easier question. It is imperative that the student at hand be given sufficient **wait time** to think and formulate ideas before the teacher prompts or leads the student. Research regarding wait time indicates that the desire to avoid "empty silence" can cause a teacher to become uncomfortable and unable to wait at least 3 seconds for students' responses, even though waiting for students to respond communicates positive expectations for them and results in more thoughtful responses, thereby enhancing achievement. When a student cannot answer a question after an appropriate amount of time, the teacher can best support the student's learning by providing one or more prompts to help him or her summon up a correct response.

Redirecting is the technique of posing a question or prompt to students for a response or to add new insights. Most often, this technique is used by skilled facilitators to invite the class to respond to a question addressed to the teacher—for example, "That's a good question. Let's ask the class for ideas about that." Redirecting might also involve extending a student's partial contribution by asking another student for additional insights—for example, "Latisha, can you add to what Brendan said?"

Drawing inferences is the process of reaching conclusions based on implications from students' input. Drawing inferences is a step beyond summarizing, which is limited to ideas that were explicitly stated in the discussion. Inferencing involves drawing logical conclusions from the students' contributions. Of course, teachers should solicit assistance from the class in formulating conclusions and strive to obtain consensus about conclusions drawn.

Here are some guidelines that promote productive classroom discussions.

Before Discussions

- Guide students to establish rules and procedures.
- Use an advance organizer to prepare students.
- When appropriate, role-play proper discussion behaviors and turn-taking.
- Arrange the furniture/desks to facilitate discussion (for example, in a U-shape or circle).

During Discussions

- Establish and model a norm of respect for others and their contributions.
- Use strategies that are age-appropriate and sensitive to cultural background, exceptionality, and learning preferences to ensure participation by all students.

- Reinforce participation with both verbal and nonverbal cues.
- Encourage and reinforce student-to-student exchanges.
- Use questions geared to lesson objectives.
- Ask the question and give sufficient wait time before calling on a student.
- Be comfortable with silence; give students time to think and formulate ideas.
- Avoid answering your own questions.
- Refrain from modifying a student's contribution to reflect your own ideas.
- Be honest, but use tact when correcting student errors.
- Keep the discussion on track by tactfully deflecting trivial or irrelevant questions.
- Be alert for nonverbal cues from students that signal lack of interest, frustration, and so on.
- Monitor your own nonverbal communication to make sure you are sending inviting signals.
- Use techniques to discourage monopolizers.
- Avoid taking sides when disagreements arise.
- Avoid put-downs or sarcasm.

After Discussions

- Involve students in reflecting on what they learned from the discussion.
- Ask students to assess their participation in the discussion.
- Make notes about what to do differently next time to improve the discussion format.

Checkpoint

Fill in the blank.

1. In classroom discussions, it is important that _____ do most of the talking.
2. In general, active classroom discourse is best promoted by the use of _____ (closed-ended, open-ended) questions.
3. Listening in a way that indicates to the speaker that you are paying attention and hearing the speaker's message is _____ listening.
4. "From what you've read, what are the pros and cons on this issue?" is an example of a _____ (convergent, divergent) question.
5. "That is an interesting question. Class, how would you respond?" is an example of _____.
6. Head nodding is a nonverbal cue that can be used when _____ for additional information.

Checkpoint Answers

1. students
2. open-ended
3. active
4. divergent
5. redirecting
6. probing

Skillful Questioning

In crafting their questions for a lesson, class discussion, or other activity, teachers should give thoughtful attention to the cognitive complexity associated with the content they are teaching. The questions they develop for their classrooms should be aligned with the content complexity levels for the TEKS that the teachers are teaching (see "Levels of Content Complexity" in Chapter 3 for a discussion of this topic). Low-complexity questions rely mainly on recall of information, moderate-complexity questions require concrete reasoning or problem solving, and high-complexity questions should elicit abstract reasoning and higher-order thinking skills.

When developing questions, teachers can turn to Bloom's Taxonomy (Bloom, 1956) of higher-order thinking skills—knowledge, comprehension, application, analysis, synthesis, and evaluation. **Knowledge-level thinking** involves recalling or remembering information. **Comprehension-level thinking** involves interpreting previously learned material. **Application-level thinking** involves applying knowledge to produce a result. **Analysis-level thinking** involves subdividing knowledge to show how it fits together. **Synthesis-level thinking** involves putting together ideas or elements to form a whole. **Evaluation-level thinking** involves judging the quality of an idea or solution. The following table contains a list of question types based on Bloom's Taxonomy.

Question Type	Student Activities	Typical Words	Examples
Knowledge/Factual	Remembering, memorizing, recognizing, recalling	*Who, what, where, when, how, find, label, relate, tell, define, list, name*	Who is the current president of the United States? Name two parts of speech.
Comprehension	Grasping the meaning, interpreting, translating from one medium to another, describing, explaining	*Summarize, interpret, explain, illustrate, outline, rephrase, translate, estimate*	In your own words, what does the term *popular sovereignty* mean? Summarize the plot of the story.
Application	Applying information to produce some result, problem solving	*Apply, construct, select, choose, produce, classify, develop, solve, demonstrate, model*	How many numbers between 1 and 20 are prime? Classify the animals in the list as herbivores, carnivores, or omnivores.
Analysis	Identifying motives, making inferences, finding evidence to support, comparing, breaking into component parts	*Analyze, compare, contrast, simplify, examine, diagram, break apart, identify, specify, infer, predict*	What are the main ways that butterflies and moths are different? Specify the steps you would use to test your theory.
Synthesis	Creating something new, writing proofs, making predictions, recognizing patterns, putting parts together to create an original whole	*Compile, create, predict, combine, construct, design, develop, invent, propose, problem-solve, adapt*	What rule describes the pattern shown between the two variables? Create an alternate ending to the story.
Evaluation	Stating an opinion, making value judgments, drawing conclusions	*Evaluate, judge, form an opinion, critique, decide, justify, prove, prioritize, rate, assess, recommend, conclude*	What is your opinion about the Supreme Court decision in *Lau v. Nichols*? Decide what you liked best about the learning activity and justify your response.

Additionally, according to research, giving students extended time in which to respond during questioning better enables them to give more comprehensive responses involving higher levels of thinking. Therefore, teachers who want their students to think at higher levels need to become comfortable with pauses and extended silence. Questions that are meant to engage mental processing beyond simple recall or recognition require ample time for students to formulate responses.

Here are some further guidelines for using questioning to promote higher-order thinking in the classroom:

- Establish a climate of trust, openness, and risk-taking in the classroom.
- Model respect for students and provide recognition for their efforts.
- Provide many opportunities for student involvement during questioning.
- Validate students' comments and questions, using them as springboards to advance learning.
- Ask the question and provide sufficient wait time (no less than 3 seconds) for thought.
- Evaluate the level of difficulty of your questions.
- Ask more divergent than convergent questions.
- Ask more analysis, synthesis, and evaluation questions than lower-level questions.
- Ask speculative and "What if?" questions.
- Ask questions that motivate students to detect and scrutinize assumptions.
- Ask questions that challenge students to examine their own ideas and beliefs.
- Ask questions that stimulate curiosity.
- Ask questions that encourage original and flexible thinking.
- Ask questions that prompt imagination and exploration of alternatives.
- Ask questions that require students to make connections among concepts that might, on the surface, appear unrelated.
- Ask students to identify key ideas and issues and to evaluate their relevance.
- Use probing to help students clarify their thinking.
- Use prompting to encourage students to keep trying or to assist students in modifying their responses.
- Redirect students' questions to the class.
- Use students' responses to make a point or to stimulate additional discussion.
- Encourage students to ask questions of each other.
- Encourage students to ask questions that challenge you, the textbook, or other students.
- Be nonjudgmental in your response to students' answers to higher-level questions.
- Avoid the following:
  - Giving up on a student by asking an easier question or moving on to another student.
  - Being rude or sarcastic, or making fun of students' responses.
  - Using nonverbal cues (for example, a frown) that show judgmental reactions to students' responses.
  - Answering your own questions.
  - Asking nonspecific questions such as "Are there any questions?" or "Does everyone understand?"
  - Asking questions that give away answers.

Checkpoint

Fill in the blank.

1. Subdividing knowledge to show how it fits together requires _____-level thinking.
2. Giving students extended time in which to respond during questioning better enables them to give more comprehensive responses involving _____ levels of thinking.
3. Questions that encourage students to keep trying are _____ questions.

Mark as True or False.

4. _____ Skillful questioning plays a vital role in fostering students' critical and creative thinking skills.
5. _____ To check for understanding, a teacher should ask, "Are there any questions?"

Checkpoint Answers

1. analysis
2. higher
3. prompting
4. True
5. False

Brainstorming

Brainstorming is a learning activity in which students generate ideas around a specific topic of interest. It is an effective way to engage students in creative thinking (see the section "Critical and Creative Thinking" that follows for a discussion of this topic). The two main rules of brainstorming are the following:

- Any idea is acceptable.
- Criticism of the ideas of others is forbidden.

Brainstorming can be an individual, small-group, or whole-class activity. Before teachers engage students in group brainstorming, teachers should prepare students by having them discuss the rules of brainstorming and how they will implement the rules during the activity. Often, teachers find it helpful to have students role-play active listening and turn-taking before brainstorming begins. During brainstorming, the teacher or a designated recorder writes down the ideas or key points. Teachers should monitor and facilitate the process without imposing their own ideas on students. Ample time should be allotted for the activity so that students have time to think in divergent ways. Repetitive responses or the slowing down of the flow of ideas signals that it is time to end the session. After group brainstorming, the ideas are organized, prioritized, and summarized.

Brainstorming can be used for various purposes. For example, before beginning a lesson, teachers can use brainstorming to activate prior knowledge about the lesson topic. They can use a brainstorming session to help the class reach consensus on a problem in the classroom. Additionally, students can be encouraged to brainstorm as a pre-activity to reading, when beginning the writing process, or when they are engaged in problem solving.

Benefits of brainstorming are that it

- activates students' prior knowledge of a topic.
- brings to light any misconceptions that students might have.
- helps students connect existing knowledge to a topic.
- improves students' communication skills.
- stimulates students' creative thinking and problem solving.
- promotes student participation.

Checkpoint

Fill in the blank.

1. Brainstorming is an effective way to engage students in _____ thinking.
2. During a brainstorming session, criticism of the ideas of others is _____.
3. Teachers can use brainstorming to _____ students' prior knowledge about the lesson topic.

Mark as True or False.

4. _____ During brainstorming sessions, "wild" ideas are acceptable.
5. _____ Before engaging students in brainstorming, teachers should make sure that students understand the rules of brainstorming.

Checkpoint Answers

1. creative
2. forbidden
3. activate
4. True
5. True

Critical and Creative Thinking

Effective teachers recognize the importance of fostering critical and creative thinking in their students. By design, teachers use adroit questioning and their knowledge of levels of content complexity and Bloom's Taxonomy to stimulate these higher-order thinking skills in their students. In addition, teachers demonstrate and model critical and creative thinking and provide numerous opportunities for students to engage in activities (for example, brainstorming) that foster these thinking skills.

Critical Thinking

Critical thinking is the mental process of making reasoned judgments and reaching objective conclusions by analyzing, organizing, comparing, synthesizing, logically examining, challenging, and evaluating assumptions and evidence. Students might learn isolated information, but without the application of critical thinking to that information, actual understanding is minimal. As Schafersman (1991) asserted, teachers transmit the subject content, but "often fail to teach students how to think effectively about this subject matter; that is, how to properly understand and evaluate it. This second ability is termed critical thinking" (p. 1). Research indicates that critical thinking can be taught and that explicit instruction in critical thinking results in increased student academic performance.

Teachers need to be aware of characteristics of critical thinkers they can build on to advance the development of critical thinking skills in their classrooms. The following personality characteristics of critical thinkers have been gathered from the works of Brookfield (1991), Cotton (1993), Paul et al. (1990), and Schafersman (1991): Critical thinkers tend to be curious, flexible, fair-minded, independent, humble, confident, honest, skeptical, analytical, cautious, and intellectually persistent. Other characteristics identified by these authors are that critical thinkers

- identify and challenge assumptions underlying beliefs, behaviors, or issues.
- recognize and explore alternatives to their present ways of thinking.
- challenge standardized or bureaucratic ways of doing things.
- question the credibility of sources of information.
- consider how context affects beliefs, behaviors, or issues.

- recognize and prioritize key ideas.
- use evidence to make plausible inferences or predictions or to reach conclusions or make decisions.
- determine what evidence is material and relevant to an argument or issue.
- distinguish fact from opinion.
- recognize bias and vested interest.
- recognize faulty reasoning and misuse of information.
- perceive anomalies, discrepancies, or contradictions.
- evaluate issues, arguments, ideas, or interpretations using self-formulated criteria.
- sometimes ask impertinent questions or suggest disquieting ideas.
- anticipate reactions to questions or suggestions.
- are self-confident and trust their own judgment.
- "hold true to hard-won beliefs and commitments" (Brookfield, 1991, p. 23).

On the surface, some of these characteristics might appear at odds with traditional classroom situations. However, effective teachers know how to balance their responsibility to regulate and control student behavior with the need to create a classroom climate that encourages critical thinking. Here are some ideas for the classroom, gathered from experts (Brookfield, 1991; Cotton, 1993; Paul et al., 1990; and Schafersman, 1991):

- Provide an atmosphere that respects and values personal expression.
- Provide a climate that is open and conducive to "thinking for oneself."
- Create an environment that supports critical inquiry.
- Establish a culture of high expectations and encouragement.
- Explicitly explain and model higher-order thinking skills (analysis, synthesis, and evaluation) for students and provide opportunities for students to practice the skills.
- Create tasks that require students to become proficient in using critical thinking to solve problems and make decisions.
- Nurture attitudes of persistence and perseverance when students are problem-solving.
- Require students to clarify and defend their solutions or conclusions.
- Use skillful questioning (for example, to create cognitive disequilibrium) that incites critical thinking.
- Provide opportunities for students to put critical thinking skills into practice within a group setting.
- Provide ample time for critical thinking to take place.

Creative Thinking

Creative thinking is the mental process of generating new ideas, recognizing and finding solutions to problems, and making informed decisions. It involves originality of thinking. Young children are naturally creative. They play pretend games, make up stories, and freely express themselves in other ways. Encouraging and nurturing this natural inclination is important to students' academic success. As they progress through the grades, students are expected to generate creative ideas in a variety of situations, such as developing alternative solutions or perspectives to a complex problem.

Teachers need to be aware of characteristics of creative thinkers that they can build on to promote creative thinking in their classrooms. The following personality characteristics of creative thinkers have been gleaned from the works of Brookfield (1991) and Davidson (2003): Creative thinkers tend to be curious, optimistic, confident, open-minded, flexible, tolerant of ambiguity, persistent, independent, uninhibited, excitable, eager, and sociable as well as being risk-takers, nonconformists, holistic learners, and divergent thinkers. Other characteristics identified by these authors are that creative thinkers

- have interests in a wide range of disciplines but can also be intensely absorbed in one area.
- persevere unrelentingly when problem-solving.

- can look at a situation from multiple perspectives.
- are willing to consider new ideas and seek out opposing viewpoints.
- make novel or unique connections between seemingly unrelated things or ideas.
- find unusual solutions to problems.
- use metaphors or analogies to frame concepts and ideas, when appropriate.
- reject standardized or bureaucratic ways of doing things.
- sometimes ask impertinent questions or suggest disquieting ideas.
- do not see the world as absolute and unchangeable.
- are future-oriented and embrace change as a positive dynamic.
- are self-confident and trust their own judgment.

As in the case for critical thinkers, on the surface, some of these characteristics might appear at odds with traditional classroom situations. However, effective teachers know how to balance their responsibility to regulate and control student behavior with the need to create a classroom climate that encourages creative thinking. Here are some ideas for the classroom (selected from Davidson, 2003; and Wilson, 2019):

- Provide an atmosphere that respects and values personal expression.
- Provide a climate that encourages questioning, exploration, experimentation, and intellectual risk-taking.
- Engage students in generating ideas in a variety of situations, such as in brainstorming or using graphic organizers.
- Create tasks that require students to become proficient in using creative processes to solve problems.
- Nurture attitudes of persistence and perseverance when students are problem-solving.
- Use skillful questioning that evokes creative thinking.
- Allow students to pose their own problems and devise their own approaches to problem solving.
- Encourage students to develop open-ended and innovative projects.
- Allow students to collaborate with others to get feedback and support for their ideas.
- Provide ample time for creativity to flourish.
- Demonstrate and model creative thinking.
- Avoid micromanaging, hovering over students, restricting choices, rewarding students excessively, emphasizing competition, and pressuring students.

Checkpoint

Fill in the blank.

1. Critical thinkers identify and _____ assumptions.
2. Critical thinkers can distinguish fact from _____.
3. To promote critical thinking, teachers should require students to clarify and _____ their solutions or conclusions.
4. Teachers should _____ explain and model higher-order thinking skills.
5. Young children are _____ creative.
6. Creative thinkers can look at a situation from _____ perspectives.
7. To promote creative thinking, teachers should provide an atmosphere that respects and values _____ expression.

Checkpoint Answers
1. challenge
2. opinion
3. defend
4. explicitly
5. naturally
6. multiple
7. personal

Logical Reasoning

Logical reasoning involves the higher-level thinking processes that are used to make decisions or draw conclusions. There are two basic ways of reasoning to reach conclusions: inductive reasoning and deductive reasoning.

Inductive reasoning is the process of drawing a general conclusion based on one or more examples. When using inductive reasoning, you look at specific examples and try to identify a pattern or trend that fits the given examples in order to determine a general rule. For example, you might observe the coldness of a number of ice cubes and conclude (through inference) that all ice cubes are cold.

In contrast, **deductive reasoning** is the process of using an accepted rule to draw a conclusion about a specific example. When using deductive reasoning, you apply a general rule to a specific case. For example, you might start by knowing that all rectangles are parallelograms and conclude (through implication) that a square is a parallelogram because a square is a rectangle. **Syllogistic reasoning** (for example, "All rectangles are parallelograms. A square is a rectangle. Therefore, a square is a parallelogram.") and **conditional reasoning** (for example, "If a figure is a rectangle, then the figure is a parallelogram. A square is a rectangle; therefore, a square is a parallelogram.") are types of deductive reasoning.

Knowing the difference between inductive and deductive reasoning is essential to evaluating arguments. An **argument** is a course of reasoning offered in support of a position. When inductive reasoning is used in an argument, inferences are used to support the position of the person making the argument. When deductive reasoning is used, accepted truths or generalizations are applied to support the favored position.

Because inductive arguments are based on observations and examples, the validity of their conclusions is always open to question. When students are evaluating inductive arguments, they should be encouraged to consider the reliability of the evidence, whether generalizations are adequately supported, and whether the inferences made are honest and reasonable. **Hasty generalization** (generalizing from a few atypical examples), **faulty analogy** (assuming that because two things are alike in some respects, they are alike in all respects), and **false cause** (assuming that a first thing caused a second thing because the first thing preceded the second thing in time) are examples of faulty reasoning that students should be taught to be watchful for when evaluating arguments.

Deductive arguments use assumed generalizations or premises to logically arrive at conclusions. If the premises are true and the logic is sound, then the conclusion of the argument is valid. When students are evaluating deductive arguments, they should be encouraged to consider the credibility and reasonableness of the premises and the soundness of the logic used. They should be watchful for premises that are based on half-truths, exaggerated claims, or propaganda. Also, two well-known illogical pitfalls that students need to be made aware of are affirming the consequent and denying the antecedent. **Affirming the consequent** refers to assuming the first part of a conditional statement must be true when the second part is true. Here is an example: "If a person smokes, then he or she will have breathing difficulties. Tara has breathing difficulties; therefore, Tara is a smoker." This line of reasoning is illogical because Tara's breathing difficulties might be unrelated to smoking; in fact, Tara might not be a smoker at all. **Denying the antecedent** refers to assuming that when the first part of a conditional statement is not true, then the second part of the statement must also be false. Here is an example: "If a person smokes, then he or she will have breathing difficulties. Tara does not smoke; therefore, Tara does not have breathing difficulties." This reasoning is illogical because Tara might have breathing difficulties that are caused by something unrelated to smoking.

Checkpoint

Fill in the blank.

1. Reasoning from the specific to the general is _____ reasoning.
2. Reasoning from the general to the specific is _____ reasoning.
3. A course of reasoning offered in support of a position is called a(n) _____.
4. The validity of the conclusions of inductive arguments is always _____ to question.

Checkpoint Answers

1. inductive
2. deductive
3. argument
4. open

Graphic Organizers

Graphic organizers are visual depictions of the interrelationships among abstract concepts or illustrations of processes. They are powerful communication tools that help students understand concepts and organize their thinking by putting information into logical, easy-to-read visual formats. Graphic organizers are naturally conducive to learning for visual learners, but research indicates other students also show improved learner achievement when teachers use graphic organizers. Furthermore, according to Brooks-Young (2006), "students who regularly use visual learning strategies show improvement in reading comprehension, problem-solving skills, ability to organize and express their thoughts, and identifying patterns and relationships in content" (p. 1). Moreover, their retention of content is enhanced. The following chart lists some common graphic organizers and how they can be used.

Graphic Organizer	Brief Description	Uses
K-W-L chart	A visual representation of the K-W-L process in the form of a chart with three columns headed "What We **Know**," "What We **Want** to Know," and "What We **Learned**." Before a learning episode on a topic, students brainstorm on what they already know about the topic and what they want to know about it. The information is listed in the proper column. After the learning episode, the students identify what they learned, and the information is listed in the proper column. Next, the students compare the information under "What We Want to Know" with what is listed under "What We Learned."	❑ To activate prior knowledge ❑ To set a purpose for learning ❑ To provide a structure for learning

Graphic Organizer	Brief Description	Uses
Web	A visual picture that shows connections of words or phrases to a topic. The teacher lists the topic and circles it, and then from the students' contributions builds a web-like structure that links words or phrases to the central circled topic.	❑ To activate prior knowledge ❑ To show connections within a topic ❑ To identify key vocabulary ❑ To help students organize their thoughts (for example, for a writing activity)
Concept map or semantic map	A visual picture that shows the interrelationships among concepts. The teacher lists a central concept and then assists students in identifying a set of associated concepts. Related concepts are linked and, sometimes, words or short phrases are added to explain the connections.	❑ To help students organize their knowledge ❑ To show the interrelationships among concepts
Venn diagram	A visual depiction of the commonalities and differences among concepts or entities. Overlapping circles are drawn to represent each concept/entity. Students brainstorm common characteristics, which are listed in the proper intersections (overlapping areas), and differences, which are listed in the respective circles, but outside the intersections.	❑ To facilitate contrast and comparison of concepts ❑ To help students see relationships ❑ To help students organize their thinking ❑ To foster higher-level thinking skills
Decision tree	A tree-like diagram of actions and their expected outcomes or consequences	❑ To facilitate decision making ❑ To develop students' predicting skills ❑ To help students organize their thinking
Cause-effect chart	A chart showing a series of events or actions and their expected outcomes or consequences	❑ To facilitate decision making ❑ To develop students' predicting skills ❑ To help students organize their thinking
Flowchart	A visual depiction of a sequence of events or a process	❑ To foster logical thinking skills ❑ To develop skill in organizing information ❑ To facilitate planning ❑ To foster attention to detail
Story tree	A tree-like structure in which each main branch represents a major element of a story (plot, setting, and so on). On the branches, students add questions (in the shape of clumps of leaves) that they should ask themselves as they read to evaluate that particular element.	❑ To guide students' critical evaluation of a work of literature ❑ To help students organize their thinking ❑ To foster self-questioning skills ❑ To promote evaluation-level thinking

When students are first introduced to a graphic organizer, a good practice is for the teacher to model how to properly use it, stopping frequently to check for understanding. Once the students are familiar with various organizer types, then the teacher can merely remind them of the organizer before the learning experience. But, at first, if the organizer is a new type, then, just as with any new learning, explaining and modeling is critical.

Traditionally, graphic organizers are produced on whiteboards, transparencies, or large sheets of paper. Brooks-Young (2006) pointed out that a downside to this approach to using graphic organizers is that creating, editing, revising, and saving work can sometimes be problematic. To overcome these limitations, teachers are moving toward the use of electronic graphic organizers such as Inspiration, Kidspiration, and CmapTools. These innovative tools are inexpensive, easy to use, and address the shortcomings of their offline counterparts.

Checkpoint

Fill in the blank.

1. Graphic organizers are _____ depictions of the interrelationships among abstract concepts or illustrations of processes.
2. A flowchart is a graphic organizer that fosters _____ thinking skills.
3. A graphic organizer that shows actions and their expected outcomes or consequences is a _____ tree.

Mark as True or False.

4. _____ Students show improved learner achievement when teachers use graphic organizers.
5. _____ Teachers should prepare graphic organizers in advance to maximize academic learning time.

Checkpoint Answers

1. visual
2. logical
3. decision
4. True
5. False

Summary

Effective teachers are effective communicators. Teachers continually send messages to students and receive messages from them. They use verbal and written language and nonverbal communication that is appropriate to students' developmental levels and social, linguistic, and cultural backgrounds. They recognize the importance of classroom discussions and use skilled questioning to facilitate deeper learning. They provide opportunities for students to engage in individual and collaborative critical and creative thinking. In addition, they use graphic organizers to visually show relationships between knowledge, facts, concepts, or ideas to promote student understanding.

Chapter 8

Instructional Delivery

> **Competency 008:** The teacher provides appropriate instruction that actively engages students in the learning process.

This chapter provides a general review of knowledge and skills related to Competency 008. Checkpoint exercises are found throughout the review material. These exercises give you an opportunity to practice what you just learned. The answers to the Checkpoint exercises are found immediately following the set of exercises. When doing the Checkpoint exercises, you should cover up the answers. Then check your answers when you've finished the exercises.

Competency Descriptive Statements

The descriptive statements for Competency 008 as given in the TExES PPR EC-12 test preparation manual (www.tx.nesinc.com/Content/Docs/160PrepManual.pdf) specify the following knowledge and skills for beginning teachers in Texas public schools:

- Employs various instructional techniques (e.g., discussion, inquiry, problem solving) and varies teacher and student roles in the instructional process and provides instruction that promotes intellectual involvement and active student engagement and learning.
- Applies various strategies to promote student engagement and learning (e.g., by structuring lessons effectively, using flexible instructional groupings, pacing lessons flexibly in response to student needs, including wait time).
- Presents content to students in ways that are relevant and meaningful and that link with students' prior knowledge and experience.
- Applies criteria for evaluating the appropriateness of instructional activities, materials, resources, and technologies for students with varied characteristics and needs.
- Engages in continuous monitoring of instructional effectiveness.
- Applies knowledge of different types of motivation (i.e., internal, external) and factors affecting student motivation.
- Employs effective motivational strategies and encourages students' self-motivation.
- Provides focused, targeted, and systematic second language acquisition instruction to English language learners in grade 3 or higher who are at the beginning or intermediate level of English language proficiency in listening and/or speaking in accordance with the ELPS.
- Provides focused, targeted, and systematic second language acquisition instruction to English language learners in grade 3 or higher who are at the beginning or intermediate level of English language proficiency in reading and/or writing in accordance with the ELPS.
- Develops the foundation of English language vocabulary, grammar, syntax, and mechanics necessary to understand content-based instruction and accelerated learning of English in accordance with the ELPS.

Instructional Methods

Not only must teachers know what they are teaching, but they also must know how to teach it. Doing so requires using a wide range of instructional methods and materials based on knowledge of content pedagogy and characteristics of the learners. The instructional objective and the needs of the students will determine which methods teachers use.

Some of the instructional methods teachers might select when teaching are direct instruction; lecture method; constructivist instruction; discovery learning; inquiry-based learning; project-based learning and problem-based learning; reciprocal teaching; simulations, role playing, and games; differentiated instruction; individualized instruction; independent student centers; peer tutoring; thematic learning; interdisciplinary instruction; and cooperative learning (see "Cooperative Learning" later in this chapter for a thorough discussion of this topic). In some instances, these methods overlap. For example, discovery learning, inquiry-based learning, project-based learning, and problem-based learning fall under the umbrella of constructivist instruction and often are used in cooperative learning settings.

Direct Instruction

Direct instruction is a teacher-led (but student-centered) instructional strategy in which the teacher as a subject-matter expert provides systematic and explicit instruction, followed by monitored and guided student practice, to ensure that students are making progress toward mastery of specific skills and content. It emphasizes teacher control of all classroom events and the presentation of highly structured lessons, enhanced by focused teacher-student interactions. Teacher modeling is used extensively (see "Modeling" later in this chapter for a discussion of this topic). Lessons are arranged sequentially into small steps and move from the simple to the more complex. The teacher provides and elicits from students examples and nonexamples to enhance understanding. Feedback is immediate and constructive, and reteaching occurs as needed. The teacher checks for understanding at key points in the lesson and adjusts scaffolding based on student feedback. A primary goal is to foster independent learning in students. Stemming from this goal, direct instruction incorporates a gradual release of responsibility—the teacher models first, then guides students in shared practice, and finally provides opportunities for students to apply a skill or complete an activity independently.

Direct instruction is appropriate for all learners. Slavin (2008) noted that "Direct instruction is particularly appropriate for teaching a well-defined body of information or skills that all students must master." He went on to say, "It is less appropriate when . . . exploration, discovery, and open-ended objectives are the object of the lesson" (p. 222). In fact, by design, direct instruction does not rely on students' ability to discover important concepts and skills. It prepares students for independent higher-order comprehension by systematically and explicitly teaching strategies for text reading and critical thinking skills.

To be clear, research consistently points to direct instruction as a highly effective instructional method. It is not a traditional lecture or simply a teacher presentation of information; and it is not drill, nor does it focus on rote learning. Rather, it consists of carefully crafted and executed teacher actions, with the primary goal being to equip students with strategies that support independent and efficient learning.

The steps of direct instruction are incorporated into the lesson cycle model, which was developed by Madeline Hunter. (See "Lesson Cycle Model" in Chapter 3 for a description of the components of this model.)

Lecture Method

In the traditional **lecture method,** the teacher uses one-way communication to attempt to convey knowledge to the learner orally. The recommended length of time for teacher lectures is 10 to 15 minutes. The lecture method is not a common approach at the elementary level, where it definitely should be avoided; however, it is often seen at the secondary level—despite research findings that indicate it is one of the least effective teaching strategies, as measured by enduring effect. Evidence suggests that teaching by lecturing results in superficial learning, low-level simple recall, or no learning at all on the part of students. Furthermore, the traditional lecture method promotes passive rather than active learning and is the least effective instructional method at all grade levels. Most knowledge and skills can be better learned by active engagement of the learner than by listening to someone talk about them. Nevertheless, teachers continue to use the lecture method, most likely because it has the advantage that the teacher can organize facts and ideas and present them in an orderly way with a minimum amount of time and effort. If learning from a lecture is to be improved, the lecture needs to be an interactive process in which the learners are given opportunities to respond, ask questions, and react to the speaker's point of view.

Constructivist Instruction

Constructivist instruction is based on the constructivist belief that learning is an active process [in which prior knowledge plays a powerful role, that it has social aspects, and that it is context specific (Olusegun, 2015)]. (See "Behaviorism and Constructivism" in Chapter 4 for an additional discussion of constructivism.) Collaboration and the teacher's guidance and support, often in the form of scaffolding, are essential features of constructivist instruction. Additionally, Brooks and Brooks (1993) offer the following principles that guide constructivist instruction:

- Encourage and accept student autonomy and initiative.
- Use raw data and primary sources along with manipulative, interactive, and physical materials.
- Use cognitive terminology such as *classify, analyze, predict,* and *create* when framing tasks.
- Allow student input to drive lessons, shift instructional strategies, and alter content.
- Find out about students' understandings of concepts before sharing your own understandings of those concepts.
- Encourage students to engage in dialogue, both with the teacher and with one another.
- Encourage student inquiry by asking thoughtful, open-ended questions and encouraging students to ask questions of each other.
- Seek elaboration of students' initial responses.
- Engage students in experiences that might engender contradictions to their initial hypotheses and then encourage discussion.
- Allow sufficient wait time after posing questions.
- Provide time for students to construct relationships and create metaphors.
- Use instructional strategies that nurture students' natural curiosity (pp. 103–117).

Constructivist instruction is exemplified in the 5E model (see "5E Model" in Chapter 3 for a detailed description of this model).

Discovery Learning

Discovery learning is designed to encourage students to be active learners while exploring new concepts, developing new skills, and figuring things out for themselves. It promotes and capitalizes on the natural curiosity of the learner. The supposition behind discovery learning is that active manipulation, thinking, and reasoning will enhance the students' understanding and increase the likelihood that they will develop appropriate generalizations and concepts.

Inquiry-Based Learning

Inquiry-based learning is a process in which students engage when they have identified a problem to be solved. The process involves the awareness of a problem, generating possible solutions, developing a hypothesis, gathering data and testing the hypothesis, analyzing and interpreting the data, and drawing conclusions and making generalizations. Inquiry-based learning requires students to use critical thinking skills including scientific thinking, higher-order thinking (analysis, synthesis, and evaluation), logical reasoning, and decision making.

Project-Based Learning and Problem-Based Learning

In both **project-based learning** and **problem-based learning,** students investigate real-world problems and then share their findings. Investigations, which are often interdisciplinary in nature, might last over a period of several weeks. The main difference in the two strategies is that in project-based learning, students create a presentation as an end-product to the investigation, whereas in problem-based learning, students present their results, but an end-product might or might not be required. Project-based learning promotes in-depth study of a topic by an individual student, a small group, or even the whole class. Problem-based learning allows students to identify a problem of interest to them. The teacher helps students select an appropriate topic and facilitates students as they assign roles and responsibilities for members of a group focused on exploring the same problem. Both project-based learning and problem-based learning challenge students to plan and organize their own learning and to use problem-solving and decision-making skills.

Reciprocal Teaching

Reciprocal teaching, developed by Palincsar and Brown (1984), is designed to increase students' reading comprehension. It consists of an interactive dialogue between the teacher and students that includes four steps: summarizing, generating questions, clarifying, and predicting.

Simulations, Role Playing, and Games

Simulations, role playing, and games are designed to allow students to learn through their experiences in a learning activity. **Simulation** is a learning experience designed to reflect reality. Students might set up a mock business, pretend to play the stock market, reenact a historic event, and so on. In **role playing,** students act out characters or situations based on real-world models. Role playing is a necessary part of simulations. Students must act out the roles they assume in the simulation. Simulations also can be computer- and/or web-based. **Games** are learning experiences that have rules and involve students in competitive situations, having winners and losers. Games, too, can be computer-based and/or web-based. Teachers can find numerous well-designed, educational games on the Internet. In addition, teachers have available a wide array of commercially produced computer simulations and games for the various subject areas. Advantages associated with simulations, role playing, and games are as follows:

- They are student-centered.
- They engage students' interest and motivation.
- Students learn by doing.
- They provide a realistic context.
- They allow for risk-taking in a safe environment.
- They promote creative and critical thinking, including decision making and problem solving.
- They provide opportunities for students to practice social and communication skills.

Differentiated Instruction

Differentiated instruction is the practice of matching instruction to students' needs. In Texas, differentiated instruction commonly is implemented through the multi-tiered response to intervention (RtI) process. RtI uses data-based problem solving to provide indicated academic interventions. Instruction is delivered to students in multiple tiers based on individual need. Initially, goals that articulate what all students should be able to do are defined in measurable terms. Progress monitoring, which includes formal and informal assessments including tests and observations, allows teachers to assess how well students are doing on specific skills. When a student successfully meets the desired goals, intervention is discontinued and instructional support continues in the general education classroom. When a student is not responding to an intervention, then a different intervention or another approach is implemented. If a more intense level of support is necessary, students are given small group or individualized instruction which further focuses on the skills needed to be successful. (See "Response to Intervention (RtI)" in Chapter 2 for an additional discussion of this topic.)

Individualized Instruction

Individualized instruction is characterized by a shift in responsibility for learning from the teacher to the student. Effective individualized instruction is tailored to meet an individual student's interests, needs, and abilities, with consideration given to the appropriateness of the content. Individualized instruction can take various forms, such as independent study or peer tutoring. It can be as simple as allowing a student to complete the same lessons as the rest of the students but at a different pace, or modifying the objective requirements for a particular student. A technology-based strategy for individualizing instruction is **computer-assisted instruction (CAI).** In CAI, the student interacts with the computer and proceeds at his or her own speed. CAI software is commonly classified as drill and practice, tutorial, simulation, problem solving, and utility programs.

Independent Student Centers

Independent student centers (or simply **learning centers**) are carefully designed, designated places in the classroom where students can go to explore and learn, either individually or with others, using a variety of materials and resources. Independent student centers are an effective way to differentiate instruction to meet the diverse needs of learners in the classroom. Teachers in the upper elementary grades, middle school, and high school set up independent student centers for exploration of topics or for practice, extension of concepts previously learned, and focused intervention. Independent student centers are an essential feature of the early-childhood environment. Besides skills-focused reading centers, classrooms might have listening, creative writing, math, science, computer, dramatic play, spelling, block, and art centers. Some guidelines for early-childhood centers include the following:

- Noisy centers should be separated from quiet centers.
- Centers should be self-contained with all materials labeled, including both print and a picture representation, and easily accessible (no higher than children's eye level).
- Rules and procedures for using centers should be developed in conjunction with students and clearly understood by them.
- Centers should be previewed (with demonstration and modeling) by the teacher one at a time in the whole-class setting.
- Each center should have a posted chart with brief verbal instructions illustrated with **pictograms** (drawings or symbols depicting an activity) telling what to do in that center.
- Usually no more than four to six children should be in a particular center at any given time.
- Books and writing materials should be incorporated into activity centers.
- Children should be given choices when selecting centers to go to at any given time.

Peer Tutoring and Cross-Age Tutoring

In **peer tutoring,** a trained student tutor teaches a same-age classmate. In **cross-age tutoring,** an older student teaches a younger student. According to Slavin (2008), both same-age tutoring and cross-age tutoring have been found to be effective. Research indicates that both the tutor and the tutee have increased academic achievement; however, it is highly important that tutors are trained beforehand and monitored during tutoring. The goal of either peer tutoring or cross-age tutoring is for both students to have academic gains; neither should feel burdened or frustrated by this instructional method.

Thematic Learning

Thematic learning results when a teacher designs one or more lessons around a central theme or topic. The theme can be an **intradisciplinary** (within a discipline) or an **interdisciplinary** (involving two or more disciplines) topic. Thematic learning helps students see relationships between and among concepts. Themes are selected for breadth and depth of coverage, their relevance to students' interests and experiences, and to convey information in connected, meaningful ways.

Interdisciplinary Instruction

Interdisciplinary instruction (also referred to as multidisciplinary, multisubject, or thematic instruction) is the result when teachers combine several disciplines into one or more lessons. In this instructional design, a central or controlling theme is identified. Teachers from various subject disciplines collaborate to develop a thematic unit around the topic of interest. At the elementary level, it is very common for teachers to identify the primary discipline, such as reading or social studies, and then incorporate other subject areas into the lesson. At the middle and secondary levels, it is common for teachers from different disciplines to form interdisciplinary teams that collaboratively plan integrated learning activities. Information and activities from other disciplines are used to illustrate, elaborate, and enrich the learning. The information should be practical and relevant to real life. The premise behind the interdisciplinary approach is that the world is not divided into distinct subject-area compartments, so teachers should design instruction that reflects the complexity of the real world in order to prepare students for life.

Although the theme acts as a central organizer, each subject discipline teacher contributes from his or her own content area. Students remain engaged in learning the knowledge and skills of the separate disciplines because a sense of meaningfulness or wholeness is generally a goal of the teachers. By relating content and skills from each of their separate disciplines to the central concept of the theme, the learning is more relevant, connected, and meaningful to students.

Since this approach is rewarding to students and teachers alike, strategies should be in place to encourage interdisciplinary instruction. The strategies to consider when implementing this approach are the following:

- Integrate information and activities from different subject domains.
- Use reading, writing, art, and mathematics across disciplines.
- Work collaboratively with other teachers to plan the unit.
- Implement the unit separately in each teacher's own classroom.

Checkpoint

Fill in the blank.

1. In direct instruction, the teacher provides systematic and _____ instruction.
2. In the traditional lecture method, the teacher uses _____ communication to attempt to convey knowledge.
3. Inquiry-based learning is a process in which students engage when they have identified a _____ to be solved.
4. Collaboration and the teacher's _____ and _____ are essential features of constructivist instruction.
5. Reciprocal teaching is designed to increase students' reading _____.
6. Simulation is a learning experience designed to reflect _____.
7. Differentiated instruction is the practice of _____ instruction to students' needs.
8. In peer tutoring, it is highly important that tutors are _____ beforehand and _____ during tutoring.

Mark as True or False.

9. _____ Discovery learning is most compatible with a behaviorist point of view.
10. _____ Learning centers are an essential feature of early-childhood classrooms.

Checkpoint Answers

1. explicit
2. one-way
3. problem
4. guidance; support
5. comprehension
6. reality
7. matching
8. trained; monitored
9. False
10. True

Cooperative Learning

Cooperative learning instruction allows students to assume responsibility for their own learning as they work together to complete a project or activity. It provides students with opportunities to develop interpersonal and small-group social skills through a variety of group formats. These skills are lifelong abilities that are vital for the democratic decisions of citizenship and the teamwork required in the workplace. Moreover, cooperative learning instruction enables learners to further develop their creative and critical thinking skills by requiring them to engage in brainstorming, problem solving, decision making, negotiation, and so on. Additionally, students are able to examine their own values, attitudes, and forms of social behavior and to consider alternative points of view.

Planning for cooperative learning group activities requires teachers to focus on their interactions with students and on the interactions among students, task specification and materials, roles, and expectations. Although there are variations in the application of the cooperative learning concept, according to Johnson and Johnson (1994), the five critical attributes of cooperative learning are the following:

- **Positive interdependence:** Everyone's success depends on the success of everyone else in the group.
- **Individual accountability:** Everyone in the group has to contribute and learn.
- **Group processing of social skills:** Group functioning is frequently monitored and adjusted to improve group effectiveness.
- **Face-to-face promotive interaction:** Group members facilitate and help each other by committing personal resources, encouragement, and assistance to others to achieve group goals.
- **Effective interpersonal interaction:** Group members regularly use interpersonal skills such as using appropriate tone, voice level, and turn-taking to show respect for others.

The main purpose underlying cooperative learning methods is to encourage students to help each other learn. Group members take responsibility for their own learning and for one another's learning. Teachers intervene only when necessary. The positive interdependence that is an essential component of cooperative learning is a strong motivating factor for students. Students perceive that the group "sinks or swims" together. The group incentive structure allows all students—even those who have a history of limited academic success—an opportunity to succeed, which can be highly motivating to students. Commonly, group membership should extend over a period of time to allow for intergroup responsibility and collaboration to build, although group membership should not be permanent for the entire year (Slavin, 2008). Cooperative learning group activities are learner-centered, with the teacher functioning as both a facilitator to promote effective group functioning and as an academic resource.

Benefits of cooperative learning include the following:

- Motivates learners by allowing them to interact with peers
- Fosters interdependency among learners
- Enhances learners' social skills and emotional intelligence
- Improves learners' communication skills and ability to interact in small-group settings
- Creates a learner-centered environment in which participants are respected and valued
- Provides a safe environment for all learners (including ELLs and learners with special needs)
- Improves learners' academic achievement
- Enables learners to benefit from each other's diverse abilities and perspectives
- Improves learners' critical thinking and problem-solving skills
- Encourages active and constructive learning
- Decreases misbehavior in the classroom

In addition, research indicates that, in particular, minority students, at-risk students, and students with a physical or mental disability benefit from involvement in cooperative learning instruction.

Despite these benefits, critics have challenged the use of cooperative learning strategies with gifted students, arguing that high-achieving students are penalized by working in mixed-ability cooperative learning groups. They suggest that high achievers feel used and frustrated by low achievers who are not motivated to perform well (National Association for Gifted Children, 2009). Nevertheless, ample research indicates that high-achieving students learn as much in cooperatively structured classes as they do in traditional classes, as long as group goals and individual accountability are incorporated into activities (Slavin, 2008). Furthermore, they benefit socially from the opportunity to work collaboratively with and help others who are not their intellectual peers. Even so, high achievers should also be given opportunities to work cooperatively with other high achievers or on independent projects.

Numerous research studies support the positive outcomes for all students when cooperative learning is used. Specifically, Marzano et al. (2000) identified cooperative learning as a high yield instructional strategy (see the section "Marzano's High Yield Instructional Strategies" that follows for a discussion of this topic). However, adequate training for teachers and students is necessary in order for cooperative learning to be implemented successfully. Teachers who want to use cooperative learning groups should do the following:

- Arrange the classroom furniture to support group interaction.
- Assign students to groups to ensure a mix of gender, ethnicity, linguistic level, and academic ability.
- Select tasks that students will find interesting, meaningful, and challenging and that genuinely require group effort to accomplish.
- Determine group size based on the tasks and goals for the group. For most activities, particularly problem-solving activities, groups of two to four work best.
- Present objectives as group objectives and communicate expectations clearly.
- Assign each group member a job or role.
- Make expectations of group behavior clear.
- Teach socials skills necessary for working with others (before and during activities).
- Make sure everyone understands what he or she is expected to do to make the group function well.
- Monitor group processes during activities.
- Monitor individual social skills during activities.
- Reward the group for successful completion of the task.
- Assess both group and individual performance.
- Assess group participation and cooperation using self-assessment, peer assessment, and teacher assessment.
- Always incorporate group goals and insist on individual accountability.
- Apply cooperative learning in a consistent and systematic manner but do not overuse it.

Four special types of cooperative learning are

- **Jigsawing:** Group members become experts on an assigned topic that they then teach to others, after reorganizing into different groups, so that eventually all members of the class know all the content.
- **Corners:** Group members meet in a designated corner of the room to discuss an assigned topic and then teach it to the rest of the class.
- **Think, pair, and share:** First, students work individually on an assigned problem-solving task; next, they pair with a partner to discuss and revise; and finally, they share their results with the entire class.
- **Debate:** Students work in teams to research a topic and formulate persuasive arguments supporting their viewpoints on an issue. Then they present their arguments in a teacher-determined format and structure.

Checkpoint

Fill in the blank.

1. Positive interdependence means everyone's success _____ on the success of everyone else.
2. Cooperative learning group activities are _____ (learner-centered, teacher-centered).
3. In jigsawing, group members become _____ on an assigned topic.

Mark as True or False.

4. _____ Cooperative learning produces higher levels of student achievement.
5. _____ As a general rule, students in cooperative learning groups should be similar with respect to their academic abilities.

Checkpoint Answers

1. depends
2. learner-centered
3. experts
4. True
5. False

Marzano's High Yield Instructional Strategies

In *What Works in Classroom Instruction* (2000), Marzano et al. identified nine evidence-based instructional strategies that have the "highest probability of enhancing student achievement" across students, grade levels, and subject areas (p. 4). These nine strategies have come to be known as "Marzano's High Yield Instructional Strategies." The following table contains a summary of the strategies.

Strategy	Brief Description	Remarks	Classroom Tools/Tasks
Identifying similarities and differences	Involving students in (teacher-led or student-directed) comparing, classifying, creating metaphors, and creating analogies	Model and scaffold activities until students become comfortable with the processes. Thereafter, monitor student-directed activities and assist/scaffold, when needed.	Venn diagrams, T-charts, comparison charts, classification tables and diagrams, teacher-led (modeled)/student-led metaphor tasks, teacher-scaffolded analogy tasks/student-directed analogy tasks
Summarizing and note-taking	Involving students in teacher-scaffolded or student-directed activities in which students distill information for later review, analysis, and synthesis	Explicitly teach summarizing and note-taking using think-alouds. Provide rules for summarizing (e.g., omit trivial details, use texting "shorthand"). Show students various formats for note-taking. When taking notes, more is better. However, discourage verbatim note-taking.	Subject notebook/journal entries, outlines, think-alouds, graphic organizers, teacher-created specialized summary frames (narrative, definition, problem/solution, etc.), teacher-prepared notes or outlines, reciprocal teaching

continued

Strategy	Brief Description	Remarks	Classroom Tools/Tasks
Reinforcing effort and providing recognition	Using teacher-directed or student-directed practices that convey to students the influence of effort on achievement; using teacher-directed practices that provide contingency-based rewards/praise for specific accomplishments	Explicitly teach students about the value of effort using personal examples or familiar stories. Make reward/praise contingent on specific accomplishments. Link rewards/praise to student effort (not just to completing work). Avoid global, meaningless praise. Gradually discontinue tangible rewards when no longer needed.	Effort-achievement charts/rubrics, pause-prompt-praise technique, symbolic tokens of recognition, tangible rewards, quality teacher praise (See "Praise" in Chapter 5 for a detailed discussion of this topic.)
Homework and practice	Using activities/assignments that extend students' learning and/or improve skill proficiency	Have a written homework policy. Provide clear instructions and well-structured assignments for homework. Grade homework and provide specific feedback. Provide class time for guided practice and well-structured independent practice *before* students try skills at home. Avoid giving "busy work" for homework or practice.	Assignments, journal reflections, speed and accuracy charts, focused practice, guided practice, independent practice (See "Homework" in Chapter 10 for a detailed discussion of this topic.)
Nonlinguistic representation	Using visual, mental, and concrete/hands-on representations/activities to represent concepts	Explicitly involve students in creating visual, mental, and concrete representations.	Graphic organizers, drawings/pictures, pictographs, mental imagery, physical models, realia (real objects), kinesthetic activities
Cooperative learning	Organizing student-led small group activities in which students work together on a collective task that has been clearly defined and explained. Students are expected to help each other learn, rather than to depend solely upon the teacher.	Explicitly teach students cooperative learning social skills. Use a variety of grouping criteria (e.g., random assignment, birthday month). Avoid grouping according to ability. Use small groups (3–4 students). Assign each group member a role or job. Monitor group processes and social skills during activities. Avoid overusing cooperative learning.	Group problem solving, group projects, jigsawing, think-pair-share, reader's theater, debate, corners (See "Cooperative Learning" earlier in this chapter for a detailed description of this instructional strategy.)

Strategy	Brief Description	Remarks	Classroom Tools/Tasks
Setting goals and providing feedback	Providing opportunities for students to set learning targets personalized from teacher-established broad learning goals; giving criterion-referenced feedback	Make goals specific but flexible. Explicitly teach students how to set goals and keep track of their own progress. Provide frequent, timely, specific feedback that explains what is correct and what is incorrect. Let students provide feedback for themselves and others.	Goal-setting guidelines, K-W-L charts, contracts, progress monitoring forms, information rubrics, processes and skills rubrics, self-assessment, peer feedback
Generating and testing hypotheses	Engaging students in making and testing informed predictions/ guesses	Use structured tasks to explicitly teach students the process of generating and testing hypotheses. Ask students to explain their thinking.	Systems analysis task, problem-solving task, historical investigation, invention process, experimental inquiry, decision making, inductive and deductive techniques
Cues, questions, advance organizers*	Facilitating students' recall of what they already know about a topic	Ask questions that evoke analytical thinking. Give explicit cues about the topic. Focus on what's important.	K-W-L charts, advance organizers, cues (hints)/ guiding questions about the lesson, think-alouds, anticipation guides, skimming for information, vocabulary activities

*Called "Activating Prior Knowledge" in Marzano et al. (2000), but since renamed in Classroom Instruction that Works (Dean et al., 2012).

Checkpoint

Fill in the blank.

1. Marzano's High Yield Instructional Strategies work across students, grade levels, and _____ areas.
2. Venn diagrams are useful when identifying _____ and _____.
3. Rewards and/or praise should be contingent on _____ accomplishments.

Mark as True or False.

4. _____ Effort is unrelated to achievement.
5. _____ Using cooperative learning every day in the same classroom is problematic.

Checkpoint Answers

1. subject
2. similarities; differences
3. specific
4. False
5. True

Modeling

Modeling is a powerful way to communicate intended learner outcomes to students. In modeling, the teacher demonstrates a skill (for example, solving a mathematical equation) or learning strategy (for example, using self-monitoring) that students will be expected to do automatically. Usually, the teacher articulates his or her thought processes (thinks aloud), and engages students in imitation of the skill or learning strategy. Modeling is followed by guided practice to help students learn to use the skill or strategy on their own.

Students can learn knowledge and skills, appropriate behaviors, and positive attitudes from teacher modeling. No matter the age of the student, explicit modeling is an effective way to help students know what to do and how to do it, from simple skills such as routine classroom procedures, to complex cognitive tasks such as analyzing a poem. Teachers model the intended learner outcome, and then give students opportunities to practice it. This strategy provides the structure to assignments that students often need to help them focus in a productive way. Of course, teachers should avoid being overly prescriptive when using modeling for assignments in which creativity and flexibility of thought are expected.

Furthermore, teachers should know that everything they do in front of students is a type of modeling. Indeed, modeling can impact students' thinking and behaviors to such a high degree that teachers have a responsibility to make sure they are being positive role models for their students. They can use this implicit modeling to encourage motivation and foster positive values (for example, kindness and respect) in their students.

Checkpoint

Fill in the blank.

1. Modeling is a powerful way to _____ intended learner outcomes to students.
2. Modeling provides the _____ to assignments that students often need to help them focus in a productive way.
3. Teachers should know that everything they do in front of students is a type of _____.
4. Teachers can use implicit modeling to encourage motivation and foster positive _____.

Checkpoint Answers

1. communicate
2. structure
3. modeling
4. values

Problem Solving

Problem solving is a systematic and usually cyclical process. One commonly used problem-solving approach (based on the work *How to Solve It* by G. Polya, 1957) consists of the following four steps:

1. Identify and clarify the problem.
2. Brainstorm possible ways to solve the problem and devise a plan.
3. Carry out the plan.
4. Look back to see whether the problem has been solved.

Of course, in practice, problem solving seldom occurs in a sequential, step-by-step manner. Problem solvers often revisit previous steps, skip steps, and even start over. This strategy has traditionally been associated with problem solving in mathematics; however, it is applicable across the curriculum as a systematic approach to resolving problems or issues.

The importance of developing students' problem-solving skills cannot be overemphasized. Problem-solving ability is critical to students' success in school and is an essential tool for the enjoyment of a full, productive, and satisfying life. Teachers should, by design, structure the learning environment to promote a climate conducive to problem solving and provide students with numerous individual and group opportunities to engage in problem-solving activities. Benefits associated with problem solving include the following:

- It promotes critical and creative thinking skills.
- It develops logical reasoning skills.
- It facilitates reflective thinking.
- It motivates students' interest in the content.
- It promotes students' understanding and retention of concepts.
- It provides an opportunity for students to discover new ways of thinking.
- It enhances students' self-confidence.
- It gives students a sense of empowerment.

Checkpoint

Fill in the blank.

1. The first step in problem solving is to _____ and clarify the problem.
2. In practice, problem solving seldom occurs in a _____, step-by-step manner.
3. Problem-solving ability is critical to students' _____ in school.

Mark as True or False.

4. _____ Problem solving promotes students' retention of concepts.
5. _____ Problem solving sharpens students' critical thinking skills.

Checkpoint Answers

1. identify
2. sequential
3. success
4. True
5. True

Scientific Inquiry

Scientific inquiry involves the use of the **scientific method** to investigate a problem of interest. This method is the process used by scientists to obtain reliable and valid information about the world we live in. It has five main steps:

1. **Define the problem:** Pose a thoughtful question about a topic or variable of interest.
2. **Research the topic:** Look up what others have found out about the topic or variable.
3. **Formulate a hypothesis:** Make an educated guess about an aspect of the topic or variable.
4. **Gather evidence:** Design and perform an investigation to test the hypothesis; collect data about the hypothesis.
5. **Draw conclusions:** Analyze the data collected and decide whether the hypothesis is supported or not supported by the results.

Benefits of scientific inquiry include the following:

- Enhances learners' understanding of the nature and methods of science
- Enables learners to visualize concepts and understand basic ideas related to the process of laboratory investigation
- Allows learners to experience the way some scientists work
- Gives learners a chance to encounter questions that might have one or more answers or possibly no answer
- Develops learners' scientific process skills
- Provides learners with an opportunity to practice and sharpen their critical thinking skills
- Encourages learners to appreciate the role of science in society

Obviously, as in problem solving, the practice of science seldom occurs in a lock-step fashion. Scientists often revisit previous steps, skip steps, and even start over. Furthermore, disagreements in scientific inquiry are a necessary part of the process and play an important role in the generation and validation of scientific ideas.

Teachers should encourage students to evaluate the plausibility of claims or interpretations from scientific investigations. Students should be made aware that only when investigators use well-designed studies can conclusions that are reliable and valid be drawn. **Well-designed studies** investigate issues that are clear and unambiguous; clearly define populations of study; use randomization in selecting representative samples of adequate size; use well-defined variables of interest; control outside factors, such as extraneous variables; and avoid **bias,** an unintentional or, perhaps, deliberate study flaw that favors particular results and that could jeopardize the validity of conclusions.

Checkpoint

Fill in the blank.

1. The first step in scientific inquiry is to define the _____.
2. A _____ is an educated guess.
3. A study flaw that favors particular results is called _____.
4. Teachers should encourage students to evaluate the _____ of claims from scientific investigations.

Checkpoint Answers

1. problem
2. hypothesis
3. bias
4. plausibility

Second Language Acquisition Instruction in Texas

Second Language Acquisition Instruction is a term that describes research-based practices and strategies that teachers use with **English language learners (ELLs).** Effective instruction in second language acquisition involves giving ELLs opportunities to listen, speak, read, and write at their current levels of English development while gradually increasing the linguistic complexity of the English they read and hear, and are expected to speak and write [19 TAC § 74.4 (4)]. In compliance with 19 TAC § 74.4 (4), teachers must provide focused, targeted, and systematic second language acquisition instruction to English language learners in grade 3 or higher who are at the beginning or intermediate level of English language proficiency in listening, speaking, reading, or writing in accordance with the English Language Proficiency Standards (ELPS) [see the subsection "English Language Proficiency Standards (ELPS)" that follows for a thorough discussion of this topic]. Teachers are responsible for ensuring that ELLs understand the instruction being provided. They must provide intensive and ongoing research-based instruction to promote the foundational English language development in vocabulary, grammar, syntax, and mechanics necessary to support content-based instruction and the accelerated learning of English. They are expected to know and understand ELL terminology and teaching strategies and to use this knowledge to plan and implement appropriate and effective instruction.

English Language Proficiency Standards (ELPS)

The **English Language Proficiency Standards (ELPS)** are second language acquisition curriculum standards that are part of the state-mandated curriculum, the Texas Essential Knowledge and Skills (TEKS) for K-12. They support the ability of ELLs to learn the academic English they need for meaningful engagement in subject-area instruction. The ELPS consist of four parts: (a) introduction, (b) school district responsibilities, (c) cross-curricular second language acquisition essential knowledge and skills, and (d) proficiency level descriptors [see "English Language Proficiency Levels" in Chapter 2 for a complete discussion of part (d)].

The ELPS are implemented as part of ongoing content area instruction and as such are integrally linked with the content area TEKS. The ELPS help teachers meet the language and subject-matter needs of ELLs simultaneously. They do not vary by subject, and with few exceptions they are the same from grade to grade. Despite their uniformity, they fully support and align with the learning of subject-specific and grade-specific English. The ELPS require content area teachers to build the English-language skills that enable ELLs to understand and use grade-appropriate English in class. For example, using the ELPS, grade 6 mathematics teachers help ELLs learn the English used in grade 6 mathematics TEKS instruction and high school biology teachers help ELLs learn the English used in high school biology TEKS instruction.

The ELPS standards for (a) to (c) are summarized below:

(a) **Introduction.**
- The English language proficiency standards in this section outline English language proficiency level descriptors and student expectations for ELLs. School districts shall implement this section as an integral part of each subject in the required curriculum. The English language proficiency standards are to be published along with the Texas Essential Knowledge and Skills (TEKS) for each subject in the required curriculum.
- In order for ELLs to be successful, they must acquire both social and academic language proficiency in English. Social language proficiency in English consists of the English needed for daily social interactions. Academic language proficiency consists of the English needed to think critically, understand and learn new concepts, process complex academic material, and interact and communicate in English academic settings.
- Classroom instruction that effectively integrates second language acquisition with quality content area instruction ensures that ELLs acquire social and academic language proficiency in English, learn the knowledge and skills in the TEKS, and reach their full academic potential.
- Effective instruction in second language acquisition involves giving ELLs opportunities to listen, speak, read, and write at their current levels of English development while gradually increasing the linguistic complexity of the English they read and hear and are expected to speak and write.
- The cross-curricular second language acquisition skills given in subsection (c) below apply to ELLs in kindergarten-grade 12.
- The English language proficiency levels of beginning, intermediate, advanced, and advanced high are not grade-specific. ELLs may exhibit different proficiency levels within the language domains of listening, speaking, reading, and writing. The proficiency level descriptors show the progression of second language acquisition from one proficiency level to the next and serve as a road map to help content area teachers instruct ELLs commensurate with students' linguistic needs.

(b) **School district responsibilities.** In fulfilling the requirements of this section, school districts shall:
- identify the student's English language proficiency levels in the domains of listening, speaking, reading, and writing in accordance with the proficiency level descriptors for the beginning, intermediate, advanced, and advanced high levels;

- provide instruction in the knowledge and skills of the foundation and enrichment curriculum in a manner that is linguistically accommodated (communicated, sequenced, and scaffolded) commensurate with the student's levels of English language proficiency to ensure that the student learns the knowledge and skills in the required curriculum;
- provide content-based instruction including the cross-curricular second language acquisition essential knowledge and skills [see subsection (c) below] in a manner that is linguistically accommodated to help the student acquire English language proficiency; and
- provide intensive and ongoing foundational second language acquisition instruction to ELLs in grade 3 or higher who are at the beginning or intermediate level of English language proficiency in listening, speaking, reading, and/or writing as determined by the state's English language proficiency assessment system. These ELLs require focused, targeted, and systematic second language acquisition instruction to provide them with the foundation of English language vocabulary, grammar, syntax, and English mechanics necessary to support content-based instruction and accelerated learning of English.

(c) **Cross-curricular second language acquisition essential knowledge and skills.**
- **Cross-curricular second language acquisition/learning strategies.** The ELL uses language learning strategies to develop an awareness of his or her own learning processes in all content areas. In order for the ELL to meet grade-level learning expectations across the foundation and enrichment curriculum, all instruction delivered in English must be linguistically accommodated (communicated, sequenced, and scaffolded) commensurate with the student's level of English language proficiency. The student is expected to use prior knowledge and experiences to understand meanings in English; to monitor oral and written language production and employ self-corrective techniques or other resources; to use strategic learning techniques (such as concept mapping, drawing, memorizing, comparing, contrasting, and reviewing) to acquire basic and grade-level vocabulary; to speak using learning strategies (such as requesting assistance, employing non-verbal cues, and using synonyms and circumlocution); to internalize new basic and academic language by using and reusing it in meaningful ways in speaking and writing activities that build concept and language attainment; to use accessible language and learn new and essential language in the process; to demonstrate an increasing ability to distinguish between formal and informal English and an increasing knowledge of when to use each one commensurate with grade-level learning expectations; and to develop and expand a repertoire of learning strategies (such as reasoning inductively or deductively, looking for patterns in language, and analyzing sayings and expressions) commensurate with grade-level learning expectations.
- **Cross-curricular second language acquisition/listening.** The ELL listens to a variety of speakers including teachers, peers, and electronic media to gain an increasing level of comprehension of newly acquired language in all content areas. ELLs may be at the beginning, intermediate, advanced, or advanced high stage of English language acquisition in listening. In order for the ELL to meet grade-level learning expectations across the foundation and enrichment curriculum, all instruction delivered in English must be linguistically accommodated (communicated, sequenced, and scaffolded) commensurate with the student's level of English language proficiency. The student is expected to distinguish sounds and intonation patterns of English with increasing ease; to recognize elements of the English sound system in newly acquired vocabulary (such as long and short vowels, silent letters, and consonant clusters); to learn new language structures, expressions, and basic and academic vocabulary heard during classroom instruction and interactions; to monitor understanding of spoken language during classroom instruction and interactions and seek clarification as needed; to use visual, contextual, and linguistic support to enhance and confirm understanding of increasingly complex and elaborated spoken language; to listen to and derive meaning from a variety of media (such as digital audio, video, DVD, and CD-ROM) to build and reinforce concept and language attainment; to understand the general meaning, main points, and important details of spoken language ranging from situations in which topics, language, and contexts are familiar to unfamiliar; to understand implicit ideas and information in increasingly complex spoken language commensurate with grade-level learning expectations; and to demonstrate listening comprehension of increasingly complex spoken English by following directions, retelling or summarizing spoken messages, responding to questions and requests, collaborating with peers, and taking notes commensurate with content and grade-level needs.

- **Cross-curricular second language acquisition/speaking.** The ELL speaks in a variety of modes for a variety of purposes with an awareness of different language registers (formal/informal) using vocabulary with increasing fluency and accuracy in language arts and all content areas. ELLs may be at the beginning, intermediate, advanced, or advanced high stage of English language acquisition in speaking. In order for the ELL to meet grade-level learning expectations across the foundation and enrichment curriculum, all instruction delivered in English must be linguistically accommodated (communicated, sequenced, and scaffolded) commensurate with the student's level of English language proficiency. The student is expected to practice producing sounds of newly acquired vocabulary (such as long and short vowels, silent letters, and consonant clusters) to pronounce English words in a manner that is increasingly comprehensible; to expand and internalize initial English vocabulary by learning and using high-frequency English words necessary for identifying and describing people, places, and objects, by retelling simple stories and basic information represented or supported by pictures, and by learning and using routine language needed for classroom communication; to speak using a variety of grammatical structures, sentence lengths, sentence types, and connecting words with increasing accuracy and ease as more English is acquired; to speak using grade-level content area vocabulary in context to internalize new English words and build academic language proficiency; to share information in cooperative learning interactions; to ask for and give information ranging from using a very limited bank of high-frequency, high-need, concrete vocabulary, including key words and expressions needed for basic communication in academic and social contexts, to using abstract and content-based vocabulary during extended speaking assignments; to express opinions, ideas, and feelings ranging from communicating single words and short phrases to participating in extended discussions on a variety of social and grade-appropriate academic topics; to narrate, describe, and explain with increasing specificity and detail as more English is acquired; to adapt spoken language appropriately for formal and informal purposes; and to respond orally to information presented in a wide variety of print, electronic, audio, and visual media to build and reinforce concept and language attainment.

- **Cross-curricular second language acquisition/reading.** The ELL reads a variety of texts for a variety of purposes with an increasing level of comprehension in all content areas. ELLs may be at the beginning, intermediate, advanced, or advanced high stage of English language acquisition in reading. In order for the ELL to meet grade-level learning expectations across the foundation and enrichment curriculum, all instruction delivered in English must be linguistically accommodated (communicated, sequenced, and scaffolded) commensurate with the student's level of English language proficiency. For kindergarten and grade 1, certain of these student expectations apply to text read aloud for students not yet at the stage of decoding written text. The student is expected to learn relationships between sounds and letters of the English language and decode (sound out) words using a combination of skills such as recognizing sound-letter relationships and identifying cognates, affixes, roots, and base words; to recognize directionality of English reading such as left to right and top to bottom; to develop basic sight vocabulary, derive meaning of environmental print, and comprehend English vocabulary and language structures used routinely in written classroom materials; to use pre-reading supports (such as graphic organizers, illustrations, and pretaught topic-related vocabulary and other pre-reading activities) to enhance comprehension of written text; to read linguistically accommodated content area material with a decreasing need for linguistic accommodations as more English is learned; to use visual and contextual support and support from peers and teachers to read grade-appropriate content area text, enhance and confirm understanding, and develop vocabulary, grasp of language structures, and background knowledge needed to comprehend increasingly challenging language; to demonstrate comprehension of increasingly complex English by participating in shared reading, retelling or summarizing material, responding to questions, and taking notes commensurate with content area and grade-level needs; to read silently with increasing ease and comprehension for longer periods; to demonstrate English comprehension and expand reading skills by employing basic reading skills (such as demonstrating understanding of supporting ideas and details in text and graphic sources, summarizing text, and distinguishing main ideas from details) commensurate with content area needs; to demonstrate English comprehension and expand reading skills by employing inferential skills (such as predicting, making connections between ideas, drawing inferences and conclusions from text and graphic sources, and finding supporting text evidence) commensurate with content area needs; and to demonstrate English comprehension and expand reading skills by employing analytical skills (such as evaluating written information and performing critical analyses) commensurate with content area and grade-level needs.

- **Cross-curricular second language acquisition/writing.** The ELL writes in a variety of forms with increasing accuracy to effectively address a specific purpose and audience in all content areas. ELLs may be at the beginning, intermediate, advanced, or advanced high stage of English language acquisition in writing. In order for the ELL to meet grade-level learning expectations across foundation and enrichment curriculum, all instruction delivered in English must be linguistically accommodated (communicated, sequenced, and scaffolded) commensurate with the student's level of English language proficiency. For kindergarten and grade 1, certain of these student expectations do not apply until the student has reached the stage of generating original written text using a standard writing system. The student is expected to learn relationships between sounds and letters of the English language to represent sounds when writing in English; to write using newly acquired basic vocabulary and content-based grade-level vocabulary; to spell familiar English words with increasing accuracy, and employ English spelling patterns and rules with increasing accuracy as more English is acquired; to edit writing for standard grammar and usage, including subject-verb agreement, pronoun agreement, and appropriate verb tenses commensurate with grade-level expectations as more English is acquired; to employ increasingly complex grammatical structures in content area writing commensurate with grade-level expectations (such as using correct verbs, tenses, and pronouns/antecedents; using possessive case correctly; and using negatives and contractions correctly); to write using a variety of grade-appropriate sentence lengths, patterns, and connecting words to combine phrases, clauses, and sentences in increasingly accurate ways as more English is acquired; and to narrate, describe, and explain with increasing specificity and detail to fulfill content area writing needs as more English is acquired.

[Source: Adapted from 19 TAC § 74.4 (c)]

Proficiency Level Descriptors (PLDs)

The ELPS proficiency level descriptors (PLDs) define how well ELLs at four proficiency levels (beginning, intermediate, advanced, and advanced high) are able to understand and use English in academic and social settings. They specify the main characteristics of each language proficiency level for each language domain. The descriptors show the progression of second language acquisition from one proficiency level to the next and serve as guides to help content area teachers craft instruction commensurate with the linguistic needs of ELLs (see "English Language Proficiency Levels" in Chapter 2 for a full discussion of the PLDs).

Texas English Language Proficiency Assessment System (TELPAS)

Texas uses the **Texas English Language Proficiency Assessment System (TELPAS)** to measure the progress of ELLs in kindergarten through grade 12 toward attaining English language proficiency in **oral language skills** (listening and speaking) and **literacy skills** (reading and writing). ELLs in kindergarten and grade 1 are evaluated on classroom-based assessments, while ELLs in grades 2 through 12 are evaluated based on writing samples and responses to online assessments. TELPAS is designed to directly support the state's educational goals for meeting the language and content needs of ELLs. The assessment is fully aligned with the ELPS and measures the ELPS student expectations in the four language domains (listening, speaking, reading, and writing) in terms of the following four levels of English language proficiency defined in the PLDs:

Beginning: None or little English language ability in academic and social settings; below grade-level proficiency

Intermediate: Limited English language ability, simple, high-frequency vocabulary used in routine academic and social settings; below grade-level proficiency

Advanced: At grade-level proficiency with second language acquisition support

Advanced high: At grade-level proficiency with minimal second language acquisition support

Checkpoint

Fill in the blank.

1. Effective instruction in second language acquisition involves giving ELLs opportunities to listen, speak, read, and write at their _____ level of English development.

2. The ELPS are second language acquisition curriculum _____.

3. The PLDs define how well ELLs at _____ proficiency levels are able to understand and use English in academic and social settings.

4. TELPAS is the state-approved assessment for English language _____.

5. TELPAS measures two oral language skills: _____ and _____.

6. TELPAS measures two literacy skills: _____ and _____.

Mark as True or False.

7. _____ An ELL whose speaking and listening skills are at the beginning level should be able to participate, with little or no support, in a class discussion about a book the teacher has read aloud.

8. _____ An ELL whose writing skills are at the advanced level should be able write a story, with little or no support, about the way his or her own family celebrates a special holiday.

Checkpoint Answers

1. current
2. standards
3. four
4. proficiency
5. listening; speaking
6. reading; writing
7. False
8. True

Second Language Development

According to Stephen Krashen and Tracy Terrell (in Nutta, 2006), when acquiring a new language, all students progress through predictable stages or levels; however, the length of time each student spends before moving to the next level can be expected to vary greatly. The following chart is an adaptation of Krashen and Terrell's stages. It contains a brief description of each level of language acquisition, some characteristic milestones of each level, and suggestions for teachers.

Level of Development	Description	Characteristic Milestones of Student	Suggestions for Teachers
Level 1: Pre-Production	This is the silent period in which students are listening to the new language, but rarely speaking it, while acquiring a receptive vocabulary of about 500 words. It might last up to 6 months.	Shy, but listens attentively; will respond nonverbally; can copy words from board or overhead; can watch, pay attention, and listen; responds to visuals/graphics; understands gestures; can show understanding by gesturing, miming, pointing, or drawing.	Focus on listening skills and acquisition of receptive vocabulary; use frequent repetition; use visuals to support verbal speech; use modeling, pictures, props, and realia (real objects); use gestures, body language, facial expressions, and miming to support verbal communication; do not force student to talk; accept nonverbal responses.

continued

Level of Development	Description	Characteristic Milestones of Student	Suggestions for Teachers
Level 2: Early Production	During this stage, students begin to use one-word responses or short phrases to communicate, while acquiring a receptive and active vocabulary of about 1,000 words. It might last up to 6 months.	Can show understanding by responding with one- or two-word answers; has limited comprehension; can use short phrases that have been memorized to communicate; can use simple communication with classmates in pairs or small groups.	Focus on providing opportunities for language development along with the same types of supports used in Level 1; ask questions that have one-word responses (for example, yes/no, either/or); use simple, high-frequency words; use fewer pronouns; avoid contractions; explain idioms and limit their use; use fewer multi-syllabic words; use a simplified sentence structure; paraphrase content into simpler language; preteach difficult or technical vocabulary before an assignment; use concrete examples when explaining concepts; accept one-word or short responses from student; provide opportunities for student to work in pairs or small groups with other students to practice speaking and negotiating meaning.
Level 3: Speech Emergence	During this stage, students use phrases and short sentences to express complete thoughts, while acquiring an expressive vocabulary of about 3,000 words, along with a receptive vocabulary of about 7,000 words. This stage takes from 1 to 3 years to reach.	Can show understanding by using phrases and short sentences; has increased comprehension; will initiate and engage in simple discourse; can ask simple questions; can understand simple stories read aloud; can follow simple directions; can read simplified text; can do fill-in-the-blank when provided a word bank; can match vocabulary to definitions; can understand charts and graphs; can write original materials, but writing will have many mechanical errors; can create original stories based on personal experience.	Continue to use supportive strategies such as frequent repetition of key terms, modeling, gesturing, using models and visual representations, and preteaching vocabulary; use simple, predictable books for reading; use graphic organizers, charts, and graphs; provide word banks for assignments such as filling in a graphic organizer or labeling a diagram; provide an outline or template for writing assignments; continue to provide opportunities for interactions with peers.

Level of Development	Description	Characteristic Milestones of Student	Suggestions for Teachers
Level 4: Intermediate Fluency	During this stage, students use BICS, the social skills of language, without difficulty and are beginning to develop CALP, academic language skills [see "Basic Interpersonal Communication Skills (BICS) and Cognitive Academic Language Proficiency (CALP)" later in this chapter for a discussion of these topics]. They are beginning to use more complex sentences and to engage in extended discourse, while acquiring an expressive vocabulary of about 6,000 words, along with a receptive vocabulary of about 12,000 words. This stage takes from 3 to 4 years to reach.	Can speak in sentences and phrases and produce connected narrative; can show understanding by speaking or writing to give opinions, defend, debate, justify, examine, predict, hypothesize, analyze, synthesize, or evaluate; has very good comprehension; will ask questions for clarification; can answer complex questions; can write essays and other creative works; can solve complex problems; can engage in research; can critique literature.	Focus on learning strategies; provide contextual support and scaffolding for academic tasks; check for prior understanding and use task analyses to make sure learning experiences are appropriate.
Level 5: Advanced Fluency	In this stage, students have achieved CALP; receptive and expressive vocabulary continues to expand, particularly with regard to content vocabulary. This stage takes from 5 to 7 years to reach.	Can perform listening, speaking, reading, and writing comparable to native speakers in social and academic situations; has very good comprehension; understands complex language.	Continue to provide scaffolding and other supports that enhance understanding for all students.

Some general tips from Badía (1996), Reiss (2001), and other experts for working with ELLs at all levels of second language development are the following:

- Learn each student's name and how to pronounce it.
- Use seating that maximizes student participation.
- Make sure that new students are oriented to the school setting and classroom rules and procedures.
- Use trained peer tutors for struggling students.
- Provide frequent opportunities for students to work in pairs or small groups to practice language skills and negotiate meaning with peers.
- Use knowledge of cultural charactcristics to promote understanding.
- Use concrete models and hands-on activities.
- Use graphic organizers, graphs, charts, maps, diagrams, sketches, photos, sequenced pictures, and other visual supports of content.
- Use explicit strategies to activate prior knowledge so that learners can relate new material to existing knowledge.

- Preteach the meaning of difficult or technical vocabulary using ELL-friendly strategies such as pointing out cognates, which are words that come from the same root word (for example, *liberty* and *libertad*), and providing examples and nonexamples.
- Use a variety of instructional strategies to make instruction relevant and meaningful to students.
- Use lessons that encourage students to use creative and critical thinking and metacognitive and study skills.
- Use lessons that require active student engagement.
- Use technology to enhance instruction.
- Give frequent, constructive feedback.
- Speak naturally, but at a slower pace, and enunciate clearly.
- Use gestures, facial expressions, pantomime, and so on to enhance your words.
- Give clear oral directions, which are supported with written directions that can be reviewed as needed.
- Restate, repeat, and paraphrase frequently.
- Monitor for understanding by watching facial expressions and other body language.
- Model acceptance of the student's culture and home language.
- Allow adequate wait time for students' responses. Do not give up on a student.
- Extend students' responses to encourage students to go beyond their original responses.
- Avoid correcting student's language attempts. Accept the student's effort and model the response correctly without comment.
- Allow students to negotiate meaning through their home language.
- Provide frequent opportunities for ELLs to have meaningful interactions in a variety of situations with native English-speaking students.
- Provide opportunities for students to learn the language in real-life, experiential settings such as the grocery store, library, community park or playground, restaurant, and public transportation.
- Don't assume that a student who has acquired proficiency in social language skills has acquired academic language skills as well.
- Use a variety of assessment methods that allow students multiple ways (for example, through speaking, writing, or performing) to demonstrate what they have learned, while minimizing the potential effect of Limited English Proficiency on assessment results.
- When scoring oral presentations, do not penalize students for dialect features, accents, and pronunciation.
- Treat students as individuals with their own unique needs and interests.
- Create a classroom environment that promotes learning and self-esteem for all students. Do not make ELLs feel singled out or stigmatized.
- Never instruct a parent to speak only English at home.
- Set high but reasonable expectations and provide ongoing instructional support.
- Differentiate instruction based on English language proficiency and/or academic need. Instruction and interventions must consider ELLs' native language proficiency and cultural background/experiences. [See "Response to Intervention (RtI)" in Chapter 2 for additional discussion of differentiating instruction.]

Checkpoint

Fill in the blank.

1. During the pre-production stage, students are _____ to the new language, but rarely speaking it.
2. Students begin to use one-word responses or short phrases to communicate during the _____ production stage.
3. During the intermediate fluency stage, teachers should focus on _____ strategies.

Mark as True or False.

4. ____ Reaching advanced fluency usually takes from 5 to 7 years.

5. ____ Although the stages of language development are predictable, the length of time students remain in any given stage varies greatly.

Checkpoint Answers

1. listening
2. early
3. learning
4. True
5. True

Krashen's Theory of Second Language Acquisition

Five hypotheses are central to Stephen Krashen's (2003) theory of second language acquisition:

- **Acquisition-learning hypothesis:** An adult's second language ability is acquired through two interrelated systems: subconscious language **acquisition** and conscious language **learning.** Subconscious acquisition requires meaningful interaction and natural communication in the second language. Conscious language learning occurs through formal instruction and is characterized by error correction and explicit teaching of rules.
- **Monitor hypothesis:** The crux of this hypothesis is that conscious learning can be used only as a monitor for the language attempts of the acquisition system. Language that is acquired through natural means is edited, either before or after production, for correctness and accuracy by the conscious learning system. Krashen pointed out that ELLs can underuse, overuse, or optimally use the monitor function. Extroverts tend to be underusers, while introverts, perfectionists, and self-conscious individuals are overusers.
- **Natural order hypothesis:** The grammatical rules and structures of a language are acquired in a predictable order.
- **Input hypothesis:** Acquiring second language ability requires that learners receive comprehensible input that slightly exceeds their current level of ability. Comprehensible input is advanced by the use of visuals, graphics, gestures, and actions, along with multiple and frequent exposure to the words and concepts.
- **Affective filter hypothesis:** Affective factors such as emotions, feelings, and dispositions can impact second language acquisition. Negative affective factors can create a "mental block" or imaginary filter in the brain that makes input unavailable for acquisition. The affective filter is said to be "up" when this occurs. The affective filter is said to be "down" when positive affective factors are predominant. According to Krashen (2003), the optimal affective conditions are as follows: The language learner is motivated, has self-confidence and a good self-image, and has a low level of anxiety.

Checkpoint

Fill in the blank.

1. According to Krashen, subconscious language acquisition requires meaningful interaction and _____ communication in the second language.

2. According to Krashen, the grammatical rules and structures of a language are acquired in a(n) _____ order.

3. According to Krashen, acquiring second language ability requires that the learner receives comprehensible input that slightly _____ the learner's current level of ability.

Mark as True or False.

4. _____ Extroverts tend to be overusers of the monitor function.

5. _____ Being nervous likely would cause the affective filter to be up.

Checkpoint Answers

1. natural
2. predictable
3. exceeds
4. False
5. True

Marzano's Six-Step Process for Academic Vocabulary Development

Marzano's six-step process for teaching academic vocabulary (Marzano and Simms, 2013, p. 14) works well with students of all ages including ELLS. Here are the steps:

1. Provide a description, explanation, or example of the new term.
2. Ask students to restate the description, explanation, or example in their own words.
3. Ask students to construct a picture, symbol, or graphic representing the term or phrase.
4. Engage students in activities that help them add to their knowledge of the terms in their vocabulary notebooks.
5. Periodically ask students to discuss the terms with one another.
6. Involve students in games that allow them to play with terms.

When using Marzano's process with ELLs, teachers will find it helpful to:

- provide non-linguistic examples.
- monitor and correct misunderstandings during the process.
- point out cognates to words in their home language.
- caution students about common confusions (e.g., homographs).
- scaffold by writing incomplete analogies for students to complete.
- use physical gestures to enhance understanding.

Checkpoint

Mark as True or False.

1. _____ Having students look up words in a dictionary is one of the steps in Marzano's six-step process.

2. _____ Involving students in games that allow them to play with terms is one of the steps in Marzano's six-step process.

3. _____ Letting students find a picture of a term on the Internet is consistent with Marzano's six-step process.

4. _____ When teaching vocabulary to ELLs, teachers should provide non-linguistic examples.

5. _____ When teaching vocabulary to ELLs, teachers should avoid correcting misunderstandings.

Checkpoint Answers

1. False
2. True
3. True
4. True
5. False

Basic Interpersonal Communication Skills (BICS) and Cognitive Academic Language Proficiency (CALP)

The language skills required for everyday activities are called **Basic Interpersonal Communication Skills (BICS).** These are the language skills that are used to communicate with others in a social environment. For example, children acquire BICS in a natural way from their friends, the media, and day-to-day experiences. After initial exposure to the second language, it takes only from 6 months to 2 years to acquire BICS (Cummins, 1994).

In contrast, **Cognitive Academic Language Proficiency (CALP),** the language skills required for academic achievement, are seldom acquired as easily as BICS. The cognitive demands of the language of the classroom are usually much higher than those of social situations. In addition, the contextual support that is often found in social situations (gestures, facial expressions, and so on) cannot be counted on for academic tasks. According to Cummins, it takes from 5 to 7 years for students to acquire CALP after initial exposure to the second language.

Cummins conceptualized language difficulty for given situations as depending on a combination of the cognitive challenge and the contextual support available. He identified four levels of increasing language difficulty, as shown in the following chart.

Level of Difficulty	Examples
Level I: Cognitively Undemanding + Context-Embedded	Having a conversation with friends; ordering food at a cafeteria; playing sports; talking at parties
Level II: Cognitively Undemanding + Context-Reduced	Ordering food over the telephone; following instructions given on a recorded message; reading a letter from a friend
Level III: Cognitively Demanding + Context-Embedded	Solving math problems using graphs, charts, figures, diagrams, or manipulatives; doing a hands-on science experiment; playing an interactive computer simulation game
Level IV: Cognitively Demanding + Context-Reduced	Proving math theorems; writing a research report; listening to a presentation on an unfamiliar topic

As students progress through the grades, cognitive demand increases and contextual support tends to decrease for academic tasks. Reiss (2001) asserted that, in the upper grades, classwork and homework are usually cognitively demanding and context-reduced. ELLs who have not yet developed CALP will experience limited success with this type of schoolwork. Content teachers of basic subject areas assigned to instruct ELLs need to have an understanding of the complexity of academic tasks in order to plan and use appropriate ELL-focused strategies in their classrooms. Particularly when academic tasks are cognitively demanding, teachers should make efforts to provide adequate contextual support such as concrete examples, demonstrations, pictures, graphs, charts, and tables to decrease the language difficulty level of the task.

Checkpoint

Fill in the blank.

1. It takes from 6 months to _____ years to acquire BICS after initial exposure to the second language.
2. It takes from 5 years to _____ years to acquire CALP after initial exposure to the second language.
3. In the upper grades, classwork and homework are usually cognitively _____ (demanding, undemanding) and context-_____ (embedded, reduced).

Mark as True or False.

4. _____ The cognitive demands of the language of the classroom are usually much higher than those of social situations.
5. _____ Providing contextual support can reduce the language difficulty level of an academic task.

Checkpoint Answers

1. 2
2. 7
3. demanding; reduced
4. True
5. True

Useful Second Language Acquisition Terms to Know

circumlocution: Conveying ideas by defining or describing when exact English words are not known.

code-switching: The alternate use of two languages interchangeably within a language utterance; for example, "Good, *hijo* (son)."

cognates: Words that are related in meaning and form to words in another language; for example, *animal* in English and *animal* in Spanish are cognates.

dialect: A variation of a language used by a particular group of people.

ESL: English as a Second Language.

expressive language skills: Speaking and writing; also called **productive language skills.**

false cognates: A pair of words in two different languages that are the same or similar in appearance but differ in meaning; for example, *boot* (boat in German) and *boot* (footwear in English).

function: The intended use of language; for example, to satisfy wants and needs **(instrumental function)**; to control the behavior of others **(regulatory function)**; to exchange information with others **(interactional function)**; to maintain contact with others **(personal function)**; to assert identity, make choices, and take responsibility **(heuristic function)**; to pretend and create images **(imaginative function)**; and/or to inform **(informative function)** (Halliday in Badía, 1996).

idioms or **idiomatic expressions:** Expressions, peculiar or characteristic of a given language, that are difficult to understand when translated literally.

jargon: The technical language of a discipline or profession.

LEP: Limited English Proficient.

lexicon: The vocabulary used in a particular profession, subject area, or social group.

literacy: The ability to read and write.

overcorrection: Overdoing a grammatical rule by applying it unnecessarily, such as adding –s to a plural form of a noun; for example, *peoples* instead of *people*.

overgeneralization: Extending a grammatical rule inappropriately, such as adding *–ed* to the end of irregular verbs; for example, *goed* instead of *went*.

pragmatics: The use of language in social contexts.

receptive language skills: Listening and reading.

register: An appropriate form of language determined by the setting and the relationship to the person or persons to whom the speaker is speaking.

semantics: The study of the meaning of words.

target language: The second language being learned.

Checkpoint

Fill in the blank.

1. "Adios, my friend" is an example of _____.
2. "The boy runned home" is an example of _____.
3. Two words from different languages that look alike and have similar meanings are _____.

Mark as True or False.

4. _____ When giving a speech at a graduation ceremony, a student likely would use a formal register.
5. _____ When talking with a friend on the telephone, a student likely would use a casual register.

Checkpoint Answers

1. code-switching
2. overgeneralization
3. cognates
4. True
5. True

Summary

Effective teachers use instructional activities and strategies that communicate subject matter knowledge in a manner that enables students to learn. They seek out and use research-based instructional methods, strategies, and procedures to deliver instruction so that students of all capabilities are able to understand the content. They use explicit and systematic instruction, as needed, and model and scaffold student learning for optimum outcomes. They incorporate the materials and technologies of the content area in learning activities for students. Moreover, they use data-driven differentiated instructional practices based on identified student learning needs and individual differences. Furthermore, Texas classroom teachers are aware of their responsibilities toward ELLs. They strive to develop ELLs' foundational skills in English language vocabulary, grammar, syntax, and mechanics, all of which are necessary for understanding content-based instruction and accelerated learning of English in accordance with the ELPS.

Chapter 9

Technology

> **Competency 009:** The teacher incorporates the effective use of technology to plan, organize, deliver, and evaluate instruction for all students.

This chapter provides a general review of knowledge and skills related to Competency 009. Checkpoint exercises are found throughout the review material. These exercises give you an opportunity to practice what you just learned. The answers to the Checkpoint exercises are found immediately following the set of exercises. When doing the Checkpoint exercises, you should cover up the answers. Then check your answers when you've finished the exercises.

Competency Descriptive Statements

The descriptive statements for Competency 009 as given in the TExES PPR EC-12 test preparation manual (www.tx.nesinc.com/Content/Docs/160PrepManual.pdf) specify the following knowledge and skills for beginning teachers in Texas public schools:

- Demonstrates knowledge of basic terms and concepts of current technology, systems, and operations (e.g., hardware, software applications and functions, input/output devices, networks, and basic design principles).
- Understands issues related to the safe and appropriate use of technology in society and follows guidelines for the legal and ethical use of technology and digital information (e.g., privacy guidelines, copyright laws, acceptable use policies, and digital etiquette).
- Applies procedures for acquiring, analyzing, and evaluating electronic information (e.g., locating information on networks, accessing and manipulating information from secondary storage and remote devices, using online help and other documentation, and evaluating electronic information for accuracy and validity).
- Knows how to use task-appropriate tools and procedures to synthesize knowledge, create and modify solutions, and evaluate results to support the work of individuals and groups in problem-solving situations and project-based learning activities (e.g., planning, creating, and editing word processing documents, spreadsheet documents, and databases; using graphic tools; participating in electronic communities as learner, initiator, and contributor; and sharing information through online communication).
- Knows how to use productivity tools to collaborate and communicate information in various formats (e.g., slide show, multimedia presentation, and newsletter) and applies procedures for publishing information in various ways (e.g., printed copy, monitor display, Internet document, and video).
- Knows how to plan, organize, deliver, and evaluate instruction that incorporates the effective use of current technology; knows how to use developmentally appropriate instructional practices, activities, and materials to integrate the Technology Applications TEKS into the curriculum.
- Knows how to promote creative thinking and innovative process to construct knowledge, generate new ideas, and create products (e.g., design multimedia presentations, explore complex systems or issues, and develop steps for the creation of products).
- Identifies and addresses equity issues related to the use of technology.

Digital Literacy

Digital literacy means having the knowledge and ability to use a range of technology tools for varied purposes; it involves both cognitive abilities and technical skills. The term includes the capacity to use, understand, and evaluate

Chapter 9: Technology

technology for use in education settings [TEC § 21.001 (2)]. Technology is a powerful tool for transforming learning. The National Education Technology Plan (NETP) articulates a vision of equity, active use, and collaborative leadership to make everywhere, all-the-time learning possible. The plan calls on all those involved in American education to ensure equity of access to transformational learning experiences enabled by technology. Further, the International Society for Technology in Education (ISTE) provides a framework for digital learning for K-12 students, teachers, and administrators. However, to fully benefit from the power of technology to accelerate, amplify, and expand the impact of effective teaching practices in our education system and to provide authentic learning experiences for students, teachers need to have the knowledge and skills to take full advantage of technology-rich learning environments (U.S. Department of Education Office of Educational Technology, 2017).

For Texas teachers, digital literacy is a requirement, not an option. They should know basic technology terminology. They should have a sound understanding of the nature, operation, and limitations of technology systems and be proficient in their use both for accomplishing teacher duties and enhancing learning opportunities for students. They need to be able to select and use appropriate technology tools (for example, content-specific software, graphing calculators, and web tools) and resources to accomplish a variety of tasks and solve problems. For example, they should know how to do the following:

- solve routine hardware, software, and connectivity problems;
- save and move files;
- use word processing, database, and spreadsheet software;
- import graphics and images;
- use e-mail to send and receive messages and attachments;
- use social media platforms (for example, Facebook, Twitter, YouTube, WhatsApp, Instagram, and Snapchat);
- use scanners, digital video, digital cameras, tablets, multitouch screens, apps, and sophisticated smartphones;
- use technology resources to design, develop, publish, and present products (for example, PowerPoint presentations, web pages, and videos) that demonstrate and communicate curriculum concepts to audiences inside and outside the classroom; and
- be able to efficiently search the Internet (see "Searching the Internet" later in this chapter for a discussion of this topic).

In addition, teachers need to know Internet safety issues (see "Internet Safety" later in this chapter for a discussion of this topic). Moreover, they should investigate and evaluate the accuracy, relevance, appropriateness, comprehensiveness, and bias of electronic information sources; keep up-to-date on advances in technologies and their effects on the workplace and society; and follow legal and ethical guidelines when using technology and discuss consequences of misuse with students. Teachers must know, and model for their students, the principles of digital citizenship.

Checkpoint

Fill in the blank.

1. Digital literacy means having the knowledge and ability to use a range of _____ tools for varied purposes.
2. The NETP articulates a vision of equity, active use, and collaborative leadership to make_____, all-the-time learning possible.
3. Teachers should investigate and evaluate the _____, relevance, appropriateness, comprehensiveness, and _____ of electronic information sources.

Mark as True or False.

4. _____ Digital literacy is an option for Texas teachers.
5. _____ Teachers are not expected to know how to solve routine hardware problems.

Checkpoint Answers

1. technology
2. everywhere
3. accuracy; bias
4. False
5. False

Benefits of Using Technology in the Classroom

New and everchanging technology continues to impact Texas EC-12 classrooms. Effective teachers know how to use developmentally appropriate instructional strategies to integrate the Technology Applications TEKS (19 TAC § 126) into the curriculum. They are aware of the following benefits of using technology in the classroom:

- offers more control and involvement of students in the learning process;
- facilitates both group and individual learning;
- makes learning more interesting to students;
- promotes students' investigative skills;
- develops students' skills to measure, monitor, and improve performance;
- enables communication with people from many parts of the world, bringing the sights, sounds, and thoughts of another language and culture into the classroom;
- provides opportunities to apply knowledge to virtual or real-life projects;
- develops students' readiness for a high-tech world of work; and
- improves the proficiency of teachers to both enhance learning opportunities for students and accomplish everyday classroom duties.

(Adapted from *Secondary Physical Education Curriculum Guide*, 2003–2004, Brevard Public Schools)

Learners of all ages can benefit from the use of technology in schools. According to the National Association for the Education of Young Children (NAEYC), research indicates that, when used appropriately, technology has positive effects on young children's cognitive and social abilities (Donohue, 2015). Technology enables students to learn alongside one another (Cazden, 2001) and to engage in transnational communities (Schreyer, in Williams and Zenger, 2012); additionally, technology provides opportunities for teachers to learn from and with their students.

In "Use of Technology in Teaching and Learning," the U.S. Department of Education (2019, August) asserted that technology brings fundamental structural changes to teaching and learning. It transforms classrooms with digital learning tools, such as computers and handheld devices; expands course offerings, experiences, and learning materials; supports learning 24 hours a day, 7 days a week; builds 21st century skills; increases student engagement and motivation; and accelerates learning. Moreover, it also has the power to transform teaching through a new model of connected teaching. This model links teachers to their students and to professional content, resources, and systems to help them improve their own instruction and personalize learning.

In addition, online learning opportunities and the use of open educational resources can increase educational productivity by accelerating the rate of learning, reducing costs associated with instructional materials or program delivery, and better utilizing teacher time. **Open educational resources** are teaching, learning, and research resources that are freely available to anyone over the Web. They are an important element of an infrastructure for learning through a wide range of online delivery options, including video instruction, podcasts, digital libraries, textbooks, and games. Of course, it is imperative that teachers who use these resources make sure they meet standards of quality, integrity, and accuracy and that they are accessible to all learners, including students with limited resources (e.g., homeless students) and students with disabilities.

Without a doubt, technology has transformed teaching. Even so, Reinhartz and Beach (1996) pointed out that technology cannot, and should not, make teachers obsolete. However, to use technology to its maximum potential in the teaching and learning process, teachers need support and training.

Checkpoint

Mark as True or False.

1. _____ The use of technology in the classroom offers more involvement of students in the learning process.
2. _____ The use of technology in the classroom is likely to hinder the learning process.
3. _____ The use of technology in the classroom promotes students' investigative skills.
4. _____ The NAEYC is opposed to the use of technology with young children.
5. _____ To use technology to its maximum potential in the teaching and learning process, teachers need support and training.

Checkpoint Answers

1. True
2. False
3. True
4. False
5. True

Technology Terms to Know

Keeping up to date on technology terminology is difficult because new terms are constantly being added. The following terms were gathered and modified from various reliable and current sources:

acceptable use policy (AUP): A policy that describes the ways users are permitted to use a computer or network. (See "Internet Safety" later in this chapter for additional discussion of AUPs.)

accessibility: Refers to the design of apps, devices, materials, and environments that support and enable access to content and educational activities for all learners.

add-on: A software application that runs within another program to change or enhance the program's performance.

app: Short for "application." A type of software used on a smartphone or mobile device that performs a specialized function.

applet: A small Java program that allows functions such as animation to be performed on a web page. See also **Java**.

application (software): A set of programming language instructions that is designed to perform specific tasks, such as word processing, on a computer.

assistive technology: Any item, piece of equipment, or product system, whether acquired commercially off the shelf, modified, or customized, that is used to increase, maintain, or improve the functional capabilities of children with disabilities (Section 34, Code of Federal Regulations).

asynchronous communication: Communication in which there is a time delay between sending and receiving messages.

attachment: A file or image that is sent along with an e-mail or text message.

augmented reality (AR): Technology that helps students interact with the real world in an enhanced experience.

back up/backup: To make a duplicate copy of a file, program, and so on; "backup" also refers to the duplicate copy made.

bandwidth: The amount of data that can be moved to a computer during a given period of time.

banner advertisement: A banner-shaped advertisement that is placed above, below, or on the sides of a website's content and that is linked to the advertiser's own website.

BI/OS: Stands for "Basic Input/Output System," the system that starts up the computer and communicates between devices within the system.

blog: An online diary; a personal chronological log of thoughts published on a web page; short for *weblog* or *web log*.

bookmark: A way to store direct links to websites on the Internet to make returning to the sites easy.

Boolean logic: A type of logic used by search engines to find information.

boot: To start up the operating system of a computer.

broadband: High-speed Internet access.

browse: To explore or search the Internet.

browser: A software application that enables the user to locate and display web pages. Web browsers can display graphics as well as text. In addition, they can present multimedia information, including sound and video, although plug-ins might be required in some cases. Firefox, Google Chrome, Microsoft Edge, and Safari are examples of browsers. See also **plug-in**.

bulletin board: A computer service that lets users post messages and read messages left by others.

bus: A circuit that connects the central processing unit (CPU) with other devices in a computer. See also **central processing unit (CPU)** and **USB**.

camcorder: A digital video camera.

CD-ROM (CD): Stands for "compact disc–read only memory." A CD is a round, laser-read, portable disc on which large amounts of data can be stored.

cellphone: A wireless telephone; a mobile telephone.

cellular wireless: A way of connecting to the Internet that does not use any ground lines.

central processing unit (CPU): The "brain" of the computer. The CPU has an arithmetic logic unit, which performs calculations and logical operations, and a control unit, which decodes and executes instructions.

chat: A real-time "conversation" in which users type in their words to "talk" to a live person.

chat room: A website where users can log in and "chat" in real time with other users on a wide range of topics such as entertainment, sports, music, public issues, and so on. All chat conversation can be viewed by other individuals in the chat room while the interchange is taking place.

child protection software: Software that blocks a student from accessing inappropriate websites on the Internet.

Children's Online Privacy Protection Act (COPPA): Federal rule designed to place parents in control over what information is collected from their young children online (15 USC §§ 6501–6506).

class website: A website where teachers, parents, and students can log in and communicate 24/7 regarding pertinent and interrelated issues such as class assignments, activity calendars, projects, and so forth.

clip art: Ready-made graphics or images such as cartoon characters, arrows, geometric shapes, and illustrations that can be electronically copied and inserted into documents.

cloud computing: Connecting to and using computer storage, resources, and applications from an off-site third-party provider.

communication apps: Apps that allow parents to be involved in the students' activities electronically; for example, Bloomz.

computer aided design (CAD): The computer-assisted production of graphics and designs.

computer-assisted instruction (CAI): Tasks of instruction accomplished with the assistance of a computer. The student interacts with the computer and proceeds at his or her own speed. CAI software is commonly classified into the following categories: drill-and-practice, tutorial, simulation, educational games, problem solving, and tool software (www.cs.csustan.edu/~lamie/sed590/CSUS Categories of CAI.htm).

computer conference: A meeting via computer networking that takes place among users who are at different locations. This type of meeting can be conducted through Skype, Google Hangouts, etc.

cookie: A piece of information sent by a web server to a web browser that the browser software is expected to save and to send back to the server whenever the browser makes additional requests from the server. See also **browser.**

crash: A sudden, unexpected system failure.

cursor: The (usually) blinking symbol that indicates where the next character entered will appear in a document.

cyberbullying: Bullying that is done through the use of any electronic communication device, including through the use of a cellular or other type of telephone, a computer, a camera, electronic mail, instant messaging, text messaging, a social media application, an Internet website, or any other Internet-based communication tool [TEC § 37.0832(2)].

cyber grooming: The term used to describe the deceptive practices that online predators use to gain their victims' trust (for example, being a sympathetic listener).

cyberspace: The electronic Internet world.

database: A software application that lets the user store information in categories (for example, personal data about students such as addresses and phone numbers). Users can sort the information and create form letters and mailing labels.

desktop: The main computer screen where images, windows, icons, shortcuts, and other graphical items appear.

desktop publishing: A sophisticated type of word processing that allows the user to produce high-quality newsletters, brochures, books, and other types of printed documents using multiple columns of text on the same page if desired.

dial-up service: A way of connecting to the Internet through a modem and a traditional telephone line. This method of Internet connection is usually sufficient for using the Web and e-mail applications but is not as effective for transferring larger files such as video clips.

digital camera: A camera that takes digital pictures rather than using film. See also **modem.**

digital citizenship: The safe, ethical, responsible, and informed use of technology (Ribble, 2015).

digital divide: The gap between students who have access to the Internet and devices at school and home and those who do not.

digital learning: Any type of learning that is facilitated by technology or instructional practice that makes effective use of technology [TEC § 21.001 (2)].

digital literacy: Having the knowledge and ability to use a range of technology tools for varied purposes, including the capacity to use, understand, and evaluate technology for use in education settings [TEC § 21.001 (3)].

digital subscriber line (DSL): A high-bandwidth technology for connecting to the Internet that permits data transmission at far greater speeds than standard dial-up service.

digital video: Video that is stored digitally.

document cameras: Cameras that are designed to expand displayable text or images for a substantial audience.

domain name: The characters used in URLs to identify particular web pages or sites located on the Internet. For example, the domain name tea.texas.gov represents the website for the Texas Education Agency. An Internet address is broken into several different portions separated by periods. The portions of the address are read in reverse order to determine the location of the server. The last portion of an Internet address is the top-level domain (TLD), which identifies the nature of the entity associated with the address. Common TLDs are .com (commercial), .org (usually a nonprofit organization), .edu (educational institution), and .gov (government). See also **uniform resource locator (URL).**

download: To receive a file from a remote location and save it on a local computer.

Dropbox: An online service that offers secure storing and sharing in a central place and can be synced across other devices.

DVD: Stands for "digital video disc." A DVD is used to store large quantities of data, usually audiovisual material like movies.

electronic mail (e-mail): (1) A system for sending messages from one individual to another via a local area network (LAN) or wide area network (WAN); (2) an electronic message. See also **local area network (LAN)** and **wide area network (WAN).**

electronic mailing list: A discussion group to which users can subscribe to receive and participate in discussions via e-mail. A well-known electronic mailing list software application is LISTSERV.

emoji: A small pictograph that expresses an emotion or that represents an object (such as ☺ for happy); emoji are the newer form of an emoticon. See also **emoticon.**

emoticon: A small icon that expresses a mood or emotion, using keyboard symbols (such as :) for happy).

end user: The individual who uses a computer application.

eportfolio: An electronic artifact to showcase student learning to an outside audience.

extension: The three characters following the dot at the end of a file name that indicates the file type (text, graphic, and so on).

FAQs: Stands for "frequently asked questions" that are created to answer the majority of questions that a newcomer to a website might have.

favorite: A way to store direct links to websites on the Internet to make returning to the sites easy.

fax machine: Stands for "facsimile machine." A device that electronically transmits and receives text or graphical materials over telephone lines.

file: A program or collection of information treated as a unit and stored electronically.

file transfer protocol (FTP): A standardized Internet procedure for transferring files from one computer to another.

filtering: The process of controlling access to particular locations on the Internet based on the IP addresses of the source and/or destination. E-mail messages and websites can also be filtered based on content. See also **IP address.**

firewall: An electronic boundary (or physical piece of hardware) that prevents unauthorized access to a protected system.

fixed wireless: Wireless devices or systems that are in fixed locations, such as an office or home, as opposed to devices that are mobile, such as cellphones.

flame: An electronic hateful and personal attack in an e-mail, chat room, bulletin board, blog, and so on.

flash memory: A type of reprogrammable computer memory (used in digital cameras, cellphones, and other such devices) that retains data when the power is turned off.

format (in word processing): The layout of a document; formatting determines how the document looks on the screen and how it will look when printed.

frames: A feature that enables website designers to divide the browser display area into two or more sections (frames).

google (v): To search for information about (someone or something) on the Internet.

Google Docs: A word processing software that is cloud-based and owned by Google. Documents can be created and stored and accessed from any computer and other mobile devices. Documents can also be shared with other users, allowing multiple people to contribute to or edit a document.

Google Drive: A safe cloud storage for storing, saving, and backing up documents, videos, and photographs.

graphics: Images or pictures.

graphing calculator: A powerful handheld calculator with a viewing screen that displays the graphs of functions entered into the calculator when appropriate commands are given.

hacker: Someone who attempts to gain illegal access to a computer system.

hardware: The physical components of a computer system.

hashtag: The symbol # used to label keywords or phrases in a social media message.

hit: A web address matching the query posed to a search engine; an occurrence of accessing a website by an Internet user.

home page: The main page of a website.

host (n): A computer system that is accessed from a remote location. The system that contains the data is called the host, while the computer at which the user sits is called the remote terminal. (v) To provide the infrastructure for a computer service.

hypertext markup language (HTML): The formatting language of the Internet, used to create web pages and specify how they will appear on-screen.

icon: A tiny graphic that represents a program, file, or folder or expresses an idea.

influencer: A user on social media who has established credibility as a person of influence.

input device: A device that is used to put information *into* a computer, such as a keyboard/keypad, mouse, microphone, digital camera, drawing tablet, scanner, or webcam.

input/output device: A device, such as a jump drive or CD, that can serve as either an input or output device. See also **input device** and **output device.**

instant message: Private, real-time electronic message exchanged between users (for example, in a chat room).

intellectual property: Copyrighted material.

interactive whiteboard: A whiteboard that acts as a large touch-screen display of a computer's desktop image.

interface: Devices or programs designed to communicate information between computing systems or programs.

Internet: Collectively, the myriad computer and telecommunications facilities, including equipment and operating software, which comprise the interconnected worldwide network of networks that employ a transmission control protocol to communicate information of all kinds [15 USC § 6501 (6)].

Internet service provider (ISP): An entity that provides paid access to the Internet.

intranet: An internal network restricted to users within an organization.

iPad: A popular touchscreen tablet made by Apple. See also **touchscreen.**

IP address: An Internet Protocol address, which represents a unique computer location on the Internet. For example, when the domain URL https://tea.texas.gov is keyed into a web browser, the browser asks a server for the actual IP address, which tells the browser how to get to the site.

Java: A programming language developed by Sun Microsystems that is specifically designed for writing programs that can be safely downloaded and used. See also **download.**

JavaScript (JS): The programming language for the Web.

jump drive: A lightweight, miniature, portable storage device for computer files; also called a thumb drive or a flash drive.

keyboard: The keys on a computer input device used to enter text.

keyboarding: Entering data into a computer using the keys on the computer input device.

Khan Academy: A popular non-profit OER (created in 2008 by Salman Khan) that produces short lessons in the form of videos. See also **open educational resource (OER).**

link: A shortcut between sites on the Internet.

local area network (LAN): A short-distance (typically, less than 500 meters) network used to link a group of computers within a room, building, or campus that allows users to communicate and share information. Ethernet is the most commonly used form of LAN. Each computer connected to a LAN is called a node. A piece of hardware, called a hub, serves as the common wiring point.

log in: The act of connecting to a computer or network system by using your personal information (usually your username and password). See also **username** and **password.**

malware: Malicious software designed to damage or disrupt a computer system.

meme: A humorous digital element (for example, a picture or video clip) that spreads rapidly online.

modem: A device that connects a computer to a telephone or cable line (or, perhaps, another wire) so that it can communicate with another remote computer or information network. Modems are classified according to the speed with which they send and receive information.

monitor: The screen part of a computer.

mouse: A device that controls the location of the cursor of a computer. See also **cursor.**

multimedia: A term that refers to the use of more than one "natural sensory" medium. Multimedia presentations use various means of delivery and include two or more of the following: text, graphics, sound, video, or animation. Using multimedia is a way to address a variety of learning styles.

netiquette: Polite, courteous behavior on the Internet (for example, no typing in all caps and no profanity).

network: A collection of computers that are connected to each other in order to share computer software, data, communications, and peripheral devices. Each computer connected in a network is called a node.

newsgroup: A discussion group on a specific topic conducted via the Internet.

online: Taking place via or on the Internet.

online social networking: An in-class platform which allows students to interact with one another as the teacher facilitates.

open educational resource (OER): A teaching, learning, or research resource that is freely available to anyone over the Web.

operating system (OS): The electronic instructions that control a computer and run the programs. This software is generally specific to a type of computer (for example, Windows 2000, UNIX Linux, and Mac OS X).

output device: A device that is used to get information *out* of a computer, such as a monitor, printer, speaker, or headphones.

P2P: Stands for peer-to-peer sharing on websites designed to allow file sharing.

packet: A fragment of a message that contains a portion of data or information. Messages sent on the Internet are broken into smaller, more easily transportable packets.

password: A secret code or word used to validate entry to a protected website.

patch: A software solution to correct a problem in a software program.

peripheral: A device (such as a keyboard, monitor, printer, and so forth) that is connected to a computer but operates separately from the central processing unit of the computer. See also **central processing unit (CPU).**

personal digital assistant (PDA): A handheld device (for example, PalmPilot or Pocket PC) that performs a combination of computing activities.

phishing: A type of scam that uses fraudulent e-mails or texts, or copycat websites, to get you to share valuable personal information—such as account numbers, social security numbers, or your login IDs and passwords.

piracy: The illegal copying of movies, music, or software.

platform: An online teaching and learning environment that engages and monitors students (for example, Blackboard, Canvas, Desire2Learn, Moodle, or Brightspace); also referred to as a *learning management system (LMS)*.

plug-in: A software piece that is used to alter or enhance a program or system (for example, to view special graphic formats or play multimedia files).

podcast: A digital audio or video file that is released episodically.

pop-up: A separate browser window that spontaneously opens as a website is being viewed.

portable document format (PDF): A file format developed by Adobe Systems that is used for many of the documents on the Internet because the original formatting of the document is preserved when the document is viewed or printed. To view a PDF file, the Adobe Acrobat Reader software, which is downloadable for free, is required.

portal: A website or service that offers an array of resources and services, such as e-mail, search engines, and online shopping.

post (n): An online message (or picture, video, etc.) on a social media platform, discussion board, bulletin board, forum, and so on; (v) to publish such a message.

presentation software: Software, such as Microsoft PowerPoint or Google Slides, that allows the user to create slides, handouts, notes, and outlines.

printer: A device that prints text or images onto paper.

productivity software: Software such as word processing, databases, spreadsheets, presentation applications, and so forth.

Promethean Activslate: A commercial interactive whiteboard.

quick response (QR) code: A matrix barcode. In education, the QR code is helpful in placeholding URLs used in the classroom, which in turn saves login time.

random access memory (RAM): The memory location in a computer where the operating system, applications, programs, and data in current use are temporarily stored.

routers: The devices or software applications that control the movement of information from point to point along a network until it arrives at its destination.

scanner: A device that converts a graphic into a digitized image. A scanner also can be used to convert a printed document into a word processing document.

screensaver: An image that appears on a computer monitor after it has not been used for a certain period of time. Originally, screensavers were used to prevent images from burning into the monitors, but with today's technology, they are largely obsolete.

search engine: A service dedicated to locating documents or files on the Internet.

search string: The sequence of words and/or symbols used to define a search on the Internet.

server: A computer or device on a network that manages network resources. For example, a file server is a storage device dedicated to storing files. Any user on the network can store files on the file server. A print server manages one or more printers, and a network server manages network traffic.

sexting: Sending sexually explicit messages or images, via mobile phones; in Texas, it can result in charges of a crime against a minor.

simulation (computer): A software program that creates an interactive, reality-based environment. It allows the user to explore, investigate, and problem-solve in a simulated real-life setting.

smartphone: A mobile phone that has advanced computing ability and connectivity features.

smart speaker systems: Internet-enabled device that captures audio questions or commands that are sent to the cloud and the device responds appropriately. Amazon's Alexa and Amazon Echo are popular classroom digital assistants.

social media: Refers to the conglomerate of websites and applications whose main purpose is to support and facilitate online social networking; for example, Twitter, Facebook, Instagram, and Reddit.

social networking: Using a dedicated website (such as Facebook or Twitter) to interact with other members of the site by posting messages, photographs, videos, and so forth.

software programs: Sets of instructions written in various programming languages that enable a computer's central processing unit to interpret and implement actions. See also **central processing unit (CPU).**

source code: The programming language instructions to a computer in their original form.

spam: Electronic junk mail or postings.

spreadsheet: A software program in which information is stored in rows and columns. Spreadsheets can perform mathematical or statistical calculations on data and create graphs, charts, and other data summaries. They can be used by teachers for making grade books and by students for recording data from experiments or inventory for a make-believe company. Microsoft Excel, Google Sheets, and Numbers (Apple/Mac) are examples.

spyware: An Internet program that secretly uses a user's Internet connection to transmit data to a company about the user's online activity.

streaming media: Video or audio content sent over the Internet and available to be played immediately.

streaming service: An online provider that delivers on-demand video or audio content via an Internet connection to a subscriber's computer, TV, or mobile device.

student response system (SRS): An interactive device that allows teachers to collect student responses or ask questions during class, such as clickers.

style (in word processing): Formatting instructions for a document; styles give a document a consistent, polished look.

surfing: Moving from site to site on the Internet in a random way while searching for topics of interest.

synchronous communication: Communication that takes place in real time with no (noticeable) delay in sending and receiving messages.

system software: Software that enables a computer to run (such as operating system software).

3D printing: Technology that offers students opportunities to print a three-dimensional model, making it easier to understand challenging concepts and ideas. Instead of printing on paper, a 3D printer builds a three-dimensional object layer by layer using a custom material.

tablet: A portable minicomputer that has most of the features of a full-size computer.

TCP/IP: Refers to communication protocols used to connect hosts on the Internet. TCP stands for Transmission Control Protocol, which is the main protocol in an IP (Internet Protocol) network.

teleconferencing: Meeting via a computer network instead of face-to-face.

texting: Sending text messages. See also **text message.**

text lingo: The shorthand used in texting (for example, LOL for "laughing out loud").

text message: A short, electronic, written message sent via a cellphone, PDA, or other handheld device. See also **personal digital assistant (PDA).**

touchscreen: A feature which allows a user to interact with a computer, tablet, smartphone, and such by touching areas on the screen.

uniform resource locator (URL): An Internet address, which consists of several parts including the protocol, the server where the web page resides, the path, and the file name of the resource. An example of a URL is www.ed.gov.

upload: To transfer data or files to the Internet.

USB: Stands for "Universal Serial Bus," a standard bus type for multiple kinds of devices, including scanners, digital cameras, and printers. See also **bus.**

U.S. Copyright Law: The United States law that protects copyright owners from unauthorized copying of their intellectual property. See also **intellectual property.**

Usenet: A decentralized, worldwide system of discussion groups, called newsgroups. See also **newsgroup.**

username: A sign-in name for a protected website; also called a login name.

virtual field trip: Through a virtual field trip, students experience guided exploration via the World Wide Web. For example, Discovery Education provides a virtual field trip to a copper mine (www.digintomining.com/virtualfieldtrips/archive) and the Smithsonian provides a virtual field trip to the National Postal Museum (https://postalmuseum.si.edu/visit/virtual-tour.html).

virtual reality: A computer-generated simulation of an environment that allows the user to interact with the environment as if it were real, even though it does not really exist.

virus: A software program designed to cause damage to a computer system's data.

virus protection software: A software application that reduces the possibility of data corruption due to a malicious virus by detecting and removing virus programs. Once installed, virus protection software must be updated frequently because individuals are continually creating new and more destructive viruses.

webcam: A video camera that feeds real-time images to a computer or computer network.

webcast: A media presentation streamed over the Internet synchronously to listeners.

web conference: A forum to listen to information on leading-edge topics.

webquest: An inquiry-based learning activity requiring students to search the World Wide Web for information on various topics of interest or centered around a theme, topic, or standard(s) selected by the teacher.

website: A virtual location on the Internet.

white space: A portion of a document (or web page, etc.) with no text or images (for example, the white space between paragraphs); white space makes the document look less crowded and makes it easier for the viewer to process the presented information.

wide area network (WAN): A network, which can be made up of interconnected smaller networks, that allows users to communicate and share information throughout a district, a state, or the world. The Internet is an example of a WAN.

widget: A gadget designed to furnish a specific piece of information, such as weather, calculators, or news.

WiFi: Short for "wireless fidelity." A technology that allows computers to connect wirelessly to the Internet.

wiki: A website that allows the creation and editing of interlinked web pages.

Wikipedia: A free web-based encyclopedia that anyone can edit, located at www.wikipedia.org.

word processing software: Computer software that enables creation of text documents (such as Microsoft Word).

worm: A destructive program that reproduces itself to cause damage to a computer system or network.

Checkpoint

Fill in the blank.

1. The U.S. Copyright Law protects copyright owners from unauthorized use of their _____ property.
2. The main page of a website is called its _____ (two words).
3. Electronic junk mail or postings are called _____.

Mark as True or False.

4. _____ A virus is a program that is designed to cause harm to a computer system.
5. _____ The Internet is a type of local area network (LAN).

Checkpoint Answers

1. intellectual
2. home page
3. spam
4. True
5. False

Searching the Internet

The following are helpful tips for searching the Internet:

- Select a search engine (for example, www.google.com). You can read about search engines and get searching tips at Search Engine Watch (www.searchenginewatch.com).
- Read the "advanced search" tips provided by the search engine.

- Use the operators **AND** and **OR** correctly. Putting **AND** between two or more terms means you want only pages that contain all terms listed. For example, to find pages that contain both the term *behaviorism* and the term *Skinner*, use the search string: behaviorism AND Skinner. *Note:* This operator is the default for some search engines. Putting **OR** between two or more terms means you want pages that contain at least one of the terms listed, which will return a very large number of hits (so it is best to avoid this search technique). *Note:* Most search engines ignore *and* and *or* if they are typed in lowercase. However, normally, Internet searches are not case-sensitive, meaning whether you use uppercase or lowercase in your terms does not matter.
- Use **+** and **−** correctly. Putting **+** immediately before a search term means you want only pages that specifically mention that term. For example, to find pages that contain both the term *behaviorism* and the term *Skinner*, use the search string: +behaviorism +Skinner. Putting a space followed by − between two terms means you want pages that contain the first term, but not the second term. For example, to find pages containing the term *behaviorism* that do *not* contain the term *Skinner*, use the search string: behaviorism − Skinner.
- Use **quotation marks** around exact phrases. For example, to find pages that contain the exact phrase *Hope springs eternal*, use the search string: "Hope springs eternal." *Note:* Exact spelling and punctuation are important with this search strategy.
- Use **truncation** to find variations of a word using *. For example, educat* will return pages containing *educate, educating, education,* and so on.
- After locating websites, evaluate the reliability and credibility of the information posted by looking at the domain name (for example, .edu or .gov) to determine what type of source produced the site. Also, check for authorship and whether the information is current.

Checkpoint

Fill in the blank.

1. Putting AND between two or more terms in a search string means you want only pages that contain _____ terms listed.
2. Putting OR between two or more terms in a search string means you want pages that contain at least _____ of the terms listed.
3. To search for variations of a word, use _____.

Mark as True or False.

4. _____ To search efficiently for the phrase *Heaven can wait,* use the search string: "Heaven can wait."
5. _____ The operators AND and OR are interchangeable.

Checkpoint Answers

1. all
2. one
3. truncation
4. True
5. False

Internet Safety

Internet safety for students is a great concern in Texas schools. The following recommendations for Internet safety are gathered and summarized from materials from the U.S. Department of Education, the Federal Bureau of Investigation (FBI), and other organizations that promote Internet safety:

- Employ a filtering system to guard against student access to inappropriate Internet sites (see "Technology Terms to Know" earlier in this chapter for a definition of **filtering**).
- Make sure that a firewall is in place (see "Technology Terms to Know" earlier in this chapter for a definition of **firewall**).
- Teach students that surfing the Internet on school computers is an inappropriate activity (see "Technology Terms to Know" earlier in this chapter for a definition of **surfing**).
- Teach students to never give out identifying information such as their name, home address, social security number, a screen name that functions as online contact information, school name, or telephone number; to never post pictures of themselves on the Internet or send pictures to people they do not personally know; to never arrange a face-to-face meeting with someone they meet online; to never respond to messages or bulletin board postings that are suggestive, obscene, belligerent, or harassing; to never download pictures from an unknown source (as there is a good chance there could be sexually explicit images); and that whatever they are told online might or might not be true (U.S. Department of Justice, Federal Bureau of Investigation, Cyber Division, 2005).
- Teach students to report to appropriate authorities any suspicious or dangerous contact that makes the students feel uncomfortable.
- Teach students to show good digital citizenship on the Internet by using netiquette (see "Technology Terms to Know" earlier in this chapter for a definition of **netiquette**).
- Teach students to document and report incidences of cyberbullying to an adult (see "Technology Terms to Know" earlier in this chapter for a definition of **cyberbullying**).
- Make sure you are vigilant in your monitoring of students' Internet activity and behavior online. The best way you can make sure students are not accessing inappropriate sites and/or engaging in inappropriate online activity is to circulate around the room and check on their online activity.
- Have a written acceptable use policy (AUP) in place. The purpose of an AUP is to be certain that everyone understands that along with the privilege of Internet usage comes the responsibility of appropriate usage. It is of foremost importance that students have specific written approval of a parent for school-based Internet access. An AUP should include the following:
  - Notice of the rights and responsibilities of computer and network users
  - Notice of legal issues, such as copyright and privacy
  - Notice of acceptable content and conduct on the network
  - Description of behaviors that could result in disciplinary action
  - Description of the range of disciplinary options, including the removal of access privileges

(Source: *Weaving a Secure Web Around Education: A Guide to Technology Standards and Security,* a publication of the U.S. Department of Education, 2003)

The AUP for a school or district applies to all users who might access the Internet, including administrators, teachers, students, parents, staff members, and other members of the community who might be given access.

Checkpoint

Fill in the blank.

1. Schools should employ a _____ system to guard against student access to inappropriate Internet sites.
2. Teach students to never give out identifying information to someone they meet _____.
3. Teachers should be vigilant in _____ students' Internet activity and behavior online.

Mark as True or False.

4. _____ Internet safety is the responsibility of the parents, not the school.
5. _____ A benefit of an AUP is the promotion of student responsibility for ethical online behavior.

Checkpoint Answers

1. filtering
2. online
3. monitoring
4. False
5. True

Summary

Teaching in today's world is a complex process. In addition to knowing content and using appropriate teaching strategies, teachers are responsible for implementing technology in the teaching and learning process. In order to use technology successfully, teachers must have knowledge, skills, and understanding of concepts related to technology. Accordingly, effective teachers create authentic learning opportunities using technology tools in lessons and material preparation.

Chapter 10

Assessment

> **Competency 010:** The teacher monitors student performance and achievement; provides students with timely, high-quality feedback; and responds flexibly to promote learning for all students.

This chapter provides a general review of knowledge and skills related to Competency 010. Checkpoint exercises are found throughout the review material. These exercises give you an opportunity to practice what you just learned. The answers to the Checkpoint exercises are found immediately following the set of exercises. When doing the Checkpoint exercises, you should cover up the answers. Then check your answers when you've finished the exercises.

Competency Descriptive Statements

The descriptive statements for Competency 010 as given in the TExES PPR EC-12 test preparation manual (www.tx.nesinc.com/Content/Docs/160PrepManual.pdf) specify the following knowledge and skills for beginning teachers in Texas public schools:

- Demonstrates knowledge of the characteristics, uses, advantages, and limitations of various assessment methods and strategies, including technological methods and methods that reflect real-world applications.
- Creates assessments that are congruent with instructional goals and objectives and communicates assessment criteria and standards to students based on high expectations for learning.
- Uses appropriate language and formats to provide students with timely, effective feedback that is accurate, constructive, substantive, and specific.
- Knows how to promote students' ability to use feedback and self-assessment to guide and enhance their own learning.
- Responds flexibly to various situations (e.g., lack of student engagement in an activity, the occurrence of an unanticipated learning opportunity) and adjusts instructional approaches based on ongoing assessment of student performance.

Effective Classroom Assessment

Assessment is a process in which information about students' progress toward learning outcomes and performance standards is collected. The purpose of assessment is to promote student learning and development. Assessment should be systematic and ongoing in the classroom in both formal and informal ways. Effective teachers know that assessment is most useful when it aims to help students by identifying their unique strengths and needs so as to inform teacher planning and instruction.

Both teachers and students benefit from the process of assessment. As teachers devise methods of assessment to measure students' knowledge and skills, they need to keep the following four major purposes of assessment in mind:

- To help students improve their performance by providing constructive feedback
- To provide students with specific criteria for success, time to respond to feedback and the quality of their work, and opportunities to self-assess and reflect on their learning
- To inform instruction by providing teachers with opportunities to align their instruction to the curriculum, reflect on the variety of learning experiences needed as they devise TEKS-based assessments, and continually adapt instruction to improve student performance based on assessment results

Chapter 10: Assessment

- To report student achievement to stakeholders interested in monitoring student performance or measuring academic accountability

(Source: Adapted from Social Studies Center for Educator Development, 1999)

The most effective classroom assessments are those that are aligned directly with curriculum and instruction and focus on student learning. *Curriculum* (plural form, *curricula*) refers to the subject areas that are included in a school's program of study. Skillful teachers use a variety of assessment methods, such as observations, checklists, documentation of students' talk, interviews, anecdotal notes, collections of students' work over time, traditional teacher-made tests, self-assessment, peer assessment, and appropriate performance tasks and projects to find out how well students know, understand, and are able to apply the curriculum. Key questions to ask about any classroom assessment are

- Does the assessment consist...
- Does the assessment...
- Does the assessment p... onstrate understanding?
- Does the assessment p... nstruction and/or providing interventions?
- Does the assessment pro... instruction or interventions are effective?
- Does the assessment reflec... nd the instructional method?

Effective teachers are aware that c... important for all students, including students identified as Eng... ecial education services. Teachers use information collected... learning strengths and needs. Additionally, assessment resu... rents in a timely manner.

Checkpoint

Fill in the blank.

1. Teachers should use a _____ of assessment approaches.
2. Assessment should align with state _____ and grade-level standards.
3. Assessment should reflect the instructional _____.
4. Teachers use assessment data to _____ instruction and/or provide interventions.

Checkpoint Answers

1. variety
2. curriculum
3. method
4. differentiate

Testing Terminology to Know

If a method of assessment is to be valuable to a teacher in making important decisions about children, it must have reliability and validity and be unbiased. **Reliability** refers to the consistency of a measurement over time and repeated measurements. If a teacher gives alternate forms of the same test periodically over several months and the students' performance scores remain relatively the same, the test has reliability. **Validity** has to do with whether the assessment instrument measures what it is supposed to measure. Validity can be determined by comparing a test score against some separate or independent observation of whatever is being measured. If a teacher wants to measure math skills, the test must measure math skills, not reading skills. The teacher also can compare the daily or weekly grades of students to their test scores. If they are similar, then the test probably has validity. An **unbiased** test is one that does not unfairly favor a particular group. For example, a test that uses references that are unfamiliar to minority cultural groups might give an unfair advantage to the dominant cultural group. Thus, such a test would be **biased.**

A **standardized test** is one that has been carefully constructed and field-tested so that, ideally, it has a high degree of reliability and validity. Directions for taking the test and conditions for administering and scoring it are uniform and rigorously monitored. A **norm-referenced test,** such as the Scholastic Aptitude Test (SAT), is one that assesses students by comparing their performance to that of a norm group. Usually, the norm group is representative of students of the same age or grade level as the test-takers. A **criterion-referenced test** assesses students by comparing their performance to a predetermined level of mastery. Texas' statewide, standardized assessments are criterion-referenced tests (see "K-12 Statewide, Standardized Assessment Program" later in this chapter for a discussion of statewide assessments). An advantage of criterion-referenced tests over norm-referenced tests is their diagnostic, placement, and remediation use. Teachers in Texas are expected to analyze student performance data to address remediation needs of individual students. Disaggregation of the data (that is, separating it) by subject, gender, race, and so on must be used by schools and teachers to identify groups of students needing remediation/interventions.

All teachers need to be familiar with the terms *mean, median,* and *mode,* known as **measures of central tendency.** These measures are used frequently for determining certain information in assessment data. When you have a set of scores, the **mean** is determined by adding all the scores and dividing this sum by the total number of scores that were added. The **median** is the midpoint when the scores are listed from lowest to highest (or highest to lowest). The **mode** is the score (or scores) that occurs most frequently. Measures of central tendency should have the same units as those of the data values from which they are determined. If no units are specified, as in test scores, then the measure of central tendency will not specify units.

All three of these measures provide a way to describe the typical or average score. The mean is usually the best indicator of the average; however, when a few scores are either very high or very low compared to the rest of the scores, the median is a better choice to use for the average. If a large number of the scores are the same, the mode can be used to report which score or scores occurred most often—but only if used in conjunction with the mean and/or median. The mode should not be used as the only measure of central tendency for summarizing assessment data.

Although measures of central tendency are important for describing data sets, their interpretation is enhanced when the spread or dispersion about the central value is known. **Measures of variability** are used to describe the amount of spread. Two important measures of variability are the range and the standard deviation. The **range** is the simplest measure of variability. In a set of scores, it is the greatest score minus the least score. The range should have the same units as those of the data values from which it is computed. If no units are specified, then the range will not specify units.

The range gives some indication of the spread of the scores, but its value is determined by only two scores. A measure of variability that takes into account all the scores is the standard deviation. The **standard deviation** is a measure of the dispersion of a set of data values about the mean of the data set. The more the data values vary from the mean, the greater the standard deviation, meaning that the data set has more spread. The standard deviation should have the same units as those of the data values from which it is computed. If no units are specified, then the standard deviation will not specify units. The standard deviation is used extensively in education, particularly with the normal curve and standardized tests.

Other measures used to describe assessment data are percentiles and quartiles. The *P*th **percentile** is a value at or below which *P* percent of the data fall. For example, the median is the 50th percentile because 50 percent of the data fall at or below the median. **Quartiles** are values that divide an ordered data set into four portions, each containing approximately one-fourth of the data. Twenty-five percent of the data values are at or below the **first quartile** (also called the **25th percentile**); 50 percent of the data values are at or below the **second quartile** (also called the **50th percentile**), which is the same as the median; and 75 percent of the data values are at or below the **third quartile** (also called the **75th percentile**).

The interquartile range is another measure of the spread of a data set. To compute the interquartile range, you first compute the first quartile (Q_1) and third quartile (Q_3) of the data set. The **interquartile range (IQR)** is the difference between the first and third quartiles; that is, IQR = $Q_3 - Q_1$. The IQR contains the center 50 percent of the data. It gives you an indication of how much the data values "stretch" from the center of the data.

A **raw score** is (most commonly) the total number of correct responses on an assessment. For example, if a test-taker answers 40 out of 50 questions on a test correctly, then his or her raw score is 40. For a constructed response test, the raw score is the sum of the scorer's ratings assigned to a test-taker's response.

A **percent-correct score** is the percentage of questions a test-taker answers correctly on an assessment. For example, if a test-taker answers 40 out of 50 questions on a test correctly, then his or her percent-correct score is 80 percent.

A **scaled score** is a conversion of the raw score onto a standardized scale that takes into account the difficulty level of the specific set of questions in comparison to the questions on different test **forms** of that assessment. For a test form with easier questions, a test-taker must answer more questions correctly to obtain a particular scaled score. For a test form with more difficult questions, a test-taker can get that same scaled score by answering fewer questions correctly.

The *z-score* for a raw score is its distance in standard deviations from the mean of the scores on the assessment. To compute a z-score, use the following formula:

$$\text{(raw score} - \text{mean)} \div \text{(standard deviation)}$$

A **percentile rank** is a derived score used to rank a student's performance in relation to a specific group (for example, a representative sample of Texas students at the same grade level). The **percentile rank** of a student's score is based on the percentage of scores in the comparison group that are the same or lower than it. For example, if the scores of 74 percent of the comparison group are the same as or lower than a student's score, the student's percentile rank is 74th. *Tip:* A percentile rank is NOT the percentage of items answered correctly.

Stanine scores usually are derived from percentiles and compare test performance using nine intervals that are numbered in order from 1 to 9. The 5th stanine is the middle interval, and corresponds to the interval between the 40th and 60th percentiles. Stanine scores from 1 to 3 are below average, 4 to 6 are average, and 7 to 9 are above average.

A **grade equivalent score** is used to describe a student's performance in comparison to the performance of an average student at a specified grade level. Be careful interpreting grade equivalent scores. For example, suppose that a fourth-grade student receives a grade equivalent score of 6.2 on a reading assessment. This student's score reflects performance on the reading assessment matching the estimated performance of an average student in the second month of sixth grade on the *same* assessment. The score does *not* mean that the fourth-grader is ready for sixth-grade reading material. Grade equivalent scores range from the beginning of kindergarten (K.0) to the ninth month of grade 12 (12.9).

In standard deviations, the **effect size** expresses the difference between the increased or decreased achievement of an experimental group (a group of students who were exposed to an intervention) with that of a control group (a group of students who were not exposed to the intervention). This means that if the effect size computed for a specific study is 1.0, the average score for students in the experimental group is 1.0 standard deviation higher than the average score of students in the control group. A useful aspect of an effect size is that it can be easily translated into percentile gains. By consulting a statistical table for converting effect sizes to percentile gains, you can determine that an effect size of 1.0 represents a percentile gain of about 34 points. This means that the performance of the average student who received the intervention was 34 percentile points higher than the average student who did not.

Checkpoint

Fill in the blank.

1. If a test measures what it purports to measure, the test has _____.
2. Standard deviation is a measure of the dispersion of a set of data values about the _____ of the data set.

3. A vocabulary test that includes terms specific to a particular socioeconomic group is likely to yield _____ results.

Mark as True or False.

4. _____ The Texas statewide, standardized assessments are criterion-referenced tests.

5. _____ A median score of 75 on a history test in a class of 22 students means 11 students scored at or below 75.

6. _____ A grade equivalent score of 7.6 obtained by a fourth-grader on a standardized math test means that the fourth-grader can do math at the seventh-grade level.

Checkpoint Answers

1. validity
2. mean
3. biased
4. True
5. True
6. False

Types of Classwide Assessments

Three broad categories of classwide assessment are diagnostic, formative, and summative. **Diagnostic assessment** occurs before instruction. It is used to gather information about what students already know about the topic to be taught. **Formative assessment** occurs during instruction. It provides feedback that is critical to teachers' instructional decision making. **Summative assessment** occurs after instruction has taken place at the end of an instructional unit, regular grading period, or school year.

Diagnostic Assessment

Diagnostic assessments include screening tests, pretests, and various informal pre-assessments such as one-on-one interviews, class discussions/interviews, self-assessments/surveys, and ungraded quizzes. Through the use of diagnostic assessments, teachers can assess students' prior knowledge, preconceptions, and/or readiness for a topic. Data collected from diagnostic assessments help teachers better plan what to teach and how to teach it.

Formative Assessment

Formative assessments include progress monitoring and various informal classroom assessments. **Progress monitoring assessments** are regularly administered (that is, dynamic, ongoing) assessments used to evaluate students' academic progress for the purpose of making data-based decisions regarding instruction and interventions. Progress monitoring should occur routinely (weekly, biweekly, or monthly) and use valid and reliable assessments that are sensitive to small changes in student academic performance. The frequency should increase for Tier 2 and Tier 3 students (see "Response to Intervention (RtI)" in Chapter 2 for a discussion of multi-tiered instruction). Data from progress monitoring assessments provide information about whether a student's or group's level of performance is progressing at an acceptable rate toward an end-of-year TEKS-aligned outcome goal. A student's **level of risk** is assessed based on the extent of discrepancy between the student's actual level of performance and the performance of peers who are achieving benchmarks.

Informal classroom assessments include teacher observations, anecdotal records, classroom questioning, checklists, guided practice, student activities, portfolios and work samples, projects and products, teacher-made quizzes and tests, and homework. The information obtained can be used to guide reteaching, adjust instruction and/or interventions, vary the pace of instruction, or adjust the curriculum. Typically, these measures are not standardized or normed, but they can be used in conjunction with formal standardized assessments to **triangulate data** (that is, use two or more different data sources) to corroborate results.

Formative assessment also includes student **progress reports,** which report students' grades to date, usually at the mid-grade reporting period. By Texas law, parents must receive accurate and timely information if their child's academic progress is consistently unsatisfactory. This requirement can alert parents to the need for a parent-teacher conference.

Summative Assessment

Summative assessments include outcome assessments and grade/performance reports. **Outcome assessments** include the end-of-year statewide, standardized assessments; standardized norm-referenced tests; and end-of-grading-period assessments. Data from these assessments are used to evaluate the effectiveness of the instructional program. The end-of-year state-, district-, and campus-level assessment data are part of the state annual report card as required by the Elementary and Secondary Education Act (ESEA, 1965), as amended by the Every Student Succeeds Act (ESSA, 2015, available at www.govinfo.gov/content/pkg/BILLS-114s1177enr/pdf/BILLS-114s1177enr.pdf).

Grade/performance reports are timely, summative assessments that convey a student's academic performance in each class or subject relative to established learning criteria. Parents use these reports to find out how well their child is doing and whether the child needs additional help in school, and students use them to evaluate their progress and set future goals. Therefore, report-card grades should provide valid and meaningful information about a student's academic performance, based on examinations, written papers, class participation, and other academic performance criteria.

Checkpoint
Fill in the blank.

1. Assessment that occurs at the end of an instructional unit is _____ assessment.
2. Assessments that are designed to identify a student's strengths and weaknesses are _____ assessments.
3. Progress reports are a type of _____ assessment.

Mark as True or False.

4. _____ Diagnostic assessments allow teachers to assess students' prior knowledge about a topic.
5. _____ End-of-year statewide, standardized assessments are summative assessments.

Checkpoint Answers
1. summative
2. diagnostic
3. formative
4. True
5. True

K-12 Statewide, Standardized Assessment Program

The Texas Education Agency (TEA) oversees the K-12 statewide, standardized assessment program. According to state law, the goal of the statewide assessment program is to provide all eligible Texas students an appropriate statewide assessment that measures and supports their achievement of the state-mandated curriculum, the Texas Essential Knowledge and Skills (TEKS) (see "TEKS" in Chapter 3 for a discussion of this topic). To maximize its effectiveness, the program adheres to the following quality standards:

- Tests are aligned to the essential knowledge and skills of the state-mandated curriculum in all subject areas tested.

- Tests are reliable and valid measures of the essential knowledge and skills and are administered in a standardized manner.
- Test results at the student, campus, district, regional, and state levels are reported in a timely and accurate manner.

(Source: 19 TAC § 101.1)

The statewide assessment program is known as the STAAR, which is an acronym for the State of Texas Assessments of Academic Readiness. The STAAR consists of criterion-referenced assessment instruments designed to assess essential knowledge and skills in reading, writing, mathematics, social studies, and science. Currently, the STAAR assesses reading and mathematics, annually in grades 3 through 8; writing, including spelling and grammar, in grades 4 and 7; social studies, in grade 8; and science, in grades 5 and 8. For high school courses, the program provides end-of-course (EOC) assessments for English I, English II, Algebra I, biology, and U.S. history.

For the STAAR assessments, students receive a **scaled score,** derived from the raw test score. Based on the scaled score, a performance level in each subject tested is reported. There are four possible performance levels that indicate students' proficiency with grade-level content. Descriptions of the four performance levels are as follows:

Masters Grade Level: Indicates mastery of the assessment's content.
Meets Grade Level: Indicates strong knowledge of the assessment's content.
Approaches Grade Level: Indicates limited success with the assessment's content.
Did Not Meet Grade Level: Indicates inadequate success with the assessment's content.

(Source: TEA, https://www.texasassessment.com/families/understanding-the-test-score/)

Checkpoint

Fill in the blank.

1. Texas's state-mandated assessments are _____-referenced assessment instruments.
2. The STAAR assesses reading and mathematics, annually in grades 3 through _____.
3. For the STAAR assessments, students receive a _____ score, derived from the raw test score.

Mark as True or False.

4. _____ The goal of the statewide assessment program is to provide all eligible Texas students an appropriate statewide assessment that measures and supports their achievement of the TEKS.
5. _____ The STAAR program provides EOC assessments for all high school courses.

Checkpoint Answers

1. criterion
2. 8
3. scaled
4. True
5. False

Alternative Classroom Assessment

Effective teachers integrate assessment into everyday classroom practice and real contexts. As an alternative to traditional assessments (see the section "Traditional Assessments" that follows), they employ multiple measures, including more authentic classroom assessments of students such as performance observations (in person, by videotape and/or audiotape); work samples (tests, papers, and projects); process observations and products; interviews; and portfolios. **Authentic assessment** incorporates real-life application tasks and enables the teacher to directly assess meaningful and complex educational performances. Authentic assessment is sometimes called **performance assessment** or **process/product assessment.** Performance assessments have long been used in the assessment of music, art, drama, and physical education. Process/product assessments are usually more evident in science, math, social studies, and language arts. In theory, authentic assessment is more likely to possess validity than traditional assessment methods because it allows the teacher to directly observe what the student has learned. Following are some commonly used authentic classroom assessment methods.

Instructionally embedded assessment (also called **teacher observation**) uses systematic observational methods along with checklists, interviews, and questioning while students are engaged in learning activities. This assessment approach is particularly essential in early-childhood classrooms in order to provide developmentally appropriate curricula and instruction. According to Gestwicki (1999), "Teachers observe children's performance and activity during real interest center times, group work, and literacy experiences. They have conversations with children to gain additional insights into their style, rate, and interest in learning. . . . Teachers do all of this over periods of time, so that they put together a consistent picture or pattern about a particular child, rather than a single observation that may or may not be representative of the child's actual accomplishment or ability" (p. 291).

A **portfolio** is a meaningful collection of student work. It provides various and comprehensive summaries of student performance in particular contexts. Portfolio assessment requires students to collect and reflect on examples of their work and provide documentation of what they can do. Teachers also can select pieces of a student's work to include in the portfolio. Keeping a portfolio is one of the best ways for students to engage in assessing their progress over time.

Projects or **products** include stories, essays, drawings, models, audio recordings, videos, PowerPoint presentations, and other mechanisms that allow students to demonstrate their acquisition of knowledge and skills.

A **checklist** of skills or performances is an assessment tool that can be used by teachers or students to monitor learning.

Conferences and **interviews** provide an opportunity for the teacher to discuss and question a student about what the student knows and is able to do. These methods also can be used between students.

Journals and **notebooks** provide a way for students to respond in writing to a prompt by the teacher and to reflect on their own learning.

Two other popular assessment methods used by teachers are student self-assessment and peer-assessment. **Student self-assessment** is performed by the student. Students can assess themselves in many ways, such as grading their own papers, group participation, and portfolio assessment. **Peer assessment** is assessment by students of their classmates' products or performances. Generally, student self-assessment and peer assessment lack validity due to factors such as the assessor's immaturity and lack of expertise. Nevertheless, students benefit from involvement in self-assessment and peer assessment because these forms of assessment give students opportunities to develop their critical thinking and evaluation-level thinking skills.

Checkpoint

Fill in the blank.

1. Authentic assessments incorporate _____ application tasks.
2. In theory, authentic assessment is more likely to possess _____ than traditional assessment methods.
3. A meaningful collection of student work is commonly called a _____.
4. In order to provide developmentally appropriate curricula and instruction in early-childhood classrooms, _____ (two words) assessment is particularly essential.

Checkpoint Answers

1. real-life
2. validity
3. portfolio
4. instructionally embedded

Traditional Assessments

Traditional assessment is a term used to describe a traditional teacher-made test composed of true-false, multiple-choice, matching, fill-in-the-blank, or constructed-response (commonly called essay) questions. Traditional assessments can provide valuable information about students' grasp of rules, facts, information, and concepts.

The key to preparing good teacher-made tests is ensuring that they accurately reflect what has been taught. Teachers should try to make sure that content that was given more emphasis in class is given more weight on the test. Research on the effectiveness of testing has consistently found that tests promote learning (Slavin, 2008). This is especially true if what is to be learned is tested soon after it is introduced. The most effective tests are those given frequently and at consistent intervals. Furthermore, frequent cumulative tests result in more learning than infrequent tests or tests given only on content covered since the last test.

Planned review and practice activities before testing also are important. These activities might include games, role-playing, simulations, computer-based exercises, hands-on practice assignments, self-checks, or quizzes. Review activities and materials should be logical extensions of instruction and should involve frequent feedback from the teacher. Most of the time, reviews should be done in pairs or groups to encourage active engagement and communication among students. Frequent short reviews, spaced over time, are more effective than concentrated practice. Moreover, weekly or monthly reviews of previously learned material will help students' retention.

When designing a test, teachers must decide what form the test questions will take. In selecting a format for the test, teachers need to consider the degree of objectivity of the test questions. **Objective** questions depend less on teacher judgment when grading, and **subjective** questions require more teacher judgment in the scoring process. In general, multiple-choice, matching, fill-in-the-blank, and true-false questions are considered objective. Constructed-response questions fall into the subjective category. To reduce inconsistency in grading, teachers should try to design tests so that subjectivity in grading is minimized. Following are some guidelines for writing the various test question types.

True-False Questions

A true-false question requires students to decide whether a statement is true or false. Here is an example:

Directions: Read each question and decide whether it is true or false. Write the letter corresponding to your answer in the blank provided.

---

1. _____ George Washington was the first president of the United States.
   - A. True
   - B. False

The correct answer is A.

Advantages: True-false questions are easy to write, can be used to test a lot of content efficiently, and are easy to grade.

Disadvantages: Writing nontrivial questions is a challenge. Most true-false questions test at lower cognitive levels. Student guessing is problematic. True-false tests have little diagnostic value.

Following are some guidelines for construction.

Teachers should DO the following:

- Write questions based on the significant ideas they've presented—important facts, principles, and concepts.
- Make sure that each question tests one, and only one, main idea, not a combination of several ideas.
- Write questions so that the main idea in the statement is readily apparent to the student.
- Use simple, easy-to-understand language.
- Write simple, clear statements.
- Write statements that have sufficient information to clearly indicate whether the statement is true or false.
- Write questions that are completely true or completely false, not partially true or partially false.
- Make the length of the questions, whether true or false, about the same.
- Cite the source when the question contains material based on opinion.
- Try to include questions that test beyond lower levels of thinking.
- Write clear and specific directions.
- Include about the same number of true questions and false questions on a test.

Teachers should AVOID the following:

- Using ambiguous language
- Stating questions negatively
- Using giveaway words like *always* or *never* that help students decide the correctness or incorrectness of the statement
- Using tricky questions or questions for which the correct answer relies on a trivial detail
- Using statements that could be read in more than one way
- Falling into a pattern for the correct answer

Multiple-Choice Questions

A traditional multiple-choice question (also called selected-response question) requires students to select the one correct or best answer from a number of possible options. Here is an example:

Directions: Read each question and select the best response. Write the letter corresponding to your answer in the blank provided.

---

1. _____ What is the area, in square inches, of a square that measures 5 inches on a side?
   - **A.** 10
   - **B.** 20
   - **C.** 25
   - **D.** 50

The correct answer is C.

Advantages: Multiple-choice questions can be used to test at lower and higher cognitive levels and are easy to grade.

Disadvantages: Preparing a well-crafted multiple-choice question is time-consuming. Coming up with plausible *distractors* (incorrect answer choices) is difficult. Writing stems that present situations briefly is challenging.

Following are some guidelines for construction.

Teachers should DO the following:

- Write questions based on the significant ideas they've presented—important facts, principles, and concepts.
- Make sure that each question tests one, and only one, main idea.
- Include no more than five answer choice options.
- Put the answer choices in a logical order (for example, alphabetically or from least to greatest).
- Use simple, easy-to-understand language.
- Write brief, concise question stems.
- Make sure that all answer choices agree grammatically with the question stem.
- Make sure that all answer choices are parallel in construction.
- Write question stems that have sufficient information to clearly indicate the correct answer.
- Write distractors that make sense and are plausible to students.
- Write distractors that are based on common misconceptions or errors.
- Make sure that the distractors are clearly wrong or inadequate.
- Make sure that one question does not help in answering another question.
- Cite the source when the question contains material based on opinion.
- Include questions that test higher levels of thinking.
- Write clear and specific directions.

Teachers should AVOID the following:

- Using ambiguous language
- Stating questions negatively
- Using giveaway words like *always* or *never* that help students eliminate incorrect answer choices
- Using *none of the above, none of these, not given,* or *all of the above* as a final answer choice
- Falling into a pattern when placing the correct answer choice in the questions

Matching Questions

A matching question requires students to match a list of items with a set of answer choices based on a relationship between the items listed and their matching answer choices (for example, countries with their capitals or terms with their characteristics/definitions). Here is an example:

Directions: Match the state with its capital. Write the letter corresponding to your answer in the blank provided.

____ 1.	Arkansas	A.	Albuquerque
____ 2.	California	B.	Austin
____ 3.	Louisiana	C.	Baton Rouge
____ 4.	New Mexico	D.	Houston
____ 5.	Texas	E.	Little Rock
		F.	Sacramento
		G.	Santa Fe

The correct answers are 1-E; 2-F; 3-C; 4-G; 5-B.

Advantages: Matching questions are easy to write, can be used to test a lot of content efficiently, are easy to grade, and are a quick way to check students' recognition of relationships.

Disadvantages: Most matching questions test at the recall level of thinking. Writing short, succinct answer choices is sometimes challenging. Coming up with plausible extra incorrect choices is sometimes difficult. As students complete the matching, guessing can enter into selecting answer choices.

Following are some guidelines for construction.

Teachers should DO the following:

- Write questions based on the significant ideas they've presented—important facts, principles, and concepts.
- Use a list of items that are similar in content.
- Write matching answer choices that are short in length.
- Put both the list of items and the answer choices on the same page in two columns.
- Use numbers to identify the items in the first column and uppercase letters to identify the answer choices in the second column.
- Use no more than 10 to 12 answer choices.
- Include one or two extra answer choices that do not match up, or let answer choices be used more than once.
- Write directions that are clear and specific (for example, "Write the letter corresponding to your answer in the blank provided."). Tell whether answer choices might be used more than once.

Teachers should AVOID the following:

- Listing items in the two columns so that they match up in a predictable manner
- Writing questions that rely on recall of trivial or insignificant details

Fill-in-the-Blank or Completion Questions

A fill-in-the-blank or completion question requires students to fill in a blank with one word or a brief answer. Here is an example:

Directions: Fill in the blank with the correct response.

1. The author of *Great Expectations* is _____.

The correct answer is Charles Dickens.

Advantages: Fill-in-the-blank questions are fairly easy to write, can be used to test a lot of content efficiently, and minimize student guessing.

Disadvantages: Most fill-in-the-blank questions test at lower cognitive levels. Writing questions that elicit only the desired correct answer is challenging. Deciphering students' writing can be problematic (when the test is paper-based, as is common for teacher-made tests). Subjectivity might enter into the scoring of responses. Deciding how to score unanticipated correct answers must be addressed.

Following are some guidelines for construction.

Teachers should DO the following:

- Write questions based on the significant ideas they've presented—important facts, principles, and concepts.
- Make sure that each question tests one, and only one, main idea.
- Write questions for which only key words or important concepts, rather than trivial words, should be placed in the blanks.
- Use simple, easy-to-understand language.
- Write questions that have sufficient information to clearly indicate one correct answer.
- Write questions that have one word or a short phrase as the correct answer.
- Make sure that one question does not help in answering another question.

- Cite the source when the question contains material based on opinion.
- Include questions that test higher levels of thinking.
- Try to put the question blank at or near the end of the question.
- Make all blanks the same length.
- Use no more than two blanks in a question.
- Leave ample space for writing the answer.
- Write clear and specific directions.

Teachers should AVOID the following:

- Using ambiguous language
- Stating questions negatively
- Using tricky questions or questions for which the correct response relies on recall of a trivial detail
- Using statements that could be read in more than one way

Constructed-Response (or Essay) Questions

A constructed-response question requires students to write an extended response to a question or prompt. Here is an example:

Directions: In the space provided, write a well-organized 250- to 300-word response addressing the following prompt:

Compare and contrast the Norse gods with the Roman gods.

Advantages: Constructed-response questions are fairly easy to write, allow the teacher to test at higher cognitive levels of thinking, allow students more opportunity to express themselves in their own way, and minimize student guessing.

Disadvantages: Constructed-response questions are time-consuming for the student to answer; thus, teachers must limit the number per test. Not as much content can be assessed with this type of question. Deciphering students' writing can be problematic (when the test is paper-based, as is common for teacher-made tests). Grading students' responses is time-consuming and difficult to do fairly and reliably.

Following are some guidelines for construction.

Teachers should DO the following:

- Write questions/prompts based on the significant principles and concepts they've presented.
- Write clear, specific, and unambiguous questions/prompts.
- Use introductory phrases such as *explain in your own words, describe the similarities and differences between, compare and contrast, present an argument for or against,* and *list and describe the major causes of.*
- Write questions/prompts that address higher levels of thinking.
- Write questions/prompts that students can reasonably answer in the time allotted.
- Write clear and specific directions.
- Allow students to use word processing to construct responses, if feasible.
- Use a rubric or scoring guide (see the sample scoring guide that follows) and explain it to students *before* they write their responses.
- Give a separate grade for mechanical skills.

Teachers should AVOID the following:

- Using broad questions/prompts
- Grading when tired or sleepy

Sample Constructed-Response Scoring Guide

All constructed-response questions will be assessed using a holistic rating scale ranging from 0 to 4 points.

4 points: The response indicates that the writer has a complete understanding of the topic. The response is accurate, complete, and fulfills all requirements of the task. The writer demonstrates control in the development of ideas and clearly specifies supporting details.

3 points: The response indicates that the writer has an understanding of the topic. The response is accurate, complete, and fulfills all requirements of the task, but the writer's attempts to develop supporting details are not fully realized.

2 points: The response indicates that the writer has a partial understanding of the topic. The response is essentially correct, but the writer does not maintain focus on the topic. Development and organization are largely incomplete or unclear.

1 point: The response indicates that the writer has a very limited understanding of the topic. The response is largely inaccurate and incomplete. Development and organization are very weak and incoherent.

Score of 0: The response is off-topic, too short to score, or otherwise unscorable at a level of 1 or above.

Checkpoint

Fill in the blank.

1. A teacher-made multiple-choice test is a type of _____ (nontraditional, traditional) assessment.
2. Most often, true-false questions test at _____ (higher, lower) cognitive levels.
3. Fill-in-the-blank questions reduce the opportunity for students to _____ correctly.

Mark as True or False.

4. _____ When writing test questions, teachers should write questions based on the significant ideas they have presented.
5. _____ Most often, matching questions test lower levels of thinking.
6. _____ Research has consistently found that testing promotes learning.

Checkpoint Answers

1. traditional
2. lower
3. guess
4. True
5. True
6. True

Homework

Another way for teachers to find out what students have learned is through homework assignments. Homework is a research-based, high yield instructional strategy (Marzano et al., 2000). Studies indicate that carefully prepared and implemented homework assignments positively impact student achievement. In the elementary and middle school grades, students should be given homework to help them develop good study habits, develop positive attitudes toward school, and realize that learning is something that happens not only at school but also at home. By the time students reach high school, the purpose of giving homework is primarily to improve their academic achievement. Further, homework is a valuable tool that allows parents to monitor their child's learning activities.

When homework is given as independent practice, it should

- be viewed as an integral part of instruction.
- be appropriate for the ability and maturity level of the students.
- be closely tied to what was taught in class.
- have a clearly articulated purpose.
- be worthwhile (not meaningless worksheets).
- be coordinated with what the students' other teachers are requiring them to do.
- be given immediately after presentation of the subject matter.
- be given frequently as a means of extending learning beyond the classroom.
- be carefully prepared and accompanied by concise written instructions, if needed.
- be clearly understood by the students before they leave class.
- be frequently checked orally in class.
- be checked and returned to students in a timely manner, when collected.
- be checked and returned to students with feedback that informs them about what they are doing correctly and what they still need to work on, when collected.
- be successfully completed by most of the students.
- *never* be given as punishment.

For elementary school students, homework assignments should be short and require only materials commonly found in the students' homes. As a general rule, a reasonable time expectation for homework is approximately ten times a student's grade level in minutes (for example, a first-grader would spend 10 minutes, a sixth-grader 60 minutes). For middle school students, homework assignments can be longer, taking from 1 to 2 hours per night. These students might also be assigned voluntary homework. These assignments should involve tasks that students of middle school age are intrinsically motivated to do (for example, assignments that use pop-culture technology). In high school, teachers should assign homework on a regular basis. It is not unreasonable to expect homework assignments in high school to call for materials not commonly found in the students' homes and to take several hours to complete. For most high school students, 7 to 15 hours of homework per week is suitable. Marzano et al. (2000) reported that, in general, homework has increased influence on students' learning as they progress through the grades.

Regardless of grade level, teachers should have written homework policies (that might be obtained from the school or district). Students and parents should be provided copies of a teacher's homework policy, and the parent should be asked to return signed acknowledgment of receipt of the policy. For students in elementary and middle school, the teacher should provide parents information about assignments and elicit their support to encourage completion of homework and monitor their child's study time. When a student consistently fails to complete homework assignments, parental contact is essential, and an appropriate plan to remediate the problem should be developed in consultation with the student, parent, and teacher. This plan should be appropriate to the student's needs and home environment.

Checkpoint

Fill in the blank.

1. Feedback on homework should inform students about what they are doing correctly and what they still need to _____ (two words).

2. In the elementary and middle school grades, two reasons students should be given homework are to help them develop good _____ habits and positive _____ toward school.

3. In high school, it is not unreasonable to expect students to do 7 to _____ hours of homework per week.

Mark as True or False.

4. _____ Homework should be offered only on a voluntary basis.

5. _____ An hour a day of homework is suitable for children in first grade.

6. _____ When students misbehave, giving homework as punishment is appropriate.

Checkpoint Answers

1. work on
2. study; attitudes
3. 15
4. False
5. False
6. False

Correcting Student Errors

For students to learn, they need to know whether what they are doing is correct. Validating students' correct responses with appropriate reinforcement such as simple acknowledgment, class agreement, or specific praise makes students aware of their own understanding. Teachers should provide timely, specific feedback based on clear and appropriate criteria. Feedback informs the students about what they are doing correctly and what they still need to work on. Moreover, teachers know how to help students use feedback to manage and direct their own learning.

When students respond incorrectly, the teacher uses a variety of strategies such as probing, restating or rephrasing the question, or asking a leading question to encourage students to take chances and keep trying. When possible, the teacher should try to find something positive to point out about the student's response prior to pointing out errors, even if it is simply to commend the student for trying.

To correct student errors, teachers use strategies that include constructive feedback, modeling, providing an explanation of additional information, or probing by asking additional questions. Corrections often provide the opportunity to discuss common errors associated with the situation. For some teachers, it is not easy to criticize students; however, teachers can be honest without humiliating or disparaging students. Providing criticism is important so that the student and the other students do not internalize misinformation or become perplexed about key concepts. Often probing, prompting, or asking a follow-up question can result in the student self-correcting his or her own error, thereby taking the responsibility for correction from the teacher and placing it on the student.

With regard to correcting students' verbal communication errors, generally teachers should avoid publicly pointing out grammatical mistakes—especially when students are very young or English language learners (ELLs). Accepting students' efforts and rephrasing them correctly when responding will be less likely to inhibit speech production. At the same time, teachers should make sure that students know they are expected to use grammatically correct constructions. Besides modeling correct usage, the teacher—even in content areas other than English language arts—can hold class discussions about common errors the teacher has observed. This approach will communicate high expectations from the teacher and help all students develop improved language skills.

Checkpoint

Fill in the blank.

1. Students need to know when they make _____.
2. "Let me rephrase the question for you" is a way a teacher can encourage a student to keep _____.
3. Teachers should try to find something _____ to say about a student's response prior to pointing out errors.
4. "Will you explain how you got that answer?" is an example of probing that could lead to a student _____ his or her own error.

Checkpoint Answers

1. errors
2. trying
3. positive
4. self-correcting

Study Skills and Test-Taking Strategies

To help students achieve success on assessments, teachers should identify and sequence learning activities that support study skills and test-taking strategies. For example, students benefit from explicit guidance on how to study. Teachers should help students learn how to set goals for learning, monitor their learning, assess their own progress, and self-check their understanding. Using modeling, demonstrations, think-alouds, and other explicit instructional techniques, teachers can show students what works, why it works, and when to use it. These skills include how to

- take notes in class.
- listen and mentally process what they hear in class.
- write summaries.
- use self-questioning and answering.
- proofread and evaluate work.
- analyze a math problem or reading assignment.
- preview and make predictions about what they are learning.
- put confusing points into their own words (paraphrase).
- use mental imagery to help them remember.
- use mnemonic devices such as acronyms, rehearsal, and chunking to enhance memorization and recall. (See Appendix B for definitions of these terms.)
- use analogies to link new information to prior knowledge.
- use graphic organizers to make concepts meaningful.
- manage and organize their study time.

Teachers need to be aware that students also need explicit help on how to prepare for and take tests. The following tips are given in *Helping Your Child with Test-Taking—Helping Your Child Succeed in School,* a publication of the U.S. Department of Education (available at www2.ed.gov/parents/academic/help/succeed/part9.html):

- Plan ahead. Start studying for the test well in advance. Make sure that you understand what material the test will cover. Try to make connections about what will be on the test and what you already know. Review the material more than once.

- Don't cram the night before. This will likely increase your anxiety, which will interfere with clear thinking. Get a good night's sleep.
- When you get the test, read the directions carefully before you begin work. If you don't understand how to do something, ask the teacher to explain.
- Look quickly at the entire test to see what types of questions are on it (multiple choice, matching, true-false, constructed response). See whether different questions are worth different numbers of points. This will help you to determine how much time to spend on each part of the test.
- If you don't know the answer to a question, skip it and go on. Don't waste time worrying about one question. Mark it, and if you have time at the end of the test, return to it and try again (p. 1).

Also, teachers should not assume that all students are experienced with the various formats of standardized and classroom tests. In particular, English language learners (ELLs) who come from other countries might be unfamiliar with the types of test formats commonly used in Texas schools and might need to be taught, for example, how to fill in an answer form for a multiple-choice test or take a computer-based test.

Checkpoint

Fill in the blank.

1. Students benefit from _____ guidance on how to study.
2. Students can use analogies to link new information to _____ knowledge.
3. Cramming the night before a test is not a good idea because it likely will increase _____.
4. ELLs who come from other countries might be _____ with the types of test formats commonly used in Texas schools.

Checkpoint Answers

1. explicit
2. prior
3. anxiety
4. unfamiliar

Assessment Guidelines

Here are helpful guidelines regarding assessment:

- Focus on important ideas, rather than on trivial details.
- Most of the time, use assessment that is formative, not summative, and then use the information to evaluate the effectiveness of instruction, differentiate instruction, and plan future instruction or interventions.
- Use a variety of assessment measures, gathered over time, that allow students multiple ways to demonstrate what they have learned.
- Use assessments at short, frequent intervals to monitor learning and adjust instruction.
- Provide constructive feedback regarding assessments in a timely manner.
- Use authentic assessment more often than traditional tests and quizzes.
- Use self-assessment and peer assessment regularly.
- Integrate assessment into instruction (as in teacher-student conferences) rather than separate from it.
- Invite parent input with regard to the assessment process and performance report format.

(Source: Zemelman et al., 2005)

Additionally, in *Where We Stand on Curriculum, Assessment, and Program Evaluation* (2009), the National Association for the Education of Young Children (NAEYC) offers the following indicators of effective assessment practices:

- Assessment practices are guided by ethical principles.
- Assessment instruments are used for the purposes for which they were designed.
- Assessment instruments are developmentally appropriate for the children being assessed.
- Assessment instruments comply with professional criteria for quality.
- What is assessed is educationally meaningful.
- Assessment has the purpose of enhancing understanding and improvement of learning.
- Assessment evidence is collected in realistic settings and situations that involve children's actual performance.
- Assessments employ various sources of evidence gathered over time.
- Screening and follow-up have a necessary link.
- Individually administered, norm-referenced testing is limited.
- Stakeholders are knowledgeable about assessment.

Here are suggestions with regard to grading:

- Use criterion-referenced grading—that is, grading in comparison to established learning criteria (for example, grade-level benchmarks for the TEKS).
- Base academic grades on academic performance only.
- Do not use work habits, neatness, perceived effort, conduct, or improvement as factors in determining academic grades.
- Convey information about factors such as effort, work habits, behavior, or improvement through comments for these elements in reports to students and parents.
- Avoid competitive grading systems such as "grading on the curve"—that is, grading a student's performance in comparison to the performance of other students.

Furthermore, in compliance with Texas Education Code § 28.0216, a school district's grading policy:

- Must require a classroom teacher to assign a grade that reflects the student's relative mastery of an assignment.
- May not require a classroom teacher to assign a minimum grade for an assignment without regard for a student's quality of work.
- May allow a student a reasonable opportunity to make up or resubmit a class assignment or examination for which the student received a failing grade.

Checkpoint

Fill in the blank.

1. Assessment should not focus on _____ details.
2. Teachers should use _____ assessment more often than traditional tests and quizzes.
3. Assessment should be developmentally _____.
4. Teachers should use multiple sources of evidence gathered over _____.
5. A Texas school district's grading policy must not require a classroom teacher to assign a minimum grade for an assignment without regard for a student's _____ of work.

Checkpoint Answers

1. trivial
2. authentic
3. appropriate
4. time
5. quality

Summary

Assessment is critical to effective decision making in schools. Assessments at all levels (state, district, school, classroom) provide information about student learning to assist educators in meeting students' needs. Teachers assess their students for a number of reasons: to gain understanding of their skills and knowledge, assign grades, make decisions about what to teach, find out which students need extra help and which students need to be challenged more, and so forth. Effective teachers keep track of their students' progress, hold students accountable for their work, and differentiate instruction to improve student learning. The assessment process is vital to successful schools and classrooms.

Domain III Sample Questions and Answer Explanations

Sample Questions

1. As a student is talking, the teacher leans forward slightly and smiles at the student. This teacher behavior is an example of

    A. prompting.
    B. active listening.
    C. praising.
    D. redirecting.

2. Which of the following activities would best promote students' creative thinking skills?

    A. In math, listing the prime numbers between 1 and 100.
    B. In reading, identifying the main idea in a paragraph.
    C. In science, designing an experiment to test brands of fertilizer.
    D. In language arts, underlining all the adjectives in a selection of text.

3. A kindergarten teacher sets up a new learning center and posts illustrated directions to explain how students are expected to use the center. Which of the following would be most effective in ensuring that the students understand the directions for the center?

    A. Before students go to the center, introduce the center to the students and model how to follow the directions given.
    B. Before students go to the center, tell them to be sure to consult the directions when they are in the center.
    C. Make sure that students go to the center in pairs, so that they can work together to figure out what to do.
    D. Praise students when they follow the directions for the center without asking for clarification from the teacher.

4. Which of the following provides contextual support for oral language?

    A. repetition
    B. paraphrasing
    C. facial expressions
    D. summarizing

5. For which of the following tasks should a scanner be used?

   A. uploading a document to the Internet
   B. downloading a file from the Internet
   C. copying a drawing to insert into a document
   D. inserting clip art into a document

6. A student would like to perform an Internet search for works containing the phrase *Never say never*. Which of the following search strings would most efficiently provide this information?

   A. +never +say +never
   B. never say never
   C. never AND say AND never
   D. "never say never"

7. A fifth-grade teacher meets with a student's parents. The student's grade equivalent score on a standardized mathematics exam is 7.4. Based on this result, the parents want to know whether their child can spend part of the day at a middle school receiving mathematics instruction with a seventh-grade class. Which of the following responses would be most appropriate for the teacher to make?

   A. Offer to set up a computerized tutorial in the classroom to teach the seventh-grade mathematics standards to the child.
   B. Explain that the student's score indicates the student's level of performance on fifth-grade level, not seventh-grade level, mathematics.
   C. Suggest that the child go to after-school seventh-grade mathematics tutorials at the middle school.
   D. Agree to arrange for the child to attend a seventh-grade mathematics class.

8. A fourth-grade teacher is using an Internet activity to introduce adding decimals. To best assess whether the Internet activity is successful in promoting students' understanding of adding decimals, the teacher should

   A. informally observe and question students as they do the activity.
   B. give a test and compare the grades of the students currently in the class to those from students in past classes to see if there is an improvement.
   C. give a pop quiz the next day to see what students learned.
   D. after the activity, conduct one-on-one interviews with the five highest-achieving students to see whether they grasp the concept of adding decimals.

Answer Explanations

1. **B.** The behaviors of leaning forward and smiling are nonverbal cues, which often are used in active listening. Thus, choice B is the correct response. The other answer choices are incorrect because these communication techniques require verbal communication.

2. **C.** Eliminate choices A, B, and D because these activities do not involve originality of thinking. Choice C is the correct response because in this activity the students must create the design for the experiment.

3. **A.** For early-childhood learners, teachers should preview centers and model the instructions for the children. Therefore, choice A is the correct response. Eliminate choices B and C because these approaches would not be as effective as the approach given in choice A. Eliminate choice D because this answer choice is not aligned with the question because it does not address how the teacher will help ensure that students understand the directions.

4. **C.** Adding visual cues such as facial expressions provides contextual support to oral language, making choice C the correct response. The strategies given in the other answer choices reinforce content but do not add context.

5. **C.** A scanner can be used to convert a graphic, such as a drawing, into a digital image, which can then be inserted into a document. Thus, choice C is the correct response. Eliminate the other answer choices because these are not tasks for which a scanner would be used.

6. **D.** Putting quotation marks around an exact phrase will return the fewest number of hits. Thus, choice D is the correct response. Eliminate the other answer choices because these search strings are not as efficient as the one given in choice D.

7. **B.** Grade equivalent scores can easily be misinterpreted, especially by parents. The teacher should explain to the parents that the score indicates the student's level of performance on fifth-grade level, not seventh-grade level, mathematics. Thus, choice B is the correct response. The responses in the other answer choices would be inappropriate because these responses reflect incorrect interpretations of the student's grade equivalent score.

8. **A.** Eliminate choice B because a comparison of current students to past students would not take into account the differences in the two groups. Eliminate choice C because some students might be thrown into a state of confusion or anxiety by the surprise quiz and, thus, be unable to demonstrate their true understanding of addition of decimals. Eliminate choice D because, by choosing only the five highest-achieving math students, the teacher is not getting a good range of the entire class's understanding of addition of decimals. By informally observing and questioning the students during the activity, the teacher can most accurately determine whether the Internet activity is helping the students understand the concept of adding decimals. Thus, choice A is the correct response.

PART 4

DOMAIN IV: FULFILLING PROFESSIONAL ROLES AND RESPONSIBILITIES

- Competency 011: *The teacher understands the importance of family involvement in children's education and knows how to interact and communicate effectively with families.*
- Competency 012: *The teacher enhances professional knowledge and skills by effectively interacting with other members of the educational community and participating in various types of professional activities.*
- Competency 013: *The teacher understands and adheres to legal and ethical requirements for educators and is knowledgeable of the structure of education in Texas.*

Chapter 11

Family Involvement

> **Competency 011:** The teacher understands the importance of family involvement in children's education and knows how to interact and communicate effectively with families.

This chapter provides a general review of knowledge and skills related to Competency 011. Checkpoint exercises are found throughout the review material. These exercises give you an opportunity to practice what you just learned. The answers to the Checkpoint exercises are found immediately following the set of exercises. When doing the Checkpoint exercises, you should cover up the answers. Then check your answers when you've finished the exercises.

Competency Descriptive Statements

The descriptive statements for Competency 011 as given in the TExES PPR EC-12 test preparation manual (www.tx.nesinc.com/Content/Docs/160PrepManual.pdf) specify the following knowledge and skills for beginning teachers in Texas public schools:

- Applies knowledge of appropriate ways (including electronic communication) to work and communicate effectively with families in various situations.
- Engages families, parents, guardians, and other legal caregivers in various aspects of the educational program.
- Interacts appropriately with all families, including those that have diverse characteristics, backgrounds, and needs.
- Communicates effectively with families on a regular basis (e.g., to share information about students' progress) and responds to their concerns.
- Conducts effective conferences with parents, guardians, and other legal caregivers.
- Effectively uses family support resources (e.g., community, interagency) to enhance family involvement in student learning.

Role with Parents

Section 26.001 (a) of the Texas Education Code (TEC) states that "Parents are partners with educators, administrators, and school district boards of trustees in their children's education. Parents shall be encouraged to actively participate in creating and implementing educational programs for their children." This law provides a framework for building and strengthening partnerships among parents, teachers, principals, district school superintendents, and other personnel.

The person with the most opportunities to build positive parent-school partnerships is the classroom teacher. The aim is to build a partnership in which the teacher is considered an expert on education and parents are seen as experts on their child, with each contributing different know-how to the partnership dynamic. Mutual respect and shared planning and decision making are key components of a joint strategy to increase student success. Teachers should be mindful that parents do not have to be formally educated to help their child. If parents indicate that they feel unqualified or incapable of being involved in their child's education, it is essential that the teacher emphasize to the parents that they are the experts when it comes to their own child.

Teachers can be effective public relations agents by reaching out to their students' parents. The art of communicating with parents is an integral part of being an effective teacher. Communication between the school and the home should be purposeful and ongoing. Positive phone calls, text messages, notes, and newsletters throughout the year to all parents telling of class happenings and their children's achievements will be appreciated. Providing parents with accessible and understandable information about their child's progress and performance can spark productive conversations between parents and their child and increase parental contact with teachers. For example, in the early grades, weekly or monthly folders of students' work sent home, eliciting parents' feedback, helps parents keep apprised of their child's progress.

Parents should feel encouraged to visit their child's school at all times. They can be invited to attend student performances and to become involved in school activities. They will care about the school when they feel ownership of it. This positive outcome can be further enhanced when teachers invite parents to be on-site volunteers or at-home volunteers. Among other things, parents can serve as tutors; share a specific skill, talent, interest, or hobby; read to students or listen to them read; make bulletin boards; set up centers or labs; perform clerical tasks; help with special activities; or serve as aides and room mothers/fathers.

Teachers and parents share responsibility for creating a working relationship that fosters student learning. When parents participate and are engaged in their child's learning and school activities, the child gets better grades, chooses healthier behaviors, and has better social skills. Also, parent engagement "makes it more likely that children and adolescents will avoid unhealthy behaviors, such as sexual risk behaviors and tobacco, alcohol, and other drug use" (Texas School Health Advisory Committee, 2016). Moreover, research suggests that parents' expressed belief about their child's academic abilities and potential for achievement significantly affects the child's perceptions of his or her own competence and learning potential, regardless of the child's age.

Another way a teacher can build positive relationships with parents is by helping them understand their child's statewide assessment results. Many parents have only rudimentary knowledge of assessment terms and concepts, so statewide assessment reports can be confusing. (See "K-12 Statewide, Standardized Assessment Program" in Chapter 10 for a discussion of this topic.)

Checkpoint

Fill in the blank.

1. The person with the most opportunities to build positive parent-school partnerships is the classroom _____.
2. Communication between the school and the home should be purposeful and _____.
3. If parents indicate to a teacher that they feel unqualified to help their child with school, the teacher should emphasize to the parents that they are the _____ when it comes to their own child.
4. Parents' expressed beliefs about their children's academic abilities _____ (do, do not) affect students' perceptions of their own competence.

Mark as True or False.

5. _____ When parents participate and are engaged in their child's learning and school activities, the child gets better grades.

Checkpoint Answers

1. teacher
2. ongoing
3. experts
4. do
5. True

Parent-Teacher Conferences

An important way that teachers interact with parents is through parent-teacher conferences. The nature of parent-teacher conferences might differ depending on the age and grade level of the student. Parents are usually more involved in their child's education during the early grades than at the middle or high school levels, when students assume more responsibility for their own educational development. Traditionally, conferences take place at the school, where the parents and teacher can meet face-to-face. Nowadays, conferences can also be accomplished through telephone calls and via computer. For busy parents whose schedules make it difficult to set up a mutually convenient time for a conference, these virtual formats might be the best way to "meet." When scheduling a conference time, the teacher should use a written paper or digital form, giving the parents some time options as well as alternative days if possible. They should allow ample time for parents to complete the form and return it. Following are some general guidelines for parent conferences.

Preparing for the Conference

- Schedule the conference at a definite day and time.
- Inform the principal.
- Invite the student to attend the conference, if appropriate and the parents agree.
- Provide parents with topics to be discussed prior to the conference.
- Have a written conference agenda to keep you on task.
- Anticipate questions you think parents might have.
- Gather information/materials that are pertinent to the conference objective (for example, samples of the student's work, anecdotal records, cumulative record).
- Make sure that the setting for the conference is warm and inviting.
- Make sure that the seating is comfortable and arranged so that there are no physical barriers between you and the parents (for example, don't sit behind a desk).
- Arrange to have an interpreter, if needed.
- Ask the principal (or the principal's designee) to attend if you anticipate difficulties.

During the Conference

- Think of the conference as partnering with parents to help the student.
- Greet the parents warmly and offer refreshments.
- Introduce yourself using your first and last name.
- Be professional at all times.
- Stay poised and focused.
- Be respectful of and sensitive to the parents' cultural and social background.
- Establish and maintain eye contact (unless you sense doing so makes the parents feel uncomfortable, defensive, or hostile).
- Be an active and empathetic listener and encourage parental input.
- Address the parents often by name.
- Use language and terminology that parents can easily understand. Avoid jargon.
- Paraphrase parents' comments to avoid misunderstandings or miscommunication, especially when dealing with parents whose home language is one other than English.
- Be tactful, but honest and sincere.
- Respect confidentiality.

- Avoid comparing the student to his or her siblings; never compare the student to other students in the class.
- Stay away from psychological references as to why the student is not doing well. Avoid "diagnosing" or "labeling" the student.
- Avoid downplaying problems when explaining difficulties to parents.
- Never discuss other students.
- Avoid becoming defensive if parents question your judgment. Keep in mind that it is normal for parents to be protective of their child.
- Share any notes taken and review them with parents, summarizing key points.
- Collaboratively develop a student-parent-teacher plan.
- Suggest what parents can do to help at home.
- Set a timetable for contacting parents with a follow-up report.
- Explain to parents the procedures and practices that will be followed.
- Arrange to provide the parents and student (if appropriate) with a written copy of the plan.
- Schedule another conference, if warranted.
- Invite parents to visit the school and participate in activities.
- Accentuate the positive. Always begin and end on a positive note.

After the Conference

- Engage in self-reflection and evaluation. (What went well? What didn't?)
- Review notes and comments and file them for future reference.
- Document, date, and file what was proposed.
- Send the mutually agreed-upon plan to parents and give a copy to the student (if appropriate).
- Write a personal note or e-mail to the parents, thanking them for their time and informing them when you will contact them with an update.
- Have a positive contact with the student as soon as possible to dispel any fears and to reassure him or her.

During the school year, continue the communication in the form of weekly or monthly phone calls, e-mails, or notes. A positive phone call will be appreciated by parents who have received only negative reports in the past. The campus policy handbook will usually contain suggestions for communicating with parents. The handbook should also inform you of what kinds of records of contact to keep.

Checkpoint

Fill in the blank.

1. The seating for a parent-teacher conference should be arranged so that there are no physical _____ between the teacher and the parents.

2. During a parent-teacher conference, the teacher should be respectful of and sensitive to the parents' _____ and _____ background.

3. A parent-teacher conference should begin and end on a _____ note.

Mark as True or False.

4. _____ In a parent-teacher conference, it is best to start off explaining the problem so as not to waste the parents' time.

5. _____ To alleviate parents' anxiety in a parent-teacher conference, a teacher should tell them that other students have similar problems.

Checkpoint Answers

1. barriers
2. cultural; social
3. positive
4. False
5. False

Consequential Texas Statutes Regarding Parents' Rights

Teachers should be aware of Texas laws that may impact their interactions with parents. Following are excerpts of several Texas Education Code statutes concerning parents' rights.

Sec. 26.002. "Parent" is a person standing in parental relation to a child. The term does not include a person for whom the parent-child relationship has been terminated or a person not entitled to possession of or access to a child under a court order.

Sec. 26.003. A parent is entitled to reasonable access to the school principal to request a change in the class or teacher to which the parent's child has been assigned, if the reassignment or change would not affect the assignment or reassignment of another student.

Sec. 26.004. A parent is entitled to access to all written records of a school district concerning the parent's child, including attendance records; test scores; grades; disciplinary records; counseling records; psychological records; applications for admission; health and immunization information; teacher and school counselor evaluations; reports of behavioral patterns; and records relating to assistance provided for learning difficulties, including information collected regarding any intervention strategies used with the child.

Sec. 26.005. A parent is entitled to access to a copy of each state assessment instrument administered to the parent's child.

Sec. 26.006. A parent is entitled to review all teaching materials, instructional materials, and other teaching aids used in the classroom of the parent's child; and to review each test administered to the parent's child after the test is administered.

Sec. 26.008. A parent is entitled to full information regarding the school activities of a parent's child [except as provided by Section 38.004 (Child Abuse Reporting and Programs)]. An attempt by any school district employee to encourage or coerce a child to withhold information from the child's parent is grounds for discipline.

Sec. 26.009. An employee of a school district is not required to obtain the consent of a child's parent before the employee may make a videotape of a child or authorize the recording of a child's voice if the videotape or voice recording is to be used only for:

- purposes of safety, including the maintenance of order and discipline in common areas of the school or on school buses;
- a purpose related to a cocurricular or extracurricular activity;
- a purpose related to regular classroom instruction;
- media coverage of the school; or
- a purpose related to the promotion of student safety.

Sec. 26.010. A parent is entitled to remove the parent's child temporarily from a class or other school activity that conflicts with the parent's religious or moral beliefs if the parent presents or delivers to the teacher of the parent's child a written statement authorizing the removal of the child from the class or other school activity. A parent is not entitled to remove the parent's child from a class or other school activity to avoid a test or to prevent the child from taking a subject for an entire semester. This section does not exempt a child from satisfying grade-level or graduation requirements in a manner acceptable to the school district and the agency.

Checkpoint

Fill in the blank.

1. A parent is a person standing in _____ relation to a child.
2. A parent is entitled to access to a copy of each state _____ instrument administered to the parent's child.
3. An attempt by a teacher to encourage or coerce a child to withhold information from the child's parent is grounds for _____.

Mark as True or False.

4. _____ A parent is entitled to review all teaching materials, instructional materials, and other teaching aids used in the classroom of the parent's child.
5. _____ Parents are entitled to full information regarding the school activities of their child.

Checkpoint Answers

1. parental
2. assessment
3. discipline
4. True
5. True

Summary

Effective teachers recognize the importance of parental engagement in children's education and know how to establish strong school-home relationships that support student achievement of desired learning goals. They are cognizant of the need to foster mutual trust and shared responsibility with parents. They view parent-teacher conferences as opportunities to partner with parents to improve student outcomes, and they are careful to respect parents' rights under state law.

Chapter 12

Professional Knowledge and Skills

> **Competency 012:** The teacher enhances professional knowledge and skills by effectively interacting with other members of the educational community and participating in various types of professional activities.

This chapter provides a general review of knowledge and skills related to Competency 012. Checkpoint exercises are found throughout the review material. These exercises give you an opportunity to practice what you just learned. The answers to the Checkpoint exercises are found immediately following the set of exercises. When doing the Checkpoint exercises, you should cover up the answers. Then check your answers when you've finished the exercises.

Competency Descriptive Statements

The descriptive statements for Competency 012 as given in the TExES PPR EC-12 test preparation manual (www.tx.nesinc.com/Content/Docs/160PrepManual.pdf) specify the following knowledge and skills for beginning teachers in Texas public schools:

- Interacts appropriately with other professionals in the school community (e.g., vertical teaming, horizontal teaming, team teaching, mentoring).
- Maintains supportive, cooperative relationships with professional colleagues and collaborates to support students' learning and to achieve campus and district goals.
- Knows the roles and responsibilities of specialists and other professionals at the building and district levels (e.g., department chairperson, principal, board of trustees, curriculum coordinator, technology coordinator, special education professional).
- Understands the value of participating in school activities and contributes to school and district (e.g., by participating in decision making and problem solving, sharing ideas and expertise, serving on committees, volunteering to participate in events and projects).
- Uses resources and support systems effectively (e.g., mentors, service centers, state initiatives, universities) to address professional development needs.
- Recognizes characteristics, goals, and procedures associated with teacher appraisal and uses appraisal results to improve teaching skills.
- Works productively with supervisors, mentors, and other colleagues to address issues and to enhance professional knowledge and skills.
- Understands and uses professional development resources (e.g., mentors and other support systems, conferences, online resources, workshops, journals, professional associations, coursework) to enhance knowledge, pedagogical skills, and technological expertise.
- Engages in reflection and self-assessment to identify strengths, challenges, and potential problems; improve teaching performance; and achieve professional goals.

Texas Teacher Standards

The **Texas Teacher Standards** are performance standards to be used to inform the training, appraisal, and professional development of teachers (TAC § 149.1001). These standards define best practices for teachers in Texas. The following list is an abbreviated version of the standards:

Standard 1—Instructional Planning and Delivery. Teachers demonstrate their understanding of instructional planning and delivery by providing standards-based, data-driven, differentiated instruction that engages students, makes appropriate use of technology, and makes learning relevant for today's learners.

- Teachers design clear, well-organized, sequential lessons that build on students' prior knowledge.
- Teachers design developmentally appropriate, standards-driven lessons that reflect evidence-based best practices.
- Teachers design lessons to meet the needs of diverse learners, adapting methods when appropriate.
- Teachers communicate clearly and accurately and engage students in a manner that encourages students' persistence and best efforts.
- Teachers promote complex, higher-order thinking, leading class discussions and activities that provide opportunities for deeper learning.
- Teachers consistently check for understanding, give immediate feedback, and make lesson adjustments as necessary.

Standard 2—Knowledge of Students and Student Learning. Teachers work to ensure high levels of learning, social-emotional development, and achievement outcomes for all students, taking into consideration each student's educational and developmental backgrounds and focusing on each student's needs.

- Teachers demonstrate the belief that all students have the potential to achieve at high levels and support all students in their pursuit of social-emotional learning and academic success.
- Teachers acquire, analyze, and use background information (familial, cultural, educational, linguistic, and developmental characteristics) to engage students in learning.
- Teachers facilitate each student's learning by employing evidence-based practices and concepts related to learning and social-emotional development.

Standard 3—Content Knowledge and Expertise. Teachers exhibit a comprehensive understanding of their content, discipline, and related pedagogy as demonstrated through the quality of the design and execution of lessons and their ability to match objectives and activities to relevant state standards.

- Teachers understand the major concepts, key themes, multiple perspectives, assumptions, processes of inquiry, structure, and real-world applications of their grade-level and subject-area content.
- Teachers design and execute quality lessons that are consistent with the concepts of their specific discipline, are aligned to state standards, and demonstrate their content expertise.
- Teachers demonstrate content-specific pedagogy that meets the needs of diverse learners, utilizing engaging instructional materials to connect prior content knowledge to new learning.

Standard 4—Learning Environment. Teachers interact with students in respectful ways at all times, maintaining a physically and emotionally safe, supportive learning environment that is characterized by efficient and effective routines, clear expectations for student behavior, and organization that maximizes student learning.

- Teachers create a mutually respectful, collaborative, and safe community of learners by using knowledge of students' development and backgrounds.
- Teachers organize their classrooms in a safe and accessible manner that maximizes learning.
- Teachers establish, implement, and communicate consistent routines for effective classroom management, including clear expectations for student behavior.
- Teachers lead and maintain classrooms where students are actively engaged in learning as indicated by their level of motivation and on-task behavior.

Standard 5—Data-Driven Practice. Teachers use formal and informal methods to assess student growth aligned to instructional goals and course objectives and regularly review and analyze multiple sources of data to measure student progress and adjust instructional strategies and content delivery as needed.

- Teachers implement both formal and informal methods of measuring student progress.
- Teachers set individual and group learning goals for students by using preliminary data and communicate these goals with students and families to ensure mutual understanding of expectations.
- Teachers regularly collect, review, and analyze data to monitor student progress.

- Teachers utilize the data they collect and analyze to inform their instructional strategies and adjust short- and long-term plans accordingly.

Standard 6—Professional Practices and Responsibilities. The Texas Teacher Standards are performance standards to be used to inform the training, appraisal, and professional development of teachers. Teachers consistently hold themselves to a high standard for individual development, pursue leadership opportunities, collaborate with other educational professionals, communicate regularly with stakeholders, maintain professional relationships, comply with all campus and school district policies, and conduct themselves ethically and with integrity.

- Teachers reflect on their teaching practice to improve their instructional effectiveness and engage in continuous professional learning to gain knowledge and skills and refine professional judgment.
- Teachers collaborate with their colleagues, are self-aware in their interpersonal interactions, and are open to constructive feedback from peers and administrators.
- Teachers seek out opportunities to lead students, other educators, and community members within and beyond their classrooms.
- Teachers model ethical and respectful behavior and demonstrate integrity in all situations.
- Teachers adhere to the educators' code of ethics in § 247.2 of this title (relating to Code of Ethics and Standard Practices for Texas Educators), including following policies and procedures at their specific school placement(s).

(Source: 19 TAC § 149.1001)

Checkpoint

Fill in the blank.

1. The Texas Teacher Standards are _____ standards to be used to inform the training, appraisal, and professional development of teachers.
2. According to Texas Teacher Standard 1, teachers should design clear, well-organized, sequential lessons that build on students' _____ (two words).
3. According to Texas Teacher Standard 2, teachers should demonstrate the belief that all students have the potential to achieve at _____ (two words).
4. According to Texas Teacher Standard 3, teachers should demonstrate content-specific pedagogy that meets the needs of _____ learners.
5. According to Texas Teacher Standard 4, teachers should organize their classrooms in a safe and accessible manner that _____ learning.
6. According to Texas Teacher Standard 5, teachers should regularly collect, review, and analyze data to monitor student _____.
7. According to Texas Teacher Standard 6, teachers should _____ on their teaching practice to improve their instructional effectiveness.

Checkpoint Answers

1. performance
2. prior knowledge
3. high levels
4. diverse
5. maximizes
6. progress
7. reflect

Chapter 12: Professional Knowledge and Skills

Teacher Appraisal in Texas

Sec. 21.351 of the Texas Education Code (TEC) mandates that the criteria on which to appraise the performance of teachers must be based on observable, job-related behavior including (1) teachers' implementation of discipline management procedures; and (2) the performance of teachers' students.

Following are key points of the state-mandated appraisal process:

- An appraiser must be the teacher's supervisor or a person approved by the district school board of trustees.
- The teacher's appraisal must be detailed by category of professional skill and characteristic and must provide separate ratings for each category.
- The appraisal process must guarantee a conference between the teacher and the appraiser in which the conference must be diagnostic and prescriptive with regard to remediation needed in overall performance and by category.
- A teacher must be appraised at least once during each school year, or less frequently if the teacher agrees in writing and the teacher's most recent evaluation rated the teacher as at least proficient and did not identify any area of deficiency; in which case, the teacher must be appraised at least once during each period of five school years.
- The district must maintain a written copy of the evaluation of each teacher's performance in the teacher's personnel file.
- Each teacher is entitled to receive a written copy of the evaluation promptly upon its completion; and, upon receipt, a teacher is entitled to a second appraisal by a different appraiser or to submit a written rebuttal to the evaluation to be attached to the evaluation in the teacher's personnel file.
- In addition to conducting a complete appraisal as frequently as required, a school district shall require that appropriate components of the appraisal process, such as classroom observations and walk-throughs, occur more frequently as necessary to ensure that a teacher receives adequate evaluation and guidance. A school district must give priority to conducting appropriate components more frequently for inexperienced teachers or experienced teachers with identified areas of deficiency.
- A teacher may be given advance notice of the date or time of an appraisal, but advance notice is not required.
- A district must use a teacher's consecutive appraisals from more than one year, if available, in making the district's employment decisions and developing career recommendations for the teacher.
- The district shall notify a teacher of the results of any appraisal of the teacher in a timely manner so that the appraisal may be used as a developmental tool by the district and the teacher to improve the overall performance of the teacher.

(Source: Taken from TEC § 21.351 and TEC § 21.352)

School districts in Texas appraise teachers through either a district-developed process approved by the district and campus site-based decision making (SBDM) committees (see "Collaborative Teams" later in this chapter for a discussion of SBDM committees), and the district board of trustees, or through the Texas Commissioner's recommended state teacher appraisal system known as the **Texas Teacher Evaluation and Support System (T-TESS).** This latter, newly adopted system correlates directly with the Texas Teacher Standards specified in 19 TAC § 149.1001 (see the previous section for information about the Texas Teacher Standards).

The T-TESS has three components to measure teacher effectiveness: goal setting and professional development plan, observation (including pre-conference, formal classroom observation, post-conference, informal observations, and "walk-throughs"), and student growth. The T-TESS rubric (available at https://teachfortexas.org/) includes four **domains** (planning, instruction, learning environment, and professional practices and responsibilities) and 16 **dimensions** (4 for planning, 5 for instruction, 3 for learning environment, and 4 for professional practice and responsibilities) that define and clarify the domains. The rubric includes specific descriptors under five possible levels of performance (distinguished, accomplished, proficient, developing, and improvement needed).

Checkpoint

Fill in the blank.

1. Texas state law mandates that the criteria on which to appraise the performance of teachers must be based on _____, job-related behavior.
2. In Texas, the appraisal process must guarantee a _____ between the teacher and the appraiser.
3. In Texas, each teacher is entitled to receive a written copy of the teacher's evaluation _____ upon its completion.

Mark as True or False.

4. _____ In Texas, a teacher must be given advance notice of the date and time of an appraisal of the teacher.
5. _____ T-TESS correlates directly with the Texas Teacher Standards.

Checkpoint Answers

1. observable
2. conference
3. promptly
4. False
5. True

Staff Development

A major contributor to continuous improvement for teachers in Texas is the staff development activities provided by districts. TEC § 21.451 mandates that districts must provide staff development for teachers that is designed to improve education in the district. The staff development must be predominantly campus-based, reflect input from district and school educators, and may include training/instruction in technology; conflict resolution; discipline strategies; preventing, identifying, responding to, and reporting incidents of bullying; digital learning; and what is permissible under law, including opinions of the United States Supreme Court regarding prayer in public schools.

Furthermore, under this section of the TEC, districts are required to provide training in suicide prevention that may be satisfied through independent review of suicide prevention training material that is offered online. Also, for teachers who work primarily outside the area of special education and need assistance in implementing the Individualized Education Program (IEP) for a student in the teacher's class, districts also must provide training that relates to instruction of students with disabilities (see the section "Collaborative Teams" that follows and "Professional Conduct with Students Receiving Special Education Services" in Chapter 13 for additional discussion about IEPs).

Checkpoint

Fill in the blank.

1. Texas state law _____ that districts must provide staff development for teachers that is designed to improve education in the district.
2. The staff development provided by Texas school districts must be predominantly _____.
3. Teachers in Texas school districts can complete mandatory suicide prevention training _____.

Mark as True or False.

4. _____ Texas school districts must provide staff development training in conflict resolution.
5. _____ Texas school districts must provide staff development training in suicide prevention.

Checkpoint Answers

1. mandates
2. campus-based
3. online
4. False
5. True

Collaborative Teams

In their roles as professionals, Texas teachers often serve on collaborative teams such as Admission, Review, and Dismissal (ARD) committees; Section 504 plan (504) teams; interdisciplinary teams; subject area teams; site-based decision making (SBDM) teams; and professional learning communities (PLC) teams.

Under the Individuals with Disabilities Education Act (IDEA), school districts must provide an Individualized Education Program (IEP) for each student receiving special education services. The IEP is a written plan, designed specifically for a child receiving special education services. The **ARD committee** is a group of individuals who make decisions about the services and accommodations or modifications provided to a student with a disability. (*Note:* In most other states, the group that develops an IEP is called the **IEP team.**) The ARD committee must include the parents of the student, at least one regular education teacher of the student (provided the student is participating in a regular education classroom), at least one special education teacher of the student, a representative of the school who is qualified to provide or supervise the provision of special services, an individual who can interpret evaluation results, the student (if appropriate), and other individuals who might be of help in designing and reviewing the IEP. Parents may invite a person who, in their judgment, has "knowledge or special expertise" about the child. The IEP documents the student's present levels of performance, establishes annual goals for the student, and specifies which special services and supports are needed, including accommodations and modifications, for the student to advance toward attaining the annual goals. The regular education teacher is a full participant in the development of the IEP, including the determination of intervention strategies and accommodations, appropriate supplementary aids and services, and program modifications. The ARD committee must meet at least once a year to review the IEP. IEPs may be reviewed more frequently as needed (for example, if a parent or teacher requests a review). Every IEP meeting must include a discussion of the least restrictive environment (LRE) appropriate for the student. A student's services can be changed only during an IEP meeting. A copy of the IEP must be accessible to each of the student's teachers, who must follow it as written.

A Section 504 plan is designed to ensure that students with physical or mental disabilities that substantially limit a major life activity are provided with the same opportunity as other students without disabilities to learn at school (Section 504 of the Rehabilitation Act of 1973). The team that determines a student's eligibility for special services under Section 504 writes the plan and is called the **504 team** for the student. Although Section 504 regulations do not mandate the composition of the 504 team, they require that placement decisions be "made by a group of persons, including persons knowledgeable about the child, the meaning of the evaluation data, and the placement options." They suggest that teams should include teachers, school counselors, school nurses, related services providers, and school psychologists, if appropriate.

An **interdisciplinary team** (also called a **grade-level team**) consists of two or more teachers from different subject areas who collaboratively plan for the students they commonly instruct. Usually, these teachers share a common planning period and meet frequently on a regular basis to plan the curriculum and discuss the progress and needs of their students. The advantages of interdisciplinary teams include the following: Members provide an expanded pool of ideas and solutions to problems; members can plan collaboratively and coordinate instructional activities; members can discuss and decide on year-long curriculum objectives, goals, and timelines; members provide support and guidance for each other; beginning teachers have the benefit of experienced teachers' advice and help; members tend to work harder on improving instructional quality; members help substitute teachers when a team member is absent; members can collaborate in dealing with individual students; and students are provided a coordinated curriculum with an opportunity to see interdisciplinary connections.

It is common for middle school and secondary school faculty who teach the same basic subject areas to meet on a regular basis as **subject area teams** to share ideas and problem-solve about concerns related to their subject areas. Subject area teams collaboratively plan and sequence instructional activities and tests for their disciplines.

A **professional learning community (PLC) team** is a formal, organized group of teachers who share common student achievement goals and meet on a regular basis during the school day to identify practical ways to improve learning and teaching practices. The group collectively reviews student data to guide development of more effective instructional strategies and identify needs for professional learning to achieve joint learning goals of the group. Collaborative groups are considered PLCs if they contribute to a culture of continuous improvement by studying and researching new practices, investigating new curricular programs, examining the impact of school initiatives, and sharing their findings with other school faculty.

A district-level or campus-level **site-based decision making (SBDM) team** is composed of teachers and other district and campus-level professional staff, parents, and other community members (per TEC § 11.251). SBDM decentralizes authority. The advantages of SBDM are improved teacher morale, better alignment of financial and instructional resources with instructional goals, increased quantity and quality of communication among stakeholders, greater flexibility for schools in meeting the needs of their students, and more realistic budget setting and increased financial prudence.

Checkpoint

Fill in the blank.

1. The ARD committee is the group of individuals who make decisions about the services and accommodations or modifications provided to a student receiving _____ (two words) services.

2. The ARD committee must meet at least once every _____.

3. A(n) _____ team consists of two or more teachers from different subject areas who collaboratively plan for the students they commonly instruct.

4. SBDM _____ authority.

Mark as True or False.

5. ____ If a teacher feels a student's IEP is not appropriate, the teacher can change the plan and report the change at the next meeting of the ARD committee.

Checkpoint Answers

1. special education
2. year
3. interdisciplinary (or grade-level)
4. decentralizes
5. False

Professional Organizations

Teachers can improve their practice by becoming members of professional organizations related to their fields of interest such as the following associations:

- National Association for the Education of Young Children (NAEYC); www.naeyc.org
- Association for Middle Level Education (AMLE); www.amle.org

193

Chapter 12: Professional Knowledge and Skills

- National Council of Teachers of English (NCTE); www.ncte.org
- National Council of Teachers of Mathematics (NCTM); www.nctm.org
- National Science Teaching Association (NSTA); www.nsta.org
- National Academy of Sciences (NAS); www.nasonline.org
- National Council for the Social Studies (NCSS); www.socialstudies.org
- International Society for Technology in Education (ISTE); www.iste.org
- Society of Health and Physical Educators (SHAPE America); www.shapeamerica.org

Joining professional organizations provides an opportunity for teachers to keep abreast of the latest research and innovative practices in their areas of expertise by networking with other professionals, attending conferences and workshops, and subscribing to professional journals.

Other noteworthy groups are the following:

- The National Education Association (NEA); www.nea.org
- American Federation of Teachers (AFT); www.aft.org
- ASCD (formerly the Association for Supervision and Curriculum Development); www.ascd.org
- Texas Classroom Teachers Association (TCTA); https://tcta.org

Checkpoint

Fill in the blank.

1. A way for teachers to improve their practice is to become members of professional organizations associated with their _____ of interest.

2. The major benefit of joining a professional organization is that it provides an opportunity to keep abreast of the latest _____ and innovative practices.

Checkpoint Answers

1. fields
2. research

Reflective Practitioners

Research studies have identified certain characteristics that are essential for effective teaching. The studies found that effective teachers are clear about instructional goals and accept responsibility for student learning; choose, adapt, and use materials effectively; have a firm command of subject matter and teaching strategies; motivate students by communicating expectations to students; incorporate higher-level thinking skills; develop empathy, rapport, and personal interactions with students; and integrate instruction with other subject areas. Furthermore, effective teachers possess personality characteristics that include enthusiasm, warmth, supportiveness of students, sensitivity, interest in people, flexibility, and self-confidence. In addition, researchers maintain that effective teachers are **reflective practitioners** (meaning they monitor and assess whether their teaching is effective).

Reflective practitioners understand that reflection and self-evaluation are important, and recognize that their own personal factors—both positive (enthusiasm, warmth, commitment to student success, and so on) and negative (negative attitudes, biases, low self-concept, and so on)—affect their effectiveness in the classroom. Before, during, and after a lesson, they are considering how they can improve. During lessons, they are observing whether students are learning, and they adjust the lesson accordingly. They are constantly making decisions based on observed student needs. They ask themselves such questions as the following: Is this the best teaching strategy to use for this lesson and these students? Is what I'm doing working? Am I being supportive and sensitive toward my students? This process is known as **reflective teaching.** Reflective teaching helps teachers become proactive in their teaching practices and develop self-confidence in their ability to promote student learning.

Some teachers keep a daily or weekly journal of their thoughts and feelings to facilitate reflection and self-evaluation. They regularly reflect on what they did, and then think about what they can do better. A **reflective journal** is an authentic and effective way for teachers to identify strengths, challenges, and potential problems. It also provides a means for a teacher to look back and see progress over time.

Besides reflective journaling, teachers can use a number of other ways to examine their teaching. For example, some teachers assess themselves by videotaping or audiotaping lessons for later reviewing and critiquing of their instructional performance. Asking a colleague or mentor to observe in the teacher's classroom is another way to obtain helpful insights. This outreach can be extended into a partnership with another teacher, in which the two teachers share ideas and provide feedback on one another's teaching.

Checkpoint

Fill in the blank.

1. Researchers maintain that effective teachers are _____ practitioners, meaning that they monitor and assess whether their teaching is effective.
2. Reflective teaching helps teachers become _____ in their teaching practices.
3. A reflective journal is a(n) _____ and effective way for teachers to identify strengths, challenges, and potential problems.

Mark as True or False.

4. _____ Videotaping or audiotaping lessons for later reviewing and critiquing can help teachers improve their instructional performance.

Checkpoint Answers

1. reflective
2. proactive
3. authentic
4. True

Summary

Legislation by Texas lawmakers has made teachers' implementation of discipline management procedures and the performance of teachers' students central components of the teacher appraisal system. In addition, they have enacted laws to ensure the quality of staff development in public education in the state. A rigorous system is in place that demands student progress as a result of professional learning activities offered by school districts. As a result, continuous improvement of teachers is an ongoing process in Texas. Besides engaging in required and voluntary professional learning opportunities, teachers grow professionally by reflecting on their practice, sharing ideas, and collaborating with colleagues. They also benefit from joining professional organizations and attending professional conferences.

Chapter 13

Professional Conduct

> **Competency 013:** The teacher understands and adheres to legal and ethical requirements for educators and is knowledgeable of the structure of education in Texas.

This chapter provides a general review of knowledge and skills related to Competency 013. Checkpoint exercises are found throughout the review material. These exercises give you an opportunity to practice what you just learned. The answers to the Checkpoint exercises are found immediately following the set of exercises. When doing the Checkpoint exercises, you should cover up the answers. Then check your answers when you've finished the exercises.

Competency Descriptive Statements

The descriptive statements for Competency 013 as given in the TExES PPR EC-12 test preparation manual (www.tx.nesinc.com/Content/Docs/160PrepManual.pdf) specify the following knowledge and skills for beginning teachers in Texas public schools:

- Knows legal requirements for educators (e.g., those related to special education, students' and families' rights, student discipline, equity, child abuse) and adheres to legal guidelines in education-related situations.
- Knows and adheres to legal and ethical requirements regarding the use of educational resources and technologies (e.g., copyright, fair use, data security, privacy, acceptable use policies).
- Applies knowledge of ethical guidelines for educators in Texas (e.g., those related to confidentiality, interactions with students and others in the school community), including policies and procedures described in the Code of Ethics and Standard Practices for Texas Educators.
- Follows procedures and requirements for maintaining accurate student records.
- Understands the importance of and adheres to required procedures for administering state- and district-mandated assessments.
- Uses knowledge of the structure of the state education system, including relationships among campus, local, and state components, to seek information and assistance.
- Advocates for students and for the profession in various situations.

Code of Ethics and Standard Practices

In Texas, the State Board for Educator Certification (SBEC), established under TEC § 21.031, regulates and oversees all aspects of teacher certification, continuing education, and standards of conduct of public school teachers. To fulfill its mandated duties, SBEC has set forth a **Code of Ethics and Standard Practices for Texas Educators** (Educators' Code). The Educators' Code is stated in three parts: Professional Ethical Conduct, Practices, and Performance; Ethical Conduct Toward Professional Colleagues; and Ethical Conduct Toward Students.

SBEC is solely responsible for enforcing the Educators' Code for purposes related to certification disciplinary proceedings, in which the primary goals that SBEC seeks to achieve are:

- to protect the safety and welfare of Texas schoolchildren and school personnel;
- to ensure teachers and applicants are morally fit and worthy to instruct or to supervise the youth of the state; and
- to fairly and efficiently resolve teacher disciplinary proceedings at the least expense possible to the parties and the state.

(Source: 19 TAC § 247.1)

Complaints of violations of the Educators' Code against teachers are reported to SBEC. If a teacher is found to be in violation of any of the standards, disciplinary actions by SBEC can range from a reprimand to permanent revocation of the teacher's certification, depending on the severity of the infraction.

Checkpoint

Fill in the blank.

1. By state law, SBEC regulates and oversees all aspects of standards of _____ of teachers.
2. In teacher disciplinary proceedings, a primary goal of SBEC is to _____ the safety and welfare of Texas schoolchildren.
3. In teacher disciplinary proceedings, a primary goal of SBEC is to ensure teachers and applicants are _____ fit and worthy to instruct or to supervise the youth of the state.
4. In teacher disciplinary proceedings, a primary goal of SBEC is to _____ and efficiently resolve teacher disciplinary proceedings at the least expense possible to the parties and the state.

Mark as True or False.

5. _____ Violation of the Code of Ethics and Standard Practices for Texas Educators can result in permanent revocation of a teacher's certification.

Checkpoint Answers

1. conduct
2. protect
3. morally
4. fairly
5. True

Professional Ethical Conduct, Practices, and Performance

In maintaining the following standards of **professional ethical conduct, practices, and performance,** teachers must respect and obey the law, demonstrate personal integrity, and exemplify honesty and good moral character:

Standard 1.1. The educator shall not intentionally, knowingly, or recklessly engage in deceptive practices regarding official policies of the school district, educational institution, educator preparation program, the Texas Education Agency (TEA), or the State Board for Educator Certification (SBEC) and its certification process.

Standard 1.2. The educator shall not intentionally, knowingly, or recklessly misappropriate, divert, or use monies, personnel, property, or equipment committed to his or her charge for personal gain or advantage.

Standard 1.3. The educator shall not submit fraudulent requests for reimbursement, expenses, or pay.

Standard 1.4. The educator shall not use institutional or professional privileges for personal or partisan advantage.

Standard 1.5. The educator shall neither accept nor offer gratuities, gifts, or favors that impair professional judgment or that are used to obtain special advantage. This standard shall not restrict the acceptance of gifts or tokens offered and accepted openly from students, parents of students, or other persons or organizations in recognition or appreciation of service.

Standard 1.6. The educator shall not falsify records, or direct or coerce others to do so.

Standard 1.7. The educator shall comply with state regulations, written local school board policies, and other state and federal laws.

Standard 1.8. The educator shall apply for, accept, offer, or assign a position or a responsibility on the basis of professional qualifications.

Standard 1.9. The educator shall not make threats of violence against school district employees, school board members, students, or parents of students.

Standard 1.10. The educator shall be of good moral character and be worthy to instruct or supervise the youth of this state.

Standard 1.11. The educator shall not intentionally, knowingly, or recklessly misrepresent his or her employment history, criminal history, and/or disciplinary record when applying for subsequent employment.

Standard 1.12. The educator shall refrain from the illegal use, abuse, or distribution of controlled substances, prescription drugs, and toxic inhalants.

Standard 1.13. The educator shall not be under the influence of alcohol or consume alcoholic beverages on school property or during school activities when students are present.

(Source: 19 TAC § 247.2)

Checkpoint
Fill in the blank.

1. Teachers should not submit _____ requests for reimbursement.
2. Teachers should neither _____ nor _____ gratuities, gifts, or favors that impair professional judgment or that are used to obtain special advantage.
3. Teachers should not _____ records.
4. Teachers should not make threats of _____ against students or parents of students.
5. Teachers should not _____ alcoholic beverages on school property or during school activities when students are present.

Checkpoint Answers
1. fraudulent
2. accept; offer
3. falsify
4. violence
5. consume

Ethical Conduct Toward Professional Colleagues

In maintaining the following standards of **ethical conduct toward professional colleagues,** teachers should exemplify ethical relations with colleagues and extend just and equitable treatment to all members of the profession:

Standard 2.1. The educator shall not reveal confidential health or personnel information concerning colleagues unless disclosure serves lawful professional purposes or is required by law.

Standard 2.2. The educator shall not harm others by knowingly making false statements about a colleague or the school system.

Standard 2.3. The educator shall adhere to written local school board policies and state and federal laws regarding the hiring, evaluation, and dismissal of personnel.

Standard 2.4. The educator shall not interfere with a colleague's exercise of political, professional, or citizenship rights and responsibilities.

Standard 2.5. The educator shall not discriminate against or coerce a colleague on the basis of race, color, religion, national origin, age, gender, disability, family status, or sexual orientation.

Standard 2.6. The educator shall not use coercive means or promise of special treatment in order to influence professional decisions or colleagues.

Standard 2.7. The educator shall not retaliate against any individual who has filed a complaint with SBEC or who provides information for a disciplinary investigation or proceeding under this chapter.

Standard 2.8. The educator shall not intentionally or knowingly subject a colleague to sexual harassment.

(Source: 19 TAC § 247.2)

Checkpoint

Fill in the blank.

1. Teachers should not knowingly make _____ statements about a colleague.
2. Teachers should not interfere with a colleague's exercise of _____, professional, or citizenship rights and responsibilities.
3. Teachers should not use coercive means to _____ professional decisions of colleagues.
4. Teachers should not _____ or knowingly subject a colleague to sexual harassment.

Checkpoint Answers

1. false
2. political
3. influence
4. intentionally

Ethical Conduct Toward Students

In maintaining the following standards of **ethical conduct toward students,** teachers should measure success by the progress of students toward realization of their potential as effective citizens:

Standard 3.1. The educator shall not reveal confidential information concerning students unless disclosure serves lawful professional purposes or is required by law.

Standard 3.2. The educator shall not intentionally, knowingly, or recklessly treat a student or minor in a manner that adversely affects or endangers the learning, physical health, mental health, or safety of the student or minor.

Standard 3.3. The educator shall not intentionally, knowingly, or recklessly misrepresent facts regarding a student.

Standard 3.4. The educator shall not exclude a student from participation in a program, deny benefits to a student, or grant an advantage to a student on the basis of race, color, gender, disability, national origin, religion, family status, or sexual orientation.

Standard 3.5. The educator shall not intentionally, knowingly, or recklessly engage in physical mistreatment, neglect, or abuse of a student or a minor.

Standard 3.6. The educator shall not solicit or engage in sexual conduct or a romantic relationship with a student or a minor.

Standard 3.7. The educator shall not furnish alcohol or illegal/unauthorized drugs to any person under 21 years of age unless the educator is a parent or guardian of that child or knowingly allow any person under 21 years of age unless the educator is a parent or guardian of that child to consume alcohol or illegal/unauthorized drugs in the presence of the educator.

Standard 3.8. The educator shall maintain appropriate professional educator-student relationships and boundaries based on a reasonably prudent educator standard.

Standard 3.9. The educator shall refrain from inappropriate communication with a student or minor, including, but not limited to, electronic communication such as cellphone, text messaging, e-mail, instant messaging, blogging, or other social network communication. Factors that may be considered in assessing whether the communication is inappropriate include, but are not limited to: the nature, purpose, timing, and amount of the communication; the subject matter of the communication; whether the communication was made openly, or the educator attempted to conceal the communication; whether the communication could be reasonably interpreted as soliciting sexual contact or a romantic relationship; whether the communication was sexually explicit; and whether the communication involved discussion(s) of the physical or sexual attractiveness or the sexual history, activities, preferences, or fantasies of either the educator or the student.

(Source: 19 TAC § 247.2)

Checkpoint

Fill in the blank.

1. Teachers should not reveal _____ information concerning students unless disclosure serves lawful professional purposes or is required by law.
2. Teachers should not intentionally, knowingly, or recklessly _____ facts regarding a student.
3. Teachers should not exclude a student from participation in a program on the basis of race, color, gender, disability, national origin, religion, family status, or sexual _____.
4. Teachers should not intentionally, knowingly, or recklessly engage in physical mistreatment, _____, or abuse of a student or a minor.
5. Teachers should not solicit or engage in sexual conduct or a _____ relationship with a student or minor.

Checkpoint Answers

1. confidential
2. misrepresent
3. orientation
4. neglect
5. romantic

Avoiding Disciplinary Action

Teachers in Texas are role models for their students and their communities. Moreover, they have an ethical and a legal responsibility to adhere to a high moral standard. This responsibility is underscored by the following statement given in the Texas Administrative Code: "A certified educator holds a unique position of public trust with almost unparalleled access to the hearts and minds of impressionable students. The conduct of an educator must be held to the highest standard" [19 TAC § 249.5 (b)(1)].

The Texas Education Agency (TEA) has produced a series of 10 Texas Educator Ethics Training videos (available on youtube.com under "TEA Teacher Ethics Training"). The videos offer commonsense advice to teachers about how to avoid disciplinary action. Below are recommendations gleaned from the videos and from general sources:

- Participate in ethics training, so that you know the Code of Ethics and Standard Practices for Texas Educators and its interpretation.
- Know federal and state laws. Keep up to date on changes.
- Know your district and school policies. Read the handbooks from cover to cover.
- Make sure that you have clear grading criteria that are in writing and distributed to students and parents.
- Make sure that you have a written discipline policy that is distributed to students and parents.
- Keep your classroom door open when conferencing with a student.

- Do not use school property (for example, computers, copiers, fax machines, and e-mail) for personal use.
- Obey the federal copyright law (see "Important Legislation and Court Cases" later in this chapter for a description of PL 94-553 Copyright Law).
- Know the legal/ethical requirements regarding the use of technologies (e.g., data security, privacy, and acceptable use policies). See "Internet Safety" in Chapter 9 for additional information.
- Follow district and school policy regarding school trips, including arranging for transportation.
- Do not leave your students unattended.
- Keep a professional relationship with your students. Don't be a buddy or a pal.
- Do not give special privileges to a few students.
- Do not have a "teacher's pet."
- Do not flirt with a student.
- Do not establish an intimate relationship with a student, even if the student is over 18 or the student's parents approve.
- Do not engage in sexually intimidating behavior toward a student.
- Do not make fun of a student, even jokingly.
- Do not harass, humiliate, or disparage a student.
- Do not make verbally abusive comments to students.
- Do not bully or intimidate students.
- Do not try to force your point of view on students.
- Do not discuss other students with a student.
- Do not ask your students to keep secrets.
- Avoid physically touching your students, especially students in the upper grades. Use verbal and nonverbal reinforcement instead.
- Do not discuss your personal life with students, even outside the classroom.
- Avoid inappropriate involvement in students' personal lives (e.g., becoming a student's confidant).
- Do not "party" with your students.
- Do not drink alcoholic beverages in front of your students.
- Do not invite students to your home.
- Do not give a student a ride in your vehicle.
- Do not offer money to a student for favors.
- Do not make phone calls, write e-mails or text messages, or send notes of a personal nature to students.
- Do not post personal messages to students on social networking sites.
- Have separate personal and professional social media accounts.
- Do not bring up controversial topics in your classroom unless the topic is clearly and defensibly related to a lesson objective *and* you have obtained prior approval from school administrators.
- Avoid vulgarity-centered assignments, even if your intent is to deter usage of vulgar language by students.
- Do not discuss religion with your students.
- Avoid stereotypical language.
- Do not talk about students with other teachers in the halls or other open places in the school.
- Do not talk about your students or the school in public places in the community.
- Dress and behave professionally in school and when attending public functions.
- Maintain ethical and decent standards in your personal life. You can be subject to disciplinary action for inappropriate behavior in your private life.
- If you are unsure whether a behavior is inappropriate, err on the side of caution and don't do it.

Checkpoint

Fill in the blank.

1. Teachers in Texas have an ethical and a legal responsibility to adhere to a high _____ standard.
2. Teachers should not use school property for _____ use.
3. Unethical or illegal conduct in a teacher's private life is grounds for _____ action.

Mark as True or False.

4. _____ It is generally held acceptable for teachers to socialize with their students who are 18 years of age or older.
5. _____ It is acceptable for a teacher to tease a student about the student's sexual orientation as long as the student is not offended.

Checkpoint Answers

1. moral
2. personal
3. disciplinary
4. False
5. False

Professional Responsibility as Advocate for Students

Good teachers understand that various external factors can affect students' behavior and performance in school. As advocates for students and their health and safety, teachers need to be alert to signs of emotional distress, suicidal tendencies, substance abuse, child abuse or neglect, or eating disorders.

Emotional distress in students can stem from various sources (for example, dysfunctional family situations, conflict within peer relationships, victimization by others, or the intrusion of a new culture—"culture shock"). **Signs of emotional distress** include sudden changes in personality, behavior, or academic performance; nervousness/anxiety; frequent mood swings, sadness, or depression; irritability; lack of concentration; overreactions; withdrawal from relationships; frequent illness; tiredness; and sudden weight loss or gain. As an immediate measure to ease emotional distress, teachers should provide a predictable and routine environment where the student feels safe and accepted.

Students can become so distressed that they may begin to contemplate suicide. **Warning signs of suicide** include changes in sleep or eating patterns; neglect of personal appearance; depression, sadness, anger, or aggressiveness; alcohol or drug abuse; self-mutilation (for example, cutting oneself); isolation (withdrawing from family or friends); changes in social media behavior; loss of interest in activities/hobbies; trouble with school or work; and perfectionism or being overly self-critical. **Urgent danger signs** are hopelessness or helplessness; talking, writing, or hinting about suicide; showing signs of lethargy, apathy, or sadness; talking about feeling trapped, in unbearable pain, or being a burden to others; exhibiting extreme changes in behavior; putting affairs in order (for example, giving away possessions); experiencing an emotionally distressing relationship breakup; showing rage or talking about seeking revenge; exhibiting destructive behavior toward self or others; buying a gun or weapon or stockpiling drugs; or suddenly being happier and calmer—giving the impression that things have improved (www.mentalhealth.gov/what-to-look-for/suicidal-behavior). With any indication of suicidal tendencies in a student, teachers should act immediately by referring the student to a school counselor or school psychologist and following up with the professional in regard to the situation. By Texas Health and Safety Code § 161.325, school personnel must intervene effectively with students by providing notice and referral to a parent so appropriate action, such as seeking mental health or substance abuse services, may be taken by the parent. (Source: Mental Health America of Texas, 2015)

According to the National Institute on Drug Abuse (NIDA) (2014), adolescent substance abuse is a major public health problem. The following behaviors, when sudden, extreme, or lasting for an extended period, are **signs of alcohol or drug abuse:** unexplained changes in personality; loss of interest in once-favorite pastimes; loss of interest in family activities previously enjoyed; decline in school or work performance or attendance; chronic tardiness; skipping school; changes in friends and reluctance or unwillingness to discuss new friends; difficulty in paying attention; forgetfulness; noticeable mood swings; aggressive behavior; edginess, irritability, nervousness, or giddiness; hypersensitivity or temper tantrums; an "I don't care" attitude; deterioration of personal grooming habits; changes in eating or sleeping habits; unexplained weight loss or gain; red or watery eyes; shaking of the hands, feet, or legs; frequent nausea or vomiting; excessive sweating; slurred speech; dilated pupils; excessive need for privacy or secrecy; an unexplained need for money or even stealing money; or a heightened sensitivity to inquiry. **Signs of performance-enhancing drugs** (for example, anabolic steroids, ephedrine, or diuretics) include an unusual gain in muscle mass; aggressive behavior or rage; deeper voice (especially in females); severe acne; complaints of stomach pain or nausea; or signs of kidney, liver, or heart damage. Having a reasonable suspicion is sufficient cause for a teacher to initiate a private conversation with the student to discuss the specific behaviors the teacher has observed. If substance abuse is clearly a problem, the teacher should take immediate action by contacting a school counselor, school psychologist, school social worker, or other appropriate professional for assistance.

Teachers in Texas have a legal obligation to report all actual or suspected cases of child abuse or neglect to the Texas Department of Family and Protective Services or any local or state law enforcement agency within 48 hours. Teachers may not rely on another person or administrator within the school district to report suspected child abuse or neglect for them. They are not expected to, and should not, investigate the situation prior to making a report. The identity of the teacher making a report is kept confidential, and he or she is immune from liability unless the report is knowingly or intentionally false. Failure to report is a class A misdemeanor and can result in a fine and criminal prosecution (Texas Family Code § 261.101-009).

The following chart from *Recognizing Child Abuse and Neglect: Signs and Symptoms* (Child Welfare Information Gateway, 2007, available at www.childwelfare.gov/pubPDFs/signs.pdf) summarizes signs and symptoms of child abuse, physical abuse, neglect, sexual abuse, and emotional maltreatment or harm.

Signs and Symptoms of Child Abuse and Neglect

Type of Abuse	The Child	The Parent
Child abuse (general)	Shows sudden changes in behavior or school performance. Has not received help for physical or medical problems brought to the parents' attention. Has learning problems (or difficulty concentrating) that cannot be attributed to specific physical or psychological causes. Is always watchful, as though preparing for something bad to happen. Lacks adult supervision. Is overly compliant, passive, or withdrawn. Comes to school or other activities early, stays late, and does not want to go home. Is frequently absent from school.	Shows little concern for the child. Denies the existence of, or blames the child for, the child's problems in school or at home. Asks teachers or other caretakers to use harsh physical discipline if the child misbehaves. Sees the child as entirely bad, worthless, or burdensome. Demands a level of physical or academic performance the child cannot achieve. Looks primarily to the child for care, attention, and satisfaction of emotional needs.

Type of Abuse	The Child	The Parent
Physical abuse	Has unexplained welts, burns, bites, bruises, broken bones, or black eyes. Has repeated occurrences of injuries, even when explanations are offered. Has fading bruises or other marks noticeable after an absence from school. Seems frightened of the parents and protests or cries when it is time to go home. Shows extremes in behavior such as being passive-aggressive. Shrinks at the approach of adults. Reports injury by a parent or another adult caregiver.	Offers conflicting, unconvincing, or no explanation for the child's injury. Describes the child as "evil" or in some other very negative way. Uses harsh physical discipline with the child. Has a history of abuse as a child.
Neglect	Is frequently absent from school. Begs or steals food or money. Lacks needed medical or dental care, immunizations, or glasses. Has noticeable below-average body weight and height. Is consistently dirty and has severe body odor. Lacks sufficient clothing for the weather. Abuses alcohol or other drugs. States that there is no one at home to provide care.	Appears to be indifferent to the child. Seems apathetic or depressed. Behaves irrationally or in a bizarre manner. Is abusing alcohol or other drugs.
Sexual abuse	Has difficulty walking or sitting. Suddenly refuses to change for gym or to participate in physical activities. Reports nightmares or bed-wetting. Experiences a sudden change in appetite. Demonstrates bizarre, sophisticated, or unusual sexual knowledge or behavior. Becomes pregnant or contracts a venereal disease, particularly if under age 14. Writes about sexual abuse in notes, journals, or other written assignments. Runs away. Reports sexual abuse by a parent or another adult caregiver.	Is unduly protective of the child or severely limits the child's contact with other children, especially of the opposite sex. Is secretive and isolated. Is jealous or controlling with family members.

continued

Type of Abuse	The Child	The Parent
Emotional maltreatment/ harm	Shows extremes in behavior, such as overly compliant or demanding behavior, extreme passivity, or aggression. Is either inappropriately adult (parenting other children or younger siblings, for example) or inappropriately infantile (frequently rocking or head-banging, for example). Is delayed in physical or emotional development. Has poor self-concept. Has attempted suicide. Reports a lack of attachment to the parent.	Constantly blames, belittles, or berates the child. Is unconcerned about the child and refuses to consider offers of help for the child's problems. Overtly rejects the child.

Teachers should also be on the alert for eating disorders in young people. Eating disorders include **anorexia nervosa** (self-starvation, eating very little even to the point of death by starvation), **bulimia** (eating and then engaging in self-induced vomiting, taking laxatives, or over-exercising), and **binge eating** (frequent episodes of overeating). Eating disorders have both mental and physical consequences that can be difficult to overcome. Both male and female students can fall victim. Some researchers suggest that individuals restrict food intake as a way to gain a sense of control over some aspect of their lives, while those who overeat do so as a way to cope with stress and relieve anxiety. Compounding the problem is popular culture's seeming adulation of thinness, which reinforces a preoccupation with diet. Signs of eating disorders are losing or gaining weight in a short period of time, complaining of abdominal pain, full or bloated feeling, faintness, or dizziness; showing tiredness or fatigue; having dry skin or hair; having tooth decay; dieting or having irregular food habits; pretending to eat and then throwing away food; over-exercising; wearing baggy clothes; going to the bathroom frequently; complaining about appearance, particularly about being or feeling fat; expressing helplessness; showing sadness, depression, or moodiness; or being a perfectionist or overly self-critical. Having a concern is reason enough for a teacher to initiate a private conversation with the student to discuss the specific behaviors he or she has observed. If the student's health is clearly at high risk, the teacher should take immediate action by contacting a school counselor or school psychologist for assistance (U.S. Department of Health and Human Services, 2005).

Another growing health issue for children in the United States is obesity. **Obesity** means having an abnormally high proportion of body fat. Obesity increases the risk of high blood pressure, stroke, cardiovascular disease, gallbladder disease, diabetes, sleep apnea and respiratory problems, arthritis, cancer, and emotional problems such as depression and anxiety (www.cdc.gov/healthyweight/effects/index.html). Teachers can promote healthful eating habits in children by being positive role models of healthful living.

Teachers cannot supply everything their students need, but their professional advocacy is valuable to the students in their care. Teachers are in a unique position to detect behaviors or situations that pose threats to students' safety or health, so it is important for teachers to become familiar with the signs and symptoms of risky or harmful activities or conditions and act when necessary. In addition, teachers can model coping skills and healthful behaviors and be warm, caring, and supportive toward their students. For some students, a trusted teacher is a lifeline to a better existence.

Checkpoint

Fill in the blank.

1. Substance abuse is a major public _____ problem.
2. Teachers _____ (should, should not) investigate before making a child abuse report.
3. Over-exercising is a sign of a(n) _____ disorder.

Mark as True or False.

4. _____ The identity of the person making a child abuse report must be, by law, reported to the parents of the child.

5. _____ Only girls develop eating disorders.

Checkpoint Answers

1. health
2. should not
3. eating
4. False
5. False

Professional Conduct with Students Receiving Special Education Services

Working with students receiving special education services and their families in a way that meets the students' special needs and that follows legal requirements is an important part of the classroom teacher's role.

According to the Individuals with Disabilities Education Act (IDEA, 2004), a **child with a disability** means a child evaluated as having an intellectual disability, a hearing impairment (including deafness), a speech or language impairment, a visual impairment (including blindness), a serious emotional disturbance, an orthopedic impairment, autism, traumatic brain injury, another health impairment, a specific learning disability, deaf-blindness, or multiple disabilities, and who, by reason thereof, needs special education and related services. In addition, for a child ages 3 through 9, the term **child with a disability** may be (at the discretion of the state and the local educational agency and as measured by appropriate diagnostic instruments and procedures) a child who is experiencing developmental delays in one or more of the following areas: physical development, cognitive development, communication development, social or emotional development, or adaptive development, and who, for that reason, needs special education and related services. However, if a child has a lack of instruction in math or reading or has Limited English Proficiency, he or she must not be identified as being a child with a disability, if any one of these is the reason for determining the child has a disability. Under IDEA, each student identified as a child with a disability must have an **Individualized Education Program (IEP)** and an **ARD committee** in place (see "Collaborative Teams" in Chapter 12 for a discussion of IEPs and ARD committees).

IDEA requires that states provide a **free appropriate public education (FAPE),** which must include specially designed instruction and related services to children with disabilities, ages 3 through 21, in the **least restrictive environment (LRE)** that is appropriate for the student. In Texas, 19 TAC § 89.1001 sets forth the state law for special education services that parallels the federal law. Both federal and state laws indicate a preference for educating students with disabilities in the regular education classroom. The regular classroom should be the first placement option for special education services to be considered: Segregation of exceptional students shall occur only if the nature or severity of the exceptionality is such that education in regular classes with the use of supplementary aids and services cannot be achieved satisfactorily. This approach is in accord with the concept of inclusion.

Inclusion refers to the commitment to educate each child, to the maximum extent appropriate, in the regular education setting by bringing the support services to the child. It requires only that the child will benefit from being in regular education class, instead of having to keep up with other students. In the spirit of inclusion, it is important that students receiving special education services who are placed in regular education classrooms are an integral part of the class and participate to the greatest extent possible in all classroom activities. They should feel welcomed and accepted by the teacher and other students, and should not be made to feel singled out or stigmatized because of their disability. In general, they should not be isolated from their classmates, and they should be given frequent opportunities to interact and work closely with them.

IDEA provides well-defined procedural safeguards for parents of students receiving special education services. **Procedural safeguards** are the rights of parents and students relating to notice, consent, independent education evaluation, records, hearings, and appeals in accordance with federal and state laws. Procedural safeguards are needed to ensure that parents have the opportunity to be partners in the decision making regarding their child. Informed parental consent for both initial evaluation and reevaluation of a child is required. The school must send written notice of the purpose, time, and place of ARD meetings to the parents. Parents are full participants in ARD meetings, their input must be solicited during the evaluation process, and they are entitled to participate in making the decision regarding their child's educational placement. A parent may be accompanied to the ARD meeting by anyone the parent deems as having knowledge or special expertise regarding the student, including an attorney. If the parents are hearing impaired or have a home language other than English, the school must provide an interpreter at the meeting. Parents have the right to sign the IEP and to indicate on the document whether they agree or disagree with the decisions made by the team; they also have the right to challenge or appeal any decision related to the identification, evaluation, or educational placement of their child. Parents have the right to inspect and review any educational records relating to their child that the school collects, maintains, or uses. In addition, they have the right to inspect and review all educational records with respect to identification, evaluation, and educational placement of the child. Parents have the right to obtain an independent educational evaluation of their child at public expense if the parent disagrees with an evaluation obtained by the school.

In order for students receiving special education services to achieve their educational goals, teachers might need to adjust their instructional strategies, make changes in the learning environment, or make other accommodations. (See "Learning Environment Accommodations for Learners with Special Educational Needs" in Chapter 5 for discussion of this topic.) In addition, teachers should be knowledgeable of the procedural safeguards for parents of students receiving special education services to ensure that the teachers do not unknowingly violate the parents' rights or misinform them concerning their rights.

Checkpoint

Fill in the blank.

1. In Texas, special education services are provided to any student who is _____ as being a child with a disability.
2. IDEA requires that states provide a free appropriate public education to children with disabilities in the _____ restrictive environment.
3. Both federal and state laws indicate a preference for educating students with disabilities in the _____ education classroom.

Mark as True or False.

4. _____ Under IDEA, Limited English Proficiency can be the sole reason for classification of a student as a student with a disability.
5. _____ Procedural safeguards with regard to students receiving special education services in Texas are the rights of the students and their parents under federal and state laws.

Checkpoint Answers

1. identified
2. least
3. regular
4. False
5. True

Texas Statutes Relevant to Teachers

Following are key points of several statutes from the TEC and the TAC that are relevant to teachers:

Sec. 21.057. PARENTAL NOTIFICATION. A school district that assigns an inappropriately certified or uncertified teacher to the same classroom for more than 30 consecutive instructional days during the same school year shall provide written notice of the assignment to a parent or guardian of each student in that classroom.

Sec. 21.355. CONFIDENTIALITY. A document evaluating the performance of a teacher or administrator is confidential and is not subject to disclosure as public information.

Sec. 21.404. PLANNING AND PREPARATION TIME. Each classroom teacher is entitled to at least 450 minutes within each 2-week period for instructional preparation, including parent-teacher conferences, evaluating students' work, and planning. A planning and preparation period under this section may not be less than 45 minutes within the instructional day. During a planning and preparation period, a classroom teacher may not be required to participate in any other activity.

Sec. 21.405. DUTY-FREE LUNCH. Each classroom teacher or full-time librarian is entitled to at least a 30-minute lunch period free from all duties and responsibilities connected with the instruction and supervision of students. Each school district may set flexible or rotating schedules for each classroom teacher or full-time librarian in the district for the implementation of the duty-free lunch period.

Sec. 21.406. DENIAL OF COMPENSATION BASED ON ABSENCE FOR RELIGIOUS OBSERVANCE PROHIBITED. A school district may not deny an educator a salary bonus or similar compensation given in whole or in part on the basis of educator attendance because of the educator's absence from school for observance of a holy day observed by a religion whose places of worship are exempt from property taxation.

Sec. 21.407. REQUIRING OR COERCING TEACHERS TO JOIN GROUPS, CLUBS, COMMITTEES, OR ORGANIZATIONS: POLITICAL AFFAIRS. A school district board of trustees or school district employee may not directly or indirectly require or coerce any teacher to join any group, club, committee, organization, or association; and may not directly or indirectly coerce any teacher to refrain from participating in political affairs in the teacher's community, state, or nation.

Sec. 21.408. RIGHT TO JOIN OR NOT TO JOIN PROFESSIONAL ASSOCIATION. Chapter 21 of the TEC does not abridge the right of an educator to join any professional association or organization or refuse to join any professional association or organization.

Sec. 21.409. LEAVE OF ABSENCE FOR TEMPORARY DISABILITY. Each full-time educator employed by a school district shall be given a leave of absence for temporary disability at any time the educator's condition interferes with the performance of regular duties. The contract or employment of the educator may not be terminated by the school district while the educator is on a leave of absence for temporary disability. "Temporary disability" in this section includes the condition of pregnancy.

Sec. 21.414. CLASSROOM SUPPLY REIMBURSEMENT PROGRAM. The commissioner shall establish a reimbursement program under which the commissioner provides funds to a school district for the purpose of reimbursing classroom teachers in the district who expend personal funds on classroom supplies.

Sec. 25.081. DAYS OF INSTRUCTION. School districts must provide at least 180 days of instruction.

Sec. 25.901. PRAYER IN SCHOOL. Students have the right to pray in a nondisruptive manner.

Sec. 25.902. MOMENT OF SILENCE. A school district can allow for a period of silence at the beginning of the school day.

Sec. 37.0832. (a)(1) BULLYING: "Bullying" means a single significant act or a pattern of acts by one or more students directed at another student that exploits an imbalance of power and involves engaging in written or verbal expression, expression through electronic means, or physical conduct that has the effect or will have the effect of physically harming a student, damaging a student's property, or placing a student in reasonable fear of harm to the student's person or of damage to the student's property; is sufficiently severe, persistent, or pervasive enough that the action or threat creates an intimidating, threatening, or abusive educational environment for a student; materially and substantially disrupts the educational process or the orderly operation of a classroom or school; or infringes on the rights of the victim at school; and includes cyberbullying.

Sec. 247.1 (e)(9), TAC: GOOD MORAL CHARACTER: The virtues of a person as evidenced by patterns of personal, academic, and occupational behaviors that, in the judgment of the State Board for Educator Certification, indicate honesty, accountability, trustworthiness, reliability, and integrity.

Checkpoint

Fill in the blank.

1. A document evaluating the performance of a teacher or administrator is _____.
2. Bullying exploits an _____ of power.
3. By Texas law, good moral character includes honesty, accountability, _____, reliability, and integrity.

Mark as True or False.

4. _____ Each classroom teacher is entitled to a duty-free lunch.

Checkpoint Answers

1. confidential
2. imbalance
3. trustworthiness
4. True

Important Legislation and Court Cases

Historically, education has undergone a series of changes prompted by legislation and decisions in court cases. Following is a listing of important legislation and court cases at the state and federal levels that teachers should know:

West Virginia State Board of Education v. Barnette **(1943)**—prohibited schools from requiring that students participate in flag salutes or other patriotic ceremonies as a part of the school curriculum.

Brown v. Board of Education of Topeka **(1954)**—banned the practice of racial segregation in schools, striking down the notion of "separate but equal" schooling.

Engel v. Vitale **(1962)**—found that school-created prayer in school, even when students pray voluntarily, is unconstitutional.

Elementary and Secondary Education Act of 1965 (ESEA)—established the federal government's expanded role in public education.

Chapter 1 (formerly Title 1) of the Elementary and Secondary Education Act of 1965 (ESEA)—provided a comprehensive plan for addressing the inequality of educational opportunity for economically disadvantaged children.

Epperson v. Arkansas **(1968)**—found prohibition of teaching evolution to be unconstitutional.

Pickering v. Board of Education **(1968)**—provided that teachers have the right of free speech on matters of public concern.

Tinker v. Des Moines Independent Community School District **(1969)**—supported students' right to free expression, ruling that students "do not shed their constitutional rights . . . at the schoolhouse gate."

Title IX of the Education Amendments of 1972—prohibited sex discrimination in any public school; also, protected students (both male and female) from sexual harassment in all of a school's programs or activities, whether they take place at school, on the bus, or at a function sponsored by the school that takes place off-campus.

Section 504 of the Rehabilitation Act of 1973—prohibits schools (and other institutions receiving federal funds) from discriminating against students with disabilities.

Family Educational Rights and Privacy Act of 1974 (FERPA)—protects the privacy of student education records. Generally, schools must have written permission from the parent or eligible student in order to release any information from a student's education record. However, FERPA allows schools to disclose those records, without consent, to school officials with "legitimate educational interest" in the child. Parents or eligible students have the right to request that a school correct records that they believe to be inaccurate or misleading. If the school decides not to amend the record, the parent or eligible student then has the right to a formal hearing. After the hearing, if the school still decides not to amend the record, the parent or eligible student has the right to place a statement with the record setting forth his or her view about the contested information. *Note:* Divorced or noncustodial parents have the same rights as custodial parents with respect to their child's school records unless a state law, court order, or binding custody agreement declares otherwise.

PL 94-142 Education for All Handicapped Children Act (1975)—mandated that children with disabilities are entitled to a free appropriate public education in the least restrictive environment.

PL 94-553 Copyright Law (1976)—restricted copying of copyrighted material including text, audio, video, graphics, computer software, and so on; under **"fair use,"** teachers can do limited copying, but the amount needs to be brief and the use must not be long term.

Anderson v. Evans **(1981)**—limited teachers' free speech rights by indicating that "a balance must be struck between the interest of the employee as an individual and the public interest served by the employer."

Castañeda v. Pickard **(1981)**—established the **"Castañeda Test"** for programs that serve Limited English Proficient (LEP) students, which includes the following criteria: (1) Theory: The school must pursue a program based on sound educational theory or, at least, as a legitimate experimental strategy; (2) Practice: The school must actually implement the program in the manner necessary to transfer theory into reality; (3) Results: The school cannot continue a program that fails to produce positive results.

Plyler v. Doe **(1982)**—decided that a state's statute denying school enrollment to children of illegal immigrants "violates the Equal Protection Clause of the Fourteenth Amendment."

New Jersey v. T. L. O. **(1985)**—permitted a school to search students and their property without a search warrant if the school has a "reasonable suspicion" of wrongdoing.

Bethel School District v. Fraser **(1986)**—permitted schools to punish students for lewd/obscene speech.

Hazelwood School District v. Kuhlmeier **(1988)**—gave schools the right to censor student speech in circumstances where the speech is contrary to the schools' "basic educational mission."

Americans with Disabilities Act of 1990—prohibited discrimination against any person with disabilities.

Lee v. Weisman **(1992)**—prohibited clergy from offering prayer at public school ceremonies.

Individuals with Disabilities Education Act (IDEA, 1997 and 2004, formerly PL 94-142)—provided updated mandates regarding students with disabilities and the rights of their parents.

McKinney-Vento Homeless Assistance Act (reauthorized 2001, 2003)—required districts to provide access to a free and appropriate education for homeless children, prohibited the segregation of homeless students (specifically stating that "districts must ensure that homeless children are not segregated or stigmatized due to their homelessness"), and protected other rights of homeless children and their families (www.ed.gov/).

Every Student Succeeds Act (ESSA, 2015)—U.S. law that governs K-12 public education policy. Like its predecessor, the No Child Left Behind Act, ESSA is a reauthorization of the 1965 Elementary and Secondary Education Act.

Noteworthy amendments to the U.S. Constitution include the following:

- **Amendment I:** Requires separation of church and state.
- **Amendment IV:** Protects against unreasonable search and seizure.
- **Amendment X:** Puts the responsibility of education at the state and local levels by the failure of the U.S. Constitution to mention education as a duty of the federal government.
- **Amendment XIV:** Provides that no state shall deprive a person of life, liberty, or property without "due process" of law. The core element of due process is fairness and includes the right to a hearing, to be represented by legal counsel, to present evidence (including witnesses), to confront the accuser, to cross-examine witnesses and challenge evidence, to have a written transcript of the proceedings of a hearing, and to appeal an adverse ruling of a hearing to a higher legal authority.

Checkpoint

Fill in the blank.

1. By case law, schools cannot require that students participate in _____ salutes or other patriotic ceremonies as a part of the school curriculum.
2. By FERPA, divorced or noncustodial parents have the _____ rights as custodial parents with respect to their child's school records.
3. The McKinney-Vento Homeless Assistance Act states that districts must ensure that homeless children are not segregated or _____.

Mark as True or False.

4. _____ By case law, teachers lose the right to make public statements of any kind when they become employed by a school district.
5. _____ By case law, teachers in Texas are held to a high moral standard.

Checkpoint Answers

1. flag
2. same
3. stigmatized
4. False
5. True

Summary

To promote and govern professional behavior of teachers in Texas, the state has adopted a Code of Ethics and Standard Practices for Texas Educators. This code addresses professional attitudes and concerns and ethical conduct toward the profession of education, professional colleagues, and students. Any teacher who is charged with and found guilty of violating any part of the code is subject to having his or her teaching certificate revoked or suspended.

Domain IV Sample Questions and Answer Explanations

Sample Questions

1. Teachers in Texas are expected to maintain positive home-school relationships. Which of the following would NOT be an appropriate way to work with families?

   A. inviting parents to visit their children's classrooms
   B. making sure that the parents know when their children are doing better than other students
   C. providing information and ideas to families about how to help their children at home with homework
   D. recruiting parents to serve as volunteers in the school

2. By Texas law, which of the following is a mandated topic for staff development training?

   A. discipline strategies
   B. conflict resolution
   C. suicide prevention
   D. digital learning

3. Of the following, which is most important as a reason for a teacher to engage in staff development?

   A. to satisfy recertification requirements
   B. to avoid being placed on professional probation
   C. to have opportunities to interact with other professionals
   D. to improve education in the district

4. Which of the following would constitute a violation of the Code of Ethics and Standard Practices for Texas Educators?

   A. A teacher writes nonspecific praise comments (for example, "Good job!") on students' papers.
   B. A teacher encourages students to consider views opposite the teacher's own views.
   C. A teacher intentionally embarrasses a student about the student's behavior.
   D. A teacher makes an unintentional error when grading a unit test.

5. Which of the following is NOT acceptable use of school property by a teacher?

   A. using a school computer to create worksheets for after-school tutorials
   B. using a school copier to make invitations to a surprise celebration for the principal
   C. using a school fax machine to fax copies of assignments to a parent
   D. using a school e-mail account to send a copy of a lesson plan to a colleague

6. Students in a social studies class have been researching the history of the U.S. flag and the Pledge of Allegiance. One student comments, "My father said that the school can't make us say the Pledge of Allegiance if we don't want to." The student's parent is

   A. correct, based on a Supreme Court decision stating that no student can be compelled to salute the flag.
   B. correct, because the student is protected under the Family Rights and Privacy Act.
   C. incorrect, because the school may require all students to salute the flag.
   D. incorrect, because, by refusing, the student would be disrupting the educational process at school.

Answer Explanations

1. **B.** Eliminate choices A, C, and D because these actions are appropriate ways to work with parents. Choice B is the correct response. Informing parents about other students' progress would be unprofessional and inappropriate.

2. **C.** Of the choices given, only suicide prevention (choice C) is a mandated topic for staff development.

3. **D.** Eliminate choice B because this response is an unprofessional reason for engaging in staff development. Choice C is a reason that a teacher might want to engage in staff development, but it is not an important reason. Choice A is an important reason for a teacher to engage in staff development, but it is not the most important reason. According to Texas law, teachers should engage in staff development to improve education in the district. Thus, choice D is the correct response.

4. **C.** Eliminate choice A because even though teachers should use specific praise comments, it is not a violation of the Code of Ethics and Standard Practices for Texas Educators for a teacher to use nonspecific praise comments. Eliminate choice B because this behavior is consistent with the Code of Ethics and Standard Practices for Texas Educators. Eliminate choice D because the teacher made the error unintentionally. Teachers should know that embarrassing students is not acceptable professional conduct. Thus, choice C is the correct response.

5. **B.** Eliminate choices A, C, and D because these uses of school property are acceptable. Using a school copier to make invitations for a celebration that is not an *official* school function falls under personal use of school property, so it is unacceptable. Thus, choice B is the correct response.

6. **A.** This question takes up the issue of a student's right to refuse to salute the flag. The Supreme Court has ruled that no student may be required to take part in a flag salute ceremony as a condition of attendance, making choice A the correct response. Choice B correctly says that the student has the right to refuse to salute the flag, but gives the wrong reason; the Family Rights and Privacy Act of 1974 does not apply to this situation. Eliminate choices C and D because these responses directly contradict the Supreme Court decision. Furthermore, in regard to choice D, no evidence in the question stem indicates that a student's refusal to say the Pledge will be disruptive. Teachers should handle such situations carefully and professionally, so that disruptions do not occur.

PART 5

TWO FULL-LENGTH MODEL PRACTICE TESTS WITH ANSWER EXPLANATIONS

- Practice Test 1
- Practice Test 2

Chapter 14

Practice Test 1

4 Hours and 45 Minutes
100 Questions

Directions: Read each item and select the best response.

---

1. A social studies teacher asks the students in the class how they could use the word HOMES to help them remember the names of the Great Lakes: Huron, Ontario, Michigan, Erie, and Superior. The students quickly recognize that the first letters of the names of the lakes can be arranged to spell HOMES. This approach to memorizing information best exemplifies using

   A. an acronym.
   B. chunking.
   C. rehearsal.
   D. rote.

2. As part of a unit focusing on health-related physical activities, a middle-grades physical education teacher plans to have students keep a reflective journal, in which they will write about how they felt, mentally and physically, after each activity. Having students keep a journal in a physical education class is best described as

   A. cross-curricular.
   B. intradisciplinary.
   C. criterion-referenced.
   D. norm-referenced.

3. Which of the following actions should the teacher take at the end of a computer simulation activity to promote students' evaluation-level thinking?

   A. Give a short quiz over the vocabulary encountered during the simulation activity.
   B. Have a whole-class discussion in which students are asked to tell why they did or did not like the simulation activity.
   C. Have students write a paragraph explaining how they participated in the simulation activity.
   D. Have students work in groups to make a list of concepts they learned from the simulation activity.

4. Students in a fourth-grade class are making drawings to illustrate their writing projects. The teacher observes a few students who are artistically talented making rude comments about the drawings of their classmates who are less artistically inclined. The teacher immediately lets the rude students know that such behavior will not be tolerated. The best follow-up response from the teacher to this situation is to

   A. allow students the option of downloading free clip art from the Internet to illustrate their writing projects.
   B. assign the rude students to work one-on-one with their classmates who are less artistically inclined to help them create better drawings.
   C. have students who make rude comments stay after class and talk with them about respecting others.
   D. hold a class meeting to establish consequences for rude behavior and enforce the consequences consistently.

5. A teacher is concerned about appropriate assessment of content-area learning for students in the class who have histories of limited academic success. To ensure fair and accurate assessment of these students, it would be most appropriate for the teacher to

   A. develop separate, more lenient criteria for assessing their progress.
   B. modify their assignments to reflect less-challenging expectations.
   C. use a variety of formal and informal assessment measures, such as observations, interviews, test scores, and samples of daily work.
   D. rely mainly on the use of students' self-assessment procedures in assessing their acquisition of knowledge and skills.

217

6. After giving an assignment, a teacher notices that a student, Carl, is frowning. The teacher walks over to Carl's desk and the following exchange occurs:

   Teacher: Do you have a question about the assignment?

   Carl: This is a stupid assignment.

   Teacher: You sound upset. Would you like to talk about it?

   In her interaction with Carl, which of the following elements of effective communication did the teacher exhibit?

   A. being sensitive to nonverbal cues and paraphrasing
   B. being sensitive to nonverbal cues and being a reflective listener
   C. being a thoughtful questioner and paraphrasing
   D. redirecting and paraphrasing

7. A high school calculus teacher decides to attend a workshop on a sophisticated mathematical software program at a state conference. The teacher's probable purpose for attending the workshop is to

   A. be a risk-taker and innovator.
   B. participate in collaborative decision making.
   C. demonstrate that the teacher has clearly defined goals.
   D. enhance the teacher's own professional knowledge and skills.

8. An interdisciplinary team of middle school teachers wants to develop lessons that promote students' higher-order thinking skills. Which of the following is most likely to promote the higher-order thinking skills of middle school students?

   A. in math, filling in the missing components of a pattern
   B. in social studies, creating a timeline showing significant events of a historical period
   C. in science, graphing data from an experiment
   D. in language arts, memorizing a favorite poem

9. A first-year third-grade teacher has received her class roster for the upcoming school year. She notes that the 19 students in her class are culturally diverse and that two students are receiving special education services—one is visually impaired, and the other has mild hearing loss. In planning her classroom layout, it is most important for the teacher to consider the

   A. materials and resources available in her classroom.
   B. availability of assistive technology equipment in the school.
   C. potential discipline problems she might encounter with such a varied group of students.
   D. instructional approaches she is planning to use in her classroom.

10. Ms. Hall, a middle school teacher, overhears two students, Jimmy and Curtis, talking about drugs. The teacher confronts the students to discuss what she heard. Following is an excerpt from their discussion:

    Ms. Hall: Jimmy, I want to talk to you about what you said to Curtis about needing some drugs.

    Jimmy: Ms. Hall, you got it all wrong. I was just kiddin' around. I don't do drugs.

    Curtis: That's right, Ms. Hall. Jimmy don't mess with drugs.

    Ms. Hall: I'm not so sure. Some of your other teachers have told me that your grades have dropped a lot since school started, Jimmy. I know for a fact that you are failing math and English!

    Jimmy: Well, I'm not doing real good in school right now, but it's not because of drugs. You gotta believe me, Ms. Hall!

    Ms. Hall: Well, you two go on to your next class. I'll talk to you about this later.

    When Ms. Hall discussed Jimmy's grades in front of Curtis, her actions were

    A. unacceptable, because the suspected drug abuse was a more important issue.
    B. unacceptable, because she revealed confidential information about Jimmy.
    C. acceptable, because Jimmy's behavior will likely change as a result.
    D. acceptable, because peer pressure from Curtis toward Jimmy to do better will likely result.

11. After a project-based learning activity in science, the teacher asks students to determine whether the activity was successful and to reflect on their roles and participation. Which of the following is a benefit of having students do this assignment?

   A. It will allow the teacher to assess students' mastery of the objective for the activity.
   B. It will promote self-reflection and self-assessment on the part of the student.
   C. It will promote a healthy, competitive spirit among students.
   D. It will allow the teacher to identify those students who exhibited leadership skills.

Read the information below to answer questions 12–13.

   A social studies teacher uses a real-life controversy in a nearby town over whether a large oil company should be permitted to drill on the site of a historic landmark as the basis for a lesson. The students spend one class period in assigned groups researching the issue using the Internet. The next day, the teacher begins the lesson with a whole-class discussion, followed by having the students form teams to debate the issue.

12. To begin the whole-class discussion, the teacher poses the following question to the class: "Should preservation of historic landmarks stand in the way of economic development?" The teacher's question is probably posed for the purpose of

   A. encouraging students to recall factual information.
   B. providing students with clues to the teacher's personal opinion about the controversy.
   C. checking students' understanding of the nature of the controversy.
   D. providing a framework for engaging students in critical thinking about the controversy.

13. The teacher's main purpose for having the class debate is to

   A. provide a means for students to practice public speaking skills.
   B. give students an opportunity to engage in collaborative problem solving.
   C. engage students in higher-order thinking in an authentic context.
   D. minimize the negative effects of historical controversies on student performance.

14. The computer science teacher volunteers to conduct a professional learning workshop for the other teachers at school on using a popular spreadsheet software program. Conducting the workshop best illustrates that the teacher knows how to

   A. use technology to enhance the mission of the school.
   B. actively share ideas with colleagues to contribute to a successful learning community.
   C. use community resources to promote professional growth.
   D. use group processes to make decisions and solve problems.

15. A science teacher observes that most of her students seem to think of scientists as men. Which of the following would be the most effective way for the teacher to counter gender stereotyping?

   A. Have the students do research papers on female scientists.
   B. Show a video about famous female scientists.
   C. Have a day in which the class learns about and celebrates women in science.
   D. Invite a variety of male and female guests who have science-related careers to visit the class throughout the year.

16. Parents of a student ask Mr. Mann, their child's teacher, to show them their child's grades and also the grades of the child's classmates. Which of the following actions would be appropriate for Mr. Mann to take in response to the parents' request?

   A. Tell the parents that he cannot legally show them other students' grades.
   B. Show the parents the grades of the other students, but caution that they must keep them confidential.
   C. Explain to the parents that there is no point in their seeing the grades because teachers have the sole right to assign grades.
   D. Tell the parents that their request must go through the principal's office first.

Read the information below to answer questions 17–18.

A second-grade teacher has an English language learner (ELL), who is at the beginning level of English language proficiency, in her classroom. The teacher is beginning a unit on the life cycle of the butterfly. For the first lesson, the teacher plans to show an educational video about the life cycle of the butterfly. The teacher knows the English language proficiency standards (ELPS) in the domains of listening, speaking, reading, and writing in accordance with the proficiency-level descriptors and is aware of her responsibility to use her knowledge of the ELPS to support the ELL's comprehension of academic content.

17. Based on the ELPS, an effective strategy for promoting the ELL's comprehension of the content of the unit is to

    A. have the ELL pre-read about butterflies at home.
    B. preteach the unit vocabulary to the whole class using visuals and gestures.
    C. have the ELL explain in simple words what he already knows about butterflies.
    D. administer a multiple-choice pretest about the butterfly life cycle to the ELL.

18. Based on the ELPS, an appropriate activity for the ELL after viewing the video would be to

    A. draw and label a diagram of the life cycle of the butterfly.
    B. write a brief description of the butterfly life cycle in a journal.
    C. put together a hardboard puzzle that depicts the four parts of the butterfly life cycle.
    D. copy definitions of key words from the video into a journal.

19. At midyear, a high school teacher asks the students to respond to the following three prompts:

    What I like best about this class

    What I like least about this class

    What I would change to make this class better

    This type of assessment is called a

    A. criterion-referenced assessment.
    B. formative assessment.
    C. needs assessment.
    D. norm-referenced assessment.

20. Students in a second-grade class have finished reading a version of the classic tale "Jack and the Beanstalk." The story is about a boy named Jack who climbs a beanstalk and meets an unfriendly giant. At the end of the story, Jack deposes the giant. Which of the following questions about the story would likely be most effective for evoking students' creative thinking skills?

    A. Why did Jack climb the beanstalk?
    B. Why do you think Jack kept returning to the giant's castle even though he was scared of the giant?
    C. What did Jack do that made his mother angry?
    D. What would have happened if the giant and Jack had become good friends?

21. To promote all students' understanding and appreciation of diversity, it would be most beneficial for a teacher to

    A. decorate the classroom with students' drawings based on readings of stories from students' home cultures.
    B. make a presentation about the holiday traditions of people from a variety of cultures.
    C. teach students numbers and other vocabulary from a variety of languages spoken in the community.
    D. invite visitors from the different cultural backgrounds represented in the class to facilitate and participate in a variety of activities.

22. Before students begin a reading assignment on the hydrologic cycle, a seventh-grade science teacher could best prepare students to understand the reading assignment by

    A. giving the students articles about the hydrologic cycle to scan through.
    B. explicitly teaching the technical vocabulary the students will encounter in the reading assignment.
    C. reminding the students to read the assignment slowly and carefully.
    D. encouraging students to look up unfamiliar words in a dictionary as they do the reading assignment.

23. To obtain detailed information about a high school student's strengths and weaknesses in a subject area, which of the following types of assessment would be best to use?

    A. diagnostic
    B. outcome measure
    C. formative
    D. summative

24. Ms. Carter, a first-year teacher, is having trouble dealing with a student who is very disruptive in her class. Ms. Carter wants to ask a colleague for advice about what she should do to discourage the student's misbehavior, but she is reluctant to discuss the problem when the opportunity arises. The most likely basis for Ms. Carter's reluctance to ask for assistance from her colleague is that she believes that

    A. she will be perceived as ill-prepared or incompetent.
    B. the best way to learn is to work through problems by herself.
    C. experienced teachers do not have time to give beginning teachers assistance after school starts.
    D. most strategies used by experienced teachers are too difficult for a beginning teacher to use.

25. In keeping with a desire to foster higher-order thinking and enhance problem-solving skills, which of the following strategies would be LEAST desirable for algebra teachers to use?

    A. Establish highly managed classroom environment that focuses on procedural knowledge.
    B. Encourage students to take time to think before deciding on a solution strategy when they are initially given a word problem.
    C. Spend more class time on problems requiring analytical skills than on basic algebraic manipulation problems.
    D. Provide opportunities for students to correct their errors rather than expecting them to rely on the teacher to determine whether their work is mathematically correct.

26. Which of the following practices would best promote social harmony among diverse students in a middle school social studies class?

    A. Avoid discussing racial or ethnic relations with the class.
    B. Use competitive games and contests.
    C. Display artifacts in the classroom that reflect students' varied cultural backgrounds.
    D. Encourage students to share ideas relevant to their cultural backgrounds during class discussions.

27. Ms. Alford is a veteran teacher with 20 years' experience. After school one day, she walks across the hall to Mr. Pennywell's room and criticizes him for allowing his students to play a game in class. Mr. Pennywell does not want to be argumentative with Ms. Alford, so he explains calmly and politely why he feels the game was a worthwhile activity for his students. The next day, the principal tells Mr. Pennywell that Ms. Alford has complained to the principal that Mr. Pennywell used profanity toward her and behaved unprofessionally during their conversation the day before. According to the Code of Ethics and Standard Practices for Texas Educators, Ms. Alford's behavior is unethical because a teacher should NOT

    A. use coercive means to influence professional decisions of colleagues.
    B. subject a colleague to sexual harassment.
    C. interfere with a colleague's exercise of citizenship rights and responsibilities.
    D. knowingly make false statements about a colleague.

28. The primary purpose of a teacher's reflective journal is to

    A. apply research to implementing effective instruction and assessment.
    B. facilitate an internal dialogue about the teacher's experiences and feelings related to teaching.
    C. provide a means to record and reflect on the teacher's own experiences of being a student.
    D. put down in writing a description of what happened during a particular lesson.

29. To improve participation in and the quality of whole-class discussions, a teacher should

　A. use *who, what, where,* and *when* questions only.
　B. recognize only those students with hands raised.
　C. ask more knowledge-level and comprehension questions.
　D. ask the question before calling on a student by name.

30. A sixth-grade social studies teacher designs a unit test, being careful to ensure that the test is aligned with the instructional content that was addressed in class and is at an appropriate level of difficulty. Upon administering and grading the test, the teacher finds that each of the students earned a score of 90 percent or better. When reflecting on these test results, the most appropriate conclusion for the teacher to draw about her teaching practices is that she

　A. needs to move at an accelerated pace of instruction for the next unit.
　B. made the test too easy and, thus, failed to differentiate adequately among the students.
　C. is an effective teacher because the students have mastered the unit content.
　D. is targeting instruction at a level that is too low for the students in the class.

31. With regard to gender differences, a teacher should plan to

　A. make allowances for gender differences by giving students freedom to pursue their own interests.
　B. use more masculine-oriented modeling to increase female students' assertiveness.
　C. treat male and female students similarly whenever appropriate.
　D. have more activities where boys and girls are grouped separately.

32. At the beginning of the second quarter of the year, a school's fourth-grade students are administered a benchmark assessment in writing. A fourth-grade teacher examines the results of the school-wide assessment and determines that two students in her class performed slightly below grade level in writing. To collect additional data for developing effective interventions, the teacher should

　A. analyze writing samples in the students' language arts portfolios for an initial time period.
　B. ask the counselor to review the assessment data with the teacher.
　C. assign peer tutors to each of the two students.
　D. monitor the students' engagement during in-class writing assignments.

Read the information below to answer questions 33–34.

　A third-grade teacher has his students silently read the following paragraph about Kendra, a young girl who moves from Texas to a new state:

> Kendra woke up early. She could hear her parents talking downstairs in the kitchen. Quickly, she began to get dressed. She wanted to explore her new neighborhood. She put on jeans, a sweater, and a coat. Then she looked for her gloves and wool scarf. She was glad her mom had taken her shopping yesterday to buy the gloves and scarf. Kendra knew she would need them often in this new place.

33. Which of the following is a convergent question about the passage?

　A. Why did Kendra's family move from Texas?
　B. Where were Kendra's parents when she woke up?
　C. What is Kendra's new neighborhood like?
　D. What state did Kendra's parents move to?

34. Which of the following is a divergent question about the passage?

　A. Why did Kendra's family move from Texas?
　B. Where were Kendra's parents when she woke up?
　C. What did Kendra wear when she got dressed?
　D. Was Kendra pleased that her mom had bought her gloves and a scarf?

35. Which of the following would NOT be an effective way to communicate high expectations to at-risk students?

   A. accepting and praising all work
   B. supporting their efforts to give oral responses
   C. allowing sufficient wait time for student responses to questions
   D. expressing expectations clearly and directly

36. When teachers challenge students to reason from basic assumptions to reach a logical conclusion, they are most likely promoting students' use of

   A. creative thinking.
   B. deductive reasoning.
   C. imaginative thinking.
   D. inductive reasoning.

37. A high school teacher is creating a lesson plan in which students will investigate their own learning styles. Learning style experts generally agree that learning style is

   A. an indication of one's intelligence.
   B. fixed and unchangeable for a particular individual.
   C. different from person to person.
   D. strictly a result of biological factors.

38. A school district wants to develop a benchmark test to see how well students are progressing toward the academic goals of the district. What type of test would be best for this purpose?

   A. aptitude
   B. criterion-referenced
   C. norm-referenced
   D. psychomotor

39. A teacher asks a question, calls on Sabrina to respond, and then waits patiently for Sabrina's answer even though Sabrina is one of the lower-achieving students. When Sabrina does not respond, the teacher rephrases the question and then continues to wait. How would you evaluate this teacher's approach to Sabrina at this point?

   A. ineffective, because it places Sabrina and the teacher in a power struggle
   B. ineffective, because it communicates a negative impression about Sabrina to the class
   C. effective, because it communicates positive expectations to Sabrina
   D. effective, because it establishes the teacher's authority in the classroom

40. A high school Algebra 1 teacher gives students the following task:

> Use what you know about adding two fractions in arithmetic to write out a plan for adding two algebraic fractions.

In giving the students this task, the teacher is most likely promoting students' use of

   A. creativity.
   B. discrimination.
   C. generalization.
   D. overlearning.

41. A language arts teacher is planning to implement a more culturally diverse approach to the study of literature in her class. An effective first step to enhance teaching by appreciating cultural diversity is for the teacher to

   A. persuade the principal to hold a campus-wide diversity awareness week.
   B. spend some time in self-reflection to examine her own attitudes and beliefs about cultural groups.
   C. examine the books she is currently using for bias or stereotyping of cultural groups.
   D. use literature that depicts main characters striving to develop bicultural identities.

42. Which of the following assessment methods is considered an authentic way to assess kindergarteners' learning in learning centers?

    A. informal teacher observation
    B. multiple-choice testing
    C. peer assessment
    D. standardized assessment

43. A teacher notices that Morgaan, one of his high-achieving students, is very inattentive in class. When he has a chance to talk with Morgaan privately, she begins to tell him about a problem she is having with a group of girls that whisper and giggle among themselves when they are around her. To encourage Morgaan to continue telling him about the situation, the teacher should

    A. immediately advise Morgaan that she needs to stand up to the rude girls.
    B. listen with a concerned look and limit interruptions.
    C. empathize with Morgaan by telling her about experiences he had with rude students when he was in school.
    D. try not to maintain eye contact with Morgaan because it might make her feel uncomfortable.

44. A social studies teacher assigns students to read an overview of the three branches of government and their functions. Next, the teacher displays the following transparency on the overhead projector:

    > BALANCE OF POWER
    >
    > Explain in your own words what you think this term means.

    This activity will benefit students most by

    A. accommodating their various learning styles.
    B. involving them in thinking about topics that are important to them.
    C. encouraging them to memorize key terminology.
    D. engaging them in higher-order thinking.

45. A history teacher is concerned about her students' low grades. She feels the low grades are mainly due to the students' lack of interest and enthusiasm in history class. Which of the following measures related to assessment would be best for motivating students to earn better grades in history?

    A. reducing the number of tests, quizzes, and homework assignments given
    B. including comments related to improvement in reports to students and parents
    C. giving feedback several weeks after administering a test
    D. using a lower standard for grading

46. In high school, students should be given homework primarily to

    A. improve their academic achievement.
    B. help them develop good study habits.
    C. foster in them positive attitudes toward school.
    D. enhance their self-discipline.

47. Students in a high school world geography class are learning about interrelationships between people and their environment. On an outside tour around their school, the students are dismayed about how much trash they see. When they return to class, a discussion about trash disposal ensues. "Is there going to be room for us with all this trash in the world?" asks Maria. The teacher responds to the whole class, "What do you think about Maria's concern?" This question to the whole class in response to Maria's question is an example of

    A. using a student's contribution to make a point.
    B. paraphrasing a student's contribution.
    C. using a student's contribution as an example.
    D. using a student's contribution to stimulate additional discussion.

48. A second-grade teacher is using a computer simulation activity to help students learn social studies concepts. A major advantage of using a computer simulation activity in social studies is that it

   A. provides an efficient means for recording and analyzing data.
   B. enhances students' mapping skills.
   C. allows students to make decisions in a safe environment.
   D. promotes low-achieving students' mastery of basic skills.

49. Ms. Curl, a new third-grade teacher, is enthusiastic about her first year. She looks forward to meeting her students and has many plans for them. The first day of class, Ms. Curl introduces herself and shares with the students some of her ideas for the classroom. As a new teacher, Ms. Curl needs to be aware of which of the following?

   A. During the first few days of school, teachers need to teach students specific procedures for how to move from group to group, how to ask for help, how to obtain needed materials, and so forth.
   B. To avoid problems later on in the year, teachers need to establish a disciplined climate in their classrooms by using frequent timeouts during the first few days of school.
   C. During the first few days of school, classroom management will be easier if the teacher works with individual students to explain classroom rules and procedures.
   D. Early on, teachers need to establish a warm and caring environment by ignoring misbehavior unless it disrupts the flow of the lesson.

50. A high school English teacher has observed a difference in the achievement of students of low socioeconomic backgrounds and that of middle-class students in her class. The teacher's observation is related to the finding of studies that show that students from low socioeconomic backgrounds usually

   A. do better in school than children from middle-class backgrounds.
   B. do about as well as children from middle-class backgrounds.
   C. do more poorly in school than children from middle-class backgrounds.
   D. enter school behind children from middle-class backgrounds but eventually close the gap in high school.

51. During a class discussion, a teacher calls only on students who raise their hands to respond. This teacher's method of recognizing students for responses is

   A. positive, because it avoids having to call on shy students who do not know the answer and might be embarrassed in front of the whole class.
   B. positive, because it is more effective than calling on students using a random process.
   C. limited, because students who don't volunteer might miss an opportunity to be actively engaged in the lesson.
   D. positive, because volunteers give a higher proportion of correct responses from which all might benefit.

52. A teacher is excited about implementing cooperative learning strategies in his classroom during the school year and is busy planning group activities that he can use with his students. Which of the following is an essential feature of cooperative learning?

   A. Using cooperative learning activities frees the teacher from monitoring student work.
   B. When using cooperative learning activities, students' rewards should be interdependently determined.
   C. Cooperative learning activities free the teacher from having to use strict grading policies.
   D. When using cooperative learning, group size should not be predetermined.

53. Students in a high school chemistry class are learning to prepare solutions of acids. Which of the following methods is the most appropriate way for the teacher to assess the students' understanding of this procedure?

   A. Use an observational checklist.
   B. Give a short quiz.
   C. Have students complete a worksheet.
   D. Have the students prepare a lab report.

54. A first-year middle-grades English teacher is trying to teach her students creative writing, but she is disappointed and frustrated when most of the students' papers are dull and uninteresting. The teacher seeks out an experienced colleague and asks for advice on how to motivate the students to write better papers. The first-year teacher's decision to consult an experienced colleague is most consistent with which of the following principles?

   A. Teachers understand the importance of creating and sustaining an efficient and supportive learning environment.
   B. Teachers benefit from working in groups to solve problems.
   C. Teachers should take advantage of opportunities for job-embedded professional development.
   D. Teachers should show the ability to articulate their own professional judgment to colleagues.

55. A third-grade teacher wants her students to learn how a hot air balloon works. Which of the following technologies would be most appropriate for this purpose?

   A. computer simulation
   B. presentation software slide show
   C. spreadsheet
   D. video

56. In regular education classrooms, academic tasks that are assigned as independent classwork or homework are typically based on

   A. low context and low cognitive demand.
   B. low context and high cognitive demand.
   C. high context and low cognitive demand.
   D. high context and high cognitive demand.

57. A third-grade teacher posts the following classroom rules:

CLASS RULES
Rule 1. Be respectful of others.
Rule 2. Work quietly.
Rule 3. Do not run indoors.
Rule 4. Complete your work.

   Which rule should be restated in a more appropriate format?

   A. Rule 1
   B. Rule 2
   C. Rule 3
   D. Rule 4

58. "Given five right triangles, each with the measure of one side missing, the students will be able to use the Pythagorean theorem to solve for the measure of the missing side in four out of five of the right triangles with no errors." This statement is an example of a(n)

   A. affective objective.
   B. cognitive objective.
   C. psychomotor objective.
   D. reflective objective.

59. As the regular education teacher of a student with a disability, a new teacher will be serving on the Admission, Review, and Dismissal (ARD) committee for the student. The teacher is aware that the student is participating in the regular education environment because this placement meets the criterion of "least restrictive environment" for the student. With regard to students with disabilities, *least restrictive environment* means that

   A. instruction to students with disabilities should be provided in the regular education classroom to the maximum extent appropriate.
   B. special education teachers should have the full responsibility for tailoring the school environment to a student's needs.
   C. a student's classroom environment should be appropriate to his or her level of disability.
   D. students with disabilities should be instructed off-campus by certified special education teachers.

60. A high school speech teacher has students conduct peer assessments of students' performances. The teacher's main purpose for using peer assessments is to

A. encourage students to explore new techniques.
B. decrease the teacher's workload and grading time.
C. allow students to deepen their understanding of the concepts.
D. provide a record of student progress over time for future reflection.

61. A student is beginning to exhibit a pattern of habitual tardiness to a high school physical education class. Which of the following should the teacher do first to address this problem?

A. Deduct points from the student's grade.
B. Give the student extra written work to complete outside of class.
C. Privately discuss the problem with the student.
D. Draw the class's attention to the student when the student arrives late.

62. Which of the following activities would be most effective in helping a teacher's English language learners (ELLs) develop awareness of differences in register?

A. having the students model verbal and nonverbal cues
B. having students practice interpreting idiomatic expressions
C. having the students role-play specific situations, such as discussing a community concern first with a classmate and then with the mayor of the city
D. having students role-play speaking in different dialects with a partner

63. A middle-grades language arts teacher encourages her students to write on topics they are interested in or care about. Which of the following is the teacher using to enhance motivation?

A. intrinsic motivation
B. negative reinforcement
C. positive reinforcement
D. reverse psychology

64. A first-year middle school teacher has a class composed of students of diverse academic ability levels. Which of the following best reflects current research regarding grouping practices for teacher instruction of the students?

A. using a combination of whole-group instruction and small-group differentiated instruction
B. using small-group instruction of high achievers and mixed-ability group instruction for the other students in the class
C. using only whole-group grade-level instruction
D. using permanently identified ability groups for instruction of all students

65. A second-grade teacher has a conference with parents whose child has been consistently off-task in the teacher's class since the beginning of the year. The teacher and parents agree that weekly updates from the teacher to the parents about the child's behavior are warranted. Of the following actions, the most appropriate way for the teacher to keep the parents informed about their child's behavior is to update the parents by

A. sending them weekly text messages.
B. creating a notebook that the child will carry home each week and bring back the following week.
C. arranging a regular time to call each week.
D. meeting with one or both parents after school once a week.

66. A teacher responds to student work that is good or that shows improvement by writing comments such as "Good job!" "Terrific!" and "Nice work!" on the students' papers. This teacher's praise would be more effective if the teacher

A. communicated the praise orally, rather than in writing.
B. specified additional areas for improvement along with the praise.
C. specifically stated what the students have done that is praiseworthy.
D. used one particular word or phrase consistently from student to student to communicate praise.

67. For a social studies unit on government, a teacher designs lesson plans around the theme of "civic ideas and practices." The teacher's idea to use a thematic approach to the unit best demonstrates that the teacher understands the importance of

- A. helping students to understand relationships within a discipline.
- B. selecting developmentally appropriate instructional strategies.
- C. nurturing a sense of community in the classroom.
- D. enhancing students' ability to apply knowledge in various contexts.

68. A fifth-grade teacher decides to hold a class meeting to address her concerns that students in the class are disruptive and unmotivated. The teacher's decision to hold a class meeting illustrates her understanding that she

- A. is a member of a learning community and knows how to work effectively with all members of that community.
- B. should promote student ownership in a smoothly functioning learning community.
- C. must communicate high expectations for student learning to create a climate of trust in the classroom.
- D. must help students become self-motivated.

69. An eighth-grade science teacher, who is using innovative teaching methods, is concerned that her students might have difficulty on the Texas statewide assessment test in science because she is not "teaching to the test." The teacher could best address this concern by

- A. setting aside part of the class period each day for explicit instruction in statewide assessment test-taking strategies.
- B. making sure that the Texas Essential Knowledge and Skills for eighth-grade science are included in her curriculum.
- C. including more drill and practice lessons over the Texas Essential Knowledge and Skills for eighth-grade science benchmarks.
- D. making sure that the students always use their textbooks, which are correlated to the Texas Essential Knowledge and Skills for eighth-grade science.

70. A middle school social studies teacher makes sure that the English language learners (ELLs) in the classroom have opportunities to use English not only for academic-related communication, but also for communicating with others, giving directions, expressing needs, and revealing feelings. This practice best demonstrates the teacher's understanding that

- A. the structure and conventions of an ELL's native language might be different from English.
- B. imagination and creativity are important components of language acquisition.
- C. ELLs will feel more comfortable using English in a relaxed atmosphere.
- D. using English across a wide range of language functions will improve proficiency.

71. A major motivational reason cooperative learning produces positive instructional outcomes is the

- A. cooperative incentive structure.
- B. model's inherent appeal to teachers.
- C. competitive task structure.
- D. homogeneous nature of the group.

72. Which of the following activities involving decimals would be LEAST desirable for a fourth-grade teacher to use in mathematics?

- A. Working individually and with partners, students solve teacher-posed real-world problems involving decimals.
- B. As a whole class, students design a project focused on decimals.
- C. As the teacher models problem solving involving decimals, students take notes and practice with the teacher.
- D. Students copy decimal problems from the textbook and use calculators to obtain the answers.

73. The Admission, Review, and Dismissal (ARD) committee meetings to review a student's Individualized Education Program (IEP), and, as appropriate, revise its provisions, must be held

- A. at least once every 3 years.
- B. at least once every 12 months.
- C. no less than twice a year.
- D. only as needed at the discretion of the school district.

74. To best maintain communication with families of students whose home language is not English, a teacher should send the families

    A. the school's website address.
    B. phone numbers of their student's bilingual classmates.
    C. the teacher's phone number and other contact information.
    D. a monthly multilingual newsletter about class events.

75. Teachers who hold high expectations for their adolescent students are likely to find that teacher expectations

    A. influence student behavior and performance.
    B. are more powerful than peer pressure.
    C. create anxiety in low-ability students and cause achievement to decline.
    D. have no impact on academic achievement.

76. A teacher has selected a cooperative learning group activity to use on the first day of school as a means to get acquainted with her students and to help the students get to know one another. The teacher is very excited about this idea because she is aware of the many positive benefits of cooperative learning. The teacher should

    A. follow up with written reports of the group activity.
    B. monitor the social interactions of the students while they are working in their groups.
    C. have the students evaluate each other's level of participation in the group activity.
    D. replace the group activity with a simple, enjoyable activity that involves the whole class.

77. Which of the following is a likely result of using fixed-ability groups that stay in place throughout the school year?

    A. The teacher will experience fewer behavior management problems.
    B. High-ability students will have an increased opportunity to become more accepting of their low-achieving classmates because they will not be held back by them.
    C. All of the students will experience achievement gains since ability grouping will allow them to experience an accelerated curriculum and advanced instruction.
    D. Students in the low-ability groups will be negatively affected.

78. A teacher ignores Carly, who blurts out answers without first raising her hand and waiting to be called on. Which technique is the teacher using with Carly?

    A. extinction
    B. negative reinforcement
    C. positive reinforcement
    D. shaping

79. If a teacher suspects a student is experiencing abuse at home, the teacher should

    A. set up a conference with the parents to see whether the teacher's suspicions are true.
    B. discuss the teacher's suspicions with some of the student's friends.
    C. notify the proper legal authorities at once and let them investigate the situation.
    D. wait a while longer and observe the student to see whether the teacher's suspicions are correct.

80. Which of the following is a primary benefit of having ELLs who are at the advanced level of English language proficiency in writing write in journals as a self-assessment tool?

    A. They can express their thoughts and feelings privately.
    B. They can look for strengths and weaknesses in their writing skills.
    C. They can critique and proofread one another's entries.
    D. They can write about everyday topics with which they are familiar.

Read the information below to answer questions 81–82.

A middle-grades health teacher is aware of the alarming rate of drug use among young adolescents. He decides to revise the 2-week unit on drug abuse that he had planned to teach. He feels this particular unit is a very important part of the curriculum, and he wants to feel confident that it will help increase the students' understanding of the dangerous effects of drug abuse. Through the Drug Abuse Resistance Education (D.A.R.E.) organization, the teacher obtains resource materials to use in the unit that stress the hazards of minors' illegal use of drugs. He also plans to invite well-known, dynamic guest speakers to visit the class to talk with students about the social pressures that sometimes lead to drug use.

81. Most likely, the teacher's lessons for the unit will be designed to enhance students'

   A. understanding of the society in which they live.
   B. ability to memorize and recall factual information.
   C. independent thinking and decision-making skills.
   D. ability to apply information learned.

82. The teacher is likely aware that a common characteristic of young adolescents is that they

   A. believe bad things happen to other people, not to them.
   B. cannot take the perspective of others.
   C. have social lives focused around their families.
   D. seldom succumb to peer pressure.

83. A high school mathematics teacher plans to use peer tutoring in her classes in the coming year. Research on the effect of peer tutoring on learning indicates that

   A. the results are much the same regardless of the expertise of the tutor.
   B. the tutors benefit, but usually the tutees do not.
   C. achievement of both the tutors and the tutees increases.
   D. neither tutors nor tutees benefit significantly, but achievement motivation increases for both.

84. Devyn is an exceptionally bright student, but he seldom completes his work, makes fun of class activities, and generally behaves disruptively. Devyn's father visits the school to complain about a lower-than-expected grade that Devyn received in science because he did not complete some homework assignments. Which of the following approaches would be appropriate for Devyn's teacher to use with this parent?

   A. explain to the parent that Devyn can do better work since he is obviously a bright student.
   B. explain to the parent that the other students do well under the school grading policy, so there is no reason to change Devyn's grade.
   C. explain to the parent that Devyn's problem is most likely related to his behavior problems in class.
   D. explain the school grading policy to the parent and show samples of Devyn's incomplete work.

85. A first-grade teacher has been keeping track of a student's reading and writing progress by using anecdotal records and checklists. Which of the following assessment tools is another informal measure the teacher might use?

   A. benchmark assessment
   B. diagnostic assessment
   C. portfolio assessment
   D. summative assessment

86. To motivate student effort and engagement, an elementary school mathematics teacher offers points, which students can save and redeem for rewards each time they answer a problem correctly. This technique is most closely associated with a(n)

   A. contingency reward program.
   B. extrinsic reward system.
   C. group reward program.
   D. intrinsic reward system.

87. A fourth-grade teacher is selecting a computer software program for science. Which of the following features would be most essential for the program to have to be effective for use by the teacher's English language learners (ELLs), most of whom are in the early production stage of English language acquisition?

   A. an introduction to keyboarding and mouse skills
   B. supplementary aids, such as quizzes and worksheets, that are age-appropriate
   C. written instructions that are easily accessible and use simple language
   D. extensive visual representations and other nonlinguistic graphic support

88. Most authorities agree that lecturing

   A. is the least effective instructional strategy for elementary school, but is very effective in middle school.
   B. should be used occasionally in elementary school to prepare students for its use in the upper-level grades.
   C. should be used in elementary school when a lot of content needs to be covered in a short time.
   D. should be avoided in elementary school.

89. During the first quarter of the year, a middle-grades English teacher spends most of the class period having the students complete practice exercises on punctuation and grammar. The teacher has become concerned because most of the students appear bored during the lessons, and off-task behavior has become a problem. Which of the following measures would be most effective in addressing the teacher's concerns?

   A. Replace the practice exercises with activities related to the students' interests and experiences.
   B. Use moderate punishment such as timeouts when students are not paying attention.
   C. Praise by name the students who are on task.
   D. Discuss the problem with individual students and ask for their cooperation.

90. Which of the following activities would be most developmentally appropriate in promoting second-grade students' multicultural awareness and appreciation?

   A. Have students learn about geographic and environmental characteristics of the countries represented by the different cultural groups in the class.
   B. Engage students in an activity in which they are able to discover common elements in their various cultural backgrounds, as well as unique features of their own culture.
   C. Have students read about cultural traditions of several countries and discuss them in class, followed by a short quiz about the reading material.
   D. Have each student memorize a song from a different country and sing it to the class, followed by a question-and-answer period during which classmates can ask questions about the song's meaning.

91. For children in the primary grades, attitudes toward an issue tend to be most influenced by their

   A. cognitive abilities.
   B. families' attitudes toward the issue.
   C. peers' attitudes toward the issue.
   D. personal experiences related to the issue.

92. A first-year early-childhood teacher is planning for the coming year. The teacher wants to use learning centers in her classroom. Which of the following is an important feature that early-childhood learning centers should have?

   A. Learning centers should be designed for students to work in isolation, away from their peers.
   B. Learning centers should be self-contained, with all materials needed contained within the center.
   C. Learning centers should include carefully designed and easy-to-read worksheets.
   D. Learning centers should be separated from the regular classroom work area.

93. Which of the following cognitive abilities should a sixth-grade teacher expect most of the students in the class to be in the process of developing?

  A. taking another person's point of view
  B. thinking hypothetically about abstract concepts
  C. thinking in concrete terms
  D. being able to mentally reverse operations

94. Which of the following principles best applies to interdisciplinary teams?

  A. Teachers should know how to communicate effectively with colleagues to create an environment that supports innovation and risk-taking.
  B. Teachers should have opportunities to learn from each other and thereby improve the educational experiences of students.
  C. Teachers should know how to apply knowledge of learning theories to classroom practices.
  D. Teachers should work with colleagues to establish strong and positive ties between the school and the community.

95. A second-grade class includes English language learners (ELLs). In which of the following situations would it be advantageous for the teacher to pair speakers of the same language?

  A. when students are working in cooperative learning groups
  B. when the most recently arrived student needs an orientation to classroom rules and procedures
  C. during labeling and drawing activities related to academic content
  D. during activities designed to promote social communication skills

96. A seventh-grade teacher has a student who is becoming the "class clown" by making distracting noises and funny faces when students are working in groups. The teacher, aware that the student has an unfortunate home life, speculates that the attention the student gets from the class makes the student feel like "one of the gang." The student's inappropriate behavior in class is probably associated with the student's fear of

  A. being rejected by peers.
  B. displeasing authority figures.
  C. failing to achieve academically.
  D. failing to learn cultural norms.

97. A first-grade teacher has planned a science unit concerning the ocean. On the first day of the unit, the children enter the classroom to see "seaweed" hanging from the ceiling, displays of seashells on tables, and pictures of ocean life on the wall. The teacher's probable purpose for transforming the classroom into a pretend ocean is to

  A. provide a concrete experience for the children.
  B. allow the children to have choices in their learning.
  C. create a safe, efficient, supportive learning environment.
  D. give students control over their learning experiences.

98. Ms. Kim, a kindergarten teacher, overhears two of the boys in her class arguing over which one is going to marry her. She is not upset and does not reprimand the boys because she realizes their behavior is normal. Ms. Kim's analysis of the situation best reflects her knowledge and consideration of

  A. students' developmental processes.
  B. the importance of developing students' positive self-esteem.
  C. allowing students to practice self-discipline.
  D. the need to model for students ways to resolve conflicts.

99. A fourth-grade English language learner (ELL) who has been determined to be at the advanced level of English language proficiency most likely still would have difficulty comprehending which of the following sentences?

A. The girl invited her friend to come to a party.
B. I'm sorry that I forgot about your birthday.
C. Your teacher will not put up with rude behavior in the classroom.
D. My brother has been unhappy all week.

100. With regard to the Admission, Review, and Dismissal (ARD) committee for a student with a disability, at least one regular education teacher of the student serves on the ARD committee. As a member of the ARD committee, the regular education teacher

A. assists with determining interventions and strategies for the student.
B. assists with interpreting the instructional implications of evaluation results.
C. serves as the representative of the school district.
D. serves only as an observer.

Answer Key for Practice Test 1

1. A	26. D	51. C	76. D
2. A	27. D	52. B	77. D
3. B	28. B	53. A	78. A
4. A	29. D	54. C	79. C
5. C	30. C	55. A	80. B
6. B	31. C	56. B	81. C
7. D	32. A	57. C	82. A
8. A	33. B	58. B	83. C
9. D	34. A	59. A	84. D
10. B	35. A	60. C	85. C
11. B	36. B	61. C	86. B
12. D	37. C	62. C	87. D
13. C	38. B	63. A	88. D
14. B	39. C	64. A	89. A
15. D	40. C	65. B	90. B
16. A	41. B	66. C	91. B
17. B	42. A	67. A	92. B
18. C	43. B	68. B	93. B
19. B	44. D	69. B	94. B
20. D	45. B	70. D	95. B
21. D	46. A	71. A	96. A
22. B	47. D	72. D	97. A
23. A	48. C	73. B	98. A
24. A	49. A	74. D	99. C
25. A	50. C	75. A	100. A

Complete Answers and Explanations for Practice Test 1

1. **A.** This question deals with study skills, a topic that falls under **Competency 010 (Assessment)**. Choice A is the correct response. An *acronym* (choice A) is a word or phrase formed from the initial letters of a list of words that is used to help you remember the words in the list—like the example given in the question of using *HOMES* to remember the names of the Great Lakes. Eliminate choice B because *chunking* involves organizing or clustering more than one piece of information in a meaningful way in order to remember it. For example, when you remember telephone numbers, you remember them as three chunks of information—the area code, the first three digits, and the last four digits—rather than as 10 separate digits. Eliminate choice C because *rehearsal* is the process of repeating information over and over again, either aloud or silently, as a means of holding it in short-term memory and preparing it for long-term memory. Eliminate choice D because *rote* is memorization through isolated drill.

2. **A.** This question addresses **Competency 003 (Instructional Design and Planning)**. Eliminate choices C and D because these choices describe types of standardized assessments, so both are off-topic. Eliminate choice B because intradisciplinary describes instruction that stays within the realm of a discipline. Thus, choice A is the correct response. Incorporating writing into physical education class is best described as cross-curricular. Instead of having students use only their physical abilities, the writing assignment integrates writing skills into the lessons.

3. **B.** This question deals with evaluation-level thinking, which falls under both **Competency 003 (Instructional Design and Planning)** and **Competency 007 (Communication)**. Evaluation-level thinking requires students to use criteria or standards to form judgments or opinions about the value of a topic or phenomenon being considered. Eliminate choices A, C, and D because, for these actions, students are not required to form judgments or opinions. A class discussion in which students are asked to form an opinion about the simulation activity and give reasons for that opinion would work well for engaging students in evaluation-level thinking. Thus, choice B is the correct response.

4. **A.** This question addresses **Competency 006 (Classroom Management)**. The teacher in question should have realized beforehand that some, and probably most, students lack drawing talent. Therefore, the teacher should have provided a means for these students to illustrate their writing projects without having to draw. In this situation, an effective strategy for encouraging a greater sense of equity and acceptance among all students is to allow them the option of downloading free clip art from the Internet to illustrate their writing projects, making differences in student artistic ability less important and apparent. This action would contribute to a positive learning climate for all students in the class. Thus, choice A is the correct response. Eliminate choice B because this action might prompt the students with less artistic talent to compare their drawings unfavorably to those of the more artistically talented students. Eliminate choice C because although this is an action that the teacher might take, it is not the *best* response. When a discipline situation involving a "perpetrator" and a "victim" occurs, the teacher should stop the perpetrator's actions, but then focus on the victim. The teacher's best follow-up response is one that helps the students who were the targets of the rude behavior. Eliminate choice D because this action would not be under consideration had the teacher anticipated the current situation might happen and planned accordingly; further, consequences for rude behavior should have already been established.

Tip: Notice that question 4 asks you to select the *best* response. A word like *best* in the question stem is a marker for a priority-setting question. In these questions there may be more than one acceptable response, but you must select the <u>one</u> best response. This tip applies to other similar marker words such as *most* or *primary*.

5. **C.** This question addresses both **Competency 002 (Diversity)** and **Competency 010 (Assessment)**. Eliminate choices A and B because these strategies would fail to communicate to students assessment criteria and standards based on high expectations for learning. Eliminate choice D because although having students engage in self-assessment is useful and appropriate, reliance on this strategy might fail to yield results that are reliable and accurate in terms of assessing students' actual knowledge and skills. In conducting classroom assessments to measure content area learning for struggling learners, teachers should strive to use a variety of assessment strategies so that the students will have varied opportunities and multiple ways to show what they have learned. Thus, choice C is the correct response.

Chapter 14: Practice Test 1

6. **B.** This question addresses **Competency 007 (Communication).** In her interaction with Carl, the teacher, noticing Carl's frown, responds to this nonverbal cue. Eliminate choices C and D because these options do not indicate that the teacher responded to a nonverbal cue. Eliminate choice A because the teacher did not paraphrase (that is, restate what Carl said in her own words). After noticing Carl's frown and going over to his desk, the teacher listens reflectively to what Carl says and responds to it. Thus, choice B is the correct response.

7. **D.** This question addresses **Competency 012 (Professional Knowledge and Skills).** Eliminate choices A and C because the question stem provides no reason to assume that the teacher wants to be a risk-taker or innovator or to demonstrate that the teacher has clearly defined goals. (*Tip:* Don't read too much into a question.) Eliminate choice B because this response also is not supported by the question—there is no indication that the teacher will participate in collaborative decision making during the workshop. Because the teacher will be learning about a sophisticated mathematical software program, the teacher's probable purpose for attending the workshop is to enhance his or her professional knowledge and skills. The teacher demonstrates awareness that Texas educators have a professional and ethical obligation to seek out opportunities for professional growth. Thus, choice D is the correct response.

8. **A.** This question addresses **Competency 003 (Instructional Design and Planning).** Eliminate choices B, C, and D because these tasks do not require higher-order thinking skills. Filling in the missing components of a pattern requires the higher-order thinking skills of analysis (involving the ability to examine relationships of the parts of the pattern to one another) and synthesis (involving the ability to predict what part is missing). Thus, choice A is the correct response.

9. **D.** This question deals with classroom layout, a topic that falls under **Competency 005 (Classroom Climate).** Eliminate choices A and B because materials, resources, and technology should not be limiting factors for teachers. In other words, the teacher should decide upon a spatial arrangement based on what the teacher thinks would provide the most effective learning environment for the students, not on what materials, resources, and technology are available. Eliminate choice C because although this aspect might be a factor for the teacher to consider, it is not as important as considering the instructional approaches the teacher is planning to use with this group of diverse learners. Thus, choice D is the correct response.

10. **B.** This question addresses **Competency 013 (Professional Conduct).** By discussing Jimmy's failing performance in front of Curtis, Ms. Hall is in violation of the principle in the Code of Ethics and Standard Practices for Texas Educators that states that teachers shall not "reveal confidential information concerning students." Thus, choice B is the correct response. Moreover, the Family Educational Rights and Privacy Act (FERPA) protects the privacy of student records. FERPA requires that schools obtain written permission from minor students' parents before releasing educational records. Discussing a student's grades in front of another student might be construed as a violation of this law. Eliminate choice A because legal, ethical, and professional standards take precedence over other considerations. Eliminate choices C and D because Ms. Hall's behavior was unacceptable.

11. **B.** This question addresses **Competency 010 (Assessment).** Eliminate choice A because this response is not aligned with the question—the students are evaluating, not the teacher. Eliminate choice C because this result would not be considered a benefit. Eliminate choice D because there is no reason to expect a connection between the students' self-reflection and their leadership skills. Thus, choice B is the correct response. By asking the students to reflect on their roles and participation in the project-based learning activity, the teacher is promoting their self-reflection and self-assessment.

12. **D.** This question addresses **Competency 007 (Communication).** Eliminate choice A because the teacher's question should elicit divergent thinking, not factual recall. Eliminate choice B because teachers should encourage students to be independent thinkers and, thus, should not give them hints about what to think about an issue. Eliminate choice C because the teacher is not questioning what the students already know about the controversy. The teacher's question is designed to create a climate of objective analysis. The teacher does not want a particular "right answer" to the question posed, but rather wants students to share their own ideas and opinions about the topic. The question is meant to provide a framework for engaging students in critical thinking about the controversy. Thus, choice D is the correct response.

13. **C.** This question deals with **Competency 003 (Instructional Design and Planning).** Notice that you must select the response that is the teacher's *main* purpose. Eliminate choice B because it is not aligned with the question—the students are debating a problem, not solving one. Although participating in a debate will

provide opportunities for students to practice public speaking (choice A) and might, in some unexpected way, minimize negative effects, if any, of historical controversies on student performance (choice D), these reasons would not be as significant as engaging students in higher-order thinking in an authentic context. Thus, choice C is the correct response.

14. **B.** This question addresses **Competency 012 (Professional Knowledge and Skills)**. Eliminate choices A, C, and D because these answer choices are not supported by the question stem—there is no indication that the computer science teacher will be addressing the mission of the school, using community resources, or making decisions and solving problems when conducting the workshop. Thus, choice B is the correct response. The computer science teacher understands that teachers have an obligation to work with each other for the advancement of mutual professional growth. The workshop will give the computer science teacher an opportunity to actively share ideas with colleagues to contribute to a successful learning community at their school.

15. **D.** This question deals with **Competency 002 (Diversity)**. Eliminate choice A because this approach has limited effectiveness in countering gender stereotyping. Eliminate choices B and C because these approaches might send the message that recognizing and celebrating the accomplishments of women scientists need to receive attention only for the day. Research indicates that, by age 9, students have well-established prejudices that are highly resistant to change; therefore, the teacher must go beyond brief and superficial measures to counter gender stereotyping—a long-term intervention is warranted. Bringing in, throughout the year, both male and female guests who have science-related careers will provide role models in science for all the teacher's students. Thus, choice D is the correct response.

16. **A.** This question deals with **Competency 013 (Professional Conduct)**. The Family Educational Rights and Privacy Act (FERPA) protects the privacy of student records. FERPA requires that schools obtain written permission from minor students' parents before releasing educational records to others. Eliminate choices B and D because these answer choices conflict with FERPA. Eliminate choice C because this action works against developing effective parent-teacher partnerships. Mr. Mann should know that his legal responsibility is to deny the parents' request to see other students' grades. Thus, choice A is the correct response.

17. **B.** This question deals with the ELPS, a topic that falls under both **Competency 002 (Diversity)** and **Competency 008 (Instructional Delivery)**. Eliminate choices A and C because beginning ELLs would struggle with doing either of these tasks. Eliminate choice D because beginning ELLs do not have sufficient English proficiency to adequately show what they know about a topic when assessed through the use of multiple-choice tests. The teacher should preteach the unit vocabulary to the whole class using visuals and gestures. This strategy is good for the whole class, and particularly for the ELLs, by helping them to become familiar with new words and place them in a meaningful context. Thus, choice B is the correct response.

18. **C.** This question deals with the ELPS, a topic that falls under both **Competency 002 (Diversity)** and **Competency 008 (Instructional Delivery)**. Eliminate choices A and B because beginning ELLs would struggle with doing either of these tasks. Eliminate choice D because even though ELLs can copy words and their definitions, this activity would not be a purposeful activity for a beginning ELL. Choice C is the correct response. Beginning ELLs understand that concrete words can be represented by pictures, so the jigsaw activity will reinforce the information from the video in a meaningful way.

19. **B.** This question falls under **Competency 010 (Assessment)**. Choice B is the correct response. The teacher's prompts constitute an informal survey, which is being used as a type of formative assessment. Eliminate choices A, C, and D because these are formal assessments. A *criterion-referenced assessment* (choice A) uses standardized tests designed to measure mastery of specific skills. A *needs assessment* (choice C) is a systematic process to identify areas in need of improvement. A *norm-referenced assessment* (choice D) uses standardized tests that focus on a comparison of students' scores to those of a "norm" group of students. A *formative assessment* (choice B) takes place before and during the learning process; it is used to give feedback to the teacher about the instructional process and may take various forms (such as an informal survey, as shown in this question).

20. **D.** This question falls under **Competency 007 (Communication)**. Eliminate choices A, B, and C because these questions do not challenge students to use creative thinking skills. The question in choice D prompts students to use their imaginations to create a new scenario between Jack and the giant, a cognitive activity that demonstrates creative thinking skills. Thus, choice D is the correct response.

Chapter 14: Practice Test 1

21. **D.** This question addresses **Competency 002 (Diversity).** Notice that you must select the answer choice that would be *most* beneficial. Eliminate choices B and C because these actions are teacher-focused and too passive for the students. You must now decide which is the better answer choice: A or D. Eliminate choice A because although a teacher might take this action to promote diversity, it would not engage the students' interest and attention as well as would taking the action given in choice D. By inviting visitors from the different cultural backgrounds represented in the class to facilitate and participate in activities with the students, a teacher is creating a classroom environment that encourages active engagement of the students, while applying the teacher's understanding that teachers should use the diversity that exists within the classroom and the community to foster students' understanding and appreciation of diversity. Thus, choice D is the correct response.

22. **B.** This question falls under **Competency 008 (Instructional Delivery).** According to research, teachers should explicitly teach the meaning of technical vocabulary before introducing a topic in which the words appear. Thus, choice B is the correct response. The suggestions given in choices A, C, and D are not supported by research.

23. **A.** This question deals with **Competency 010 (Assessment).** Eliminate choices B and D because these types of assessment usually do not provide sufficient information about a student's difficulties for diagnostic purposes. Formative assessments (choice C) can identify areas of strengths and weaknesses, but they do not give as much detailed information as do diagnostic assessments. Diagnostic assessments (choice A) provide teachers with specific information about an individual student's strengths and needs relative to subject matter skills and subskills. Such tests are effective tools for assessing a student's strengths and weaknesses. They provide specific information that can be used to customize instruction and/or interventions for particular students. Thus, choice A is the correct response.

24. **A.** This question deals with **Competency 012 (Professional Knowledge and Skills).** Eliminate choices B, C, and D because these beliefs might prevent Ms. Carter from asking for assistance, but the *most* likely reason is that she is fearful that she will be perceived as ill-prepared or incompetent to teach. Like many first-year teachers, Ms. Carter is too embarrassed to ask for help because she doesn't want the other teachers to know she is having a problem. Instead of being reluctant to seek assistance from her colleagues, Ms. Carter should view them as a rich source of support and guidance. Thus, choice A is the correct response.

25. **A.** This question deals with **Competency 003 (Instructional Design and Planning).** Eliminate choices B, C, and D because these are desirable strategies. When students are encouraged to take time to think before deciding on a solution strategy for a problem (choice B), they spend more time thinking about and analyzing the problem. Allowing more time for problems requiring analytical skills than for basic algebraic manipulation problems (choice C) would be more conducive to higher-order thinking and problem solving. When students rely on themselves to determine whether their work is mathematically correct (choice D), they engage in critical thinking in order to clarify their mathematical thinking. According to Van De Walle et al. (2009), procedural knowledge is knowledge of the rules and procedures that are used to carry out routine mathematical tasks and of the symbolism that is used to represent mathematical concepts. A highly managed classroom environment focused on procedural knowledge likely would result in less risk taking and less higher-level thinking from students. Thus, A is the correct response.

26. **D.** This question relates to **Competency 005 (Classroom Climate).** Creating an environment that respects and confirms the dignity of students as human beings is essential in meeting the needs of diverse students. Encouraging students to share ideas relevant to their cultural backgrounds during class discussions would allow the class to celebrate and respect the diversity in the classroom and, thereby, promote harmonious relations among the students. Thus, choice D is the correct response. Eliminate choice A; as when dealing with other inappropriate behavior, teachers should respond immediately to expressions of racism. Eliminate choice B because competitive games might result in group disharmony. Eliminate choice C because although displaying artifacts is an acceptable practice, it would not be as effective as that given in choice D.

27. **D.** This question addresses **Competency 013 (Professional Conduct).** Eliminate choices A, B, and C because these answer choices are not supported by the stimulus. Ms. Alford intentionally made false statements about Mr. Pennywell. She is in violation of the principle in the Code of Ethics and Standard Practices for Texas Educators, which states that a teacher shall not knowingly make false statements about a colleague. Thus, choice D is the correct response.

28. **B.** This question addresses **Competency 012 (Professional Knowledge and Skills).** Choice B is the correct response. A reflective journal is a private, written record of a teacher's experiences and feelings related to teaching. It promotes reflection and self-evaluation and is an authentic and effective way for teachers to identify strengths, challenges, and potential problems. It also provides a means for a teacher to look back and see progress over time. Eliminate choices A, C, and D because none of these choices is a primary purpose of a teacher's reflective journal.

29. **D.** This question deals with **Competency 007 (Communication).** Eliminate choices A and C because the quality of discussions will not be improved with these lower-level question types. Eliminate choice B because this action works against student participation. Choice D is the correct response. Asking a question first and then calling a student's name for a response is an effective approach teachers can use to keep students mentally involved in the discussion. When the question comes before the student's name, all students are given the opportunity to think and process their responses because the teacher has not yet identified the student who will be asked to respond. Research shows that asking the question first increases the number of responses as well as elicits more correct and longer responses.

30. **C.** This question deals with **Competency 010 (Assessment).** Because the teacher was careful to design the assessment so that it was aligned with the instructional content that was addressed and was at an appropriate level of difficulty, she should be pleased with the results. The most appropriate conclusion for the teacher to draw from the assessment data from the unit test is that the students have mastered the unit content, indicating that the teacher has performed effectively in achieving the desired learning outcomes. Thus, choice C is the correct response. The students are doing well at the current pace, so there would be no reason to pick up the pace of instruction (eliminate choice A). Because the test was aligned with the instructional content and at an appropriate level of difficulty, the data do not support that the test was too easy or that the teacher is targeting instruction at a level that is too low (eliminate choices B and D).

31. **C.** This question relates to **Competency 002 (Diversity).** Eliminate choice A because this approach is problematic; students might pursue interests traditionally associated with their gender roles to avoid being ridiculed by classmates. Eliminate choice B because it promotes sex-role stereotyping. Eliminate choice D because grouping boys and girls separately is generally not a recommended practice. Choice C is the correct response. Teachers should treat male and female students generally the same, unless a clear legitimate reason exists to do otherwise.

32. **A.** This question relates to **Competency 010 (Assessment).** Eliminate choices B, C, and D because these measures are not ways to gather data about a student's writing ability. Choice A is the correct response. Analyzing the writing samples in the students' portfolios will provide information about students' writing strengths and deficiencies from which the teacher can develop appropriate interventions.

33. **B.** This question deals with **Competency 007 (Communication).** Questions can be categorized as **convergent** (closed-ended) or **divergent** (open-ended), depending on whether the teacher is seeking knowledge of information or is trying to generate ideas and stimulate thinking, respectively. Only the question in choice B is convergent because it elicits a single response ("the kitchen"). Eliminate choices A, C, and D because the questions in these answer choices are divergent questions.

34. **A.** This question addresses **Competency 007 (Communication).** Questions can be categorized as **convergent** (closed-ended) or **divergent** (open-ended), depending on whether the teacher is seeking knowledge of information or is trying to generate ideas and stimulate thinking, respectively. Only the question in choice A is divergent because it allows for many different responses. Eliminate choices B, C, and D because the questions in these answer choices are convergent questions.

35. **A.** This question deals with conveying high expectations, a topic that falls under **Competency 004 (Learning Principles).** At-risk students are low-performing students who are potential dropouts. Teachers should understand factors inside the classroom, such as teacher expectations, that influence these students' perceptions of their own worth and potential. Eliminate choices B, C, and D because these choices contain ways that represent consensus in educational research and theory about maximizing teaching and learning for all students, but especially in working with at-risk students. Teachers should encourage these students to express themselves orally (choice B) because of the need for schools to provide opportunities for development of effective oral communication skills, which are sometimes lacking in the home environments of at-risk students. Because disengagement is problematic with at-risk students, the teacher should provide a confidence-building environment, including giving them sufficient wait time (choice C) and expressing

expectations clearly and directly (choice D). Praise serves to inform students of what they are doing right; therefore, it is critical that the praise be given for correct responses and appropriate behavior. Especially with at-risk students, accepting and praising all work will not be effective in facilitating learning and will send a confused message about teacher expectations. Thus, choice A is the correct response.

36. **B.** This question deals with logical reasoning, a topic that falls under **Competency 007 (Communication)**. Eliminate choices A and C because these ways of thinking involve coming up with new ideas, which would not be expected when students are reasoning from general statements to reach a logical conclusion. Eliminate choice D because *inductive reasoning* involves looking at a number of specific examples and trying to identify a pattern or trend that fits the given examples in order to determine a general rule. Choice B is the correct response. *Deductive reasoning* starts with basic assumptions or facts and proceeds to a logical conclusion.

37. **C.** This question deals with learning styles, a topic that falls under **Competency 002 (Diversity)**. Learning style is said to be the manner in which an individual perceives and processes information in learning situations. Knowledge of learning style theory might assist teachers in designing educational conditions in which most students are likely to learn. Learning style experts generally agree that every person has an individual learning style (choice C); that learning style is an indicator not of intelligence (eliminate choice A) but of how a person learns; that learning style strengths might change over time and with training (eliminate choice B); and that although certain learning style characteristics are biological in nature, others are developed through experience (eliminate choice D). Thus, choice C is the correct response.

38. **B.** This question addresses **Competency 010 (Assessment)**. Eliminate choice A because an *aptitude test* is a standardized test designed to predict future performance in a subject area. Eliminate choice C because *norm-referenced tests* are standardized tests that focus on comparing students' scores to those of a "norm" group of students, so this type of test would not necessarily show achievement of district academic goals. Eliminate choice D because *psychomotor tests* assess physical, not academic, skills. *Criterion-referenced tests* (choice B) are used to compare scores against a predetermined minimum standard of competency. A test of this type would be the best way to assess student progress toward the academic goals of the district. Thus, choice B is the correct response.

39. **C.** This question falls under **Competency 007 (Communication)**. Eliminate choices A and B because the teacher's approach is not ineffective. By giving Sabrina sufficient wait time, the teacher is sending a positive message to Sabrina—that the teacher values her input. Eliminate choice D because it is not aligned with the question. Thus, choice C is the correct response. The teacher's approach is effective because it communicates positive expectations to Sabrina. By rephrasing the question and continuing to wait, the teacher is not giving up on Sabrina. Slavin (2008) pointed out that "Research has found that teachers tend to give up too rapidly on students whom they perceive to be low achievers, a practice that tells those students that the teacher expects little from them" (p. 233).

40. **C.** This question deals with **Competency 008 (Instructional Delivery)**. The teacher wants the students to take a skill previously learned in one setting and use it in a new setting. The ability to carry learning over from one setting to a different setting is called *generalization* (choice C). Therefore, the task given to the students is most likely to promote generalization. Thus, choice C is the correct response. The other answer choices do not apply as well to the task as choice C. *Creativity* (choice A) involves putting together ideas to come up with new ideas or understandings. *Discrimination* (choice B) involves recognizing differences. *Overlearning* (choice D) is practicing beyond the point of mastery to improve retention.

41. **B.** This question relates to **Competency 002 (Diversity)**. Notice that you must select the *first* step that a teacher should take. Eliminate choice A because holding a campus-wide diversity week might send the message that recognizing and celebrating differences need to receive attention only during that time period. Indeed, research findings indicate that such measures might be too brief or superficial to make an impact. Choices C and D contain measures that the teacher should take to implement a more culturally diverse curriculum; however, your knowledge of effective multicultural practices should tell you that before proceeding with her plans, the teacher should *first* examine her own personal beliefs and feelings about cultural groups. Many teachers are unaware of their own biases and prejudices. Thus, choice B is the correct response.

42. **A.** This question addresses **Competency 010 (Assessment)**. Eliminate choices B and D because these assessment methods are not developmentally appropriate for kindergarteners. Eliminate choice C because

peer assessment by kindergarteners is unlikely to yield reliable, authentic data. *Informal teacher observation* (choice A) allows the teacher to assess in a natural and ongoing way. This method is an authentic way to assess because the teacher collects information about what the children are learning by directly observing them. Thus, choice A is the correct response.

43. **B.** This question deals with **Competency 007 (Communication).** Eliminate choice A because quickly offering advice would be a disservice to Morgaan. Eliminate choice C because by interrupting Morgaan to share his own personal experiences, the teacher interrupts her thought processes and impedes communication. Eliminate choice D because maintaining eye contact is a way to promote communication and indicates active listening. Choice B is the correct response. Listening with a concerned look and limiting interruptions will send the message to Morgaan that what she is saying is important to the teacher and will encourage her to continue talking with him about her problem with the other girls.

44. **D.** This question falls under **Competency 003 (Instructional Design and Planning).** Eliminate choice A because there is no evidence in the question stem to indicate that the teacher is using multisensory approaches that might appeal to students with different learning styles and preferences. Eliminate choice B because no evidence in the question stem indicates that the assignment topic is important to the students (although it might very well be)—don't read too much into a question. Eliminate choice C because although the assignment might encourage students to memorize key terminology, it benefits students most by engaging them in higher-order thinking such as finding connections among concepts, drawing valid conclusions, and formulating ideas. Thus, choice D is the correct response.

45. **B.** This question deals with **Competency 010 (Assessment).** Eliminate choices A and D because these approaches are likely to have a negative impact on how the students think about themselves. Eliminate choice C because feedback is more effective and more meaningful when it occurs immediately after testing. Although in Texas public schools, the academic grade is based on academic performance only, the teacher might consider including comments related to improvement in reports to students and parents. This approach is likely to increase motivation and interest by making it possible for all students, regardless of ability, to be reinforced and recognized for effort. Thus, choice B is the correct response.

46. **A.** This question deals with homework, a topic that falls under **Competency 010 (Assessment).** One important method for teachers to find out what students have learned and to increase their academic achievement is through assigning homework. For students in the elementary and middle school grades, homework should be given to help them develop good study habits, develop positive attitudes toward school, and realize that learning is something to do not only at school but also at home. By the time students reach high school, the purpose of giving homework is primarily to improve their academic achievement. Thus, choice A is the correct response. The other answer choices are not primary reasons for giving homework in high school.

47. **D.** This question relates to **Competency 007 (Communication).** Eliminate choices A and C because the teacher is not making a point with Maria's concern or using it as an example; the teacher is merely calling attention to it. Eliminate choice B because the teacher did not modify Maria's question. The teacher uses Maria's question as a springboard for further class discussion. Thus, choice D is the correct response.

48. **C.** This question relates to **Competency 009 (Technology).** Computer simulation is a form of learning with computers in which the user may experiment with a simulated situation that strongly resembles reality. In social studies, the software programs create interactive environments that expand historical, geographical, and economic themes and opportunities while leaving the user in control. A major advantage of computer simulation is that, when using it, students are immersed in a reality-based situation that requires them to use problem solving, critical thinking skills, and decision making in a safe environment. Thus, choice C is the correct response. None of the other answer choices are major advantages of computer simulation—in fact, these outcomes would not be considered advantages associated with using computer simulation, although one or more might be incidental or, in some cases, designed outcomes of particular simulation activities.

49. **A.** This question deals with **Competency 006 (Classroom Management).** Eliminate choice B because this answer choice is not consistent with establishing a positive social and emotional atmosphere in the classroom. Eliminate choice C because during the first days of school, effective classroom managers are involved with the whole class. Eliminate choice D because effective classroom managers respond immediately to stop any misbehavior. The first days of school are critical in establishing classroom order.

During the first days of school, effective classroom managers spend much of the time teaching students specific classroom procedures. Thus, choice A is the correct response.

50. **C.** This question relates to **Competency 002 (Diversity)**. Eliminate choices A, B, and D because these responses are inconsistent with research findings that indicate, on average, that children from lower socioeconomic-class backgrounds are less likely to achieve as well in school as children from higher socioeconomic backgrounds (American Psychological Association, 2010). Regarding the difficulties for children from lower socioeconomic-class backgrounds, Slavin (2008) explained that these children (on average) are less likely to be as well prepared when entering school, and their upbringings emphasize behaviors and values different from those (such as individuality and future time orientation) expected of them in schools. Further, researchers have found that middle-class teachers often have low expectations for low-socioeconomic-class students, which is likely to influence those students' perception of their own worth and potential and, in turn, might result in low achievement for these students. Slavin (2008) made the point that teachers should be aware that in contrast to children from mainstream, middle-class backgrounds, children from lower socioeconomic-class backgrounds often are at a disadvantage in the typical school environment; and teachers should make efforts to recognize the potential of these students to achieve. Thus, choice C is the correct response.

51. **C.** This question deals with **Competency 007 (Communication)**. Eliminate choice A because teachers should provide appropriate and nonthreatening opportunities for all students to be involved in the lesson, even those who sometimes are reluctant to do so. Eliminate choice B because an effective method of calling on students is to use a random process, so that all participate and are kept attentive during the teaching act. Eliminate choice D because allowing volunteers to dominate the lesson will establish a classroom climate in which some students will be likely to assume a passive role during classroom discourse; further, the teacher will not be able to adequately assess whether those not participating are learning. Choice C is the correct response. The teacher's strategy is limited because students who don't volunteer will miss the opportunity to actively participate in the lesson.

52. **B.** This question deals with cooperative learning, a topic that falls under **Competency 008 (Instructional Delivery)**. Teachers need to be able to identify activities (such as cooperative learning activities) that support the knowledge, skills, and attitudes to be learned in their subject areas. They should understand principles, procedures, advantages, and limitations associated with those activities. Teachers should closely monitor student work (eliminate choice A), adhere to strict grading policies (eliminate choice C), and determine group size (eliminate choice D) before assigning students to groups. Choice B is the correct response. When cooperative learning is used, rewards for students are based on group performance, so students "sink or swim" together interdependently. Research results underscore that such practices have a positive impact on student behavior and academic achievement (Slavin, 2008).

53. **A.** This question addresses **Competency 010 (Assessment)**. Choice A is the correct response. Directly observing the students preparing the solutions and using a checklist to record their implementation of the procedure is a powerful way to find out what the students know and understand about preparing acid solutions. This method is a performance assessment. It is more likely to yield valid and reliable information about the students' learning than the methods given in choices B, C, and D.

54. **C.** This question relates to **Competency 012 (Professional Knowledge and Skills)**. Eliminate choices A and D because these answer choices are not aligned with the question. Eliminate choice B because the teacher did not make her decision in a group setting. Thus, choice C is the correct response. By seeking out advice from an experienced colleague, the teacher is taking advantage of an opportunity for on-the-job professional development.

55. **A.** This question addresses **Competency 009 (Technology)**. Given this is a third-grade class, you must select the answer choice that is *most* appropriate for the topic and the learners' abilities. Eliminate choices B and D because even though these technologies do provide images, they are not the *most* appropriate way for children at this age to learn how a hot air balloon works. Brain research suggests that watching a slide show or a video is a poor way for children to learn because the children assume a passive role with these technologies. Eliminate choice C because a spreadsheet would not provide an image of a hot air balloon. The children need to see a hot air balloon to help them understand how one works. Spreadsheets are most useful when mathematical or statistical calculations are needed. Choice A is the correct response. In this particular instance, computer simulation software is especially useful because it affords students the

opportunity to experiment with the scientific principles that explain how hot air balloons work in a safe environment without the danger from fire or other hazards.

56. **B.** This question deals with language difficulty, a topic that falls under **Competency 008 (Instructional Delivery)**. Eliminate choices A and C because academic tasks usually have high cognitive demand, not low cognitive demand. Eliminate choice D because academic tasks assigned as independent classwork or homework in a regular education classroom typically are presented in a low context. Choice B is the correct response. Academic tasks that are assigned as independent classwork or homework are typically based on low context and high cognitive demand.

57. **C.** This question addresses **Competency 006 (Classroom Management)**. Classroom rules should be stated in positive terms. Choices A, B, and D are consistent with this guideline. Using negative terms often results in students exhibiting the undesirable behavior that you want them to avoid. Rule 3 should be reworded to say, perhaps, "Walk when indoors." Thus, choice C is the correct response.

58. **B.** This question addresses **Competency 003 (Instructional Design and Planning)**. The statement in the question is an example of an instructional objective. Instructional objectives are classified as *affective, cognitive,* or *psychomotor*. Eliminate choice A because *affective objectives* involve feelings and dispositions. Eliminate choice C because *psychomotor objectives* involve physical activity on the part of the student. Eliminate choice D because this choice is not a type of lesson objective. Choice B is the correct response. *Cognitive objectives* involve thinking capabilities such as solving right triangles using the Pythagorean theorem.

59. **A.** This question relates to **Competency 013 (Professional Conduct)**. Choice A is the correct response. According to the Individuals with Disabilities Education Act (IDEA; formerly PL 94-142), placement in the "least restrictive environment" means placement of the student in the regular classroom to the maximum extent appropriate. Eliminate choice B because when a student who is receiving special education services is placed in the regular education classroom, the responsibility of providing an appropriate environment for the student should not be placed entirely on the special education teacher. Eliminate choice C because it is not always in the best interest of the disabled student to participate in a regular classroom environment. By law, the ARD committee must place the student in a classroom with his or her peers, unless the student's disability is so severe that education in a regular classroom setting cannot be achieved satisfactorily. Eliminate choice D because for students who can function in a regular classroom setting, this choice would violate their rights under IDEA.

60. **C.** This question addresses **Competency 010 (Assessment)**. Notice that you must select the teacher's *main* purpose. Eliminate choice A because it is not aligned with the question. Eliminate choice B because these outcomes of peer assessment benefit the teacher, but are not the teacher's main reason for using peer assessment. Eliminate choice D because the point of peer assessments is to provide feedback at the moment, not for a future time. Choice C is the correct response. Peer assessments allow students to critically evaluate others' performances and thereby deepen their own understanding of the concepts.

61. **C.** This question deals with **Competency 006 (Classroom Management)**. Notice that you must decide what the teacher should do *first*. The teacher should know how to promote student membership in a smoothly functioning learning community and to facilitate a positive social and emotional atmosphere in the classroom. Eliminate choices A and B because these actions are punitive approaches to discipline and should be avoided. Eliminate choice D because this action is an inappropriate teacher behavior. When dealing with a discipline problem, the student's dignity must be preserved. In dealing with the student's tendency to be tardy, the teacher should keep in mind that in order to solve the problem, the teacher needs to understand the problem. The student is the most direct and accessible source of information about the problem; so, the *first* step for the teacher to take is to talk with the student to determine the student's awareness of the problem, the meaning that it holds for the student, and how the teacher and student can reach a mutual solution to the problem. Thus, choice C is the correct response.

62. **C.** This question deals with second language acquisition, a topic that falls under **Competency 008 (Instructional Delivery)**. *Register* is the social level at which language is spoken. The context of the situation determines the socially appropriate register for the speech used. Only choice C provides an opportunity for the ELLs to consciously consider appropriate speech for two different social situations. The activities in choices A, B, and D do not involve register. Thus, choice C is the correct response.

63. **A.** This question deals with motivation, a topic that falls under **Competency 004 (Learning Principles)**. The question stem does not support choice B, C, or D. *Negative reinforcement* is the technique of strengthening

243

a behavior in someone by releasing that person from an undesirable situation. There is no indication in the question that the teacher is releasing the students from an undesirable situation (eliminate choice B). *Positive reinforcement* is the technique of strengthening a behavior by giving a desirable reward. There is no indication in the question that the students are receiving rewards from the teacher (eliminate choice C). In *reverse psychology,* a person (say, a teacher) tries to get another person (say, a student) to do something by asking the student to do the opposite of what the teacher really wants the student to do. Nothing in the question indicates that the teacher wants the students to do the opposite of what she is asking them to do (eliminate choice D). Choice A is the correct response. The teacher enhances *intrinsic motivation*—that is, self-motivation or motivation from within the student—by allowing students to have choices in their learning and by making what they are doing personally meaningful to them.

64. **A.** This question relates to **Competency 002 (Diversity).** Eliminate choice B because, although some evidence suggests that high-ability learners might gain from ability grouping, the approach described would shortchange the other students in the class. However, this does not mean that high-ability students should have to learn and work at the same pace as struggling students, nor does it mean that they should not be given opportunities to work alone or cooperatively with other high achievers and pursue topics to a greater level of cognitive challenge. Eliminate choice C because it disagrees with research indicating that students who are academically challenged benefit from small-group instruction. Eliminate choice D because permanent ability grouping might negatively affect the attitudes, achievement, and opportunities of struggling students. Students placed in groups should be progress-monitored continually to make sure their group placement is appropriate. Thus, choice A is the correct response. Using a combination of whole-group instruction and small-group differentiated instruction best reflects current research regarding grouping practices. This research is reflected in the RtI approach used in Texas schools.

65. **B.** This question relates to **Competency 011 (Family Involvement).** Choice B is the correct response. Creating a notebook that the child will take home and bring back is the most appropriate way to update the parents. This approach allows both the teacher and the parents to review and reflect on the notebook's contents at times convenient for them. They can also note comments to each other about entries in the notebook. Eliminate choice A because, while text messages are a quick and easy way to reach parents (assuming the parents have access to texting technology), this format does not lend itself to review and reflection. Eliminate choices C and D because unforeseen events too often disrupt these types of rigid arrangements.

66. **C.** This question deals with praise, a topic that falls under **Competency 005 (Classroom Climate).** Eliminate choice A because written praise can be as effective as oral praise. Eliminate choice B because praise does not specify what students need to work on. Eliminate choice D because using the same phrase over and over again from student to student is a type of meaningless praise. Effective praise is positive and specifies the behavior or accomplishment that is worthy of praise. Thus, choice C is the correct response.

67. **A.** This question addresses **Competency 003 (Instructional Design and Planning).** Choice A is the correct response. By designing a unit around civic ideas and practices, the teacher will be giving students the opportunity to learn about relationships within this central theme of social studies. Eliminate choices B and C because these answer choices are not aligned with the question. Eliminate choice D because this answer choice is not supported by the stimulus as clearly as choice A.

68. **B.** This question relates to **Competency 006 (Classroom Management).** Eliminate choices A, C, and D because these answer choices are not aligned with the question. The teacher knows that providing an opportunity for the students to recognize the problem and suggest solutions is likely to promote student ownership in a smoothly functioning learning community. Thus, choice B is the correct response.

69. **B.** This question relates to **Competency 003 (Instructional Design and Planning).** Eliminate choice C because research about best practices indicates that drill and practice should be de-emphasized in the science classroom. Eliminate choice D because reliance on the textbook can stifle the students' opportunities to co-construct their learning in a learning-centered environment. You must now choose between choices A and B. Use the strategy of rereading the question before making your decision. The question says you must select the *best* way for the teacher to address her concern. Eliminate choice A because although the teacher might set aside part of the class period each day for explicit instruction in statewide assessment test-taking strategies, it is most important that she make sure that the grade-level Texas Essential Knowledge and Skills—upon which the statewide assessment in science is based—are included in her curriculum. Thus, choice B is the correct response.

70. **D.** This question deals with second language acquisition, a topic that falls under **Competency 008 (Instructional Delivery)**. Eliminate choices A and B because these answer choices are not aligned with the question stem. You must now choose between choices C and D. Use the strategy of rereading the question before making your decision. The question stem tells you that the teacher is giving the ELLs opportunities to use English for a variety of purposes. Choice D is more aligned with this idea than choice C. According to Badía (1996), "Acquiring a language requires the opportunity to use it in meaningful context with speakers of the language in a variety of situations" (p. 3). The teacher, who understands that using English across a wide range of language functions will improve proficiency, demonstrates this principle of language acquisition. Thus, choice D is the correct response.

71. **A.** This question deals with cooperative learning, a topic that falls under **Competency 008 (Instructional Delivery)**. Eliminate choice B because it is off-topic. Whether it is appealing to teachers does not affect student motivation. Eliminate choice C because cooperative learning emphasizes group accomplishments, not competition. Eliminate choice D because effective cooperative learning groups should be heterogeneous in membership. Thus, choice A is the correct response. The positive interdependence that is an essential component of cooperative learning is a strong motivational incentive for the students. Students perceive that it is to their advantage if others students in their group learn and to their disadvantage if other students in their group do poorly. Also, a group incentive structure allows all students, even those who usually perform poorly, an opportunity to succeed, which can be highly motivating for these students.

72. **D.** This question relates to **Competency 008 (Instructional Delivery)**. Notice that you must select the choice that is *least* desirable. Eliminate choices A, B, and C because these answer choices are consistent with effective teaching practices. Choice D is a textbook-centered approach. Copying textbook problems and using calculators to obtain the answers would likely discourage active inquiry and result in less risk taking and less higher-level thinking from the students. Thus, choice D is the correct response.

73. **B.** This question addresses **Competency 013 (Professional Conduct)**. According to the Individuals with Disabilities Education Act (IDEA; formerly PL 94-142), the ARD committee must meet at least once every 12 months. Thus, choice B is the correct response. Eliminate choices A and C because these timelines are incorrect. Eliminate choice D because the timeline for ARD committee meetings is determined by federal law and is not left to the discretion of the school district.

74. **D.** This question addresses **Competency 011 (Family Involvement)**. The newsletter is the only option that ensures communication with the families will be effective. Eliminate choices A, B, and C because these actions do not ensure that the families will understand information that is conveyed through these means. The teacher can contact ESOL personnel on campus or in the district for information on how to create a multilingual newsletter. Thus, choice D is the correct response.

75. **A.** This question deals with teacher expectations, a topic that falls under **Competency 004 (Learning Principles)**. Eliminate choice B because research indicates that for young adolescents, peer influence usually overrides adult influence. Eliminate choice C because anxiety in small doses can improve academic achievement, as long as students are not held to an unrealistic level of expectation. Eliminate choice D because teacher expectations affect student self-concept and motivation, which, in turn, affect academic achievement. Teachers need to be aware of the "self-fulfilling prophecy," which predicts that, with time, a student's behavior and achievement will conform more closely to the expectations the teacher has for that student. Thus, choice A is the correct response.

76. **D.** This question deals with **Competency 006 (Classroom Management)**. According to research, effective classroom managers are initially involved with the whole class; have clear, specific plans for introducing rules and procedures; use simple, enjoyable tasks; and respond immediately to stop any misbehavior. Therefore, the teacher should not break students into groups on the first day. Choices A, B, and C are incorrect because these answer choices contain measures a teacher might take when using a cooperative group activity, which this teacher should not be doing on the first day of school. Thus, choice D is the correct response.

77. **D.** This question relates to **Competency 002 (Diversity)**. Teachers should be aware that behavior management problems are a potential roadblock when within-class ability grouping is used because other students are expected to work independently while the teacher works with a particular group (eliminate choice A). Eliminate choice B because research indicates that fixed within-class ability grouping widens the gap between high-ability and low-ability students. Thus, it is unlikely that the high-ability students will

Chapter 14: Practice Test 1

become more accepting of the low-ability students. Eliminate choice C because numerous experts contend that inflexible ability grouping is detrimental to low achievers because they often get locked into a low-level curriculum. Thus, choice D is the correct response.

78. **A.** This question relates to behaviorism, a topic that falls under **Competency 004 (Learning Principles)**. Eliminate choice B because *negative reinforcement* is the technique of strengthening a behavior by release from an undesirable situation. Eliminate choice C because *positive reinforcement* is the technique of strengthening a behavior by giving a desirable reward. Eliminate choice D because *shaping* involves positive reinforcement of a successful completion of steps toward a desired learning goal or behavior. Choice A is the correct response. *Extinction* is the technique of withdrawing reinforcers to discourage undesirable behavior in the classroom. The teacher is withdrawing recognition of the student (a reinforcer) to discourage the undesirable behavior of calling out in the classroom.

79. **C.** This question addresses **Competency 013 (Professional Conduct)**. Choice C is the correct response. Teachers in Texas have a legal obligation to report all actual or suspected cases of child abuse or neglect to the Texas Department of Family and Protective Services or any local or state law enforcement agency within 48 hours. They are not expected to, and should not, investigate the situation prior to making a report. Therefore, the teacher should not investigate on his or her own by discussing his or her suspicions with the student's parents (eliminate choice A) or the student's friends (eliminate choice B). Eliminate choice D because the teacher should not delay in making the report; failure to report is a Class A misdemeanor.

80. **B.** This question addresses both **Competency 002 (Diversity)** and **Competency 010 (Assessment)**. Eliminate choices A and D because these choices are off-topic. They do not relate to self-assessment. Eliminate choice C because this choice is about peer-assessment, not self-assessment. Thus, choice B is the correct response. By reviewing their journal entries, ELLs can identify strengths and weaknesses in their writing. In doing so, they self-assess the development of their writing skills over time.

81. **C.** This question deals with **Competency 003 (Instructional Design and Planning)**. Eliminate choice A because it is not supported by the question; the teacher's unit is focused on drug use, not on society in general. The teacher is aware that students will be more likely to avoid drug use if they are able to think for themselves and make informed, intelligent decisions, choice C. Eliminate choices B and D because although these might be additional outcomes, most likely the teacher's lessons will be designed to enhance students' independent thinking and decision-making skills. Thus, choice C is the correct response.

82. **A.** This question deals with characteristics of adolescents, a topic that falls under **Competency 001 (Developmentally Appropriate Practice)**. Eliminate choices B, C, and D because these characteristics do not describe adolescents; rather, they describe younger children. A typical psychosocial characteristic of adolescents is that they believe bad things happen to other people, not to them (the *invincibility fable*). Thus, choice A is the correct response.

83. **C.** This question relates to **Competency 008 (Instructional Delivery)**. Eliminate choices A, B, and D because these choices disagree with research findings. Teachers who are aware of the influence of peers on students' social and intellectual development can take advantage of this factor by using peer tutoring. Research investigating the effects of peer tutoring on student achievement has shown that, in general, the achievement of both tutors and tutees increases. Thus, choice C is the correct response.

84. **D.** This question addresses **Competency 011 (Family Involvement)**. Successful parent-teacher conferences can be the key that enhances a student's growth and promotes learning. Eliminate choices A and C because teachers should avoid diagnosing students to parents. Eliminate choice B because the teacher should not discuss other students' performance with Devyn's father. Choice D is the correct response. The teacher should explain her grading policy and show samples of Devyn's incomplete work. The teacher needs to emphasize that she expects students to be responsible and turn in work that is complete.

85. **C.** This question addresses **Competency 010 (Assessment)**. Of the assessment tools given in the answer choices, only portfolio assessment is an informal measure. Thus, choice C is the correct response.

86. **B.** This question deals with motivation, a topic that falls under **Competency 004 (Learning Principles)**. The teacher is using extrinsic motivation by offering a tangible reward. Thus, choice B is the correct response. Eliminate choices A and C because in contingency and group reward programs, rewards for the whole class (or group) are contingent on everyone's effort and participation. Eliminate choice D because intrinsic

rewards (for example, personal satisfaction) occur within an individual. It should be noted that authorities disagree about the use of rewards as a motivational strategy. Some are concerned that students' interest in gathering rewards may sabotage genuine interest in the subject area. Also, teachers find it difficult to determine rewards that are appropriate and, at the same time, desirable by students. A practice guide on Response to Intervention (RtI) for mathematics prepared by the What Works Clearinghouse suggested "As students learn and succeed more often in mathematics, interventionists can gradually fade the use of rewards because student success will become an intrinsic reward" (Gersten et al., 2009, p. 46).

87. **D.** This question deals with second language acquisition, a topic that falls under **Competency 008 (Instructional Delivery).** Eliminate choices A, B, and C because these features would require a level of reading ability that is probably beyond that of most students in the early production stage. Content area materials that are most effective for ELLs, especially those who are in the early production stage of English language acquisition, use nonlinguistic aids, such as charts, maps, illustrations, drawings, and pictures. It would be most critical for the software program to have extensive visual representations and other nonlinguistic graphic support to be effective for use by the teacher's ELLs. Thus, choice D is the correct response.

88. **D.** This question addresses **Competency 008 (Instructional Delivery).** Eliminate choice A because most authorities agree that lecturing is the least effective instructional strategy for all prekindergarten through grade 12 classrooms. Further, it is an inappropriate instructional strategy for use with elementary school students, so eliminate choices B and C. Lecturing should be avoided in elementary school. Thus, choice D is the correct response.

89. **A.** This question relates to **Competency 006 (Classroom Management).** Eliminate choice B because punitive-based measures fail to preserve the dignity of the student, which is an essential component of effective classroom management. The likely reason for the students' lack of interest is the long engagement in repetitive and boring tasks. Generally, students pay closer attention and become more involved when the topics relate directly to their experiences and interests. The teacher should engage the students in activities related to their interests and experiences. Thus, choice A is the correct response. Eliminate choices C and D because although these answer choices are measures that the teacher might take, they would not be as effective as that given in choice A.

90. **B.** This question addresses **Competency 001 (Developmentally Appropriate Practice).** Appreciation of another's culture in a child of this age can best be approached by showing similarities and differences with the child's familiar cultural forms. Eliminate choice A because this activity would be limited to physical characteristics of countries, and besides, it focuses on differences. Eliminate choice C because the countries selected might not represent any of the cultural groups in the class. Eliminate choice D because second-graders would have difficulty with this activity. Choice B is the correct response. Having students participate in a class activity in which they discover cultural similarities and differences in their own classroom could readily be expanded into a discussion about the diversity of American culture. By seeing that they have things in common, the students will be less suspicious of each other's cultures, and by identifying features that are unique, they will still be able to retain their cultural identities. This activity would be the most developmentally appropriate and meaningful of all the described activities.

91. **B.** This question deals with characteristics of children, a topic that falls under **Competency 001 (Developmentally Appropriate Practice).** Eliminate choices A and D because generally children at this age are too young to have the cognitive abilities or experiences to form strong opinions on issues. They rely more on the opinions of their family members (choice B), such as parents or older siblings, in forming their own attitudes. As they mature into young adolescents, the attitudes of their peers will begin to exert more influence, but not at this stage of their development (eliminate choice C). Thus, choice B is the correct response.

92. **B.** This question deals with learning centers, a topic that falls under **Competency 008 (Instructional Delivery).** Eliminate choice A because young children benefit from working in collaboration with others. Eliminate choice C because centers should involve "hands-on" activities, not worksheets (a poor practice). Eliminate choice D because learning centers should be an integral part of the early-childhood classroom. When students are working in centers, they should not have to leave the center to go get materials. All materials needed should be contained within the center. Thus, choice B is the correct response.

93. **B.** This question relates to **Competency 001 (Developmentally Appropriate Practice).** The teacher's students are sixth-graders, so most of them are between 11 and 12 years old. Eliminate choices A, C, and D because

247

these cognitive abilities are normally acquired during earlier stages of cognitive development. Choice B is the correct response. Most sixth-graders are in the process of developing the ability to think hypothetically about abstract concepts. They are able to handle contrary-to-fact propositions and can develop and test hypotheses.

94. **B.** This question addresses **Competency 012 (Professional Knowledge and Skills).** Eliminate choices A and C because these answer choices are not aligned with the question. You must now choose between choices B and D. Use the strategy of rereading the question before making your decision. The question is about interdisciplinary teams. Choice B is more aligned with the role of interdisciplinary teams than is choice D. Teachers on an interdisciplinary team recognize that they are members of a learning community and know how to work effectively with each other to promote student learning. By implementing the use of interdisciplinary teams that meet regularly to discuss concerns and plan together, a school is affording the teachers an opportunity to learn from each other and thereby improve the educational experiences of students. Thus, choice B is the correct response.

95. **B.** This question deals with working with ELLs, a topic that falls under **Competency 008 (Instructional Delivery).** Eliminate choice A because cooperative groups should be "composed of students of different ethnic backgrounds and at diverse cognitive and linguistic levels, who challenge and encourage each other" (Badía, 1996, p. 4). Eliminate choice C because most ELLs, even those in the preproduction stage of English language acquisition, can do labeling and drawing activities without assistance. Eliminate choice D because ELLs should be encouraged to interact with their non–ELL classmates during activities designed to promote social communication skills. Choice B is the correct response. When a recently arrived student needs an orientation to classroom rules and procedures, assigning a same-language classroom "buddy" who can assist the new student with classroom orientation is a good idea.

96. **A.** This question relates to **Competency 006 (Classroom Management).** The students are seventh-graders, so most of them are between 12 and 13 years old. Choice A is the correct response. A major source of anxiety for adolescents this age is fear of rejection by peers because peer relations are so important. By comparison, displeasing authority figures (choice B), failing to achieve academically (choice C), and failing to learn cultural norms (choice D) are less important sources of anxiety for most adolescents.

97. **A.** This question addresses **Competency 003 (Instructional Design and Planning).** Eliminate choices B and D because these answer choices are not supported by the question. The teacher did not involve the students when transforming the classroom into a pretend ocean. Eliminate choice C because this answer choice is not aligned with the question. Choice A is the correct response. When planning how to begin the unit, the teacher is likely to have been aware that providing the children with a concrete experience would make their study of the ocean more meaningful.

98. **A.** Essentially, this question deals with the psychosocial development of young children, a topic that falls under **Competency 001 (Developmentally Appropriate Practice).** The teacher's response reflects her knowledge and consideration of students' developmental processes, so choice A is the correct response. The other answer choices are not aligned with the question.

99. **C.** This question deals with English language proficiency levels, a topic that falls under **Competency 003 (Instructional Design and Planning).** Eliminate choices A, B, and D because the vocabulary and grammar in these sentences would be understandable to students who have been determined to be at the advanced level of English language proficiency. The sentence in choice C contains the idiom "put up with," which means "tolerate." An idiom is an expression used by speakers of a language that usually doesn't make sense if taken literally. ELLs, even those who test as advanced level proficient, have difficulty with idioms because the meaning cannot be determined simply by translating the words. Thus, choice C is the correct response.

100. **A.** This question addresses **Competency 013 (Professional Conduct).** Choice A is the correct response. According to the Individuals with Disabilities Education Act (IDEA; formerly PL 94-142) and Texas law, the regular education teacher on the ARD committee must participate as a full member of the team (eliminate choice D), including assisting in determining interventions and strategies for the student, choice A. Eliminate choices B and C because the regular education teacher on the ARD committee does not assume these responsibilities.

Chapter 15

Practice Test 2

4 Hours and 45 Minutes
100 Questions

Directions: Read each item and select the best response.

1. Students in a social studies class are having a whole-class discussion about the preservation of historical landmarks in their community. What are students likely to learn from the class discussion?

   A. Historical landmarks have little economic value.
   B. Accurate information is critical for effective communication.
   C. Community problems can be solved through thoughtful discussion.
   D. Working with others can lead to better and quicker solutions to problems.

2. A new teacher is using innovative instructional methods in his English class. To best ensure a supportive attitude from the principal, the teacher should

   A. invite the principal to visit his class to observe his teaching methods and their effects.
   B. present the principal with copies of scientifically based research that supports the teacher's instructional methods.
   C. send weekly reports to the principal to keep the principal apprised of the progress of the teacher's students.
   D. organize parents to send e-mails to the principal supporting the teacher's instructional methods.

3. After a science experiment, a high school teacher asks students to respond to the following two prompts:

   1. Justify the results of your experiment.
   2. Formulate a theory based on the results of your experiment.

   The major benefit to students from this assignment is that it

   A. helps them recall facts and basic concepts.
   B. allows them to apply their learning in a new context.
   C. provides a means for the teacher to assess their learning.
   D. promotes their higher-order thinking skills.

4. When planning learning experiences for diverse students, which of the following is an important guideline for teachers to keep in mind?

   A. Teachers should avoid incorporating the cultural backgrounds of their students into the curriculum.
   B. Teachers should recognize that, within a particular cultural group, individual variation is to be expected.
   C. Students from different cultural backgrounds will share few common educational interests and aspirations.
   D. Students' cultural backgrounds have little impact on how students construct knowledge or interact in the classroom.

249

5. With regard to administration of the mandatory statewide assessments, which of the following actions by a teacher would be considered unethical?

   A. to present lessons in advance that focus on the Texas Essential Knowledge and Skills
   B. to use a seating chart to plan and record student seat assignments in the testing room
   C. to remain in the testing room when the students are taking the assessment
   D. to question students on test content or test items after the days set aside for state testing have passed

6. A student who scores at the 80th percentile on a standardized achievement test has

   A. scored the same as or better than 80 percent of a norm group.
   B. scored better than 20 percent of a norm group.
   C. correctly answered 80 percent of the test questions.
   D. correctly answered 20 percent of the test questions.

7. As students in a social studies class watch a video about the importance of recycling, the teacher periodically stops the video and poses questions about the ideas presented. This strategy is most likely motivated by the teacher's understanding that

   A. teachers should demonstrate and model the use of higher-order thinking skills.
   B. teachers' efforts to maintain and reinforce student involvement correlate with students' cognitive engagement.
   C. students stay on task when they are aware that they are being monitored.
   D. students need structured, well-managed environments.

8. The most appropriate way for a teacher to share an innovative instructional strategy with school colleagues is to

   A. send an e-mail to all teachers describing the strategy and offering to demonstrate it in their classrooms.
   B. speak with the principal about demonstrating the strategy as part of a workshop for all interested teachers.
   C. speak with the superintendent about ways the strategy could be implemented throughout the school district.
   D. explain the strategy at the next school board meeting.

9. Which of the following is most likely to promote the creative thinking skills of high school students?

   A. in algebra, recognizing an equivalent representation of a numerical quantity
   B. in economics, locating details on a graph, chart, or diagram
   C. in science, predicting the logical next step
   D. in English, writing an original short story

10. A student who exhibits a cognitive style that is right-brain dominant is likely to learn best through instruction based on

    A. presentation of content in small, step-by-step increments.
    B. detailed verbal explanations and instructions.
    C. visual and kinesthetic global activities.
    D. objective, short-answer questioning.

11. During a technology workshop, Mr. Bishop, the art teacher, tells the workshop presenter that he has been using a popular computer graphics software package in his classes and that his students thoroughly enjoy it. However, Mr. Bishop goes on to say that he has discovered that the school does not own any licensed copies of the software. What action, if any, should Mr. Bishop take?

   A. Immediately remove all copies of the software from the computers in the classroom.
   B. Continue to use the software, but contact the manufacturer about obtaining licensed copies.
   C. Continue to use the software, but contact the district technology specialist and discuss the problem.
   D. Continue to use the software and say nothing, because educators are allowed to use software without obtaining licensed copies.

12. Which of the following types of assessment includes a variety of samples of a student's work, collected over time, that shows the student's growth and development?

   A. checklist
   B. daily quizzes
   C. portfolio
   D. running record

13. After students finish reading *Charlotte's Web*, the teacher asks, "Do you think Fern loved Wilbur?" A student replies, "Of course!" The teacher then says, "Tell us how you know that Fern loved Wilbur."

   What communication technique is the teacher using in her last statement?

   A. paraphrasing
   B. probing
   C. redirecting
   D. summarizing

14. Mr. James, a new high school American history teacher, has asked Ms. Flores, a mentor teacher, to observe a session of his history class because he has had difficulty motivating students to stay on task during cooperative learning activities. Mr. James can most effectively help Ms. Flores prepare for the classroom observation by providing her with a

   A. seating chart that indicates the students who tend to be "ringleaders" of the off-task behavior.
   B. lesson plan for the class session that she will be observing.
   C. written detailed description of the problems he is having with students.
   D. list of all students' names along with designation of their current grades in the class.

15. A language arts teacher attended a summer workshop on critical thinking. The teacher plans to incorporate ideas from the workshop into her lessons. Which of the following language arts tasks would best elicit students' critical thinking skills?

   A. using a dictionary to find the meaning of words
   B. identifying and summarizing the major events in a narrative
   C. evaluating the effectiveness of a written response according to audience and purpose
   D. identifying standard English grammatical structures in a written work

16. A teacher has a class composed of students from varied cultural backgrounds. DVDs, CDs, games, magazines, and books related to students' home cultures would be most effectively used as resources for the purpose of

   A. integrating cultural content into content area instruction.
   B. matching students according to similar cultural communication styles.
   C. determining students' personal interests related to their home cultures.
   D. improving communication with the parents of students.

17. A parent of a student in Ms. Chen's algebra 1 class wants to meet with Ms. Chen to discuss his son's performance and progress in her class. Ms. Chen prepares for the parent-teacher conference by collecting samples of the student's work and assessments, along with the learning objectives for the current grading period. Ms. Chen's method of preparation for the conference likely is to be most effective in helping her to

   A. facilitate a productive meeting with the parent.
   B. ensure accurate communication between the student and his parent.
   C. foster in the student a positive attitude toward algebra.
   D. promote in the student a sense of responsibility for his learning.

18. On which of the following test question types does guessing have the most effect?

   A. constructed response
   B. fill in the blank
   C. multiple choice
   D. true-false

19. When facilitating class discussions, teachers should

   A. ask more questions of students sitting in the back of the room to make sure they are involved in the discussion.
   B. mainly use questions that elicit specific, concrete information about the topic of discussion.
   C. establish positive interactions that support students' responses.
   D. provide the correct answer if no one responds immediately.

20. A new high school English teacher joins the Texas Council of Teachers of English Language Arts (TCTELA). Which of the following is the most significant benefit of joining a professional organization in one's content field?

   A. increased opportunities to stay abreast of current developments in the field
   B. increased opportunities to obtain grants for school-based projects in the field
   C. expanded access to experienced mentors in the field
   D. expanded access to quality lesson plans and other instructional resources in the field

21. Students in a third-grade class are working in groups doing an experiment in which they drop a ball from various heights and measure the greatest height the ball reached when it bounced. Before the experiment begins, the teacher asks the students to formulate a hypothesis about what they expect to happen. After they have collected all their data, the students create a graph that shows maximum height reached when the ball was dropped from different heights. Afterward, which of the following prompts regarding the experiment would be most effective for assessing students' higher-order thinking skills?

   A. Did you always measure the bounce to either the top or the bottom of the ball?
   B. Did the ball bounce more times when it was dropped from a higher height?
   C. Write a justification for the information shown in your graph.
   D. Without referring to the instructions provided to you, write a set of step-by-step procedures that another person could follow to perform the experiment.

22. During a science unit on simple machines, a girl in the class complains to the teacher, "This is boy stuff. Why do I have to do it?" Several of the other girls in the class nod in agreement. The teacher ponders how best to deal with this incident. She should *first*

   A. check herself to make sure she is not modeling any gender stereotyping.
   B. lead a class discussion about science-related career opportunities.
   C. check classroom materials to make sure they do not reflect gender stereotyping.
   D. attend a workshop about promoting gender equity.

23. A school district permits teachers to borrow computers from their schools to take home. According to the Code of Ethics and Standard Practices for Texas Educators, if a teacher in the district borrows a computer from the school, it would be unethical for the teacher to

   A. keep the computer for more than one business day.
   B. fail to delete his or her files before returning the computer.
   C. fail to use the computer for authorized school business only.
   D. fail to repair any damage that might occur to the computer when it is in his or her home.

24. Which of the following assessment methods is most likely to yield valid information about what students know and understand?

   A. informal observation with a checklist
   B. student self-assessment
   C. peer assessment
   D. student journaling

25. A teacher begins a language arts class by saying, "Today, your 10-minute writing activity is on the subject of school uniforms. Please begin writing in your journals, and stop when I give the signal." Some of the students begin the writing assignment, but most of the students have puzzled expressions and are not writing. The teacher addresses the class, "Do you have a question about the assignment?" One student responds, "What do you want us to write? We don't understand."

   Which of the following tenets would have been most helpful for the teacher to consider when crafting the writing assignment?

   A. Effective teachers communicate instructional tasks clearly to students.
   B. Effective teachers know how to shape the classroom into a community of learners engaged in active inquiry.
   C. Effective teachers use a variety of modes and tools of communication.
   D. Effective teachers appreciate the cultural dimensions of communication.

26. A new high school teacher wants to learn how to more effectively facilitate whole-group class discussions. Which of the following measures probably would most helpful for that purpose?

   A. Ask colleagues for their opinions on whether holding whole-group class discussions is a worthwhile instructional activity.
   B. Search the Internet for guidelines on how to effectively facilitate whole-group discussions and practice the advice provided.
   C. Study articles in professional journals on how to effectively facilitate whole-group discussions.
   D. Arrange to observe a colleague who effectively uses whole-group discussions.

27. Which of the following science tasks would best elicit students' higher-order thinking skills?

   A. solving a problem after choosing an appropriate formula
   B. retrieving information from a chart, table, diagram, or graph
   C. drawing a conclusion based on data analysis
   D. recognizing examples and nonexamples of concepts

28. Middle school students who are at risk of academic failure benefit most when

   A. teachers help the students understand the structure and organization of school at the middle level.
   B. the students are given opportunities to experience academic success on assignments they perceive as meaningful and challenging.
   C. the students are routinely grouped together to do class assignments to avoid being put in competition with their higher-achieving peers.
   D. teachers minimize the use of any form of assessment to avoid causing stress due to low achievement.

29. A first-grade teacher plans to introduce a new mathematics concept in her class of 20 students that includes two students who are struggling learners. Which of the following approaches is most likely to provide the teacher with useful data to differentiate instruction for these two students?

   A. Discussing with her grade-level colleagues the acquisition of the mathematics concept by first-graders.
   B. Writing anecdotal notes of each student's attention span during the introduction of the mathematics concept.
   C. Having all of her students complete a teacher-made checklist about the mathematics concept during a class cooperative group activity.
   D. Analyzing each struggling learner's performance on previously taught concepts to identify areas of strength and weakness.

30. A social studies teacher has planned a thematic unit titled "Saving the Planet." The teacher begins the unit with the topic of natural resources. Of the following graphic organizers, which would be most useful for determining students' prior knowledge about natural resources?

   A. decision tree
   B. flowchart
   C. story tree
   D. web

31. In general, a teacher's expectations would tend to have the LEAST effect on a middle school student's

   A. academic performance.
   B. behavior.
   C. peer relations.
   D. self-concept.

32. In giving students problems in which they must generalize an algebraic or geometric pattern, a mathematics teacher is most likely promoting students' use of

   A. conditional reasoning.
   B. deductive reasoning.
   C. inductive reasoning.
   D. syllogistic reasoning.

33. As a culminating activity for a unit on nutrition, a high school interdisciplinary team plans to have an informal social event at school for their classes. Which of the following is most likely to occur when the social event takes place?

   A. Field-independent learners and field-dependent learners will be equally active during the event.
   B. Field-independent learners will tend to be more passive than field-dependent learners during the event.
   C. Field-dependent learners will tend to be more passive than field-independent learners during the event.
   D. Both field-independent learners and field-dependent learners will be passive during the event.

34. It is inappropriate for a teacher to share information about a minor student without written permission from the student's parent when a

   A. school counselor who has been seeing the student wants to examine the educational records kept by the teacher on the student.
   B. colleague who is conducting a research project wants to use non-personally identifiable information from the educational records kept by the teacher on the student.
   C. colleague who is a former teacher of the student wants to look at the educational records kept by the teacher on the student.
   D. noncustodial parent wants to review the educational records kept by the teacher on the student.

Read the information below to answer questions 35–36.

A high school world history studies teacher has observed that during whole-class discussions, the English language learners (ELLs) in the classroom rarely volunteer comments.

35. In facilitating class discussions, it is important the teacher is aware that

   A. asking ELLs less challenging questions they can get right will make them more willing to participate in future discussions.
   B. ELLs who are more willing to speak in class are usually more proficient language users than those who are reluctant to speak.
   C. cultural factors as well as language ability affect the extent to which ELLs speak out in class.
   D. probing for further explanation or clarification when ELLs give responses should be avoided, so that they will not be embarrassed in front of their peers.

36. To encourage all students to think critically and consider a variety of ideas during class discussions, the teacher should ask

   A. affective domain questions.
   B. convergent questions.
   C. divergent questions.
   D. who, what, where, and when questions.

37. A teacher who has academically gifted students in the class can best prepare to work with these students by keeping in mind they need

   A. opportunities for independent learning that encourage them to apply creative and critical thinking.
   B. time to work independently when their peers are working in small groups.
   C. structured activities that reinforce basic skills more often than their peers.
   D. external rewards, because they often lack intrinsic motivation to learn.

38. A fifth-grade student has a grade equivalent score of 7.6 on a standardized reading test. The student's grade equivalent score indicates that the student

   A. is ready for seventh-grade reading material.
   B. is in the top 7.6 percent of students who took the test.
   C. did as well on the test as an average seventh-grader in the sixth month of the school year would do on a standardized seventh-grade reading test.
   D. did as well on the test as an average seventh-grader in the sixth month of the school year would do on the same standardized reading test that the fifth-grade student took.

39. During an informal conversation, a second-grade English language learner (ELL) tells his teacher, "My *madre*—I mean, my mother—she work on grocery store." Which of the following would be the most appropriate teacher feedback in response to the student's statement?

   A. "Oh, so the Spanish word for 'mother' is *madre*? That's good to know."
   B. "What should you do to the verb *work* when it comes after the word *she*?"
   C. "Your mother works in a grocery store? What does she do there?"
   D. "Should you say 'on a grocery store' or 'in a grocery store'?"

40. Assigning students to work with a partner, a middle school language arts teacher challenges each pair with the following question: "How many uses can you think of for a book?"

In giving students this task, the teacher is most likely promoting their use of

   A. convergent thinking.
   B. divergent thinking.
   C. deductive reasoning.
   D. generalization.

41. In which of the following classes is the activity LEAST consistent with a tactile/kinesthetic modality preference?

   A. In language arts, students put on a play and dress in costumes.
   B. In mathematics, students do a survey on favorite jean brands and summarize results.
   C. In social studies, students participate in a simulation activity acting out a historical event.
   D. In science, students work in small groups to compare the heat reflection properties of various fabrics.

42. During group presentations, after students have worked in cooperative learning groups to investigate the properties of magnets, a fifth-grade teacher notices that two students, Rosa and Katie, are whispering to each other instead of paying attention to the presentations. When the girls look in the teacher's direction, the teacher gives them a stern look. Immediately, the girls quit whispering and direct their attention to the presentations. The teacher's behavior is an example of

   A. extinction.
   B. negative reinforcement.
   C. nonverbal communication.
   D. modeling.

43. During daily mathematics activities, an English language learner (ELL) demonstrates an adequate proficiency in using place-value concepts. However, the student scores very poorly on items assessing understanding of place value on a standardized test. The student's mathematics teacher could best interpret this conflicting result by *first* taking which of the following steps?

   A. Calculate the deviation between the student's standardized test score and the student's average daily score to determine whether the student's overall performance is on grade level.
   B. Give the student the standardized test again, and compare the student's performance on the two tests to determine whether the test results are reliable.
   C. Analyze whether the daily mathematics activities are aligned with the way the standardized test assesses place value.
   D. Use additional multiple methods to investigate the student's actual understanding of place-value concepts.

44. Especially with young children, praise is most effective when it is

   A. global and given frequently.
   B. global and given infrequently.
   C. specific and given frequently.
   D. specific and given infrequently.

Read the information below to answer questions 45–47.

An eighth-grade health education teacher is beginning a unit focusing on the development of healthy lifestyles. An important goal of the unit is for students to learn to make responsible decisions related to risky behaviors. The teacher begins the unit by having the students brainstorm ways to respond to pressure from peers to engage in unsafe activities such as drug or alcohol use.

45. The teacher can maximize the benefit of the brainstorming activity by asking the students to

   A. back up suggestions with personal experiences in their own lives.
   B. present any ideas that come to mind and refrain from judging the ideas of others.
   C. focus on presenting ideas that are unique instead of elaborating on the ideas of others.
   D. avoid presenting ideas that are probably unworkable and focus instead on realistic ideas.

46. To help the students develop decision-making skills, the teacher involves them in role-play activities modeled on situations they are likely to encounter. This approach demonstrates the teacher's understanding that students at this developmental stage

   A. are highly responsive to suggestions from adults for modifying their behaviors.
   B. cannot imagine any situation they have not personally experienced.
   C. learn better when skills are practiced in a meaningful context.
   D. have little concern about what others think of them.

47. As part of the healthy lifestyles unit, the teacher presents a series of lessons on the science of nutrition. The teacher observes that the two English language learners (ELLs) in the class are having difficulty understanding this material. Given that the two ELLs are at the intermediate level of English language proficiency, which of the following strategies would be most effective to help them comprehend the content?

   A. Give the ELLs an English language dictionary and have them write definitions of key vocabulary words before each lesson.
   B. Pair each ELL with a native English speaker and have them read the material about the science of nutrition together.
   C. Show a short video clip about the day's topic at the beginning of a lesson.
   D. Read the material about the science of nutrition to the whole class as they follow along silently.

48. Students in a sixth-grade health class are learning about interpersonal skills. One student asks, "What do we do when a friend is mean to us?" The teacher addresses the whole class, "What do you think you should do when a friend is mean to you?"

   What technique is the teacher using in the last question to the whole class?

   A. paraphrasing
   B. probing
   C. redirecting
   D. summarizing

49. For which of the following purposes would a teacher use truncation during an Internet search?

   A. to increase the accuracy of the search
   B. to narrow the search
   C. to represent variant forms of the same word
   D. to find an exact phrase

50. A second-grade teacher has set up learning centers in the classroom. In addition to work periods that make use of the learning centers, the teacher allots a block of time every day for students to have free choice to select the centers to which they want to go. To avoid overcrowding in popular centers, the teacher devises a system of organization that limits the number of students who are permitted to use a center at any one time. To accommodate as many students as possible, a bell is rung periodically during the free-choice time to signal that it is time to move to a different center. On occasion at free-choice time, some students in the class get upset when they cannot immediately go to their favorite centers. A few students even get into arguments over the centers. In general, which of the following management strategies would best promote appropriate student behavior during free-choice time?

   A. modeling social skills with all students and helping them work out compromises to conflicts
   B. helping students who cannot go to their favorite centers find alternative centers they are likely to enjoy
   C. being flexible about the number of students who are permitted to use a center at any one time, so that students who are upset do not have to wait to go to their favorite centers
   D. devising a plan for managing centers that allows all students to work in their favorite centers at least once a week

51. Which of the following strategies would be best for increasing adolescents' motivation to learn?

   A. Provide learning opportunities that relate to their interests and experiences.
   B. Offer public recognition as an incentive for good work.
   C. Stress the importance of good grades to achievement of future success.
   D. Withdraw privileges for failure to complete work.

52. Children in a prekindergarten class complain to the teacher that the markers in the art center do not write anymore. One child says that someone dipped the markers in glue. Another child says that the caps were left off. What should the teacher do to address this situation?

    A. Ask the children to tell the teacher when they see someone misusing the markers.
    B. Hold a class meeting and guide the children to generate a set of rules for the art center.
    C. Replace the markers, but tell the children that if the markers are misused again, they will not be replaced.
    D. Speak privately to the children who are misusing the markers and warn them that they will not be able to go to the art center if they continue to misuse the markers.

53. A second-grade teacher has selected an expository text on vegetable garden plants of Texas to read to her students. The teacher can best prepare the students for the text on vegetable garden plants by

    A. helping the students make a chart in which they list what they already know and what they want to learn about vegetable garden plants.
    B. having the students memorize a list of key vocabulary words related to vegetable garden plants.
    C. drawing a diagram of a corn plant on the board and eliciting the students' help in labeling the parts.
    D. telling the students that it is important for them to learn about vegetable garden plants because humans depend on these plants for food.

54. The use of different language forms that depend on the setting, the relationship of the speaker to the person he or she is addressing, and the function of the interaction is known as

    A. discourse.
    B. lexicon.
    C. register.
    D. semantics.

Read the information below to answer questions 55–56.

Mr. Ruiz is an eighth-grade teacher. He has scheduled a parent-teacher conference with Cardi's parents about her low performance on a criterion-referenced reading test. The teacher understands the importance of family involvement in their child's education and looks forward to working with the parents to help Cardi. He has prepared a written agenda for the conference to keep the meeting on track, and has gathered information and materials that are pertinent to the purpose of the conference.

55. As the meeting begins, the parents tell the teacher they are concerned that Cardi comes home upset every day and says that no one likes her. Which of the following would be the most appropriate response from Mr. Ruiz?

    A. Paraphrase the parents' comment and ask for further information about the situation.
    B. Show concern and then move on to the planned agenda.
    C. Tell the parents they should schedule a meeting with the school counselor to discuss the situation.
    D. Assure the parents that most middle school students feel that way occasionally.

56. Which of the following statements by Mr. Ruiz would be the best way to explain to the parents what the results of Cardi's criterion-referenced reading test show?

    A. "The results show Cardi's individual performance and effort in reading up to this point in the school year."
    B. "The results show how Cardi compares in reading achievement with children of the same age and grade in schools nationwide."
    C. "The results show Cardi's mastery of specific concepts and skills in reading."
    D. "The results show that Cardi has selected her best work to showcase her performance in reading."

57. A teacher encourages family members to serve as volunteer tutors in the school. Which of the following would be the most likely purpose for such an arrangement?

A. to give family members a sense of ownership in the school
B. to create family awareness of problems in the school
C. to allow students, while at school, the opportunity to discuss their problems with a family member
D. to improve student behavior in the community at large

58. A teacher has a class of mixed-ability and diverse cultural backgrounds. When assigning students to groups for cooperative learning activities, the teacher makes sure the groups are diverse in ability level, gender, and cultural background. Grouping students this way is most likely to

A. help students learn to deal with prejudice.
B. promote critical thinking and problem solving in group activities.
C. nurture a sense of community in the classroom.
D. enhance students' ability to be thoughtful questioners.

59. "Given a paragraph, the student will identify all the nouns with 90 percent accuracy." This statement is an example of a(n)

A. affective objective.
B. cognitive objective.
C. psychomotor objective.
D. reflective objective.

60. A high school teacher has a student who seems especially unmotivated and has been performing poorly in class. Before talking with the student, which of the following should the teacher do first to find out additional information that would help in dealing with the student?

A. Review the student's educational records.
B. Discuss the problem with the school counselor.
C. Talk with the student's friends.
D. Arrange a conference with the student's parents.

61. A kindergartener is shown a tall, thin jar and a short, wide jar, both of which hold exactly one pint. When the teacher questions her about the two jars, the student's answers indicate that she believes the taller container holds more liquid. Based on this evidence, the teacher likely would conclude that the student

A. is developmentally delayed.
B. has a vision problem.
C. lacks the ability to conserve.
D. needs to be evaluated by a special education specialist.

62. A key goal of a teacher's classroom management strategy should be to

A. provide an environment that eliminates unfamiliar or unexpected occurrences.
B. motivate students to proceed from simple to complex in their approach to learning.
C. encourage students to monitor and self-manage their own behavior.
D. allow students to decide which topics will be studied and for how long.

63. The stage of development in language acquisition wherein the second language learner works to receive and understand the new language but produces little or no expressive language is known as

A. preproduction.
B. early production.
C. speech emergence.
D. intermediate fluency.

64. A seventh-grade science teacher's instructional methods include inquiry and discovery learning in the context of cooperative learning groups. These instructional methods will most likely

A. provide structure to learning activities.
B. sequence instruction.
C. establish group morale.
D. foster independent learning.

65. During a whole-class discussion, a student is creating a minor disruption by tapping a pencil on the desk. Which of the following interventions should the teacher use *first* with the student?

   A. Say the student's name and give the student a signal to stop the behavior.
   B. Make eye contact with the student and give a stern gaze but continue with the lesson uninterrupted.
   C. Ask the student to stop the pencil tapping.
   D. Stop the class discussion and send the student to the principal's office.

66. Which of the following situations is an example of scaffolding to promote student learning in a fifth-grade social studies classroom?

   A. The teacher sets up a reading center containing biographies of significant individuals in American history.
   B. The teacher gives students weekly geography quizzes to review important information covered during recent lessons on North American geography.
   C. The teacher assigns students to cooperative learning groups to create a presentation on an American invention or innovation.
   D. The teacher reviews and posts a timeline of key events to provide students with context for learning about factors leading up to the American Revolution.

67. Two middle school teachers agree to create an interdisciplinary science and social studies unit with coordinated learning activities between their classes. The teachers should begin their planning of the unit by *first*

   A. checking on the availability of materials and resources.
   B. deciding on student learning goals that both will emphasize in their classrooms.
   C. activating students' prior knowledge related to the unit theme.
   D. deciding on appropriate instructional strategies to address the varied needs and abilities of all their students.

68. During a whole-group activity about the characters in a book that students in a third-grade class have read, most of the students are actively participating in the activity, with the exception of one student, who is rolling a small ball on the desk. Which of the following would be the *best* approach for the teacher to use with this student?

   A. Ignore the off-task behavior completely, so as not to lose the momentum of the class activity.
   B. Walk by the student's desk, unobtrusively take the ball, and then find time later to talk with the student.
   C. Stop the activity and reprimand the student in a calm voice.
   D. Stop the activity, walk to the student's desk, and quietly ask the student to put the ball away.

69. A high school economics teacher is planning a unit on the development of a market economy. Which of the following would be most effective for assessing students' prior knowledge about the unit topic?

   A. using an advance organizer
   B. giving students time to do some reading on the topic
   C. having small-group discussions
   D. inviting in a guest speaker

70. An English language arts teacher's decision to use a thematic approach for teaching a unit on literature *best* demonstrates the teacher's understanding of the importance of

   A. helping students to make connections between and among concepts within a discipline.
   B. using multiple activities that engage and motivate students at appropriate developmental levels.
   C. providing learning situations that will encourage students to practice skills and gain knowledge needed in a diverse society.
   D. enhancing students' ability to apply knowledge in various contexts.

71. Which of the following practices is likely to have a negative impact on a beginning English language learner's acquisition of English?

   A. encouraging the student to use English instead of the primary language when at home
   B. creating an academically challenging environment
   C. having high expectations for all learners
   D. using nonverbal cues, including gestures and facial expressions

72. A social studies teacher plans to use a simulation activity in a lesson about supply and demand. Which of the following is a major limitation of using simulation activities?

   A. They focus too much on basic skills.
   B. They often require a considerable amount of time.
   C. Students usually do not find them interesting or fun.
   D. Students find the realism too threatening.

73. Under the Individuals with Disabilities Education Act (IDEA; formerly PL 94-142), which of the following is a right of the parents of a child with disabilities who is receiving special education services in a public school?

   A. the right to participate in the decision-making process regarding the educational placement of their child
   B. the right to select the public school their child will attend
   C. the right to interpret the instructional implications of evaluation results
   D. the right to determine the most appropriate accommodations or modifications for their child

74. A first-grade teacher is concerned about Joaquin's self-concept. He does not have many friends because he insists on being in charge at play time. Which of the following actions by the teacher would be most effective in helping Joaquin change his behavior and in improving his self-concept?

   A. Privately praise him when he plays cooperatively with others at play time.
   B. Tell him he has to let other children be in charge at play time.
   C. Send him to timeout when he starts demanding to be in charge at play time.
   D. Suggest to him that he play alone at play time.

75. A teacher is considering using a tutorial software with a few struggling learners. The software presents information in small units, followed by one or two questions, and then immediate feedback to the student on his or her responses. Such software is most useful for which of the following purposes?

   A. allowing students to monitor their own progress
   B. prompting students to set higher standards of personal achievement
   C. fostering students' development of critical thinking skills
   D. encouraging students to explore creative solutions to problems

76. Students in a high school sociology class are designing a questionnaire to survey students in the school about the removal of vending machines from the school building. Allowing the students to compose the questions for the questionnaire is likely to enhance their interest in the survey project by

   A. relating their learning to community issues.
   B. enabling them to pursue topics of personal interest.
   C. helping them to set their own learning goals.
   D. giving them a sense of control over their learning experiences.

77. A high school biology teacher is having students engage in a cooperative learning group activity. After the students complete the activity, each student group will make a presentation to the entire class to share the group's results. The teacher plans for the presentations to take place during the last 15 minutes of class, so the group activity must not run over into this time period. Which of the following would be the best way for the teacher to remind the students about the time, so that the group activity is completed in time for the presentations to take place?

   A. Remind them at the very beginning of the activity.
   B. Remind them every 5 minutes.
   C. Remind them every 10 minutes.
   D. Remind them 5 minutes prior to the necessary end time for the activity.

78. A fifth-grade teacher plans a unit designed to strengthen students' skills in pattern recognition and critical thinking. The teacher plans to use appropriate instructional activities in whole-group and small-group settings. As part of the initial planning process, the teacher's *first* step in defining instructional objectives for the new unit should be to

   A. select appropriate instructional activities for fostering growth in pattern recognition and critical thinking.
   B. analyze the benefits and limitations of various whole-group and small-group instructional strategies.
   C. assess students' general areas of strengths and needs in pattern recognition and critical thinking.
   D. implement procedures for promoting positive and productive group interactions.

79. During the first week of school, a teacher observes behavior in a student that causes the teacher to suspect that the student might have a learning disability. With regard to this student, the teacher has a responsibility to

   A. notify special education staff that the student needs special education support services in the teacher's classroom.
   B. notify the student's parents that they need to initiate a request for the student to be evaluated to determine whether the student is eligible for special education services.
   C. initiate a request for the student to be evaluated to determine whether the student is eligible for special education services as soon as possible.
   D. initiate a request for the student to be evaluated to determine whether the student is eligible for special education services only when it is clear that the student's needs cannot be met through the regular education program.

80. Which of the following is a necessary element of inquiry-based learning in science?

   A. students writing group reports after researching a science topic together
   B. a teacher showing a video presentation of a science principle related to a lesson
   C. students forming hypotheses prior to a lab investigation
   D. a teacher leading a question-and-answer session on a scientific principle

81. When an English language learner (ELL) has developed the ability to understand a message in a second language, the student has developed

   A. expressive language.
   B. oral language.
   C. pragmatic language.
   D. receptive language.

82. Students in a social studies class are designing a learning project about ways the environment affects human systems. In assisting the students in designing their learning experiences for the project, it is most important that the teacher make certain that the tasks and activities for the project

   A. address the grade-level standards set forth in the Texas Essential Knowledge and Skills for social studies.
   B. be planned by the students and address only the grade-level Texas Essential Knowledge and Skills standards for social studies that the students have identified as most relevant and consistent with the project.
   C. address only the grade-level Texas Essential Knowledge and Skills standards for social studies that are simple enough so that even students who are academically at risk can participate in a meaningful way.
   D. be preplanned by the teacher to ensure that the learning experiences are congruent with the grade-level Texas Essential Knowledge and Skills standards for social studies.

83. A third-grade teacher begins a mathematics lesson about polygons by reading to students the book *The Greedy Triangle* by Marilyn Burns. This book tells a story about triangles and other multi-sided figures such as polygons. The probable purpose for this way of beginning the lesson is to

   A. gain students' attention.
   B. communicate the objective for the lesson.
   C. present the lesson content.
   D. assess student learning.

84. A teacher is concerned about Victor, a student who recently enrolled in school. Victor acts listless most of the time and appears uninterested in class activities. The teacher talks with the assistant principal about Victor and learns that Victor and his family are living in a homeless shelter. After repeated attempts, the teacher is able to talk by telephone with Victor's mother about the teacher's concerns regarding Victor. The teacher's best response to Victor's unstable home situation is to give highest priority to

   A. stressing to Victor's mother that he needs a more stable home environment right away.
   B. offering to put Victor's mother in touch with a church organization that provides housing for homeless families.
   C. ensuring that Victor has one or two close friends in the class with whom he can interact on a regular daily basis.
   D. providing an accepting and supportive environment for Victor in the classroom.

85. Students in a kindergarten class are going on a field trip to a fire station. The teacher asks a paraprofessional to accompany them and videotape the field trip. To ensure that the video will be a useful instructional tool, the teacher should *first*

   A. assign questions to the students to ask as they are being videotaped.
   B. write a narrative for the video.
   C. discuss with the paraprofessional the sequence of events that need to be recorded.
   D. discuss with the paraprofessional the purpose of the video.

86. Which of the following assessments is most effective in determining the extent to which students use specific problem-solving strategies in math?

   A. norm-referenced achievement test
   B. criterion-referenced skills test
   C. self-monitoring checklist
   D. holistic scoring rubric

87. To improve the effectiveness of his communication with English language learners (ELLs), a new fourth-grade teacher attends a workshop on Stephen Krashen's comprehensible input hypothesis. Which of the following strategies best supports comprehensible input for ELLs?

    A. incorporating gestures, visuals, and manipulatives
    B. giving noncorrective responses
    C. extending wait time
    D. using idiomatic expressions

88. Which of the following practices by a teacher would best promote a student's development of positive self-esteem?

    A. frequently praising the student for "doing a good job" when returning the student's assignments
    B. giving the student tangible rewards for finishing assignments on time
    C. pointing out the student's achievements in front of classmates
    D. routinely presenting the student with challenging tasks that, with effort, the student can accomplish successfully

89. Teachers holding class meetings to deal with problems in the classroom is most in accord with which of the following?

    A. Teachers should take opportunities to clarify consequences for inappropriate behavior.
    B. Teachers should promote student ownership in a smoothly functioning learning community.
    C. Teachers should model respect for diversity and individual differences.
    D. Teachers should use a variety of means to convey high expectations for all students.

90. A middle school English language arts teacher uses a holistic scoring rubric to assess students' weekly one-page essays. The teacher assigns an overall score of 1 to 5 based on five criteria: organization, grammar, punctuation, spelling, and clarity. Which of the following is an important limitation of using this assessment method on a regular basis?

    A. It is time-consuming for the teacher to use.
    B. It does not provide students information from which they can determine whether their writing is improving.
    C. It does not provide specific feedback on the criteria used in the rubric.
    D. It does not result in a score that can be converted to a letter grade.

91. A social studies teacher begins a unit on the similarities and differences of Native American groups in Texas by devoting time to collecting ideas from the whole class about what they already know about the topic from their own previous experiences. This approach is beneficial to students primarily because it will help them

    A. memorize detailed information quickly and efficiently.
    B. make value judgments about relevant concepts.
    C. make connections between what they already know and new learning.
    D. determine which events caused other events to happen.

92. A first-grade teacher is working with her students on a learning project about the significant aspects of the lives and accomplishments of selected men and women in the period of history before 1880 (for example, Sacajawea, George Washington, Betsy Ross, Abraham Lincoln, and Harriet Tubman). Which of the following activities related to the project would be of greatest benefit to the students?

    A. having the students play a game in which they name a historical figure when their turn comes
    B. reading aloud a children's biography of a historical figure of the relevant time period
    C. having the students color pictures of historical figures of the relevant time period to post on their classroom wall
    D. showing a video about the Revolutionary War or the Civil War

93. Students in a third-grade class have been gathering information about planets from websites. During an Internet session, a student in the class tells the teacher, "My mom doesn't want me doing this. She says there are bad things on the Internet." The teacher is aware that the school computers are equipped with Internet child-safety filtering software, but she has not explained what this means to the students. Nonetheless, the teacher also is probably aware that, for young children this age, attitudes toward an issue, such as whether using the Internet is a "good" or "bad" idea, tend to be most influenced by their

   A. cognitive abilities.
   B. families' attitudes.
   C. peers' attitudes.
   D. personal experiences.

94. Teachers in a middle school set up a homework hotline that students and their families can use to obtain information about homework assignments for each class. Which of the following is the most significant benefit of this strategy?

   A. It will promote students' sense of ownership of their own learning.
   B. It will strengthen families' ability to be partners with the teachers in their children's education.
   C. It will enhance the teachers' ability to create classroom environments that are responsive to diverse student needs.
   D. It will emphasize to both students and families that the teachers have high expectations for students' achievement.

95. The language that is used to communicate with others in a social environment is known as

   A. cognitively demanding communication.
   B. cognitive academic language.
   C. basic interpersonal communication.
   D. context-reduced language.

96. What is an important advantage of having students assume the major responsibility for planning a class learning project?

   A. It provides the teacher an opportunity to learn about and correct students' misconceptions regarding the topic of the project.
   B. It makes students partners with the teacher in assessing their academic progress.
   C. It facilitates the development of a project plan that best addresses individual students' strengths and weaknesses.
   D. It promotes the development of autonomy, initiative, and self-reliance in students.

97. A fourth-grade teacher has observed that Ayisha, who has natural artistic talent, is rushing through her classwork so that she can spend time in the creative arts center. Which of the following is the best way for the teacher to deal with this situation?

   A. Have Ayisha bring her work to the teacher to check over before she can go to the creative arts center.
   B. Tell Ayisha she can go to the creative arts center if she promises to complete her classwork properly at home.
   C. Provide Ayisha a checklist that she must complete before going to the creative arts center.
   D. Give Ayisha a lower grade for classwork not finished properly.

98. An English language learner (ELL) experienced a decline in academic performance upon moving into the upper elementary grades. Which of the following factors should the student's teachers consider as the most reasonable explanation for this occurrence?

   A. an increased focus on academic language in the upper elementary grades
   B. an increased focus on social language skills in the upper elementary grades
   C. a decreased level of interest in learning on the part of the student
   D. a decreased level of academic support from the student's parents

99. In working with a student who has a severe physical disability and is receiving special education services, the regular education teacher should place primary emphasis on

  A. fostering the student's development of emotional and social skills that will help the student cope with his or her disability.
  B. helping the student to learn specialized strategies that can enhance his or her ability to function physically.
  C. using strategies and materials that allow the student to participate as fully as possible in all class activities.
  D. identifying and using engaging alternative learning opportunities for the student whenever possible.

100. Which of the following approaches would be the most effective way for a teacher to promote dental hygiene in kindergarten students?

  A. Show a video on dental hygiene and discuss it with the kindergarteners.
  B. Read simple, illustrated books about proper dental care in an interactive manner to the kindergarteners.
  C. Explore with the kindergarteners a website that has illustrations and animations on dental hygiene.
  D. Bring in large models of teeth and toothbrushes and have the kindergarteners practice proper dental care with the models.

Answer Key for Practice Test 2

1. B	26. D	51. A	76. D
2. A	27. C	52. B	77. D
3. D	28. B	53. A	78. C
4. B	29. D	54. C	79. D
5. D	30. D	55. A	80. C
6. A	31. C	56. C	81. D
7. B	32. C	57. A	82. A
8. B	33. B	58. C	83. A
9. D	34. B	59. B	84. D
10. C	35. C	60. A	85. D
11. A	36. C	61. C	86. C
12. C	37. A	62. C	87. A
13. B	38. D	63. A	88. D
14. B	39. C	64. D	89. B
15. C	40. B	65. B	90. C
16. A	41. B	66. D	91. C
17. A	42. C	67. B	92. B
18. D	43. C	68. B	93. B
19. C	44. C	69. A	94. B
20. A	45. B	70. A	95. C
21. C	46. C	71. A	96. D
22. A	47. C	72. B	97. C
23. C	48. C	73. A	98. A
24. A	49. C	74. A	99. C
25. A	50. A	75. A	100. D

Complete Answers and Explanations for Practice Test 2

1. **B.** This question deals with a class discussion, which falls under **Competency 007 (Communication)**. Eliminate choice A because a discussion is unlikely to lead to an absolute conclusion, given the fact that no undisputed facts are provided. Eliminate choices C and D because the students are discussing a problem, not solving it. During the discussion, the teacher should monitor the effects of messages, simplifying and restating when necessary, and encourage the students to communicate effectively. The teacher should emphasize to the students that the critical elements of verbal communication are *accuracy of language, accuracy of information, standardization of language,* and *clearly defined expectations*. Thus, choice B is the correct response.

2. **A.** This question addresses **Competency 013 (Professional Conduct)**. Eliminate choice C because this approach would be excessive and burdensome to the principal. Eliminate choice D because this action would be unprofessional. You must now choose between choices A and B. Eliminate choice B because although this might be a measure the teacher could take, it would not be as effective as the approach given in choice A, which allows the principal to see firsthand what the teacher is doing and how it is impacting student learning. Thus, choice A is the correct response.

3. **D.** This question relates to both **Competency 007 (Communication)** and **Competency 008 (Instructional Delivery)**. Notice that you must select the *major* benefit to students from the assignment. The two prompts address higher-order thinking skills. When students justify the results of their experiment, they use evaluation-level thinking. When they formulate a theory based on the results of their experiment, they use synthesis-level thinking. Thus, the prompts promote students' creative and critical thinking skills (choice D). Eliminate choice A because even though a student might recall facts and basic concepts in order to address the prompts, this type of lower-level thinking would not be the *major* benefit of responding to the prompts. Eliminate choice B because it is not supported by the question stem. Eliminate choice C because the prompts will likely be used as an informal assessment tool by the teacher, but the *major* benefit to students comes from engaging in higher-order thinking skills. Thus, choice D is the correct response.

4. **B.** This question addresses **Competency 002 (Diversity)**. Eliminate choice A because incorporating students' cultural background into the curriculum contributes to an effective learning environment by validating and confirming the students' home cultures, thereby enhancing their feelings of acceptance in the classroom. Eliminate choice C because educational interests and aspirations vary widely among individual students, even within a cultural group, and often overlap with those of students of other cultures. Eliminate choice D because the way a student learns and interacts in the classroom is influenced—at least in part—by cultural norms and the norms learned as a member of a particular cultural group. Thus, choice B is the correct response. Teachers should recognize that each student is a unique person and that, within a cultural group, students can be expected to exhibit a broad range of strengths, interests, and needs.

5. **D.** This question addresses **Competency 013 (Professional Conduct)**. Eliminate choices A, B, and C because these are actions that teachers are expected to do. Choice D is the correct response. The requirements for administration of the mandatory statewide assessments prohibit anyone from questioning students on test content or test items after testing is complete, even after the days set aside for state testing have passed. This action by a teacher would be unethical.

6. **A.** This question relates to **Competency 010 (Assessment)**. For standardized tests, percentile scores are scores that reflect a student's standing relative to a norm group. The 80th percentile is the same as or better than 80 percent of the scores of the norm group. Thus, choice A is the correct response. The other answer choices are incorrect interpretations of a percentile score.

7. **B.** This question relates to **Competency 008 (Instructional Delivery)**. Eliminate choice A because it not supported by the question stem. Eliminate choices C and D because these answer choices relate to keeping students on task. Although the teacher's questioning strategy will likely result in better classroom behavior, this outcome probably is not the main reason for stopping the video and prompting students to consider the ideas presented. Maintaining an orderly, disciplined classroom is an important teacher function; however, the teacher's primary concern should be with promoting students' academic achievement. Choice B is the correct response. The teacher is most likely motivated by the understanding that teachers' efforts to maintain and reinforce student involvement correlate with students' cognitive engagement. Giving students opportunities to think about and discuss ideas presented in the video will help them create new understandings and reflect on old ones. By posing key questions, the teacher is likely to keep the students focused, involved, and engaged in learning.

8. **B.** This question falls under **Competency 012 (Professional Knowledge and Skills)**. The most appropriate way for a teacher to share an innovative instructional strategy with school colleagues is to speak with the principal about demonstrating the strategy as part of a workshop for all interested teachers. Thus, choice B is the correct response. The measures given in the other answer choices are not appropriate ways to share ideas with colleagues.

9. **D.** This question deals with creative thinking, a topic that falls under **Competency 007 (Communication)**. Eliminate choices A, B, and C because these tasks do not require creative thinking skills. Creative thinking is thinking that results in a new idea, product, or creation. Writing an original short story would promote students' creative thinking skills. Thus, choice D is the correct response.

10. **C.** This question deals with brain hemisphericity, a topic that falls under **Competency 002 (Diversity)**. Research indicates that brain hemisphericity has a strong influence on an individual's ability to process information. Right-brain-dominant learners respond best to visual and kinesthetic instruction, process information holistically, see patterns and relationships, think from whole to part, prefer to see the "big picture" before exploring small details, depend on images and pictures for meaning, and can work on several parts of a task at the same time. Hence, visual and kinesthetic global activities would work best with these learners. Thus, choice C is the correct response. The instructions described in the other answer choices would not be as compatible with the way right-brain-dominant learners process information.

11. **A.** This question deals with **Competency 013 (Professional Conduct)**. Teachers should be aware that using unlicensed software is illegal. Mr. Bishop should immediately remove all copies of the software from the computers. He should follow the principle of the Code of Ethics and Standard Practices for Texas Educators that states teachers "shall be of good moral character." Thus, choice A is the correct response. The actions given in the other answer choices would not satisfy Mr. Bishop's legal and ethical responsibility.

12. **C.** This question addresses **Competency 010 (Assessment)**. A *portfolio* assessment includes a variety of samples of a student's work, collected over time, that shows the student's growth and development. Thus, choice C is the correct response. Although the assessments given in the other answer choices might be included in a portfolio, none of these alone constitutes a variety of samples of a student's work.

13. **B.** This question addresses **Competency 007 (Communication)**. Eliminate choice A because *paraphrasing* is saying what students say, but in different words. Eliminate choice C because *redirecting* is posing a question or prompt to other students for a response or to add new insights. Eliminate choice D because *summarizing* is the technique of reducing students' ideas to key points. Thus, choice B is the correct response. The teacher is using the technique of *probing*, which is used to ask students to clarify or justify answers.

14. **B.** This question addresses **Competency 012 (Professional Knowledge and Skills)**. Mr. James can most effectively help Ms. Flores prepare for the classroom observation by providing her with a lesson plan for the class session that she will be observing. The lesson plan will help Ms. Flores know what to expect when she observes the lesson. Thus, choice B is the correct response. Eliminate choices A, C, and D because these measures would not be as effective in helping Ms. Flores prepare for the classroom observation.

15. **C.** This question relates to both **Competency 003 (Instructional Design and Planning)** and **Competency 007 (Communication)**. Eliminate choices A and D because these tasks are at the knowledge level of thinking. Eliminate choice B because this task is at the comprehension level of thinking. Evaluating the effectiveness of a written response according to audience and purpose requires evaluation-level thinking, which is a type of critical thinking. Thus, choice C is the correct response.

Chapter 15: Practice Test 2

16. **A.** This question falls under **Competency 002 (Diversity)**. Choice A is the correct response. The teacher can most effectively make use of the DVDs, CDs, games, magazines, and books as resources for the purpose of integrating cultural content into content area instruction. For the purposes given in choices C and D, other means would be more effective. The purpose given in choice B is one that, in general, teachers should avoid.

17. **A.** This question addresses **Competency 011 (Family Involvement)**. Eliminate choices C and D because these responses do not align with the question stem. Eliminate choice B because it is off-topic. Thus, choice A is the correct response. Providing materials for the parent to examine during the meeting will provide a context for a constructive meeting with the parent by enhancing the parent's understanding of his son's performance and progress in relation to course expectations, thereby facilitating productive collaboration to support the student's learning.

18. **D.** This question addresses **Competency 010 (Assessment)**. Teacher-made tests can provide valuable information about what students have learned; however, teachers should be knowledgeable of the uses and limitations of different types of test questions. When designing tests, teachers need to be aware that guessing can compromise the validity of results. Although guessing can be a factor with any type of test item, it has the most effect on true-false items. Thus, choice D is the correct response.

19. **C.** This question falls under **Competency 007 (Communication)**. Eliminate choice A because effective teachers should attempt to ask questions of all students equally, regardless of where they are seated. Eliminate choice B because these types of questions require only lower-level thinking. Eliminate choice D because effective teachers avoid answering their own questions. Choice C is the correct response. When facilitating class discussions, effective teachers want to draw ideas from the students. To that end, they establish positive interactions that support students' responses.

20. **A.** This question deals with **Competency 012 (Professional Knowledge and Skills)**. Eliminate choices B and C because it is questionable whether joining a professional organization would have the results given in these answer choices. Now you must choose between choices A and D. Although expanded access to quality lesson plans and other instructional resources in a teacher's field is a benefit of joining a professional organization in one's content field, it is not the *most* significant benefit of doing so. Competent teachers should demonstrate an awareness of current developments in their field of specialization. Therefore, choice A is the correct response.

21. **C.** This question relates to **Competency 010 (Assessment)**. Eliminate choices A and B because these questions elicit short answers that require only lower-level thinking. Eliminate choice D because although this question requires students to think about the procedures and might result in an extended answer, it does not require higher-level thinking. Choice C is the correct response. Writing a justification for the information shown in the graph requires students to engage in analysis, synthesis, judgment, and creative thought.

22. **A.** This question relates to **Competency 002 (Diversity)**. Notice that you must select the answer choice that the teacher should do *first*. Eliminate choices B and D because although these are actions that the teacher might take, they are not as important or necessary as the actions given in choices A and C. You must now choose between choices A and C. Even though the teacher is a woman, she might have unconscious biases or prejudices toward girls' abilities in science. Eliminate choice C because this is something the teacher should do, but not before she examines her own personal beliefs and feelings about female students' abilities in science. Thus, choice A is the correct response.

23. **C.** This question addresses **Competency 013 (Professional Conduct)**. According to the Code of Ethics and Standard Practices for Texas Educators, teachers should not use equipment committed to their charge for personal gain or advantage. Thus, choice C is the correct response. Eliminate choices A, B, and D because none of these actions is a violation of the Code of Ethics and Principles of Professional Conduct.

24. A. This question addresses **Competency 010 (Assessment)**. Teachers should be knowledgeable of the uses and limitations of different types of assessment. Choice A is the correct response. Informal observation is an authentic assessment method in which teachers directly observe students performing or working on an activity. The teacher might use a checklist listing skills or performances that are critical to the task. Seeing students actually perform behaviors to demonstrate skills and knowledge is more likely to yield valid results than the methods given in the other answer choices. Eliminate choices B, C, and D because generally *student self-assessment, peer assessment,* and *student journaling* lack validity due to factors such as the assessor's immaturity and lack of expertise. Nevertheless, students benefit from involvement in these assessment methods because these forms of assessment give students opportunities to develop their critical thinking and evaluation-level thinking skills.

25. A. This question relates to **Competency 007 (Communication)**. Eliminate choice B because it is not supported by the stimulus. The teacher is asking the students to write on a topic, not to engage in inquiry. Eliminate choice C because the teacher's problem is not with the teacher's means of communication, but rather with the message. Eliminate choice D because it is not supported by the stimulus; you are not told the cultural makeup of the class. Choice A is the correct response. The teacher should have explained the 10-minute writing assignment more precisely, so that the instructional task would have been clearer to the students. Instead of asking the students to write on the subject of school uniforms, which is rather broad and somewhat vague, the teacher might have clarified the assignment by saying, "Write why you would or would not be in favor of our school adopting school uniforms." Effective teachers communicate instructional tasks clearly to students.

26. D. This question relates to **Competency 012 (Professional Knowledge and Skills)**. Eliminate choice A because this answer choice is not aligned with the question. This measure would not help the teacher learn how to more effectively facilitate whole-group class discussions. The measures given in choices B, C, and D are all ways the teacher can learn about appropriate techniques for facilitating whole-class discussions; however, the measure that probably would *most* help the teacher in improving his or her practice is to observe firsthand a colleague who effectively uses whole-group discussions. Thus, choice D is the correct response.

27. C. This question falls under **Competency 003 (Instructional Design and Planning)**. Eliminate choice A because this task is at the application level of thinking. Eliminate choice B because this task is at the knowledge level of thinking. Eliminate choice D because this task is at the comprehension level of thinking. Generalizing or drawing conclusions requires analysis-level thinking, which is a type of higher-order thinking. Thus, choice C is the correct response.

28. B. This question falls under **Competency 002 (Diversity)**. Eliminate choices C and D because these measures would shortchange the at-risk students. Now you must choose between choices A and B. Eliminate choice A because although this measure is one teachers might take, it would not provide as much benefit to the middle school students who are at risk as giving them opportunities to experience academic success on assignments they perceive as meaningful and challenging. This practice will help improve the self-esteem of the at-risk students, who, having confronted repeated failure in the past, might have simply quit trying. Thus, choice B is the correct response.

29. D. This question falls under **Competency 002 (Diversity)**. Eliminate choice A because discussions with colleagues about the acquisition of the mathematics concept by typical first-graders will be of little help, if any, to the teacher for differentiating instruction for the two specific first-graders in the class. Eliminate choice B because gathering information about attention span might gauge the students' interest (or lack thereof) in the concept, but would provide little, if any, useful information for differentiating instruction. Eliminate choice C because a checklist filled out within a group setting might reflect influence from other group members, and therefore could fail to accurately indicate a student's needs. Analyzing the students' previous performances will provide useful data about each student's instructional needs, and thereby aid the teacher in providing differentiated instruction for them. Thus, choice D is the correct response.

30. **D.** This question falls under **Competency 007 (Communication)**. A *graphic organizer* is a visual depiction of abstract concepts or processes. Eliminate choice A because a *decision tree* is used to guide students in the decision-making process. Eliminate choice B because a *flowchart* is used to show a sequence or flow of events, actions, or processes. Eliminate choice C because a *story tree* is used to guide students' critical evaluation of a work of literature. Thus, choice D is the correct response. A *web* would be an excellent graphic organizer for the teacher to use to determine students' prior knowledge about natural resources. In webbing, students list words or phrases that are connected to the central topic. This activity will reveal the students' prior knowledge and disclose their misconceptions about natural resources.

31. **C.** This question deals with teacher expectations, a topic that falls under **Competency 004 (Learning Principles)**. Eliminate choices A and B because research studies support the self-fulfilling prophecy hypothesis that teachers get what they expect, so their expectations affect middle school students' achievement and behavior. Eliminate choice D because middle school students have a fragile self-confidence that can be impacted, either positively or negatively, by teacher expectations. Choice C is the correct response. With regard to middle school students, peer relations and peer influences tend to be relatively impervious to the impact of teachers. This circumstance is probably due to the great need that young adolescents have for peer acceptance.

32. **C.** This question falls under **Competency 007 (Communication)**. Eliminate choice B because *deductive reasoning* starts with basic assumptions or facts and proceeds to a logical conclusion. Eliminate choices A and D because *conditional* and *syllogistic* reasoning fall under deductive reasoning. Choice C is the correct response. *Inductive reasoning* involves looking at specific examples and trying to identify a pattern or trend that fits the given examples in order to determine a general rule. Since the students are to generalize an algebraic or geometric pattern, the teacher is most likely promoting students' use of inductive reasoning.

33. **B.** This question addresses **Competency 002 (Diversity)**. According to research by Witkin and Goodenough (1981), field-independent learners tend to be passive in social situations; in contrast, field-dependent learners tend to be active in social situations. Thus, choice B is the correct response. The other answer choices disagree with research about field dependency.

34. **B.** This question addresses **Competency 013 (Professional Conduct)**. The Family Educational Rights and Privacy Act (FERPA) protects the privacy of student records. Eliminate choice D because noncustodial parents have the right to review their child's educational records. Eliminate choices A and C because according to FERPA, a teacher may share a minor student's educational records with a school official without written permission from the minor students' parent, provided that the school official has a "legitimate educational interest" in reviewing the records—that is, the official needs to review the educational records "in order to fulfill his or her professional responsibility." Thus, it is inappropriate for teachers to share students' educational records with their former teachers without written permission from parents. Hence, choice B is the correct response.

35. **C.** This question relates to **Competency 008 (Instructional Delivery)**. Eliminate choices A and D because these measures would shortchange the English language learners (ELLs) and communicate low expectations to them. Eliminate choice B because students who say little might, in fact, be just as proficient language users as more talkative students. They might have reasons other than lack of proficiency in English for not speaking up more often. The varied cultural backgrounds of students who are ELLs make assessing their grasp of spoken English difficult. Among other explanations, it might simply be that the culture in which they acquired their first language mandates silence or reticence in a wide range of social situations, including open discussions. Thus, choice C is the correct response.

36. **C.** This question falls under **Competency 007 (Communication)**. Eliminate choice A because *affective* refers to feelings and emotions. Eliminate choices B and D because these types of questions elicit closed responses at lower levels of thinking. Choice C is the correct response. *Divergent questions* are open-ended and, thus, would elicit a variety of ideas during a class discussion.

37. **A.** This question falls under **Competency 002 (Diversity)**. Eliminate choices C and D because these options contain ideas that are not characteristic of gifted children. Eliminate choice B because gifted students should not be isolated when the class is involved in group activities. However, they also should be afforded opportunities for independent learning that encourage them to apply creative and critical thinking. Thus, choice A is the correct response.

38. **D.** This question addresses **Competency 010 (Assessment)**. Grade equivalent scores can easily be misinterpreted. This student's score reflects performance on the reading assessment matching the estimated performance of an "average" student in the sixth month of seventh grade on the *same* assessment. The student's score indicates his or her level of performance on fifth-grade-level reading, not seventh-grade-level reading. Thus, choice D is the correct response. The responses in the other answer choices reflect incorrect interpretations of the student's grade equivalent score.

39. **C.** This question deals with second language acquisition, a topic that falls under **Competency 008 (Instructional Delivery)**. Eliminate choice A because although this is an appropriate response from the teacher, it is not the most appropriate feedback for the situation. The responses given in choices B and D would not be appropriate ways to correct the student's errors because they likely would inhibit the student's attempts at language production by raising negative affective filters. The most appropriate way for the teacher to correct the student's errors is through modeling a corrected version of what the student attempted to say. Thus, choice C is the correct response.

40. **B.** This question falls under **Competency 007 (Communication)**. Eliminate choice A because *convergent thinking* is a type of closed-ended thinking, which would not lead to the generation of many new ideas. Eliminate choice C because *deductive reasoning* involves drawing conclusions from known facts or generalizations. Eliminate choice D because *generalization* is the ability to carry learning over from one setting to a different setting. The teacher wants the students to come up with many new ideas, so she poses an open-ended question. Choice B is the correct response. The task given to the students is most likely to promote *divergent thinking*.

41. **B.** This question deals with learning styles, a topic that falls under **Competency 002 (Diversity)**. Notice that you must select the answer choice that is *least* consistent with a tactile/kinesthetic modality preference. Tactile/kinesthetic learners prefer to learn by touching objects, by feeling shapes and textures, and by moving things around. Eliminate choice A because the students will be acting out a play, which is tactile/kinesthetic. Eliminate choice C because the students will be participating in a simulation, which is tactile/kinesthetic. Eliminate choice D because the students will be involved in a hands-on activity, which is tactile/kinesthetic. Choice B is the correct response. The mathematics activity affords the least opportunity for the learners to be physically involved, so this activity is least consistent with a tactile/kinesthetic modality preference.

42. **C.** This question relates to **Competency 007 (Communication)**. Eliminate choice A because *extinction* is the technique of withdrawing reinforcers to discourage undesirable behavior in the classroom. Eliminate choice B because *negative reinforcement* is the technique of strengthening a behavior by release from an undesirable situation. Eliminate choice D because *modeling* is the tactic of demonstrating a skill or behavior that the teacher wants the students to mimic. Choice C is the correct response. The teacher uses *nonverbal communication* (that is, a stern look) to convey a message of disapproval.

43. **C.** This question relates to **Competency 010 (Assessment)**. An important question to ask about an assessment is the following: "Does the assessment reflect the instructional methods?" In order to best interpret the conflicting results obtained with the standardized test, the teacher should *first* analyze whether the daily mathematics activities are aligned with the way the standardized test assesses place value. Thus, choice C is the correct response. The actions given in the other answer choices would not be as useful in helping the teacher interpret the discrepancy that has occurred.

44. **C.** This question falls under **Competency 005 (Classroom Climate)**. According to Slavin (2008), teachers should use praise frequently (eliminate choices B and D), especially with young children, and the praise should specify the particular behavior or accomplishment that warrants the praise (eliminate choice A). Thus, choice C is the correct response.

45. **B.** This question falls under **Competency 007 (Communication)**. *Brainstorming* is a teaching/learning strategy in which students generate ideas, judgment of the ideas of others is forbidden, and ideas are used to create a flow of new ideas. In brainstorming, it is important that students are encouraged to think freely without risk of criticism of their ideas. Eliminate choices A, C, and D because these approaches would restrict students' thinking. Choice B is the correct response. The teacher can best maximize the benefit of the brainstorming activity by asking the students to present any ideas that come to mind and refrain from judging the ideas of others.

Chapter 15: Practice Test 2

46. **C.** This question relates to **Competency 001 (Developmentally Appropriate Practice)**. Current knowledge about how young adolescents learn indicates that they learn best when they are involved in active, experiential learning in a meaningful context. Role-playing provides such a context. Thus, choice C is the correct response. The other answer choices contain ideas that are not typical of young adolescents. Eliminate choice A because early adolescents are beginning to question adult standards. Eliminate choice B because this characteristic is typical of very young children; most adolescents are capable of imagining a situation they have not personally experienced. Eliminate choice D because young adolescents have a deep concern about what their peers think of them.

47. **C.** This question deals with the English Language Proficiency Standards (ELPS), a topic that falls under both **Competency 002 (Diversity)** and **Competency 008 (Instructional Delivery)**. Eliminate choice A because even though vocabulary knowledge is directly linked to comprehension, copying definitions from the dictionary is an ineffective strategy for building understanding of unfamiliar words. Eliminate choice B because just reading the material with a partner doesn't assure comprehension is taking place. The ELLs may be hearing the material, but not comprehending it. Eliminate choice D because reading aloud doesn't guarantee the material will be comprehensible to the ELLs. Again, the ELLs may be hearing without understanding. Choice C is the correct response because, according to the ELPS, intermediate-level ELLs are still dependent on visual cues and topic familiarity. Showing a video is an effective strategy for preparing the ELLs (and their classmates, as well) for a topic that is unfamiliar to them.

48. **C.** This question addresses **Competency 007 (Communication)**. Eliminate choice A because *paraphrasing* is saying what students say, but in different words. Eliminate choice B because *probing* is the technique of asking students to clarify or justify answers. Eliminate choice D because *summarizing* is the technique of reducing students' ideas to key points. Choice C is the correct response. The teacher is using the technique of *redirecting*, which is posing a question from a student to other students for a response or to elicit ideas.

49. **C.** This question addresses **Competency 009 (Technology)**. Eliminate choices A, B, and D because none of these choices is the purpose of using truncation. Truncation is used to search for a word and variant forms of that word. Thus, choice C is the correct response.

50. **A.** This question addresses **Competency 006 (Classroom Management)**. Eliminate choices B and D because these measures are unlikely to placate the students who are acting up. Eliminate choice C because this measure would reward students for acting up, sending a wrong message to them and to the rest of the class. Teachers should use effective strategies to create positive and productive learning environments in which students are responsible and self-disciplined. Teachers can help students learn behavioral skills needed to solve problems without adult intervention by modeling social skills with all students and helping them work out compromises to conflicts. Thus, choice A is the correct response.

51. **A.** This question falls under **Competency 004 (Learning Principles)**. Choice A is the correct response because providing learning opportunities that relate to adolescents' interests and experiences will help them find their own (intrinsic) motivation for learning, thereby fostering a long-term desire to learn. The strategies in the other answer choices are extrinsic motivational strategies, which likely would not be as effective in the long term as a strategy that promotes intrinsic motivation. Indeed, some research suggests that students who are encouraged to think about public recognition (choice B), grades (choice C), or privileges (choice D) become less inclined to explore ideas, think creatively, and take on challenging tasks—all undesirable outcomes from a teacher's perspective.

52. **B.** This question falls under **Competency 006 (Classroom Management)**. Eliminate choices C and D because these are measures that threaten or punish children, practices that should be avoided by teachers. Such practices are in disagreement with experts who suggest response to student misbehavior is most effective when it maintains or enhances students' dignity and self-esteem and encourages them to be responsible for their own behavior. Eliminate choice A because this measure is a teacher-centered approach that does not allow the children to self-manage their behavior. Further, it will likely create additional conflict in the classroom. In establishing a smoothly functioning learning community in the classroom, teachers should involve students—even children as young as preschool age—in establishing rules and standards for behavior. Holding a class meeting and guiding the children to generate a set of rules for the art center will help them learn to take responsibility for their learning environment. Thus, choice B is the correct response.

53. **A.** This question relates to **Competency 008 (Instructional Delivery)**. Effective teachers understand how students learn and recognize instructional strategies that promote student learning. Eliminate choice B because whereas pre-reading activities for a lesson must provide explicit and systematic instruction in key vocabulary words that the students will encounter in the lesson, having students memorize key vocabulary before a unit begins is not recommended. Eliminate choice D because this approach involves too much teacher-telling, without giving students the opportunity to do the thinking in the classroom. Eliminate choice C because it limits students' thinking to one type of vegetable plant—corn. The teacher can best prepare the students for new learning by having them write down (1) what they already know about vegetable plants, to facilitate linking new information to prior knowledge; and (2) what they want to learn about vegetable plants, to give them ownership of their learning and make it purposeful. These actions are steps 1 and 2 in the K-W-L process that effective teachers use to promote students' active engagement in learning and construction of meaning. In step 3, students recall what they learned. K-W-L stands for what students Know, Want to know, and have Learned. Thus, choice A is the correct response.

54. **C.** This question deals with second language acquisition, a topic that falls under **Competency 008 (Instructional Delivery)**. Eliminate choice A because *discourse* is simply conversation or verbal expression. Eliminate choice B because *lexicon* refers to the vocabulary used in a particular profession or area of study. Eliminate choice D because *semantics* is the study of word meanings. Choice C is the correct response. *Register* describes the use of different language forms (for example, formal versus informal) that depend on the setting, the relationship of the speaker to the person he or she is addressing, and the function of the interaction. A register is a situationally appropriate form of a language.

55. **A.** This question deals with parent conferences, which fall under **Competency 011 (Family Involvement)**. Parent conferences are an important way for teachers to build positive partnerships with parents. Choice A is the correct response. The teacher should express sympathy to the parents and then ask for further information about the situation. The parents' child might be experiencing harassment or bullying, both of which are prohibited by law in Texas schools. The other answer choices would be inappropriate responses from the teacher.

56. **C.** This question falls under **Competency 010 (Assessment)**. Eliminate choice A because this choice describes portfolio assessment. Eliminate choice B because this choice describes a norm-referenced test. Eliminate choice D because this choice describes a self-selected item to be used for assessment, perhaps as part of a portfolio. Choice C is the correct response. A criterion-referenced test shows a child's mastery of predetermined concepts or skills in a subject area.

57. **A.** This question addresses **Competency 011 (Family Involvement)**. Eliminate choices B and D because although these outcomes might occur incidentally, neither would be the most likely purpose for arranging to have family members serve as volunteer tutors in the school. Eliminate choice C because it would be inappropriate for volunteer tutors to assume such a role, and teachers should guard against it by training the volunteers before they work with students. Because family members have a vested interest in the school, they are a valuable resource to teachers. Teachers should apply strategies for engaging family members in various aspects of the educational program, such as encouraging them to serve as volunteers in the school. Such an arrangement likely would cultivate strong family-school partnerships, thereby giving family members a sense of ownership in the school. Thus, choice A is the correct response.

58. **C.** This question falls under both **Competency 005 (Classroom Climate)** and **Competency 008 (Instructional Delivery)**. Eliminate choices A, B, and D because these answer choices are not supported by the question stem—don't read too much into a question! The teacher demonstrates knowing how to turn diversity in the classroom to advantage. By creating diverse learning groups that must work together, the teacher is fostering communication and collaboration among students, thereby promoting their understanding of each other. These interactions will nurture a sense of community in the classroom. Thus, choice C is the correct response.

59. **B.** This addresses **Competency 003 (Instructional Design and Planning)**. The statement in the question is an example of an instructional objective. Instructional objectives are classified as *affective, cognitive,* or *psychomotor*. Eliminate choice D because a *reflective objective* is not a type of instructional objective. Eliminate choice A because *affective objectives* involve feelings and dispositions. Eliminate choice C because *psychomotor objectives* involve physical activity on the part of the student. Thus, choice B is the correct response. *Cognitive objectives* involve thinking capabilities such as identifying nouns in a paragraph.

60. A. This question deals with **Competency 005 (Classroom Climate)**. Notice that you must select what the teacher should do *first* to find out additional information that would help in dealing with the student. This means that there might be other answer choices that would be appropriate for the teacher to do, but you have to pick the one the teacher should do first. Eliminate choice C because this action would be inappropriate and a violation of the student's right to privacy. Eliminate choices B and D because these are steps the teacher might take later, but not before the teacher talks with the student. Choice A is the correct response. To be well prepared for the conference with the student, the teacher should first review the student's educational records.

61. C. This question falls under **Competency 001 (Developmentally Appropriate Practice)**. Choice C is the correct response. The child has not yet developed conservation, which is normal for a kindergarten student. According to Piaget, students no longer have problems with conservation when they reach the concrete operational stage, ages 7 to 11. The other answer choices are not supported by the information given in the question.

62. C. This question deals with **Competency 006 (Classroom Management)**. Eliminate choice A because this result is unrealistic and not necessarily desirable; unfamiliar or unexpected occurrences can sometimes provide a change of pace in a classroom. Eliminate choice B because, for example, when students are engaged in discovery learning, they often proceed in a nonlinear fashion, rather than in a simple-to-complex progression. Eliminate choice D because although it is appropriate that students have input in deciding which topics will be studied and for how long, the teacher has a responsibility—which should not be relinquished to students—to ensure that the learning activities address the state-mandated curriculum. Choice C is the correct response. Teachers should identify and apply effective techniques for encouraging students to monitor and manage their own behavior.

63. A. This question deals with second language acquisition, a topic that falls under **Competency 008 (Instructional Delivery)**. In the natural approach to language acquisition (Nutta, 2006), the stages of second language development are *preproduction, early production, speech emergence,* and *intermediate fluency*. The stage of development wherein the second language learner works to receive and understand the new language but produces little or no expressive language is known as the preproduction or "silent period." Thus, choice A is the correct response. The stages given in the other answer choices follow the preproduction stage.

64. D. This question deals with the topic of instructional methods, which falls under **Competency 008 (Instructional Delivery)**. Eliminate choices A, B, and C because although these results might occur, they would not necessarily result from the use of inquiry and discovery learning or cooperative learning groups. These instructional methods are most likely to foster independent learning in the students because they give students responsibility for their own and for each other's learning. Thus, choice D is the correct response.

65. B. This question addresses **Competency 006 (Classroom Management)**. Notice that you must select the intervention that the teacher should use *first* with the student. The teacher should react quickly and calmly to the student's disruptive behavior; however, the teacher's *first* intervention should be the least intrusive. Eliminate choices A, C, and D because these measures interrupt the class discussion. Choice B is the correct response. The teacher should try nonverbal interventions, like a stern gaze, before moving to more intrusive measures. The stern gaze will likely send a clear cue to the student that continuation of the disruptive behavior will result in consequences.

66. D. This question falls under **Competency 004 (Learning Principles)**. Scaffolding is the support and assistance provided for learning and problem solving, such as verbal cues or prompts, visual highlighting, diagrams, checklists, reminders, modeling, partially completed learning charts or tasks, and examples. Choice D is the correct response. The timeline of events posted by the teacher provides students with a tool to help record information accurately and independently while, at the same time, integrating new information into a broader historical context. The teacher actions in the other answer choices are appropriate, but none is an example of scaffolding.

67. **B.** This question falls under **Competency 003 (Instructional Design and Planning)**. Notice that you must select what the teachers should do *first* to begin their planning of the unit. Teachers must recognize key factors to consider in planning instruction (for example, instructional goals and objectives, students' prior knowledge, available time and other resources, and instructional strategies). The key factors the teachers should consider *first* as they plan the unit are appropriate learning goals and objectives. Thus, choice B is the correct response. This is the first step in planning because it provides a framework into which information about materials and resources (choice A), activating prior knowledge (choice C), and responsive instructional strategies (choice D) will fit.

68. **B.** This question addresses **Competency 006 (Classroom Management)**. Eliminate choice A because effective classroom managers respond immediately to stop or redirect inappropriate behavior. Eliminate choices C and D because educational research suggests that teachers should follow the principle that misbehaviors should be corrected with the simplest intervention that will work while avoiding unnecessary disruption of instructional activities. The teacher should walk by the student's desk and unobtrusively take the ball because this action stops the misbehavior without interrupting the momentum of the lesson. Thus, choice B is the correct response.

69. **A.** This question falls under **Competency 004 (Learning Principles)** and **Competency 010 (Assessment)**. Schema theory (Slavin, 2008) emphasizes the important role that prior knowledge plays in students' learning. Students construct meaning based on their background knowledge about a topic and integrate new knowledge into their existing prior knowledge. Teachers should ascertain prior knowledge and design instructional activities accordingly. Eliminate choice B because although this approach would help activate students' prior knowledge, it would not assess prior knowledge. Eliminate choice D because the students would be expected to listen to the guest speaker, not tell what they know about the topic. Eliminate choice C because the teacher could use small-group discussions to assess prior knowledge, but using an advance organizer (for example, a graphic organizer such as a concept map) would be a better strategy because it would help the students see the structure of key concepts and topics, which might not occur in the small-group discussions. Thus, choice A is the correct response.

70. **A.** This question is related to **Competency 003 (Instructional Design and Planning)**. Choice A is the correct response. By using a thematic approach for teaching literature, the teacher will give students an opportunity to see relationships between and among concepts within a central theme of the subject area. Eliminate choices B and C because these answer choices are not supported by the question stem. Eliminate choice D because it is not supported by the concept of a thematic approach as clearly as choice A.

71. **A.** This question deals with second language acquisition, a topic that falls under **Competency 008 (Instructional Delivery)**. Eliminate choices B, C, and D because these answer choices are appropriate and positive practices to use with English language learners (ELLs). Choice A is the correct response. Encouraging the student to use English instead of the primary language when at home is likely to have a negative impact on a beginning ELL's acquisition of English because it fails to show respect and value for the student's home language. Teachers should strive to develop ELLs' pride in their home languages and cultures.

72. **B.** This question relates to **Competency 009 (Technology)**. Eliminate choice A because simulations usually address higher-level concepts and skills. Eliminate choice C because students usually enjoy participating in simulation activities and find them interesting and fun. Eliminate choice D because, for a few students, the realism might be too threatening for some simulations. However, this circumstance is not a *major* limitation—given that most simulations are artificial situations with the risks encountered in real life removed. Teachers should identify activities that support the knowledge, skills, and attitudes to be learned in a subject area. In social studies, simulation activities are a good choice because they help students develop empathy and learn to see situations from different perspectives; however, a major limitation is that they often require a considerable block of time. Thus, choice B is the correct response.

73. **A.** This question falls under **Competency 013 (Professional Conduct)**. The Individuals with Disabilities Education Act (IDEA) gives parents the right to participate (which does *not* mean they have unilateral decision-making power) in meetings regarding the identification, evaluation, eligibility, re-evaluation, and educational placement of their child. Thus, choice A is the correct response. The "rights" in the other answer choices are not specified under the IDEA.

74. **A.** This question falls under **Competency 006 (Classroom Management)**. Choice A is the correct response. By privately praising Joaquin when he performs the desired behavior, the teacher will reinforce the behavior and increase its likelihood of occurring again, thereby improving Joaquin's relationships with his classmates. This outcome and the teacher's praise will work toward improving Joaquin's self-concept. Eliminate choice B because this approach is too teacher-centered—it does not promote self-management. Eliminate choice C because punitive-based measures fail to preserve the dignity of the student, which is an essential component of effective classroom management. Eliminate choice D because this is an inappropriate teacher response.

75. **A.** This question addresses **Competency 009 (Technology)**. By sequencing the content into small units of information and providing immediate feedback to the student on his or her grasp of the content, the software would allow students to monitor their progress as they proceed through the program. Thus, choice A is the correct response. Eliminate choices B, C, and D because these answer choices are not supported by the question stem.

76. **D.** This question falls under **Competency 004 (Learning Principles)**. Teachers should apply procedures for enhancing student interest and helping students find their own motivation. Notice that the question is asking why the act of composing their own questions is motivational for the students. Eliminate choice A because this answer choice does not respond to the question—the questions in the survey might relate to community issues, but the act of composing the questions does not. Eliminate choices B and C because these answer choices are not supported by the question stem—the students are composing questions, not pursuing topics of personal interest or setting their own learning goals. Choice D is the correct response. The teacher understands that intrinsic motivation is enhanced when students are given a measure of control over their learning experiences.

77. **D.** This question relates to **Competency 006 (Classroom Management)**. Eliminate choice A because although the teacher should inform students of the time limitation for the activity, the reminder needs to be near the end of the activity since students are unlikely to remember the time limitation once they become involved in the activity. Eliminate choices B and C because these measures would be distracting to students while they are working on the activity. Choice D is the correct response. The best way to remind students is to give them a 5-minute warning prior to the necessary time for the activity to end.

78. **C.** This question addresses **Competency 003 (Instructional Design and Planning)**. Notice that you must select the answer choice that should be the teacher's *first* step in defining instructional objectives for the new unit. Eliminate choices A, B, and D because these measures should come after objectives have been determined. Choice C is the correct response. The purpose of instruction is to increase knowledge or performance on the part of the student. In order to create clearly defined objectives, the teacher needs to have a sound basis by which success can be measured—by first determining students' general areas of strengths and needs in pattern recognition and critical thinking.

79. **D.** This question falls under **Competency 013 (Professional Conduct)**. Eliminate choice A because the student has not yet been identified as a student in need of support services. Eliminate choice B because this action would be inappropriate. At the start of the school year, the teacher in question has not had time to explore ways to help the student, so eliminate choice C. Choice D is the correct response. The teacher should initiate a request for the student to be evaluated to determine whether the student is eligible for special education services only when classroom strategies fail to enhance student learning—that is, when it is clear that the student's needs cannot be met through the regular education program.

80. **C.** This question falls under **Competency 008 (Instructional Delivery)**. Notice that the question asks that you select a *necessary* element of inquiry-based learning. Choice C is the correct response because inquiry-based learning requires that students form hypotheses prior to investigations. Eliminate choice A because writing reports can have value, but this activity is not a necessary element of inquiry-based learning. Eliminate choice B because a video might be used to spark interest, but showing a video is not a necessary element of inquiry-based learning. Eliminate choice D because while class question-and-answer sessions are useful, they are not a necessary element of inquiry-based learning.

81. **D.** This question deals with second language acquisition, a topic that falls under **Competency 008 (Instructional Delivery)**. Eliminate choice A because *expressive language* involves speaking or writing. Eliminate choice B because *oral language* is spoken language. Eliminate choice C because *pragmatic language* refers to social language. *Receptive language* (choice D) is the ability to receive and understand messages. Choice D is the only answer choice that specifically describes the ability to receive messages. Thus, choice D is the correct response.

82. **A.** This question deals with **Competency 003 (Instructional Design and Planning)**. Choice A is the correct response. In order for the standards set forth in the Texas Essential Knowledge and Skills (TEKS) to be learned, they must be taught. Teachers may choose from a variety of instructional methods, including engaging students in in-depth studies of topics, to convey the social studies curriculum. Nevertheless, whichever method of instruction they choose, it is most important that they make certain that learning is clearly focused on the important facts, concepts, generalizations, and skills set forth in the TEKS. They should not relinquish this important charge to students (eliminate choice B). Eliminate choices C and D because these approaches shortchange students. In choice C, the learning experiences resulting from this answer choice likely will fail to address grade-level expectations of high content complexity. Choice D is a teacher-directed measure that would not give students the opportunity to take initiative and responsibility for investigation of the topic. In learning projects, students take charge of their own learning—they become self-managed—but the teacher still plays a vital role and, ultimately, must ensure that learning is geared toward the state curriculum.

83. **A.** This question relates to **Competency 008 (Instructional Delivery)**. Eliminate choices C and D because these purposes occur at a later point in the lesson, after the introduction. Eliminate choice B because although a teacher should communicate the objective in the introduction of the lesson, there is no evidence to indicate that the book *The Greedy Triangle* will communicate the objective for the lesson. Choice A is the correct response. The probable purpose for beginning the introduction by reading the book is to activate student interest and motivate students to engage in learning—in other words, to gain students' attention.

84. **D.** This question falls under **Competency 011 (Family Involvement)**. Eliminate choices A and B because it would be inappropriate for the teacher to imply that Victor's family situation is unsuitable by suggesting that it be changed or that the family seek charity. Eliminate choice C because teachers usually do not control friendship patterns in their classrooms. Although the teacher might encourage students to become friends with Victor, the teacher cannot ensure that friendships will develop, as the language in choice C implies. The teacher should be aware that Victor's unstable home environment might continue indefinitely and should understand that this situation likely has created stress that is impacting Victor's behavior at school. The teacher can best meet Victor's needs by giving highest priority to providing an accepting and supportive environment for Victor at school. Thus, choice D is the correct response.

85. **D.** This question falls under **Competency 008 (Instructional Delivery)**. Notice that you must select the action that the teacher should do *first* to ensure that the video will be a useful instructional tool. Eliminate choices A, B, and C because these actions neglect to take into consideration the age of the students and the spontaneity that is sure to occur on a field trip. To ensure that the video will be a useful instructional tool, the teacher should first discuss with the paraprofessional the purpose of the video. This measure will help the paraprofessional make good decisions about what to include in the video while the students are on the field trip. Thus, choice D is the correct response.

86. **C.** This question addresses **Competency 010 (Assessment)**. Choice C is the correct response. A self-monitoring checklist can be used to cue students to use specific strategies while problem solving. The student checks off each step (such as "I read the problem and underlined key information") as it is completed. The student turns in the checklist along with the solved problem to the teacher. Eliminate choices A and B because these are standardized instruments to assess skills, not strategies. Eliminate choice D because a holistic scoring rubric assigns a single score to all components considered as a whole, not individually.

Chapter 15: Practice Test 2

87. A. This question deals with second language acquisition, a topic that falls under **Competency 008 (Instructional Delivery)**. Krashen (2003) maintained that one acquires language by receiving comprehensible input (understandable messages). Eliminate choice D because this measure works against students' comprehension of input. Eliminate choices B and C because although these measures are appropriate to use with ELLs, they do not specifically support comprehensible input. Choice A is the correct response. Comprehensible input can be enhanced by incorporating gestures, visuals, and manipulatives.

88. D. This question falls under both **Competency 004 (Learning Principles)** and **Competency 005 (Classroom Climate)**. Experts suggest that self-esteem improves as a student grows more competent in school tasks and that, in contrast, confronted with repeated failure, a student simply will quit trying. Therefore, most of the time, teachers should give students tasks that, with effort, they can accomplish and present them with content that is accessible at their level of understanding. At the same time, teachers can challenge students with tasks just beyond their independent level (in the *zone of proximal development*), as long as they provide the *scaffolding* (assistance) necessary to help the student succeed. To facilitate this process, learning experiences should be developmentally appropriate and meaningful for the student, making it more likely that he or she will persist until achieving success. Thus, choice D is the correct response. Eliminate choices A, B, and C because these approaches involve reinforcing students with praise, rewards, or recognition—all of which are more closely related to motivation. Choice A is incorrect also because praise should be given for a specific desirable behavior or accomplishment, not for generally "doing a good job." The approaches in choices B and C might contribute in some indirect way to self-esteem, but these approaches are not as likely to promote a student's development of positive self-esteem as the approach given in choice D. Furthermore, the approach given in choice B should be used cautiously because some research suggests that extrinsic rewards might work against intrinsic motivation for tasks that are already intrinsically motivating.

89. B. This question relates to **Competency 006 (Classroom Management)**. Eliminate choice A because class meetings to solve problems that arise should focus on *solutions,* not on consequences. Eliminate choices C and D because there is no evidence in the question stem to support these responses. Choice B is the correct response. Holding class meetings illustrates a teacher's understanding that providing an opportunity for the students to recognize and clarify the problem, and then suggesting solutions, is likely to promote their ownership in a smoothly functioning learning community. Involving students in solving problems that arise is likely to lead to lasting solutions that the class embraces because this practice allows the students to have a say in deciding how the problem should be handled.

90. C. This question addresses **Competency 010 (Assessment)**. Effective feedback to students should inform them of what they are doing correctly and what they need to work on. Choice C is the correct response because a holistic scoring method does not provide specific feedback on the criteria used in the rubric. Eliminate choice A because a holistic scoring method is designed for scoring students' work quickly. Eliminate choice B because students can get an overall sense of whether they are improving from the weekly scores. Eliminate choice D because the teacher can, for example, convert the scores to percentages (1 out of 5 equals 20 percent) and then to letter grades.

91. C. This question deals with **Competency 008 (Instructional Delivery)**. Notice that you must select the *primary* benefit of devoting time to collecting ideas from the whole class about what they already know about the topic from their own previous experiences. Devoting time to collecting ideas from the whole class about what they already know about the topic from their own previous experiences will activate students' prior knowledge, which will facilitate their ability to link new information and ideas to what they already know. Thus, choice C is the correct response. There is no evidence in the question stem to support the other answer choices—don't read too much into a question! Eliminate choices A, B, and D because there is no basis to think that the students will benefit from the teacher's approach in any of these ways; even if in some incidental manner they were to do so, the primary benefit is indisputably given in choice C.

92. **B.** This question deals with **Competency 008 (Instructional Delivery)**. Eliminate choices A and D because these activities are not developmentally appropriate for first-graders; further, regarding choice D, brain research suggests that, in general, watching a video is a poor way for students to obtain information because it is too passive. Eliminate choice C because coloring pictures is not a mentally engaging experience. When teaching social studies, teachers should use a variety of rich materials such as biographies, poetry, songs, and artwork related to the time periods under study. In a read-aloud, the teacher reads a book aloud to the whole class in an interactive and animated manner. A read-aloud of a children's biography of a historical figure of the relevant time period is an appropriate and meaningful activity that will enhance the students' understanding of the historical figure as a real person. Thus, choice B is the correct response.

93. **B.** This question deals with the topic of psychosocial characteristics of children, which falls under **Competency 001 (Developmentally Appropriate Practice)**. The teacher's students are third-graders, so most of them are between 8 and 9 years old. Eliminate choices A and D because in general, children of this age are too young to have the cognitive abilities or experiences to form strong opinions on issues. Eliminate choice C because although it is the case that as these children mature into young adolescents, the attitudes of their peers begin to exert considerable influence, it is not characteristic at this stage of their development. They rely more on the opinions of their family members, such as parents or older siblings, in forming their attitudes. Thus, choice B is the correct response.

94. **B.** This question falls under **Competency 011 (Family Involvement)**. Eliminate choice A because teachers promote students' sense of ownership of their own learning by, for example, allowing them to make choices about their learning opportunities, but not by setting up a way for them to obtain information about their homework assignments. Eliminate choices C and D because these answer choices are not supported by the question stem. Choice B is the correct response. Parental involvement is an integral part of a successful school program. Thus, the most significant benefit of the homework hotline is that it will strengthen families' ability to be partners with the teachers in their children's education.

95. **C.** This question deals with second language acquisition, a topic that falls under **Competency 008 (Instructional Delivery)**. The language that is used to communicate with others in a social environment is known as basic interpersonal communication. Thus, choice C is the correct response. According to Cummins (1994), usually children learn basic interpersonal communication skills (BICS) with ease, taking only from 6 months to 2 years to acquire them after initial exposure to the second language. Eliminate choices A, B, and D because these options describe language typically used in the classroom.

96. **D.** This question addresses **Competency 003 (Instructional Design and Planning)**. Eliminate choice A because when students engage in learning projects, teachers expect that they might have misconceptions about the topic, but the teachers do not correct the students regarding the misconceptions; instead, they allow the students the opportunity to self-correct as they proceed. Eliminate choice B because assessment of academic progress occurs at a later time, not during planning. Eliminate choice C because there is no evidence in the question stem indicating that the project plan will address specific strengths or weaknesses of individual students. Choice D is the correct response. Allowing students to assume the major responsibility for planning their class learning project provides them an opportunity to structure and manage their own learning, thereby promoting their development of autonomy, initiative, and self-reliance.

97. **C.** This question falls under **Competency 006 (Classroom Management)**. Teachers should provide structure that will help students be self-disciplined and self-managed in the classroom. Eliminate choice A because this approach is too teacher-centered—it does not promote self-management. Eliminate choice B because Ayisha is at an age where she needs to prioritize her responsibilities wisely and thus, not put the creative arts center first. Eliminate choice D because although the teacher could justify giving Ayisha a lower grade, this approach would not be the *best* way to deal with the situation; further, it would penalize Ayisha for her enthusiasm about art and her need to express herself through it. Thus, choice C is the correct response. The teacher can encourage Ayisha to be self-managed in completing her work by providing a checklist that she must complete before going to the creative arts center.

98. **A.** This question deals with the academic performance of English language learners, a topic that falls under both **Competency 002 (Diversity)** and **Competency 008 (Instructional Delivery).** Notice that you must select the answer choice that is the *most reasonable* explanation. The ELL's teachers should be aware of the differences between social- and academic-language proficiency. According to Cummins (1994), after initial exposure to the second language, it takes ELLs only 6 months to 2 years to acquire basic social-language skills, but it takes significantly longer (from 5 to 7 years) for them to develop academic-language proficiency. The ELL in this scenario likely has yet to acquire academic-language proficiency, making it difficult to grasp concepts in classroom situations where academic-language proficiency is a necessity. Therefore, the most reasonable explanation of the ELL's decline in academic performance is that there is an increased focus on academic language in the upper elementary grades. Thus, choice A is the correct response. Eliminate choices B, C, and D because they lack the logical credibility of choice A.

99. **C.** This question falls under **Competency 013 (Professional Conduct).** Choice C is the correct response. Students with disabilities who are receiving special education services should be full participants in the regular education classroom to the greatest extent possible. Therefore, the teacher should place primary emphasis on using strategies and materials that allow the student to participate as fully as possible in all class activities. The actions in the other answer choices would be inappropriate.

100. **D.** This question deals with **Competency 001 (Developmentally Appropriate Practice).** Choice D is the correct response. Children at this age learn best when they have direct, hands-on experiences with concrete objects. Using nonlinguistic representations (such as the tooth models) is an evidence-based high yield instructional strategy (Marzano et al., 2000). Eliminate choices A, B, and C because these options do not involve concrete objects, so they would not be as effective as bringing in large models and having the children practice proper dental care with the models.

Appendix A

References and Helpful Resources

Abrams, D. (2013). *Diversity & Inclusion: The Big Six Formula for Success.* Create Space Independent Publishing Platform: Author.

American Psychological Association. (2010). *Learner-Centered Psychological Principles: A Framework for School Redesign and Reform.* Washington, DC: American Psychological Association.

Badía, A. (1996). *Language Arts through ESOL: A Guide for ESOL Teachers and Administrators.* Tallahassee, FL: Department of Education.

Beech, M. (2010). *Accommodations: Assisting Students with Disabilities,* Third Edition. Florida Department of Education. Retrieved from https://files.eric.ed.gov/fulltext/ED565777.pdf.

Bindreiff, D. (2017). "A Brief Intervention to Increase the Use of Precorrection and Praise by Elementary School Teachers" (Doctoral dissertation). Retrieved from https://pdxscholar.library.pdx.edu/cgi/viewcontent.cgi?article=4649&context=open_access_etds.

Bloom, B. (1956). *Taxonomy of Educational Objectives Handbook.* New York: Longman.

Borek, J. (2003). "Inclusion and the Multiple Intelligences: Creating a Student-Centered Curriculum." *The Quarterly*, 25, 24–28.

Borgmeier, C. (2006). *Classroom Behavior Management Packet: Extending PBS into the Classroom.* Retrieved from http://swpbis.pbworks.com/f/Classroom+Management+Packet+OR+PBS.pdf.

Brookfield, S. (1991). *Developing Critical Thinkers: Challenging Adults to Explore Alternative Ways of Thinking and Acting.* San Francisco: Jossey-Bass.

Brooks, J., and Brooks, M. (1993). *In Search of Understanding: The Case for Constructivist Classrooms.* Alexandria, VA: Association for Curriculum and Development.

Brooks-Young, S. (April, 2006). "Technology in the Classroom: Tap Student Creativity with Electronic Graphic Organizers." *Today's Catholic Teacher*.

Brophy, J. (1983). "Classroom Organization and Management." *The Elementary School Journal, 83*(4), 265–285.

Carnegie Foundation. (1988). *An Imperiled Generation: Saving Urban Schools.* Lawrenceville, NJ: Princeton University Press.

Cazden, C. (2001). *Classroom Discourse: The Language of Teaching and Learning,* Second Edition. Portsmouth, NH: Heinemann.

Child Welfare Information Gateway. (2007). *Recognizing Child Abuse and Neglect: Signs and Symptoms.* Retrieved from https://www.childwelfare.gov/pubPDFs/signs.pdf.

Clay, M. M. (2002). *An Observation Survey of Early Literacy Achievement,* Second Edition. Auckland, N.Z.; Portsmouth, NH: Heinemann.

Cotton, K. (1993). *Fostering Intercultural Harmony in Schools.* Research findings (Issue 7 of School Improvement Research Series). Portland, OR: Northwest Regional Educational Laboratory, School, Community and Professional Development Program.

Council for Exceptional Children. (1990). *Giftedness and the Gifted: What's It All About?* Retrieved from https://files.eric.ed.gov/fulltext/ED321481.pdf.

Appendix A: References and Helpful Resources

Cummins, J. (1994). "The Acquisition of English as a Second Language," in Spangenberg-Urbschat, K., and Pritchard, R. (eds). *Kids Come in All Languages: Reading Instruction for ESL Students.* Newark, DE: International Reading Association.

Davidson, D. (2003). *Developing Creativity.* Retrieved from www.ctahr.hawaii.edu/oc/freepubs/pdf/CF-3.pdf.

Davis, K., Christodoulou, J., Seider, S., and Gardner, H. (2012). *The Theory of Multiple Intelligences.* Retrieved from howardgardner01.files.wordpress.com/2012/06/443-davis-christodoulou-seider-mi-article.pdf.

Dean, C. B., Hubbell, E. R., Pitler, H., and Stone, B. J. (2012). *Classroom Instruction that Works: Research-Based Strategies for Increasing Student Achievement,* 2nd Edition. ASCD, Alexandria, VA 22311-1714 USA.

Diamanti, K., Duffey, T., and Fisher, D. (2018). *Creating a Safe and Respectful Environment in Our Nation's Classrooms.* Washington, DC: National Center on Safe Supportive Learning Environments.

Donnelly, M. (1987). *At-Risk Students.* Retrieved from www.ericdigests.org/pre-928/risk.htm.

Donohue, C. (2015). *Technology and Digital Media in the Early Years: Tools for Teaching and Learning.* New York: Routledge.

Dunn, K., and Dunn, R. (2006). *Learning Styles: Dunn and Dunn Model.* Retrieved from http://americantesol.com/DunnLearningStyles.pdf.

Epstein, M., Atkins, M., Cullinan, D., Kutash, K., and Weaver, R. (2008). *Reducing Behavior Problems in the Elementary School Classroom: A Practice Guide* (NCEE #2008-012). Washington, DC: National Center for Education Evaluation and Regional Assistance, Institute of Education Sciences, U.S. Department of Education. Retrieved from https://issuu.com/quetechceus/docs/reducing-behavior-problems-in-the-elementary-schoo.

Erikson, E. (1968). *Identity, Youth, and Crisis.* New York: Norton.

Gallagher, J. (1994). *Teaching the Gifted Child.* Boston: Allyn and Bacon.

Gersten, R., Beckmann, S., Clarke, B., Foegen, A., Marsh, L., Star, J. R., and Witzel, B. (2009). *Assisting Students Struggling with Mathematics: Response to Intervention (RtI) for Elementary and Middle Schools* (NCEE 2009-4060). Washington, DC: National Center for Education Evaluation and Regional Assistance, Institute of Education Sciences, U.S. Department of Education. Retrieved from ies.ed.gov/ncee/wwc/PracticeGuide.aspx?sid=2.

Gestwicki, C. (1999). *Developmentally Appropriate Practice: Curriculum and Development in Early Education.* Albany, NY: Delmar.

Gilligan, C. (1982). *In a Different Voice: Psychological Theory and Women's Development.* Cambridge, MA: Harvard University Press.

Good, T., and Brophy, J. (2002). *Looking in Classrooms,* 9th Edition. New York: Harper & Row.

Gregorc, A. (2002). *Mind Styles: Anthony Gregorc.* Retrieved from web.cortland.edu/andersmd/learning/gregorc.htm.

Gresham, F. M. (2003). *Responsiveness to Intervention: An Alternative Approach to the Identification of Learning Disabilities.* University of California-Riverside. Retrieved from www.rtimdirect.com/pdf/gresham.pdf.

Houston, D., and Beech, M. (2002). *Designing Lessons for the Diverse Classroom: A Handbook for Teachers.* Tallahassee, FL: Florida Department of Education.

Huizinga, J. (1949). *Homo Ludens: A Study of the Play-Element in Culture.* Retrieved from http://art.yale.edu/file_columns/0000/1474/homo_ludens_johan_huizinga_routledge_1949_.pdf.

Jensen, E. (1998). *Teaching with the Brain in Mind.* Alexandria, VA: Association for Curriculum and Development.

Johnson, R., and Johnson, D. (1994). *An Overview of Cooperative Learning.* Retrieved from www.ioe-rdnetwork.com/uploads/2/1/6/3/21631832/johnson_and_johnson_an_overview_of_cooperative_learning.pdf.

Kagan, J. (1966). "Reflection-Impulsivity: The Generality of Dynamics of Conceptual Tempo." *Journal of Abnormal Psychology,* Vol. 71, No. 1, 17–24.

Kindsvatter, R., Wilen, W., and Ishler, M. (1996). *Dynamics of Effective Teaching,* 3rd Edition. White Plains, NY: Longman.

Kizlik, B. (2014). *Direct Teaching Information.* Retrieved from www.adprima.com/direct.htm.

Kohlberg, L. (1981). *The Philosophy of Moral Development.* New York: Harper & Row.

Kounin, J. (1970). *Discipline and Group Management in Classrooms.* New York: Holt, Rinehart and Winston.

Krashen, S. (2003). *Explorations in Language Acquisition.* Portsmouth, NH: Heinemann.

Krathwohl, D., Bloom, B., and Bertram, B. (1973). "Taxonomy of Educational Objectives, the Classification of Educational Goals." In *Handbook II: Affective Domain.* New York: David McKay Co., Inc.

Lemlech, J. (2002). *Curriculum and Instructional Methods for the Elementary and Middle School,* 5th Edition. Upper Saddle River, NJ: Merrill.

Marzano, R., Gaddy, B., and Dean, C. (2000). *What Works in Classroom Instruction.* Retrieved from www.sinc.stonybrook.edu/Class/est572td/whatworks/whatworks.pdf.

Marzano, R., and Simms, J. (2013). *Vocabulary for the Common Core.* Bloomington, IN: Marzano Research Laboratory.

Maslow, A. (1954). *Motivation and Personality.* New York: Harper & Row.

Mehan, H. (1979). *Learning Lessons: Social Organization in the Classroom.* Cambridge, MA: Harvard University Press.

Mental Health America of Texas. (2015). *Coming Together to Care: A Suicide Prevention and Postvention Toolkit for Texas Communities.* Retrieved from https://texassuicideprevention.org/wp-content/uploads/2015/09/2015_Toolkit_Online.pdf.

National Association for the Education of Young Children. (1996). *Developmentally Appropriate Practice in Early Childhood Programs Serving Children from Birth through Age 8: A Position Statement.* Retrieved from https://www.naeyc.org/sites/default/files/globally-shared/downloads/PDFs/resources/position-statements/PSDAP.pdf.

National Association for the Education of Young Children. (2009). *Where We Stand on Curriculum, Assessment, and Program Evaluation: A Position Statement.* Retrieved from www.naeyc.org/files/naeyc/file/positions/StandCurrAss.pdf.

National Association for Gifted Children. (2009). *Position Statement: Grouping.* Retrieved from www.nagc.org/sites/default/files/Position%20Statement/Grouping%20Position%20Statement.pdf.

National Institute on Drug Abuse. (2014). *Principles of Adolescent Substance Use Disorder Treatment: A Research-Based Guide.* (NIH Publication No. 14-7953). Retrieved from www.drugabuse.gov/publications/principles-adolescent-substance-use-disorder-treatment-research-based-guide.

Nutta, J. (2006). *The Natural Approach: Stages of Second Language Development.* Retrieved from tapestry.usf.edu/nutta/data/content/docs1/naturalapproachnarrative.pdf.

Olusegun, B. D. (2015). *Constructivism Learning Theory: A Paradigm for Teaching and Learning.* Retrieved from https://pdfs.semanticscholar.org/1c75/083a05630a663371136310a30060a2afe4b1.pdf.

Palincsar, A., and Brown, A. (1984). "Reciprocal Teaching of Comprehension-Fostering and Comprehension-Monitoring Activities." *Cognition and Instruction, 1*(2), 117–175.

Paul, R., Binker, A., Jensen, K., and Kreklau, H. (1990). *Critical Thinking Handbook: A Guide for Remodeling Lesson Plans in Language Arts, Social Studies and Science*. Rohnert Park, CA: Foundation for Critical Thinking.

Payne, R. (2006). *Understanding and Working with Students and Adults from Poverty*. Retrieved from homepages.wmich.edu/~ljohnson/Payne.pdf.

Polya, G. (1957). *How to Solve It: A New Aspect of Mathematical Method*. Princeton, NJ: Princeton University Press.

Reinhartz, J., and Beach, D. (1996). *Teaching and Learning in the Elementary School: Focus on Curriculum*. Upper Saddle River, NJ: Merrill.

Reiss, J. (2001). *ESOL Strategies for Teaching Content: Facilitating Instruction for English Language Learners*. Upper Saddle River, NJ: Merrill.

Ribble, M. (2015). *Digital Citizenship in Schools: Nine Elements All Students Should Know*, 3rd Edition. Washington, DC: International Society for Technology in Education.

Ritts, V., and Stein, J. (2011). "Six Ways to Improve Your Nonverbal Communications." Retrieved from https://paperap.com/paper-on-six-ways-to-improve-your-nonverbal-communications/.

Rotter, J. (1996). "Generalized Expectancies for Internal versus External Control of Reinforcement." Psychological Monographs. Vol. 80(1).

Schafersman, S. (1991). *An Introduction to Critical Thinking*. Retrieved from smartcollegeplanning.org/wp-content/uploads/2010/03/Critical-Thinking.pdf.

Slavin, R. (2008). *Educational Psychology*, 9th Edition. Boston: Allyn and Bacon.

Smith, M. (2008). "Howard Gardner and Multiple Intelligences." *The Encyclopedia of Informal Education*. Retrieved from infed.org/mobi/howard-gardner-multiple-intelligences-and-education/.

Social Studies Center for Educator Development. (1999). *Texas Social Studies Framework: Kindergarten-Grade 12*. Austin, TX: Texas Education Agency.

Texas Education Agency. (2000). *Strategies to Teach Social Studies SSCED Toolkit*. Retrieved from www.uintahbasintah.org/papers/ssstrategies.pdf.

Texas Education Agency. (2006). *Texas Star Chart*. Retrieved from https://tea.texas.gov/starchart/.

Texas Education Agency. (2018). *Notice of Procedural Safeguards for Parents of Students with Disabilities*. Retrieved from https://framework.esc18.net/documents/pro_safeguards_eng.pdf.

Texas School Health Advisory Committee. (2016). *Research and Recommendations on Health Issues and Parent Involvement and Engagement in Student Academic Success*. Austin, TX: Texas Health and Human Services.

Thamraksa, C. (2005). *Metacognition: A Key to Success for EFL Learners*. Retrieved from www.bu.ac.th/knowledgecenter/epaper/jan_june2005/chutima.pdf.

Thompson, S., Morse, A., Sharpe, M., and Hall, S. (2005). *Accommodations Manual: How to Select, Administer, and Evaluate Use of Accommodations for Instruction and Assessment of Students with Disabilities*, 3rd Edition. Retrieved from https://files.eric.ed.gov/fulltext/ED545138.pdf.

Tyler, R. (1949). *Basic Principles of Curriculum and Instruction*. Chicago, IL: University of Chicago Press.

U.S. Department of Education. (1991). *What Work Requires of Schools: A SCANS Report for America 2000*. Retrieved from wdr.doleta.gov/SCANS/whatwork/whatwork.pdf.

U.S. Department of Education. (2003). *Weaving a Secure Web around Education: A Guide to Technology Standards and Security*. Retrieved from nces.ed.gov/pubs2003/2003381.pdf.

U.S. Department of Education. (2011). Individuals with Disabilities Education Act of 2004 (Public Law 108-446, 20 U.S.C. 1400). Retrieved from idea.ed.gov.

U.S. Department of Education. (2014). *Guiding Principles: A Resource Guide for Improving School Climate and Discipline*. Retrieved from www2.ed.gov/policy/gen/guid/school-discipline/guiding-principles.pdf.

U.S. Department of Education. (2019, August). "Use of Technology in Teaching and Learning." Retrieved from www.ed.gov/oii-news/use-technology-teaching-and-learning.

U.S. Department of Education Office of Communications and Outreach. (2005). *Helping Your Child with Homework*. Retrieved from www2.ed.gov/parents/academic/help/homework/index.html.

U.S. Department of Education Office of Communications and Outreach. (2005). *Helping Your Child with Test-Taking—Helping Your Child Succeed in School*. Retrieved from www2.ed.gov/parents/academic/help/succeed/part9.html.

U.S. Department of Education Office of Educational Technology. (2017). *Reimagining the Role of Technology in Education: 2017 National Education Technology Plan Update*, Washington, DC: Author.

U.S. Department of Health and Human Services. (2005). *Bodywise Handbook: Eating Disorders Information for Middle School Personnel*. Retrieved from https://permanent.access.gpo.gov/lps100469/BodyWise.pdf.

U.S. Department of Health and Human Services. (2006). *Substance Abuse—A National Challenge: Prevention, Treatment and Research at HHS*. Retrieved from https://archives.drugabuse.gov/news-events/news-releases/2000/12/fact-sheet-substance-abuse-national-challenge-prevention-treatment-research-hhs.

U.S. Department of Homeland Security. (2014). *Net Cetera: Chatting with Kids about Being Online*. Retrieved from https://www.consumer.ftc.gov/articles/pdf-0001-netcetera_0.pdf.

U.S. Department of Justice, Federal Bureau of Investigation, Cyber Division. (2005). *A Parent's Guide to Internet Safety*. Retrieved from https://www2.fbi.gov/publications/pguide/pguidee.htm.

U.S. Department of Justice, Federal Bureau of Investigation, Cyber Division. (2016). *Simple Steps for Internet Safety*. Retrieved from https://www.fbi.gov/news/stories/simple-steps-for-internet-safety.

Van De Walle, J., Karp, K., and Bay-Williams, J. (2009). *Elementary and Middle School Mathematics: Teaching Developmentally,* 7th Edition. Boston: Allyn and Bacon.

Vygotsky, L. (1978). *Mind and Society: The Development of Higher Mental Processes*. Cambridge, MA: Harvard University Press.

Webb, N. L. (2002). *Depth-of-Knowledge Levels for Four Content Areas*. Retrieved from facstaff.wcer.wisc.edu/normw/All%20content%20areas%20%20DOK%20levels%2032802.pdf.

Wiggins, G., and McTighe, J. (2005). *Understanding by Design*, 2nd Edition. Alexandria, VA: Association for Supervision and Curriculum Development (ASCD).

Williams, B., and Zenger, A. (2012). *New Media Literacies and Participatory Popular Culture Across Borders*. New York: Routledge.

Wilson, L. (2019). *Killing or Fostering Creativity in Children*. Retrieved from http://thesecondprinciple.com/creativity/children-creativity/killingcreativityinchildren/.

Wingo, G. (1965). *The Philosophy of American Education*. Boston: D. C. Heath and Co.

Witkin, H., and Goodenough, D. (1981). *Cognitive Styles: Essence and Origins*. New York: International Universities Press, Inc.

Zemelman, S., Daniels, H., and Hyde, A. (2005). *Best Practice: Today's Standards for Teaching and Learning in America's Schools* (2005). Portsmouth, NH: Heinemann.

Appendix B

General Educational Terms

Note: This appendix is a collection of general educational terms. Additional terms related to the various chapter topics are in their respective chapters.

ability: The degree of competence present in a student to perform a given physical or mental act.

ability grouping: The grouping of students for instruction by ability or achievement for the purpose of reducing heterogeneity.

abstract concepts: Those concepts that can be acquired only indirectly through the senses or that cannot be perceived directly through the senses.

Academic Excellence Indicator System (AEIS): The state data collection system that compiles and reports information on the students in each Texas school and district.

academic learning time: The time a student is actually on-task, or successfully engaged in learning.

academic literacy: The ability to comprehend subject-area texts and literature encountered in school.

acceleration: Rapid promotion through advanced studies; enables students to progress more rapidly through the standard curriculum.

accommodation: The adjustment of an existing way of doing something to fit a new experience. Piaget used this term to describe how children change old ways of thinking to fit new information into their existing schema.

accommodations: Changes in instructional methods and materials, assignments and assessments, time demands and scheduling, and the learning environment that ensure that students with disabilities have the opportunity to participate as fully as possible in the general curriculum and ultimately earn a standard diploma.

accountability: A concept in which schools are held responsible for the quality of instruction and the progress of their students.

acculturation: The process of a cultural group or individual taking on traits from another culture without loss of cultural identity.

achievement: Level of attainment or proficiency.

achievement motivation: The generalized tendency to strive for success without extrinsic reward.

achievement test: A standardized test designed to measure levels of knowledge, understanding, abilities, or skills acquired in a particular subject already learned.

acronym: An abbreviation formed from the first letter of each of the words in a phrase; for example, ELL is an acronym for English language learner.

active listening: Being in tune with the words and thoughts of the speaker.

Admission, Review, and Dismissal (ARD) committee: Under IDEA, the group of individuals who make decisions about the services and accommodations or modifications provided to a student with a disability, and who develop, review, or revise a student's Individualized Education Program (IEP).

advance organizers: Preview questions and comments that provide structure for new information to be presented to increase learners' comprehension.

adverse childhood experiences (ACEs): Term used to describe all types of abuse, neglect, and other potentially traumatic experiences that occur to children under the age of 18.

affective domain: The realm of feelings, emotions, and attitudes in people.

affective objectives: Instructional objectives that emphasize changes in interest, attitudes, and values, or a degree of adjustment, acceptance, or rejection.

Appendix B: General Educational Terms

affiliation motive: The intrinsic desire to be with others.

algorithm: A set of rules or procedures for performing a task.

alignment: Matching learning activities with desired outcomes or matching what is taught to what is tested.

allocated time: The time set aside for specific school activities, such as teaching or lunch.

alternate assessment: The assessment procedure used for a student receiving special education services who does not participate in the statewide assessment program, as documented on the student's Individualized Education Program (IEP).

alternative assessment: Assessment that is different from conventional test formats (for example, *see* **authentic assessment**).

alternative education program: An educational program, provided in a setting other than a student's regular classroom, that provides for disruptive students to be separated from other students.

American Sign Language (ASL): A widely used language system employed by the hearing impaired.

analysis: Learning that involves the subdividing of knowledge to show how it fits together.

anecdotal record: A written record of a student's progress over time based on teacher observation with notes.

anticipation guide: A set of statements, some true and some false, that students discuss as a pre-reading activity.

anxiety: A feeling of uneasiness associated with the fear of failure.

application: Learning that requires applying knowledge to produce a result; problem solving.

aptitude test: A standardized test designed to predict future performance in a subject area.

assertive discipline: A classroom management approach that stresses the need for teachers to communicate classroom rules firmly, but without hostility.

assessment: The process of measuring the degree to which instructional objectives have been attained.

assimilation: The process of fitting a new experience into existing ways of doing things; also, in language acquisition, the process of a cultural group taking on traits from another culture at the expense of cultural identity.

assistive technology device: Any item, piece of equipment, or product system that is used to increase, maintain, or improve functional capabilities of individuals with disabilities (20 U.S.C. Chapter 33, § 1401 [25])—for example, Braille writers and speech synthesizers.

at-risk student: A low-performing student who, for a variety of reasons, is in jeopardy of academic failure and might drop out of school at some point.

attending behavior: Use of verbal and nonverbal cues by listeners that demonstrate they are listening with attention to what is being said.

attention deficit disorder (ADD): A condition characterized by an inability to concentrate.

attention deficit hyperactivity disorder (ADHD): A condition in which the individual is extremely active, impulsive, distractible, excitable, and has great difficulty concentrating on what he or she is doing.

attitude: A predisposition to act in a positive or negative way toward people, ideas, or events.

attraction: Friendship patterns in the classroom area.

authentic assessment: Assessment of students' performances in real-life application tasks.

automaticity: The level reached when performance of a task requires little mental effort.

barrier-free environment: An environment designed to enhance accessibility for students with a disability (for example, one that has no obstructions and is equipped with nonslip surfaces and ramps).

baseline score: A score calculated as a point of comparison with later test scores; a relatively stable indicator of typical performance in a content area.

basic education: The general educational program in Texas schools.

basic skills: The foundational knowledge and skills students are expected to acquire in elementary and middle school, in such areas as reading and mathematics.

behavior: What someone does.

behavior modification: The use of learning theory to reduce or eliminate undesirable behavior or to teach new responses.

behavioral learning theory: Explanations of learning that emphasize observable changes in behavior.

behaviorism: A school of psychological thought that seeks to explain learning through observable changes in behavior.

benchmark: A statement of expected knowledge and skills.

between-class ability grouping: A system of grouping in which students are assigned to classes according to achievement and abilities.

bilingual: Capable of using two languages, but usually with differing levels of skills.

bilingual education program: A full-time program of dual-language instruction that provides for learning basic skills in the primary language of the students enrolled in the program and for carefully structured and sequenced mastery of English language skills.

blended learning: Refers to courses consisting of both traditional classroom and online instruction.

Bloom's taxonomy: A system that describes six levels of learning: knowledge, comprehension, application, analysis, synthesis, and evaluation.

brain-based learning: Using "brain-compatible" strategies for learning based on how the brain works.

brain hemisphericity: Refers to a person's preference for processing information through either the left or right hemisphere of the brain.

brainstorming: A teaching strategy in which students generate ideas, judgment of the ideas of others is forbidden, and ideas are used to create a flow of new ideas.

burnout: The condition of losing interest and motivation in teaching.

centration: Focusing attention on only one aspect of an object or situation.

character education: Deliberate instruction in basic virtues or morals.

charter school: A school run independently of the traditional public school system but receiving public funding.

check-in/check-out (CICO): A strategy for building connections in which a teacher (or staff member) checks a student in and out each day to provide a positive communication link between home and school.

Child Find: A mandate of the Individuals with Disabilities Education Act (IDEA) that requires state and local education agencies to identify, locate, and evaluate all children with disabilities residing in the state, regardless of the severity of their disabilities, who are in need of special education and related services.

choral response: Response to a question made by the whole class in unison; useful when there is only one correct answer.

chronological age: Age in calendar years.

chunking: A memory technique in which information is organized into easily memorized subparts.

classical conditioning: A form of conditioning in which a neutral stimulus (such as the bell in Pavlov's experiment) comes to elicit a response (such as salivation) after it is repeatedly paired with reinforcement (such as food).

classroom climate: The atmosphere or mood surrounding classroom interactions.

Appendix B: General Educational Terms

classroom control: The process of influencing student behavior in the classroom.

classroom management: The teacher's system of establishing a climate for learning, including techniques for preventing, redirecting, or stopping student misbehavior.

clique: A small, exclusive group of peers.

clock hour: A period of 60 minutes (minimum of 50 minutes) of instructional time.

closed-ended question: A question that has a limited number of correct responses.

cloze procedure: An open-ended comprehension assessment method in which a selected word or words are eliminated from a text selection, while the student is instructed to fill in the missing word or words.

coaching: Teaching by an expert who gives feedback on performance; can be as effective as athletic coaching; results in about 83 percent retention of learning.

Code of Ethics and Standard Practices for Texas Educators: Standards of ethical conduct for Texas teachers.

cognition: The mental operations involved in thinking.

cognitive: Refers to mental activity (such as thinking, reasoning, or remembering).

cognitive development: Increasing complexity of thought and reasoning.

cognitive dissonance: Mental confusion that occurs when new information received conflicts with existing understandings.

cognitive domain: The psychological field of mental activity.

cognitive objectives: Instructional objectives that require mental capabilities.

cognitive sciences: The area of study that focuses on how people think and learn.

cohesiveness: The collective feeling that the class members have about the classroom group; the sum of the individual members' feelings about the group.

compensatory education: Federally funded education for disadvantaged students.

competency test: Test of performance of certain functions, especially basic skills, usually at a level required by the state or school district.

complex thinking strategies: Thinking strategies such as problem solving, decision making, investigating, and reflecting.

comprehension: Learning that involves making meaning of previously learned materials.

compulsory school attendance: Legally state-mandated school attendance for every child from the ages of 6 to 18 (TEC, § 25.085).

computer-assisted instruction (CAI): Instruction in which a computer is used to present instructional material.

concept: An abstract idea common to a set of objects, conditions, events, or processes.

concept map: A procedure for organizing and graphically displaying relationships among ideas relevant to a given topic.

concrete concepts: Concepts that can be perceived directly through one of the five senses.

conditioned reinforcers: Reinforcers that are learned.

conflict resolution: A type of intervention designed to help students resolve conflicts in a mutually agreeable way.

connectionism: A model for how learning occurs that theorizes that knowledge is stored in the brain as a network of connections.

consequence: A condition that follows a behavior designed to weaken or strengthen the behavior.

conservation: The logical thinking ability to recognize an invariant property under different conditions.

constructivism: A learner-centered approach to teaching that emphasizes teaching for understanding predicated on the concept that students construct knowledge for themselves based on what they already know and by interactions with their environment.

content validity: The degree to which the content covered by a measurement device matches the instruction that preceded it.

continuous reinforcement schedule: A reinforcement schedule in which every occurrence of the desired behavior is reinforced.

conventional level: Kohlberg's second level of moral judgment, characterized by accepting society's rules for right and wrong and obeying authority figures.

convergent question: A question that has a limited number of correct responses.

convergent thinking: Thinking that occurs when the task or question is so structured that the number of possible appropriate conclusions is limited (usually to one conclusion).

cooperative learning: A teaching strategy in which students work together on assigned tasks and are rewarded on the basis of the success of the group.

coordinated early intervening services (CEIS): Services provided to K-12 students (with emphasis on K-3 students) who are not currently identified as needing special education or related services, but who need additional academic and/or behavioral support to succeed in a general education environment.

corporal punishment: The moderate use of physical force or physical contact by a teacher or principal as may be necessary to maintain discipline or to enforce school rules.

correlation: The degree of relationship between two variables; usually expressed numerically as a number between −1 and +1. Positive correlation occurs when (generally) high values on one variable correspond to high values on another; negative correlation occurs when (generally) high values on one variable correspond to low values on another.

creative thinking: The mental process of putting together information to come up with new ideas or understandings.

criterion-referenced test: A standardized test that assesses the level of mastery of specific knowledge and skills that are anchored to specific standards.

critical thinking: Complex thinking skills that include the ability to evaluate information, generate insights, and reach objective conclusions by logically examining the problem and the evidence.

cross-age tutoring: Student-to-student tutoring in which an older student teaches a younger student.

cues: Signals.

cultural pluralism: The condition in which all cultural groups are valued components of the society and the language and traditions of each group are maintained.

culturally fair test: A test designed to reduce cultural bias.

dangle: A lesson transition during which the teacher leaves a lesson hanging while tending to something else in the classroom.

decentralization: A term that refers to decision making being done at a lower level rather than, traditionally, at the highest level.

decision making: Choosing from among several alternatives.

deductive learning: Learning that proceeds from the general to the specific.

deductive reasoning: Reasoning that proceeds from general principles to a logical conclusion.

deficiency needs: Maslow's term for the lower-level needs in his hierarchy: survival, safety, belongingness, and self-esteem.

Appendix B: General Educational Terms

delayed reinforcement: Reinforcement of a desired action that took place at an earlier time.

descriptive data: Data that describe a population or sample but do not present a value judgment or conclusion.

development: Growth, adaptation, or change over the course of a lifetime.

diagnostic procedure: A procedure to determine what a pupil is capable of doing with respect to given learning tasks.

diagnostic test: An assessment that provides information that can be used to identify specific areas of strength and weakness.

differential reasoning: Reasoning that requires recognizing differences.

differentiated instruction: Instruction that is adapted to accommodate individual students' needs and abilities.

direct instruction: An explicit instructional delivery model.

disability: Any hindrance or difficulty imposed by a physical, mental, or emotional problem that substantially limits one or more major life activities.

discipline: In teaching, the process of controlling student behavior in the classroom.

discourse: The interactive exchanges including talking, sharing, explaining, justifying, defending, agreeing, and disagreeing among the students and the teacher in the classroom.

discovery learning: An instructional strategy in which students learn through their own active explorations of concepts and principles.

disengagement: Withdrawal or detachment.

disjunctive concepts: Concepts that have two or more sets of alternative conditions under which the concept appears.

distance education: The use of telecommunications to deliver live instruction by content experts to remote geographic settings.

distributed practice: Practice repeated at intervals over time.

divergent thinking: The type of thinking whereby an individual arrives at a new or unique answer that has not been completely determined by earlier information.

diversity: The condition of having a variety of groups in the same setting.

drill and practice: Repeated performance of a task for the purpose of reinforcing learning.

due process: Procedural safeguards afforded students, parents, and teachers that protect individual rights.

dyscalculia: A math-related learning disability characterized by an inability to grasp and remember math concepts, rules, and formulas, despite conventional instruction, adequate intelligence, and sociocultural opportunity.

dysgraphia: A deficiency in the ability to write, primarily in terms of handwriting, but sometimes in terms of coherence.

dyslexia: A disorder manifested by a difficulty in learning to read, write, or spell, despite conventional instruction, adequate intelligence, and sociocultural opportunity.

early childhood: The period from the end of infancy to about age 8.

educational goal: A desired instructional outcome that is broad in scope.

educational placement: The setting in which a student receives educational services.

educational records: Official records, files, and data directly related to a student and maintained by the school or local education agency.

effective school correlates: A body of research identifying the characteristics of effective and ineffective schools. They are (a) safe and orderly environment, (b) climate of high expectations for success, (c) instructional leadership, (d) clear and focused mission, (e) opportunity to learn and student time on-task, (f) frequent monitoring of student progress, and (g) home/school relations.

effective schools research: Educational research focused on identifying unusually effective schools, studying the underlying attributes of their programs and personnel, and designing techniques to operationalize these attributes in less effective schools.

effective teacher: A teacher who is able to bring about intended learning outcomes.

egocentric: Believing that everyone sees the world as you do.

egocentrism: Piaget's term for the preoperational child's inability to distinguish between his or her own and another's perceptions; also, in adolescents, a preoccupation with self.

Elementary and Secondary Education Act (ESEA): A sweeping 1965 law that provides federal funding for elementary and secondary compensatory education programs.

emotional disability: A disorder in which the capacity to manage individual or interactive behaviors is limited, impaired, or delayed, and is exhibited by difficulty that persists over time and in more than one setting in one or more of the following areas: the ability to understand, build, or maintain interpersonal relationships; the ability to react/respond within established norms; the ability to keep normal fears, concerns, and/or anxieties in perspective; the ability to control aggressive and/or angry impulses or behavior.

emotional intelligence (EI): A type of social competence that involves being self-aware, managing one's emotions, being self-motivated and exhibiting self-control, having empathy for others, and managing relationships.

empathy: The ability to understand the feelings of another person.

empirical questions: Questions that require investigation in the real world to answer.

engaged time (time on-task): The actual time individual students spend as active participants in the learning process.

English for Speakers of Other Languages (ESOL): A term used to describe special programs or classes for English language learners.

English for Speakers of Other Languages (ESOL) program: A program of intensive instruction in English from teachers trained in recognizing and dealing with language differences.

English for Speakers of Other Languages (ESOL) Pull-Out program: A program of instruction in English in which students leave their English-only content classes to spend part of their day receiving ESOL instruction. Students might have different home languages.

enrichment: The process of providing richer and more varied content through strategies that supplement the standard curriculum; involves assignments or activities designed to broaden or deepen the knowledge of students who master classroom lessons quickly.

epistemology: The study of how knowledge is acquired.

equal opportunities for success: In cooperative learning, calculations of team achievement designed to ensure that equal individual improvement results in equal individual contribution to the team score, despite differences among teammates in absolute achievement.

equilibration: The process of restoring balance between what is understood and what is experienced.

equity: Equal access to educational opportunities built on a focus on closing achievement gaps and removing barriers that students face based on their race, ethnicity, or national origin; sex; sexual orientation or gender identity or expression; disability; English language ability; religion; socioeconomic status; or geographical location.

essentialism: Educational philosophy that holds that a common core of knowledge and ideals should be the focus of the curriculum.

ethnicity: The ethnic identity (e.g., Hispanic or non-Hispanic) of an individual or group.

ethnocentrism: The belief that one's culture is better than any other culture.

Eurocentrism: The belief that European culture is superior to that of others.

evaluation: The cognitive process of establishing and applying standards in judging materials and methods.

evaluation question: A question that requires that a judgment be made or a value be put on something.

evaluative comprehension: Forming an opinion on the effectiveness of a text selection with regard to its message or purpose.

evaluative reasoning: Reasoning that requires forming an opinion or making a judgment.

Every Student Succeeds Act (ESSA, 2015): U.S. law that governs K-12 public education policy. Like its predecessor, the No Child Left Behind Act (NCLB), ESSA is a reauthorization of the 1965 Elementary and Secondary Education Act (ESEA).

exceptionality: The special need of a student that qualifies for special education services. *See also* **special education.**

explaining behavior: Planned teacher talk designed to clarify any idea, procedure, or process not understood by a student.

expressive language skills: Speaking and writing.

externalizing behaviors: Actions directed outward toward others (such as aggression, bullying, and theft).

external locus of control: Having a belief that events are caused by factors outside of one's control.

extinction: The gradual disappearance of a behavior through the removal or the withholding of reinforcement.

extrinsic motivation: Motivation created by events or rewards outside the individual.

facts: Well-grounded, clearly established pieces of information.

factual questions: Questions that require the recall of information through recognition or rote memory.

Family Educational Rights and Privacy Act (FERPA): The federal law that protects the privacy of student education records (20 U.S.C. § 1232g; 34 CFR Part 99).

feedback: Information from the teacher to the student, or vice versa, that provides disclosure about the reception of an intended message; also, information from the teacher to the student that informs the student of what he or she is doing correctly and what he or she still needs to work on.

fidelity of implementation: The degree to which instructional strategies and delivery follow the intent and design of a curriculum or program.

field-dependent: Learning style in which patterns are perceived as wholes.

field-independent: Learning style in which separate parts of a pattern are apparent.

fine-tuning: Making small adjustments in the planned procedures for a lesson during its teaching.

fixed-interval reinforcement schedule: A pattern in which reinforcement is given after a desired observable behavior has occurred only at certain periodic times; often results in a great deal of work (cramming) at the last minute, just before the reinforcement is given. For example, final exams are fixed-interval reinforcements.

fixed-ratio reinforcement schedule: A pattern in which reinforcement is given after a desired observable behavior has occurred a fixed number (1, 5, 10, or so on) of times; effective in motivating students to do a great deal of work, but runs the risk of losing its value if the reinforcing is done too frequently. For example, giving students stars after they read 10 books is fixed-ratio reinforcement.

flip-flop: A lesson transition in which the teacher changes back and forth from one subject or activity to another.

focus: Component in a lesson in which the teacher secures the attention of the students and communicates the lesson objectives.

focusing question: A question used to focus students' attention on a lesson or on the content of a lesson.

formative assessment: Assessment that takes place both before and during the learning process; used to guide the content and pace of lessons.

Free Appropriate Public Education (FAPE): Provision of IDEA (formerly PL 94-142) that guarantees special education and related services to children with disabilities, at public cost.

frequency measurement: A measure of the number of times specified, observable behaviors are exhibited in a constant time interval.

frontloading: A teaching strategy that provides learners guidance and reminders before they engage in instructional tasks.

gender bias: Conscious or unconscious favorable treatment of females or males based on their sex.

general curriculum: The curriculum that is taught in regular education classes in Texas public schools.

generalization: The carryover of learning from one setting to a different setting.

gifted student: A student who has superior intellectual development and is capable of high performance.

goals: Extremely broad statements of school or instructional purposes.

Goals 2000: A federal program that codified national educational goals. (See "Goals 2000: Educate America Act," available at www2.ed.gov/legislation/GOALS2000/TheAct/index.html.)

goal structure: The degree to which students have to cooperate or compete for classroom rewards.

grade-level team: A group of teachers who share responsibility for planning, instructing, and evaluating a common group of students.

graphic organizers: Visual, hierarchical overviews designed to show relationships among abstract concepts or to illustrate processes. Types include concept or semantic maps, webs, decision trees, Venn diagrams, flowcharts, cause-effect charts, story trees, and K-W-L charts.

group contingencies: Strategies in which the entire class is rewarded on the basis of everyone's behavior; removes peer support for misbehavior.

group discussion: Verbal interaction with other learners.

group-focus behaviors: Behaviors teachers use to maintain a focus on the group, rather than on an individual student, during individual recitations.

group investigation: A cooperative learning strategy in which students brainstorm a set of questions on a subject, form learning teams to find answers to the questions, and make presentations to the whole class.

growth needs: The term for the following three higher-level needs in some versions of Maslow's hierarchy of needs: intellectual achievement, aesthetic appreciation, and self-actualization.

guided practice: Refers to practice by students under the direct guidance of the teacher.

halting time: A teacher's pause in talking, used to give students time to think about presented materials or directions.

handicap: Any hindrance or difficulty imposed by a physical, mental, or emotional disability.

hands-on: Describes work by students with tools, manipulatives, models, physical representations, and so forth.

Hawthorne effect: A phenomenon in which subjects of a research study alter their behavior as a result of being aware of their participation.

Head Start: A federal program that provides economically deprived preschoolers with education, nutrition, health, and social services.

heritage language: A non-English language to which a student has had exposure outside the formal education system, such as the language of immigrants (for example, Spanish) and indigenous peoples (for example, Navajo).

Appendix B: General Educational Terms

heterogeneous grouping: A method of grouping in which students with mixed abilities, interests, achievement levels, and/or backgrounds are grouped together.

hidden curriculum: The unintended and nonacademic learning that occurs in schools.

holistic evaluation: Determination of the overall quality of a piece of work or an endeavor.

home language: The language spoken by the parents of a student.

home schooling: The practice of parents teaching their children at home rather than sending them to public school.

homogeneous grouping: A method of grouping in which students with similar abilities, interests, achievement levels, and/or backgrounds are grouped together.

humanistic education: Educational system designed to achieve affective outcomes or psychological growth; oriented toward improving self-awareness and mutual understanding among people.

hypermedia: A nonlinear presentation of information that allows users to access related materials or images from a single computer screen.

hypothesize: To make an educated guess to explain a phenomenon.

idealism: The educational philosophy that embraces a belief in unchanging principles and eternal truths.

identity diffusion: The inability of an adolescent to develop a clear sense of self.

identity foreclosure: An adolescent's premature choice of a role.

IEP team: Individualized Education Program team; another name for the ARD (Admission, Review, and Dismissal) committee.

illiterate: The condition of being unable to read or write or perform everyday tasks (for example, understanding a bus schedule).

imagery: Details and descriptions that authors use to create a sensory experience for the reader and to improve the reader's comprehension and retention.

imaginary audience: An aspect of adolescent egocentrism that follows the belief that the adolescent is the focus of attention of others around him or her.

I messages: Clear teacher messages that tell students how the teacher feels about problem situations and that implicitly ask for corrected behaviors.

imitation: Carrying out the basic rudiments of a skill when given directions and supervision.

immorality: Conduct that is inconsistent with the standards of public conscience and good morals. It is conduct sufficiently notorious to bring the individual concerned or the education profession into public disgrace or disrespect and to impair the individual's service in the community.

improvement scores: Scores calculated by comparing the entering achievement levels with the performance after instruction.

impulsivity: The tendency to respond quickly, but often without regard for accuracy or consequences.

incapacity: Lack of emotional stability, lack of adequate physical ability, lack of general educational background, or lack of adequate command of one's area of specialization.

inclusion: When a student is receiving education in a general education regular class setting with appropriate services provided.

incompetency: The inability or lack of fitness to perform duties required by law as a result of inefficiency or incapacity.

independent practice: Refers to practice by students on their own without direct teacher guidance. For example, homework is independent practice.

independent study: An instructional strategy in which students are allowed to pursue a topic in depth on their own over an extended period.

indirect teaching: Learner-centered teaching using such strategies as discovery and inquiry-based learning.

individual accountability: In cooperative learning, making sure that all individuals are responsible for their own learning.

Individualized Education Program (IEP): A written plan developed to meet the educational needs of a student with one or more disabilities.

individualized instruction: An instructional strategy characterized by a shift in responsibility for learning from the teacher to the student.

Individuals with Disabilities Education Act (IDEA): Far-reaching legislation that provides special education and services for children with disabilities; formerly PL 94-142.

inductive reasoning: The process of drawing a general conclusion based on several examples.

inefficiency: Repeated failure to perform duties required by law; repeated failure on the part of a teacher to communicate with and relate to children, to such an extent that pupils are deprived of minimum educational experience.

inference: A conclusion derived from, and bearing some relation to, assumed premises.

inferential comprehension: Grasping the implied message in a text selection.

informal observation: An assessment method in which teachers directly observe students performing or working on an activity.

information processing model: A model for how learning occurs based on theories about how the brain processes information.

informational objectives: Abbreviated instructional objectives in which only the student performance and the product are specified.

inquiry: Obtaining information by asking.

inquiry learning: A learner-centered instructional strategy in which the learners design the processes to be used in resolving a problem.

in-service training: The professional learning workshops, demonstrations, and so forth provided by districts to keep teachers current.

instructional event: Any activity or set of activities in which students are engaged (with or without the teacher) for the purpose of learning.

instructional grouping: Dividing a class into small subunits for purposes of teaching.

instructional objective: A clearly written statement of what students are expected to know and be able to do as the result of an instructional learning experience.

instructional setting: Place where teaching and learning occur.

instructional strategy: A strategy for delivering instruction.

instructional time: Blocks of class time used for productive learning activities.

integrated language arts: Teaching reading, writing, and spelling, not as separate subjects, but as an unsegregated whole.

intelligence: General ability to learn and understand.

intelligence quotient (IQ): A measure of intelligence for which 100 is the score assigned to those of average intelligence.

interdisciplinary instruction: Teaching by themes or activities that cross subject area boundaries; most frequently, involves bringing ideas, concepts, and/or facts from one subject area to bear on issues or problems raised in another (also called multidisciplinary approach).

interference: A process that occurs when information to be recalled gets mixed up with other information.

intermediate grades: Usually, grades 3 through 5.

intermittent reinforcement schedule: A pattern in which correct responses are reinforced often, but not following each occurrence of the desirable behavior.

internalization: The extent to which an attitude or value becomes a part of the learner.

internalizing behaviors: Actions directed toward one's self (such as being shy, nonresponsive, and nonparticipating).

interval reinforcement schedule: A pattern in which reinforcement is dispensed after desired observable behavior has occurred for a specified length of time.

intonation: The rise and fall of the voice when speaking or reading aloud.

intrinsic motivation: An internal source of motivation associated with activities that are rewarding in themselves.

intuition: Knowing without conscious reasoning.

invented spelling: Spelling based on how a word sounds; used when the writer does not know the conventional spelling of the word.

inventory questions: Questions asking individuals to describe their thoughts, feelings, and manifested actions.

invincibility fable: An aspect of adolescent egocentrism that follows the belief that bad things happen to other people, not to them.

jigsaw: A cooperative learning strategy in which students become "experts" and teach other students.

judgment: Estimate of present conditions or prediction of future conditions; involves comparing information to some referent.

knowledge learning: Cognitive learning that entails the simple recall of learned materials.

knowledge questions: Questions requiring the student to recognize or recall information.

labeling: Assigning a category (especially a special education category) to an individual.

laboratory learning model: An instructional model focusing on hands-on manipulation and firsthand experience.

language experience approach: An approach to teaching, reading, and language arts that uses words and stories from the student's own language and experiences.

large muscle activity: Physical movement involving the limbs and large muscles.

leadership: Those behaviors that help the group move toward the accomplishment of its objectives.

learned helplessness: The learned belief, based on experience, that one is doomed to failure.

learning: A relatively permanent change in an individual's capacity for performance as a result of experience.

learning center: A defined space in the classroom where materials are organized in such a way that children learn without the teacher's constant presence and direction.

learning cycle model: An instructional approach such as the 5E model that includes the following components: engage, explore, explain, extend/elaborate, and evaluate.

learning disability: In general, a discrepancy between a child's intelligence and his or her academic ability.

learning environment: The surrounding conditions in which instruction takes place.

learning style: Orientation for approaching learning tasks and processing information.

least restrictive environment (LRE): The placement mandated under IDEA that requires that students with disabilities be educated in a regular classroom to the maximum extent appropriate.

lecture: Planned teacher talk designed to convey important information in an effective and efficient manner.

lesson cycle model: An instructional approach that includes the following components: focus, explanation, check for understanding, re-teach, guided practice, check for mastery, independent practice, enrichment, and closure. The components of the lesson cycle do not necessarily all occur in a single lesson, nor must a particular sequential order be followed.

lesson plan: The teacher's plan for delivering instruction.

Likert scale: Usually, a five-point attitude scale with linked options: strongly agree, agree, undecided, disagree, and strongly disagree.

Limited English Proficient (LEP): Used to describe a student whose home language is something other than English and whose English language skills are such that the student has difficulty performing ordinary classwork.

literal comprehension: Understanding the explicit message in a text selection.

local education agency (LEA): A public authority that acts as an administrative agency to provide control of, and direction for, K-12 public education.

long-term memory: Component of the memory system that can hold a large amount of information for a long time.

magnet school: A public school that focuses on special themes (science, mathematics, language arts, and so on), providing a specialized education program and drawing students from multiple school zones.

mainstreaming: Including students with special needs in regular education classrooms for part or all of the school day.

maintenance: The continuation of a behavior.

mandated time: The set amount of time, established by the state, during which school is in session.

massed practice: Repeated practice over and over in a concentrated period.

mastery learning: A teaching strategy designed to permit as many students as possible to achieve objectives to a specified level, with the assignment of grades based on achievement of objectives at specified levels.

mastery learning model: An instructional approach that emphasizes the mastery of stated objectives by all students by presenting the material in a logical progression and allowing learning time to be flexible.

measurement: The assignment of numerical values to objects, events, performances, or products to indicate how much of a characteristic being measured they possess.

melting pot theory: The belief that other cultures should assimilate and blend into the dominant culture.

mental age: An age estimate of an individual's level of mental development, derived from a comparison of the individual's IQ score and chronological age.

mental set: A student's attitude toward beginning the lesson.

mentors: Experienced teachers who support, guide, and advise the development of less experienced teachers.

metacognition: The process of thinking about and monitoring one's own thinking.

methodology: The patterned behaviors that form the definite steps by which the teacher influences learning.

middle school: School that has been planned for students ranging in age from 9 through 14 and generally has grades 5 through 8, with grades 6 through 8 being the most popular organization.

mindfulness: Focusing intentionally and without judgment on the present moment.

minority group: An ethnic or racial group that is a minority within a larger society.

miscue analysis: A formal examination of a student's deviations (reading a word incorrectly, inserting a word, skipping a word, and so on) from written text when reading.

mission statement: A broad statement of the unique purpose for which an organization exists and the specific function it performs.

mnemonic: A method to assist memory, such as using acronyms, rehearsal, or chunking.

modality: *See* **sensory modality strength.**

modeling: The teacher tactic of demonstrating a skill or behavior that the teacher wants the students to mimic.

modifications: Changes that are made in the curriculum for students who cannot meet state standards for their grade level.

monitor: To oversee a situation, activity, or process.

moral turpitude: Crime that is evidenced by an act of baseness, vileness, or depravity in the private and social duties, which, according to the accepted standards of the time, a person owes to society in general. The doing of the act itself, and not its prohibition by statute, fixes the moral turpitude (TAC, § 519.7).

morphology: The study and description of word patterns.

motivation: The willingness or drive to exhibit a behavior, such as to engage productively in a learning experience.

movement management behaviors: Those behaviors that the teacher uses to initiate, sustain, or terminate a classroom activity.

multicultural education: A structured process designed to foster understanding, acceptance, and constructive relations among people of various cultures.

multimedia: Software that combines text, sound, video, animation, and graphics into a single presentation.

multiple intelligences: A theory that proposes several different intelligences as opposed to just one general intelligence; other intelligences that have been described are verbal-linguistic, musical-rhythmic, logical-mathematical, visual-spatial, bodily-kinesthetic, interpersonal, intrapersonal, naturalistic, and existential.

multi-tiered systems of support (MTSS): A framework structured into (usually) three tiers to provide instruction and support of increasing levels of intensity within a school campus to improve academic and behaviorial outcomes of students.

National Education Association (NEA): The largest professional employee organization in the United States, the purpose of which includes working for improved education and enhancing the status of teachers.

negative reinforcement: Strengthening a behavior by release from an undesirable situation.

negligence: Lack of ordinary care in one's actions; failure to exercise due care.

no-lose tactic: A problem-resolution tactic whereby a teacher and one or more students negotiate a solution such that no one comes out the loser.

nondiscriminatory testing: Assessment that properly takes into account a child's cultural and linguistic background.

noninstructional responsibility: Duties assumed by or assigned to teachers that are outside of their regular teaching responsibilities.

nonverbal cues: Eye contact, facial expressions, gestures, movement toward someone, placing a hand on someone's shoulder, or another physical act that communicates a message without the use of speech or writing.

nonverbal reinforcement: Using some form of physical action as a positive consequence to strengthen a behavior.

normal curve: A bell-shaped curve that describes the distribution of scores or measurements; approximately 95 percent of the data fall within two standard deviations of the mean.

norming group: A large national sample of people who are similar to those for whom a particular standardized test is designed and who take the test to establish the group standards; serves as a comparison group for scoring the test.

norm-referenced test: A standardized test that focuses on a comparison of a student's score to the average of a norm group.

norms: Rules or practices that apply generally to all members of a group.

novice: A person who is inexperienced in performing a particular activity.

object permanence: The ability to recognize that objects continue to exist even when they can no longer be seen or touched.

objective: A clear and unambiguous description of instructional intent.

observable behavior: An overt act by an individual.

observation: The process of looking and listening, noticing the important elements of a performance or a product.

on-task behavior: Student behavior that is appropriate to the task.

open-ended question: A question that has an unlimited number of correct responses.

orthography: The practice or study of correct spelling.

outcome-based education (OBE): An effort designed to focus and organize all of the school's programs and instructional efforts around clearly defined outcomes that students are able to demonstrate.

overlapping: Attending to and supervising more than one thing at a time.

overlapping behaviors: Those behaviors by which the teacher indicates that he or she is attending to more than one thing when several things are going on at a particular time.

overlearning: Practicing beyond the point of mastery to improve retention.

pacing: Determining the speed of performance of a learning task.

paired-associate learning: A task involving the linkage of two items in a pair so that when one is presented, the other can be recalled.

paradigm: A pattern or model; sets of rules that establish boundaries.

paraphrasing: Restating in one's own words.

paraprofessional: A person who lacks the credentials of a fully certified teacher, but who has training to perform as an aide under the supervision of a certified teacher.

parent: Either or both parents, a guardian, or any person standing in parental relation to a child, or any person who has legal charge over a child in place of the parent.

parenting styles: The different ways parents interact with their children, including (a) authoritarian (parents are restrictive, place limits and controls on the child, and offer very little give-and-take); (b) authoritative (parents are warm and nurturing and encourage the child to be independent, but still place limits, demands, and controls on the child's actions); (c) permissive/indulgent (parents allow great freedom to the child and are undemanding, but are responsive and involved in the child's life); and (d) permissive/indifferent (parents are neglectful, unresponsive, and highly uninvolved in the child's life).

pedagogy: The art and science of teaching.

peer assessment: Assessment by students of their classmates' products or performances.

peer teaching: A procedure that provides teachers with an opportunity to practice new instructional techniques in a simplified setting, teaching lessons to small groups of their peers (other prospective or experienced teachers).

Appendix B: General Educational Terms

peer tutoring: An instructional practice in which same-age students assist with the instruction of other students needing supplemental instruction.

peers: Students equal in age, grade, class, and so forth.

percentile: A score at or below where a given percentage of the scores fall. For example, the 75th percentile is the score at or below where 75 percent of the scores fall.

performance assessment: Assessment that measures a student's ability to perform a specific cognitive or physical task correctly.

performance-based instruction: Instruction designed around evaluating student achievement against specified and predetermined behavioral objectives.

personal fable: An aspect of adolescent egocentrism that follows the belief that their personal situation is unique and that no one else understands them.

personalized learning: Individualized instruction that is customized to match characteristics of the learner such as his or her strengths, needs, skills, interests, and cultural background.

perspective taking: Assuming another person's viewpoint.

phonics approach: A literacy instructional strategy that emphasizes sounding out words based on letter-sound relationships.

pitch: The highness or lowness of sound.

planned ignoring: Withholding the positive reinforcers of an undesirable behavior.

planning: Decision-making process in which the teacher decides what, why, when, and how to teach; composed of three elements: task analysis, planning for student behaviors/outcomes, and planning for teacher behaviors/strategies.

portfolio: A collection of a student's work and achievements that is used to assess past accomplishments and future potential.

positive behavioral interventions and supports (PBIS): A three-tiered prevention-based framework that uses data, problem solving, and decision making to provide a continuum of evidence-based interventions based on students' behavioral needs.

positive reinforcement: Strengthening a behavior by giving a desirable reward.

postconventional level: Kohlberg's first level of moral judgment, characterized by making decisions based on one's own needs and desires.

PQ4R: A study strategy in which students preview the reading, create questions, read to answer questions, and reflect, recite, and review the original material.

pragmatics: The study of what words mean in context.

precision: Psychomotor ability to perform an act accurately, efficiently, and harmoniously.

primacy effect: The tendency to be able to recall the first things in a list.

primary motives: Forces and drives, such as hunger, thirst, and the need for security, that are basic and inborn.

principal: The instructional leader of the school.

principal autonomy: A system wherein the principal is authoritarian and makes all the decisions.

principle: A rule that explains the relationship between or among factors.

private speech: Children's self-talk.

probing: The communication technique of eliciting additional information from a student, often for the purpose of obtaining clarification of or justification for the student's contribution to a discussion or response to a question.

probing questions: Questions following a response that require the respondent to provide more support, be clearer or more accurate, or offer greater specificity or originality.

problem solving: A strategy that involves the application of knowledge and skills to produce a result or solution.

procedural safeguards: The rights of parents of students with disabilities.

procedure: A sequence of steps and activities that have been designed to lead to the acquisition of learning objectives.

productive questions: Broad, open-ended questions, with many correct responses, that require students to use their imagination, think creatively, and produce something unique.

professional autonomy: Freedom of professionals or groups of professionals to function independently.

professional learning: The process of engaging in activities that promote growth in one's profession.

programmed instruction: A program in which students work through specially constructed print or electronic self-instructional materials at their own pace.

progressivism: A learner-centered educational philosophy, popularized by John Dewey, based on the belief that the interaction of the student with the environment creates experiences that encourage the student to learn by doing.

progress monitoring: The use of assessments to keep track of a student's progress toward meeting learning goals during the school year.

promotion: Moving up to the next grade.

prompting: The communication technique of giving hints and clues to aid students in answering questions or in correcting an initial response.

puberty: Developmental stage at which a person becomes capable of reproduction.

Public Education Information Management System (PEIMS): The electronic system that collects all data requested and received by TEA about public education in Texas.

Public Law 94-142: Federal law requiring that all schools receiving federal funds must provide for every child with a disability a free, appropriate public education in the least restrictive environment.

pull-out programs: Programs in which students with special needs are taken out of regular classes for instruction.

punishment: Using unpleasant consequences to weaken or extinguish an undesirable behavior.

Pygmalion effect: The tendency of individuals who are treated as capable or incapable to act accordingly.

qualified reinforcement: Reinforcement of only the acceptable parts of an individual's response or action or of the attempt itself.

questionnaire: A list of written statements regarding attitudes, feelings, and opinions that are to be read and responded to.

rating scale: A scale of values arranged in order of quality, describing someone or something being evaluated.

ratio reinforcement schedule: A pattern in which reinforcement is dispensed after a desired observable behavior has occurred a certain number of times.

realia: Objects and materials from everyday life that are used as teaching aids.

reality therapy: Therapy in which individuals are helped to become responsible and able to satisfy their needs in the real world.

receiving: Affective learning that involves being aware of and willing to freely attend to a stimulus.

receiving skills: Skills used when listening to someone.

recency effect: The tendency to be able to recall the last things in a list.

receptive language skills: Listening and reading.

reciprocal teaching: An instructional approach in which the teacher helps students learn to ask teacher-type questions; designed to increase comprehension.

redirecting: The technique of directing a student away from the student's current activity; also, in communication, the technique of asking several individuals to respond to a question in light of or to add new insight to the previous responses.

referent: That to which you compare the information you have about an individual to form a judgment.

referral: A request for an individual evaluation of a student who is suspected to be in need of special education services (after strategies in the regular education classroom have failed to meet the needs of the student).

reflection: Giving direct feedback to individuals about the way their verbal and nonverbal messages are being received; also, quiet thought or contemplation that includes analysis of past experience.

reflective listening: The act of listening with feeling as well as with cognition.

reflective practitioner: A teacher who systematically reflects on his or her own performance in the classroom and development as a teacher.

reflectivity: Examining and analyzing oneself and one's thoughts before taking action.

regular class: A typical classroom designed to serve students without disabilities.

rehearsal: Repetition (often done mentally) of information to aid retention.

reinforcement: Using consequences to strengthen the likelihood of a behavior or event.

reinforcement schedule: The frequency with which reinforcers are given. Common schedules are fixed-ratio, which includes continuous reinforcement; variable-ratio; fixed-interval; and variable-interval.

relational concepts: Concepts that describe relationships between items.

reliability: The consistency of test scores obtained in repeated administrations to the same individuals on different occasions or with different sets of equivalent items.

remediation: Additional instruction given to struggling students that supplements regular instruction.

repertoire: A set of alternative routines or procedures, all of which serve some common purpose and each of which serves some additional, unique purpose.

reproduced data: Data that have been recorded in video, audio, or verbatim transcript form and can be reproduced when desired.

resiliency: The ability to cope with difficult and challenging situations and to "bounce back" from them.

responding: Affective learning that involves freely attending to a stimulus as well as voluntarily reacting to it in some way.

response to intervention (RtI): A process that studies the response of students to different types of instructional interventions at differing levels of intensity.

restructuring: A radically altering reform of schools as organizations and the way schooling is delivered.

reteach: Instruction in the original objective that is substantially different from the initial instruction; differences may be reflected in an adjustment or modification of time allocation, practice depth, length, or instructional modality.

retrieval strategy: Strategy used by a learner to remember something.

reversibility: The ability to change direction in thinking and go back to a starting point.

ripple effect: The spreading of behaviors from one individual to others through imitation.

role playing: An activity in which students act out roles.

rote learning: Memorization of facts or associations.

routine: An established pattern of behavior.

rubric: A set of criterion-referenced guidelines for scoring a student's work.

running record: An assessment tool that uses a coding system to record a student's exact oral reading performance.

salad-bowl theory: The belief that various cultures should mix, but still retain their unique characteristics.

same-age tutoring: Peer tutoring in which one student teaches another student (usually a classmate) of the same age.

scaffolding: Providing temporary support for learning and problem solving, such as giving clues, reminders, encouragement, and examples.

SCANS Report: A report issued in 1992 by the Secretary's (of Education) Commission on Achieving Necessary Skills that recommended changes in the school curricula and teaching methods in order to better prepare students for the workplace.

schema: Mental models that guide behavior.

schizophrenia: Abnormal behavior patterns and personality disorganization accompanied by less-than-adequate contact with reality.

School Improvement Plan (SIP): A plan developed each school year that sets forth the school's plan for improving student performance.

secondary motives: Forces and drives, such as the desire for money or grades, that are learned through association with primary motives.

Section 504 Plan: A written education plan for students who are not qualified for special education, but who might need special accommodations.

self-actualization: Reaching one's fullest potential.

self-concept: How a person thinks of himself or herself.

self-directed learning: Learning by designing and directing one's own learning activities.

self-efficacy: The confidence a person has that he or she has the power within himself or herself to be successful.

self-esteem: The value a person places on what he or she is; self-worth.

self-fulfilling prophecy: A phenomenon that occurs when one's biased beliefs about what should occur influence the results to conform to one's expectations.

semantics: The study of the meanings created by words, phrases, sentences, symbols, and such.

sending skills: Skills used when speaking to someone.

sensory modality strength: The predominant way an individual takes in information through the five senses (see, hear, smell, taste, touch).

seriation: The ability to sequentially order objects from smallest to largest, shortest to tallest, and so forth.

set induction: Teacher actions and statements at the outset of a lesson to get students' attention, trigger interest, and establish a conceptual framework.

sexual harassment: Unwelcome written or verbal comments or physical gestures or actions of a sexual nature.

shaping: The behavior modification technique of achieving a desired learning goal or behavior by using positive reinforcement at incremental steps along the way.

short-term memory: Component of the memory system that can hold a limited amount of information for a short period.

silent time: The time the teacher waits following a student response before replying or continuing with the discussion.

simulation: An enactment of an artificial situation or event that represents real life as much as possible, but with most of the risk and complicating factors removed; works best when students are assigned roles and the teacher acts as a facilitator but does not become actively involved in the make-believe situation.

site-based decision making (SBDM): The decentralization of decision-making authority from the state to the district and school levels.

small muscle activity: Physical movement involving the fine muscles of the hand.

social cognition: The ability to understand other people's feelings and actions.

social-emotional learning (SEL): The process of acquiring self awareness, self management, social awareness, relationship skills, and responsible decision making.

social objective: A requirement of the cooperative learning model dealing with the social skills, roles and relationships, and group processes that students need to accomplish the learning task.

sociodrama: A form of role playing that focuses on a group solving a problem.

socioeconomic status (SES): The relationship of an individual's economic status to social factors, including education, occupation, and place of residence.

special education: Programs designed to serve children with mental and/or physical disabilities under the Individuals with Disabilities Education Act (IDEA); the term used in Texas to designate special services for students with disabilities.

standard diploma: The diploma that is awarded for meeting the general requirements for high school graduation.

standardized test: A commercially developed test that samples behavior under uniform procedures; used to provide accurate and meaningful information on students' levels of performance.

state accountability system: A system that a state uses to measure schools' and districts' progress; in Texas, the Texas Academic Performance Reports (TAPR; previously the Academic Excellence Indicator System (AEIS)) provide accountability data.

story tree: A graphic organizer that is used to guide students' critical evaluation of a work of literature.

structural analysis: A strategy for determining the meaning of a word by breaking the word into its component subunits (for example, *un-success-ful*).

structuring the task: Specifying the processes and procedures students are to follow to be successful with a learning experience.

sub-group: A group of students categorized by a particular characteristic, such as race, ethnicity, English proficiency, disability status, or income.

success: Attainment, achievement, or accomplishment.

summarizing: Stating key points of a speaker's message.

summative assessment: Assessment that follows instruction and evaluates at the end of a unit, semester, and so on; used to guide programs, curricula, and the like.

symbolic medium: A representational medium for acquiring concepts through symbols such as language.

synthesis: Thinking that involves putting together ideas or elements to form a whole.

synthesis question: A question that requires the student to put together elements and parts to form a whole.

target mistake: The error that occurs when a teacher stops the wrong student or desists the wrong misbehavior.

task analysis: Analyzing a task to determine its underlying and prerequisite subskills.

taxonomy: A classification system; used here in reference to a classification system of educational objectives or skills.

teachable moment: A peak learning moment that usually occurs unexpectedly.

teacher certification or licensure: A process through which individuals are recognized by the state as having acquired the necessary skills and knowledge to teach in that state; in Texas, individuals seeking educator certification must pass the appropriate Texas Examinations of Educator Standards (TExES) exams as part of this process.

teacher empowerment: The concept of putting decision making in the hands of teachers, the school personnel closest to students.

teacher expectations: A teacher's opinion of the likelihood that students will be successful.

teacher-made test: An assessment instrument developed and scored by a teacher to meet particular classroom needs.

teaching style: The way a teacher teaches; that teacher's distinctive mannerisms complemented by his or her choices of teaching behaviors and strategies.

Teams-Games-Tournaments (TGT): A cooperative learning strategy in which teacher presentation is followed by team practice and individual mastery is tested in tournaments, with two or three students of matched achievement, rather than tests.

terminal behavior: That which has been learned as a direct result of instruction.

terminal goals: Goals one can expect to reach at the end of a given learning experience.

test: A device used to determine whether learning objectives have been met.

Test of English as a Foreign Language (TOEFL): A standardized test used to assess English language skills; frequently required of foreign students applying for admission to colleges and universities in the United States.

Texas Administrative Code (TAC): The official compilation of all rules adopted by each Texas state agency.

Texas Commissioner of Education: The head of the Texas Education Agency.

Texas Education Agency (TEA): The state agency that oversees public education in Texas in accordance with the Texas Education Code.

Texas Education Code (TEC): The state laws governing education in Texas.

Texas Primary Reading Inventory (TPRI): A diagnostic one-on-one early reading assessment designed to assess the reading development of K-3 students.

Texas Statutes or Codes: The laws of the state of Texas.

Texas Virtual School Network (TXVSN): An accredited, online Texas public school serving students in grades 3-12; TXVSN is provided through TEA.

thematic teaching: The organization of teaching and learning around a specific theme or topic. Although themes may be used in a single subject area, such as English, sociology, or literature, two or more subject areas may be integrated using a single thematic approach.

theoretical knowledge: Concepts, facts, and propositions that make up much of the content of the disciplines.

think-pair-share: A cooperative strategy in which students work individually, next with a partner, and then share with the rest of the class.

timeout: A form of punishment in which the student is removed for a short while from the rest of the class (to sit in the corner, stand out in the hall, and so on); used when the teacher believes the student misbehaves because he or she wants attention.

token reinforcement system: A system in which students perform actions or behaviors desired by the teacher in order to earn neutral tokens that can be exchanged periodically for rewards.

tracks: Classes or curricula targeted for students of a specified achievement or ability level.

trust: A value relationship between and among individuals; includes such subordinate terms as confidence, reliance, stability, and absence of deception.

unit plan: A plan for a sequence of several lessons dealing with the same general topic.

universal design for learning (UDL): An approach to teaching that aims to meet the needs of all students, including those with learning and attention challenges.

usability: In regard to a test, practical considerations, such as cost, time to administer, difficulty, and scoring procedure.

validity: The ability of a test to measure what it purports to measure.

value data: Data that involve a value judgment on the part of an observer.

values clarification: A teaching program that focuses on students' understanding of and expression of their own values.

valuing: Affective learning that involves voluntarily giving worth to an object, phenomenon, or stimulus.

variable: A characteristic that varies from entity to entity.

variable-interval reinforcement schedule: A pattern for giving reinforcements in which the time at which reinforcement will occur is unpredictable; effective for maintaining a high rate of behavior and highly resistant to extinction. For example, a teacher checking students' work at random intervals is variable-interval reinforcement.

variable-ratio reinforcement schedule: A pattern for giving reinforcements in which the number of desired responses before reinforcement is given is unpredictable; effective in motivating individuals to work a long time, even after reinforcement has stopped, and highly resistant to extinction. For example, a teacher checking random samples of students' work is variable-ratio reinforcement.

verbal component: The actual words and meaning of a spoken message.

verbal reinforcement: Using positive comments as consequences to strengthen a behavior or event.

vocal component: The meaning attached to a spoken message, resulting from such variables as voice firmness, modulation, tone, tempo, pitch, and loudness.

wait time: The amount of time a teacher waits for a student to respond to a question; also, a term used to describe the time a teacher waits before calling on a student to answer after posing a question to the whole class.

whole-class discussion: A discussion among the whole class with the teacher as facilitator; seating arrangements should be U-shaped or in a circle.

within-class ability grouping: A system for accommodating differences between students by dividing a class into groups for instructional purposes (such as reading groups).

withitness: A teacher's awareness of what is going on in all parts of the classroom.

year-round school program: A school program whose calendar provides for instruction for the entire year, with short vacation periods throughout the year.

you messages: Teacher messages that students may perceive as a verbal attack.

zero-tolerance policy: A policy that results in mandatory expulsion of students found to have committed certain offenses (for example, bringing a firearm or weapon to school).

zone of proximal development: The level of development one step above the current level; learning in this zone requires assistance of a peer or adult.